Dialectics and Gender

Dialectics and Gender

Anthropological Approaches

EDITED BY

Richard R. Randolph, David M. Schneider, and May N. Diaz

Westview Press
BOULDER & LONDON

A Westview Special Study

This Westview softcover edition is printed on acid-free paper and bound in softcovers that carry the highest rating of the National Association of State Textbook Administrators, in consultation with the Association of American Publishers and the Book Manufacturers' Institute.

Copyright © 1988 by Westview Press, Inc., except Chapter 18 (© Vincent Crapanzano).

Published in 1988 in the United States of America by Westview Press, Inc., 5500 Central Avenue, Boulder, Colorado 80301

Library of Congress Cataloging-in-Publication Data
Dialectics and gender: anthropological approaches/edited by Richard
  R. Randolph, David M. Schneider, and May N. Diaz
     p. cm.
  Includes bibliographies.
  ISBN 0-8133-7571-1
  1. Sex role—Cross-cultural studies. 2. Social change—Cross-
cultural studies. I. Randolph, Richard R. II. Schneider, David
Murray, 1918–   . III. Diaz, May N.
GN479.65.D53 1988
305.3—dc19   88-12058
                                                                          CIP

Printed and bound in the United States of America

The paper used in this publication meets the requirements of the American National Standard for Permanence of Paper for Printed Library Materials Z39.48-1984.

6   5   4   3   2   1

This book is dedicated to
Robert and Yolanda Murphy

CONTENTS

DIALECTICS AND GENDER:
AN INTRODUCTION AND CONTEXT

Richard R. Randolph
University of California, Santa Cruz

Gang rape, clitoridectomy, abduction of women, ritual belittling of men, modern feminist criticism, and the "war between the sexes" are some of the subjects examined in this volume. Contradiction, antinomy, opposition, and conflict are also here. Many of the writers in this volume have studied or taught at Columbia and many are cultural materialists who believe that culture arises from a material base. Others write in the hermeneutic or interpretive tradition, a theoretical edifice where "very few bricks touch the ground" (*pace* Edward Sapir). Freudians are between these covers as are Marxists; structuralists and pragmatists are here as well. Marvin Harris may approve of some of the material produced here and Clifford Geertz may wink in recognition at some of the interpretations offered. There should be something for everyone to disagree with.

What does unite the authors here is their appreciation of the works and lives of Robert and Yolanda Murphy. There is no disguising the fact that this book, in its conception and as it now exists, is a *Festschrift*. The contributors here have all been influenced by the works of the Murphys. In this collection colleagues and former students have taken themes and ideas from the Murphys' writing and teaching and have applied them to their own ethnographic research. Working without benefit of a conference each author has offered his or her own tribute to the Murphys.

Inspired by the dialectical insights of Hegel, Simmel, Freud and Levi-Strauss, the Murphys see in oppositions such as gender, supererogatory cultural constructions that are never completely reducible to nature's constraints. Dialectical approaches, whether Hegelian or Marxian, see contradictions in the culture, or the society, or the political economy, that are forces for change. If contradictions and antinomies are resolved at some higher stage, or later form, that is only to begin the process of the generation of further contradictory opposition. The Murphy version of dialectics, while primarily Hegelian, owes something to Freud and Levi-Strauss. Structuralism of the Levi-Straussian variety features dialectics at its core. James Boon has coined the term "structuralectics" in his analysis of anthropological theory. Dividing modern anthropological approaches into structural and pragmatic strains, Boon writes, dialectically

> Structuralism has difficulty decoding bitterness, disgust, politicized controversy, factious competition... . Pragmatism has difficulty interpreting empty metaphors, apparently nonsensical images, play for play's sake, inversion for inversion's sake -- which are structuralism's forte(1982:145).

Structuralists and pragmatists are certainly included in this volume and that is almost surely because the work of the Murphys is at once pragmatic and structural. Robert Murphy's *The Body Silent* (1987) and his *Dialectics of Social Life* (1971) do not suffer the weaknesses of either pragmatism or structuralism. They explore "metaphor" and "inversion" but also "politicized controversy" and "factious competition." The same is true of *Women of The Forest* (1974) by Yolanda and Robert Murphy.

Conflict could have been a theme around which to organize this volume. That is because the Murphys have also been influenced by the work of Georg Simmel, and Robert Murphy has made a point of teaching his students that solidarity and equilibrium are only half the story. *Dialectics of Social Life* can be seen as an attempt to break out of British structural-functionalism which privileges models of equilibrium and shows how the parts contribute to the maintenance of the whole "except, of course, when they don't" (*pace* David Schneider).

The papers in this volume are, then, sensitive to dialectical process even if it would be too much to say that the various authors share the same view of dialectics. Some are primarily structural and deal with puzzles encoded in myth or ritual while others are more pragmatic and deal with the politics of large state-sized units (Joseph). Some deal with conflict in the form of overt war between Indians and colonial powers (Balée) or between Indian groups (Ferguson) while most deal with smaller scale conflicts that are usually not fatal, i.e., the war between the sexes. But Vincent reminds us that fatalities occur on this battlefield as well.

Gender is a particularly salient dimension along which humans organize themselves into opposing camps only to come together to reproduce themselves biologically and socially. Judith Shapiro surveys recent feminist literature on the subject of gender. Without settling the issue of whether there are universal aspects of femaleness or maleness, she stresses that gender always has a cultural side that is never given by nature alone. It is to attend to the cultural construction of gender, then, that she calls anthropologists and feminists. Shapiro's chapter serves as a good introduction to many of the specifically ethnographic papers that come later in the book.

In Chapter Two Alexander Alland, in a piece that is at once psychoanalytic and structural, surveys Australian, New Guinean, African and Amazonian data and finds sacred flutes or trumpets forbidden to women and owned by men who have expropriated them from the women. Diffusion will not account for the distribution of the forbidden musical instruments. Alland argues that though the symbols may look alike their meaning varies. Symbols may be phallic but phalluses do not mean the same thing in all cultures.

The more general articles by Shapiro and Alland are followed by sixteen articles focused on single ethnographic areas: nine from Amazonia, four from Africa, and three from the Arab Middle East.

As the Murphys have detailed, ambivalences occur because all children have mothers but some must become female like their mothers, while males must not. Psychoanalytic approaches to adult sex role acquisition, then, provide one starting point for comparative work on gender. Alland's and the Johnsons' contributions use Freudian understandings in their examinations. In the Johnsons' chapter Freudian psychology is combined with aspects of the political economy to attempt to isolate the variables involved in the production of hyper-masculine males.

Burkhalter adds the dimension of play and humor to the "war between the sexes." Surely this aspect of gender relationships has received too little notice in anthropology, if not in the arts. His paper and those by Worley and Gregor remind us that in most cases the war is rather playful. Worley's paper on the Twareg builds on the pioneer work by the Murphys on these matrilineal Islamic people among whom the men wear the veils and the women own the beds. A careful comparison of the Bedouin Arabs with the Twareg is an obvious desideratum.

Chernela's paper is part of a growing genre that explicitly investigates women's culture. She compares versions of the same story, one told by a man and one by a woman and discusses the different perspectives of the two storytellers. Gregor's paper raises interesting questions about people's awareness that their own cultural rules may be arbitrary. His tale is of a woman who is brutally punished for playing the forbidden flutes. Yet she lives to take revenge on the husband who helped to punish her. My own piece on the Bedouin also suggests that people are aware that their own most cherished values are relative after all.

Many of the articles in this book feature narratives: myths, tales, stories. Levy's article investigates the narrative process itself. He describes the narration of myth and shamanic curing sessions in detail. He argues that histrionics are uniquely powerful in establishing links between the ordinary world of human beings and the supernatural world of gods and spirits. Here the problem of gender is suppressed in favor of the problem of belief. The histrionics of the shaman are seen as crucial to the perpetuation of the enchanted thought world of the Shipibo of the

Peruvian Amazon.

Leacock is included as a dissenter. He finds that dialectical theory does not help him understand the competition he encounters in his work on religion in Brazil. Perhaps it is fair to say that certain kinds of description preclude certain kinds of explanation. The reader will have to judge.

Another theme uniting several of the contributions in this book is the importance of human work. Robert Murphy, modifying the cultural-ecological approach of Julian Steward, has often privileged the category of human work in his anthropological theorizing. This is no simple economic determinism; in Murphy's hands it is an attempt to tie other cultural formations to more explicitly life-sustaining activities in a non-reductionist way. Articles by Vincent, Joseph, Ferguson, Worley, the Johnsons, and particularly that by Lennihan emphasize an interest in work.

Many of the papers in this book deal with societies in which the inhabitants understand that adult gender is not simply an anatomical matter. Ritual activity is needed to create proper men and women. Elliott Skinner's article explores the meaning of "female circumcision" in Africa and argues that the practice can be understood as a symbolic statement of equality that women make to men. Men make boys into human men by circumcising them. Women make girls into human women by circumcising them. The altered genitalia themselves become symbols of gender.

The Murphys have written factually about gang rape in Amazonia, perhaps the quintessential form of male aggression against women. Interested in new forms of ethnographic writing, Vincent Crapanzano offers a fictional account of a gang rape by Moroccan soldiers in France. His short story also reminds us that factual ethnographies, like ethnographic fictions, are made by their authors.

The essays in this book and the works and lives of the Murphys reveal that gender can organize "the procrustean and deadly struggle of the sexes"(Murphy 1971:212) but it can also be the basis of unity, intimacy, teamwork and solidarity.

ACKNOWLEDGMENTS

Grants from the Academic Senate Faculty Research Committee and the Dean of the Social Sciences Division at the University of California at Santa Cruz made the production of this book possible. The editors wish to thank the authors for their patience when that was needed and for their promptness in responding to our solicitations when that was needed. We also wish to thank all those who submitted articles we were unable to use. Andrew Castro, Debbie Johnson, Vickie Arbogast, Zoe Sodja, and Joni Tannheimer were very helpful as assistants and text editors. Thanks to Shelly Errington for last minute help.

1

GENDER TOTEMISM

Judith Shapiro
Bryn Mawr College

Introduction

Beliefs about the ways in which women and men differ from one another constitute one of the most significant and compelling illusions in a society's ideological repertoire. Gender ideologies commonly perform their cultural work by locating male/female differences in the natural or sacred order of things, postulating that the respective roles played by men and women, and the respective characteristics they exhibit, flow from inherent differences between the sexes. The work that such ideologies perform, moreover, reaches far beyond allocating men and women to their appointed places in society. Ideas about maleness and femaleness operate within a wider cultural matrix. To use Clifford Geertz' often-repeated formulation of the role of cultural symbols in general, they are models of and models for other domains of social action and experience.

Feminist critiques of gender ideologies, in general, attack both the naturalistic and the sacred/moral underpinnings of traditional wisdom about sex and gender. The basic theoretical consensus among feminist scholars is that gender should be viewed as a social and cultural construct. There are, however, not surprisingly, many different voices within the feminist movement, and some have argued quite strongly that the sexes differ in terms of their inherent psychological, social and moral qualities. A concept of gender as socially and culturally constructed is itself not incompatible with an emphasis on male/female differences: cultural forces may be construed to produce two very different kinds of social creature.

My purpose here is to explore how certain general currents of feminist scholarship are fed by the streams of traditional gender ideology. The point is not only to consider continuities of content, but structural continuities in the way in which beliefs about gender articulate with other

1

social conventions. I will state at the outset my own intellectual and political predisposition against approaches to gender that emphasize the differentness of women and men; the reader may judge whether such a predisposition is supported by the analyses and arguments that follow.

In pursuing a critique of theories of gender differences, I do not presume to deny that there are differences between women and men, but rather to assert that the differences, whatever they may be, are not what they seem. I will also be addressing, albeit more tangentially, the question of whether particular empirical differences that have been observed should be viewed as deep and relatively impervious to change, or as labile and responsive to social context.

Totemism and the Uses of Gender

As "natives," we tend to see the gender oppositions current in our culture in terms of differential characteristics attributable to women and men respectively. If, however, we manage to achieve a more detached perspective on our beliefs--and it is anthropology's claim that the royal road to such a perspective is through cross-cultural research--we can perceive that the qualities we think of as distinguishing women and men belong to a web of metaphors that have, in fact, to do with many things other than gender *per se*. The opposition between male and female serves as a source of symbolism for a diversity of cultural domains; at the same time, gender differences themselves are defined through categories of the economy, the polity--in brief, of the wider social universe in which they are located.

The properties of gender as a metaphorical system can be illuminated through a comparison with belief systems referred to under the rubric of totemism. The term totemism, drawn from the Algonkian languages of native North America, entered into the vocabulary of anthropology, psychoanalysis, and the more general interested public to designate the exotic beliefs of primitive peoples who held that a special and sacred bond existed between human beings and members of other species. Totemic beliefs that attracted particular attention were taboos on killing or consuming members of the species with which one's own group was linked, and prohibitions on marriage between members of the same totemic group. In the classic 19th and early 20th century studies, including Freud's *Totem and Taboo*, totemism served as a springboard for evolutionist accounts of social organization, psychic life, and the regulation of sexual relationships. As anthropological theorizing came to be dominated by a variety of functionalist perspectives, totemic beliefs were viewed within the context of resource use and the maintenance of solidarity both within and between social groups.

In 1962, Claude Lévi-Strauss presented a comprehensive and masterful reanalysis of totemism. He argued that what had long been viewed as a "primitive" form of religion should instead be seen as the reflection of a universal human propensity to order the social world with the help of models drawn from nature. According to Lévi-Strauss, the world of animal and plant species, which in some ways resembled one another and in other respects differed, offered a particularly suitable model for representing relationships among human groups. In response to functionalist attempts at explaining totemism in utilitarian terms--arguments that natural species became the object of ritual, totemic observances because of their importance for the survival of the group--Lévi-Strauss responded that plants and animals are not merely "good to eat," but "good to think" (Lévi-Strauss [1962] 1963: 89).

Totemism is thus essentially about metaphor, about the way in which the natural world provides a powerful logical model for representing the human social world. We de-exoticize totemism not by reducing it to a matter of practical interest, but by recognizing in it a mode of thought that characterizes certain products of Western culture as well, Social Darwinism and sociobiology being two notable examples (see Sahlins 1976).

Lévi-Strauss' analysis of totemism was a paradigm case of structuralist method. Whereas others had concentrated on the relationship between individual groups, or persons, and the particular totems with which they were associated, Lévi-Strauss concentrated on the wider set of relations that defined the system as a whole. The significance of totemism lay not in the relationship that group x was believed to have with species y, but rather in the structural relationship between human social differences, on the one hand, and the diversity of natural species, on the other. To put Lévi-Strauss' line of argument in linguistic terms, since it was in fact primarily from structural linguistics that he took his inspiration, meaning is to be sought not in the relationship between individual signs and their referents, but in the system whereby signs, and hence referents, are related to each other.

The Lévi-Straussian perspective on totemism provides a lens for viewing the gender oppositions we find in some form or another in all human cultures. Following the logic of Lévi-Strauss' argument, we can say that the biological opposition between female and male, like the array of animal species, provides a powerful natural model for representing differences between social groups and oppositions between culturally significant categories. In terms of Lévi-Straussian structuralism, with its particular emphasis on binary opposition, sex is, in fact, especially suited to this structural symbolic work. Binarism aside, however, the main point is to shift focus from the properties of groups to the nexus of relationships. Instead of focusing on the characteristics of women as a group or men as a group ("What do members of the Bear Clan have in common?" "How are the members of the Bear Clan like bears?"), the issue becomes one of seeing how a series of categorical oppositions, including the one between female and male, map onto and construct each other. To return again to the parallel with language, instead of seeking meaning by attempting to identify the referents of individual signs--a strategy common to philosophers and ordinary folk alike--we look to the relational properties of the system.

In viewing gender differences within such a structuralist framework, it is important to keep in mind the political and hierarchical dimensions of the classificatory systems at issue. We are dealing not with symmetrically opposed categories, but with oppositions that draw invidious distinctions of a complex and often contradictory nature, distinctions that can be mobilized in a variety of ways for a variety of purposes.

Let us now turn to a consideration of some recent trends in feminist politics and scholarship.

Feminism and the Defense of Difference

One of the dominant tendencies within feminist thought in recent years has been to emphasize differences between women and men, and to engage in a project of seeking out, defining, and according value to qualities characteristic of women. Popular and widely read writers like Adrienne Rich, Andrea Dworkin, Robin Morgan, and Mary Daly, whose major work appeared in the mid to late 1970's, propounded a feminist version of the feminine mystique (see, for example, Rich 1976, Dworkin 1976, Morgan 1978, and Daly 1978). More recently, feminist scholars in a variety of fields, notably philosophy and psychology, have been inquiring into the cognitive and epistemological dimensions of gender in an ideological climate receptive to theories that stress differences between the sexes.

In the general feminist literature, an insistence on male/female differences and a focus on the special qualities of women came to be associated with the label of "cultural feminism."[1] The distinctive feature of this orientation is the notion that women have a "culture" of their own, a counter-culture to the dominant culture of men. The struggle for social change becomes a struggle to transform a world dominated by men's values into a world more in line with the values of women.

The specific terms in which women and men are opposed to one another are often familiar and traditional. The major difference is that women's qualities are celebrated rather than denigrated in an attempt to overthrow--or, rather, reverse--the traditional hierarchy between maleness and femaleness. Despite this difference, however, the disturbing continuity between cultural feminism and politically conservative ideologies of gender has revealed itself clearly in such areas as the anti-pornography movement and in a tendency for some feminists to be comfortable with, or at least unconcerned about, biological determinist approaches to gender differences.

Even among feminists who explicitly assert the cultural and symbolic nature of gender oppositions, theories of gender may be advanced that are not so different in their general implications from biologistic ones. Perhaps the most interesting and intellectually rich example is the body of French feminist writings inspired by the psychoanalytic and semiotic perspectives of Jacques Lacan.[2]

In the Lacanian synthesis of Freud and Saussure, the universe of sex and sexual difference becomes a universe of signs and meanings. The anatomical grounding of such dramas of the engendered human condition as penis envy and castration anxiety ostensibly gives way to a symbolic and cognitivized account of the genesis of male and female identity. The physical penis is replaced by the semiotically constituted phallus, sign of difference. Since, however, physical sex differences remain the point of attachment for the semiotic and linguistic superstructure erected by Lacan, his processual and dialectical account of masculinity and femininity universalizes sex/gender differences in a way not entirely unlike other, more reductionist, psychoanalytic theories. Moreover, while Lacan semioticizes sex, he also sexualizes the world of language and meaning. In terms of the argument I am developing here, Lacanian psychoanalysis represents a literalization of gender metaphors.

The feminist response to Lacan's work has been an ambivalent one. His theories about the symbolic construction of masculinity and femininity, and his view of male privilege as resting on imposture and illusion, are appealing. On the other hand, the phallus remains the privileged signifier in Lacan's semiotic system, and despite the analytic care one may take in distinguishing between penis and phallus, only men, after all, have something that can pass for the phallus in a pinch. Nor can feminists take too much comfort in assertions about the chimerical nature of male superiority and female inferiority, since such assertions frequently find a place within traditional, androcentric ideologies of gender. Cynicism about male power is a common form of phallocentric *mauvaise foi.*

Feminist responses to Lacan's work have been varied, but many rest on an attempt to privilege female sexuality, much as American cultural feminism rests on an attempt to privilege female experience more generally. In both cases, the upshot is a persistence of familiar gender stereotypes. A great deal of French feminist writing is characterized by an uncritical acceptance of the same long-standing folk beliefs about female sexuality that characterize Lacan's own writings, in particular, the idea that women are insatiable creatures of boundless desires whose sexuality is inherently subversive.[3]

While such beliefs may appear to offer a source of power, they are ultimately a trap. For one thing, they tend to fall into line with familiar nature/culture oppositions in which women tend to be aligned with the forces of nature and men with the domain of culture. We will return to this issue below. It is also important not to be misled by the surface anarchy and playfulness found in feminist writing inspired by Lacan, and also by the work of Jacques Derrida. Beneath an apparently carnivalesque approach to language and thus, implicity, to order in general, persists the prison house of traditional gender constructs.

A common feature of the various feminist orientations I have been discussing here is that sex is seen as the major dimension of differentiation among human beings. Cultural differences, including differences in definitions of gender and in the ordering of relationships between women and men, do not figure in any theoretically central way. Many feminists, in fact, consider such differences to be relatively insignificant. "Women" are treated as a natural category and the differences between women in different societies are submerged within the global sisterhood that arises from global patriarchy.

The assumption made by some feminists, either implicitly or explicitly, that women around the world are in a position to understand one another in a direct and immediate way because of their common life experiences is an assumption of which we should be particularly wary. Besides implying that women are in some sense pre-cultural beings, such universalism also generally amounts to an imposition of our own political agenda on women of very differing cultural backgrounds and social circumstances. Theories that seek some positive and universal definition of womanhood are, to be sure, a powerful source of solidarity among women, and can constitute a rhetorically effective attack on the structure of values that celebrate masculinity over femininity. At the same time, they rest on a view of sex differences that we would do well to deconstruct, both in the interests of arriving at a better understanding of gender, and also, I would argue, in the interests of formulating the kind of politics we will be most comfortable living with in the long run.

Emphasizing the differences between women and men can be seen as one of two major strategies within the feminist movement, the other being to downplay the significance of gender, to see its role in systems of social hierarchy as a form of irrationality that can be overcome once we realize its costs. This latter approach, which is in harmony with the homogenizing cultural logic of capitalism and the principle of the equivalence of individuals in the marketplace, has been particularly appealing to upwardly mobile middle-class feminists aspiring to professional careers. Since there is nothing intrinsic to women or men that makes them differentially qualified for such professions as law, medicine, or corporate management, it should be a relatively straightforward matter to demonstrate the unreasonableness of excluding women.

An emphasis on the common humanity of women and men, and the denial that there are significant differences between them is also basic to socialist feminism. It accords with a concern for social equality and with the view that the most significant social distinctions are those based on class. Sexual inequality is absorbed into the analysis of class inequality and sometimes said to depend upon it, a position not borne out by the cross-cultural study of gender.

The problem with these positions, whether they be socialist or capitalist/reformist, is that they share a common underestimation of the significance and function of gender oppositions in society, and how they figure in wider systems of social stratification. If it is a distortion of one kind to say that women who wish to move into the social roles occupied by men are alienated from their own qualities as women; it is a distortion of another kind to assert that gender is extraneous to the definition of occupational roles. An alternative to both of these views is to appreciate the social and cultural uses to which gender oppositions are put.

If we now turn from general feminist writings to research on gender that has been carried out in a variety of disciplines in recent years, we find a similar focus on the ways in which women differ from men. The two examples I will discuss here--philosophy of science and developmental psychology--are of particular interest, since feminist scholarship in these fields has raised basic questions about the relationship between gender and modes of thought.

Gender and Epistemology

Feminist criticism in the field of philosophy has ranged from reformist discussions of sex discrimination in the profession to the daring and radical view that women and men think in basically different ways. Feminist philosophers of the natural and social sciences have argued that these disciplines have taken their intellectual shape from male concerns and would develop in profoundly different directions if pursued in ways more commensurate with female experience.[4]

In pursuing this line of argument, some feminists draw a parallel with Marxist analyses of how class determines consciousness. Women, like the proletariat, are said to be in a position to see through the ideological veil that surrounds our social practices and to be capable of a more authentic vision of reality (see, for example, Hartsock 1983).[5] The argument takes a universalizing turn when it comes to revolve around shared female experiences, notably motherhood. Sara Ruddick, for example, has attempted to define the characteristic features of what she calls "maternal thinking," which she sees in terms of attentiveness to the other, respect for difference, and responsiveness to feeling (Ruddick 1980, 1986).

Philosophers of science have drawn heavily on recent work in developmental psychology, in particular the work of Carol Gilligan and Nancy Chodorow, about which more will be said below, in order to explore how the process of achieving gender identity may be linked to cognitive styles. The present mother and absent father are said to lead to different processes of gender role acquisition for girls and boys. The concrete, relational matrix in which girls learn to be women is contrasted with a more abstracted presentation of the male role to the boy which, in turn, is connected to the differential propensities of women and men for contextual and analytical reasoning. The boy's need to distinguish himself from the mother in order to establish his own gender identity becomes the root for a variety of intellectual preoccupations that characterize mainstream philosophical and scientific thought: a concern for drawing unambiguous boundaries between categories, and a rigid opposition between objectivity and subjectivity. (See, for example, Hartsock 1983 and Keller 1985, Chapter 4.)

Objectivism and the type of rationality that has characterized scientific inquiry, linked by this line of argument to a masculine ego-development project, are at the same time commonly viewed as the quintessential distinguishing features of Western modes of thought. Male dominance in Western science, and in Western culture more generally, is taken by some feminist philosophers to mean that there is something essentially masculine about the Western world view. Similarly, non-Western societies, which often tend to get lumped together into a single category--"the West versus the Rest," as anthropologists have come to refer to this type of oppositional thinking--are described by some feminists as exhibiting modes of thought common to women, including women in the West (see, for example, Harding 1986b).

We see here a particularly clear example of gender totemism at work. A series of category oppositions--abstract/concrete, analytical/contextual, self/other, autonomy/inter-connectedness, Western/non-Western, male/female--are mapped on to one another and become mutually defining. The system tends to appear in distorted form to those who use it, since they focus attention on the content of the categories and associate the equations and oppositions with actual properties of the groups being contrasted. There are, of course, notable exceptions to this generalization, one being Evelyn Fox Keller, whose analyses of the compelling force of gender imagery in scientific discourse converge with the general argument made here (Keller 1985). Although Keller has been interested in exploring sex-linked psychodynamic aspects of the scientific vocation along the lines outlined above, she has, at the same time, made a point of distinguishing gender metaphorization from actual differences between the way men and women think and behave (see, for example, Keller 1985: 88). Genevieve Lloyd's analysis of how the concept of reason has become "genderized" in Western philosophy similarly sheds critical light on the interplay between gender symbolism and beliefs about differences between the sexes (Lloyd 1983 1984).

The particular equations of masculinity with the West, on the one hand, and femininity with the Third World, on the other, echo the ideas of Victorian social evolutionists who linked the opposition between women and men to the opposition between primitive and civilized societies, and also to the opposition between proletariat and bourgeoisie. In both cases, the gender dichotomy helps to constitute our understanding of class and colonialism, and vice versa. Our concepts of gender enter into and are shaped by a web of cultural preoccupations around such issues as social inequality and cultural evolution. While the current version of this scheme is anti-colonialist in intention--the civilized/savage dichotomy has given way to the colonizer/colonized dichotomy--it remains profoundly colonialist in its basic orientation, since other societies function merely as a screen on which we project our own images.

Up to this point, I have been raising questions about some of the specific differences that have been said to characterize the way women and men think. Let me now address the issue from another angle, and consider how we might analyze gender differences that do appear to emerge from ethnographic accounts and empirical research. I take as my point of departure an essay by the British anthropologist Edwin Ardener, which has had a considerable influence on the anthropological literature on gender since its publication in 1972.

In seeking to account for the degree of male bias that is so characteristic a feature of ethnographic research and writing, Ardener argued that anthropologists, because of their training and theoretical presuppositions, have a predilection for the type of information provided to them by male informants. In Ardener's view, men, because of their position in society, are more willing and more able to produce the kinds of bounded models of the social universe that anthropologists find intellectually congenial. Women, who exist more on the margins of the social structures delimited in male ideology, do not draw boundaries in the same manner. Since the social perspectives of women fail to correspond to what ethnographers are prepared to understand, women seem inarticulate and their views are, to a large extent, ignored.

Ardener's argument should be understood as an attempt to address gender differences from the perspective of the sociology of knowledge. It is in no sense an argument about inherent biological differences between the sexes. Moreover, it makes the very important point that the study of social inequality should address itself to the allocation of symbolic as well as material resources in a society. In pointing out that the perspectives of men enjoy a dominant status, while those of women remain "muted," to use his term, Ardener was drawing attention to the crucial question of which groups in society control the means of ideological production.

At the same time, it should be noted that the gender differences imputed by Ardener to women's and men's respective positions in society operate at a relatively deep level. They are differences in world view, in cognitive style. The issue is not merely what different groups of people are accustomed to express, or what they express in particular social contexts, but what they are capable of expressing.

There is an instructive parallel between Ardener's arguments and Basil Bernstein's well-known and controversial analyses of working-class speech (Bernstein 1961, 1970). According to Bernstein, working-class speech was characterized by a distinctive structure that differed from the structure of middle-class speech. Expressed as a contrast between a "restricted code" and an "elaborated code," the differences involved such matters as communicational adequacy and a speaker's potential to achieve self-reflective knowledge. Bernstein tied differential access to linguistic skills to differences in the socialization practices characteristic of working-class and middle-class families, focusing on the deep and presumably enduring consequences of childhood experiences. When Bernstein's ideas were taken up by American educators convinced of the "verbal deprivation" of Black American schoolchildren, they were taken on by the sociolinguist William Labov, who argued for the grammatical equivalence of Black English and Standard English as codes, and also for the importance of the immediate social context as determining an individual's linguistic behavior (Labov 1969). Labov documented the high cultural priority placed on rhetorical skills within the Black urban community and attributed the inarticulateness of Black children in school to the alien and alienating atmosphere in which they find themselves.

Similarly, returning to Ardener's argument, one might choose to emphasize the influence of the immediate social context on the way in which women express themselves rather than seek social effects on deeper cognitive levels. The speech setting and the identity of the addressee are among the significant variables to be considered. Not all ethnographers have found women inarticulate. The kind of effort and imagination required of those seeking to work more satisfactorily with women may be more social than cognitive and, as one male ethnographer has had occasion to acknowledge (Gregory 1984), most of his male colleagues have found excuses not to bother.

An example of how Ardener's observations might be placed within a different contextual framework is provided by a recent study of Andean women's political participation, which draws upon Ardener's notions of "muting." The authors, Kay Warren and Susan Bourque, analyze the social variables that yield different patterns of political action and different levels of political articulateness on the part of women in the two communities they offer for comparison, one an agrarian community and the other a commercial town (Warren and Bourque 1985). They also show how differences ascribed by Ardener to gender might more appropriately be applied to individuals, and provide accounts of why particular women within a given social setting might become more "muted" than others. Their data, moreover, include an example of how a genre specific to women (songs sung at *rodeos* in the agrarian community of Mayobamba) operate at a metalevel of social commentary that sets them apart from other forms of political communication engaged in by men, or by women and men jointly.

In evaluating arguments about the epistemological significance of gender, we might gain a sense of perspective from attempts to explore the influence of culture and language on modes of thought, the best known of these attempts being the work of the anthropological linguist, Benjamin Lee Whorf. Among the major points argued by Whorf is that certain categories philosophers have viewed as basic to human experience--

notably, categories of time and space--vary significantly in accordance with the underlying grammatical structures of different languages.[6]

It is useful to compare Whorf's intellectual project with current arguments for grounding knowledge in gender-linked experience, since one gets a sense of the degree of specificity and detail that would be needed to make such arguments compelling. One also sees that the very kinds of oppositions that are currently being used to designate universal, pan-cultural differences between men and women--a focus on objects versus a focus on processes, concentration on isolated elements versus concentration on the relationships between them--are the kinds of constructs that are most convincingly relativized through the analysis of deep grammatical patterns.

The general question that arises is whether differences in perspective that reflect gender are as likely to operate at as deep or general a conceptual level as differences of culture and of language. A prior question, of course, is how much difference really exists. Some feminist theorists have argued that the similarities that do exist between the intellectual and scientific productions of women and men reflect the alienation of many women from their own authentic female experience, and their subjection to the hegemonic structures of masculinity. The alternative is to view the determinism that shapes our cognitive ends as more a matter of culture and language. In other words, when the sexes think alike, it is because they are products of the same cultural traditions, and not because some women are really men in drag.

Developmental Psychology

One of the more influential bodies of work to come out of the field of developmental psychology in recent years is Carol Gilligan's series of studies on the relationship between gender and moral reasoning (Gilligan 1982). Gilligan has sought to document two contrasting styles of moral reasoning, one revolving around the concept of rights and the other around the concept of responsibilities, and to explore the differential propensity of men and women to invoke one or the other of these moralities. In analyzing differences between the responses of male and female subjects in interviews and in a variety of experimental tasks, Gillian has argued that men tend to be preoccupied with abstract standards of justice and individual rights, whereas women tend to view moral conflicts in their social context and to focus on the demands of relationships.

Gilligan intends her work as a corrective to the androcentrism in earlier developmental research, most particularly the work of Lawrence Kohlberg and his associates on moral reasoning, but also Daniel Levinson's studies of adult life stages, in which men have been the tacit focus of investigation and thus the model for theories of moral and social development. Such theories, which reflect a long-standing tendency in psychology to equate humanity with masculinity and hence to view women as somehow problematic or deficient[7] , yield schemes in which women appear to be at a lower stage of development than men.

With respect to moral reasoning, Gilligan has sought to retrieve at once the undervalued claims of social responsibility and the generally unheard "voice" of women. She has argued for replacing Kohlberg's hierarchical view of moral judgment with a relativistic concept of different moralities that complement one another, and that are both necessary components for a balanced and mature approach to moral issues. In fact, her writings alternate between a rhetoric of complementarity and one that privileges the relationship-oriented morality of women, perhaps because of a felt need to compensate for the asymmetries of the past.

Gilligan's work on moral judgment dovetails with Nancy Chodorow's analyses of gender differences in personality. According to Chodorow (1974, 1978), women have distinctive personality characteristics that can be traced to the shaping influence of the mother-daughter bond. In both cases, differences in social experience are said to lead to profound and enduring differences in cognitive and emotional functioning. In both cases also, there is a tendency--more marked perhaps in the work of others who have taken up Gilligan's and Chodorow's ideas--to shift attention from the social situational bases of gender differentiation to gender differentness itself, and to speak of certain moral or emotional qualities as defining traits of womanhood.[8]

An extensive critical literature has grown up around Gilligan's work, in which a variety of theoretical, methodological, and substantive issues have been addressed.[9] The continuity between Gilligan's writings and traditional gender stereotypes has been noted, as has her failure to take account of significant variables other than gender in her research-- notably, differences associated with class, educational background, race and ethnicity. She has been criticized for the issues on which she has chosen to focus (abortion, for example, may not be the most appropriate topic for research aimed at contrasting the views of women and men), and the relatively unoperationalized way in which subjects' responses are categorized.

Some critics have maintained that the conclusions Gilligan draws about gender differences are not in fact supported by her own material. Others have noted that her adherence to an evolutionist developmental model has led her, as it led Kohlberg, to see patterns of moral reasoning in terms of a self-contained set of progressively unfolding stages, with a consequent failure to take account of the specific and immediate social settings in which moral decisions are made. The generally decontextualized way in which the research has been carried out, its reliance on hypothetical cases, has tended to reduce the study of moral decision-making to a study of self-conscious discourse about morality.

In terms of the argument being developed here, Gilligan's work provides a particularly striking example of how gender symbolism operates in research on gender difference, that is, of how gender metaphors appear as empirical generalizations about male/female difference. The totemic aspect of this enterprise becomes clearer if we compare Gilligan's writings with David Riesman's classic analysis of American culture, *The Lonely Crowd.*

Combining social and psychological perspectives, Riesman attempted to describe and analyze the historical transformation of American character in terms of an opposition between "inner-directedness" and "other-directedness." He contrasted the will to power with the will to popularity; the impulse to impose oneself upon the world with the impulse to ingratiate oneself with others and to be liked. According to Riesman, these contrasting character types corresponded to different moments in American history; the change reflected changes in our economic, political and social order. As the hey-day of laissez-faire capitalism gave way to large-scale corporate bureaucracy, the robber baron gave way to the manager. In a particularly felicitous phrase, Riesman noted the shift "from the invisible hand to the glad hand."

In his preface to a later edition of *The Lonely Crowd*, which addressed readers' responses to the study, Riesman claimed that he had tried to be relativistic about the two character types, to show that each had both strengths and weaknesses. He admitted, however, that "quite possibly *The Lonely Crowd* did not sufficiently stress [the values of other-directedness]; at any rate, the great majority of readers in the last ten years have decided that it was better to be an inner-directed cowboy than an other-directed advertising man, for they were not on the whole being faced with the problems of the cowboy, but rather those of the advertising man." (xvii-xviii) Riesman went on to remark that "no lover of toughness and invulnerability should forget the gains made possible by the considerateness, sensitivity, and tolerance that are among the positive qualities of other-direction." (xx) Yet Riesman knew he was up against some obstacle in trying to place a positive value on other-directedness. It was difficult, he pointed out, "to give a picture of human relatedness that would be visionary without being formal or *sentimental*" (xliv; italics added).

In order to understand Riesman's dilemma, it helps to understand the covert functioning of gender symbolism in his analysis. While the contrasts that he is examining are not ostensibly tied to masculinity or femininity--Riesman is concerned with the occupational roles of men; women are virtually absent from the study--they do, nonetheless resonate with our cultural notions of maleness and femaleness, and such resonances reveal themselves in his prose. This submerged linkage between gender and social character came to the surface in Christopher Lasch's subsequent attempt to combine sociohistorical and psychoanalytic perspectives in an analysis of contemporary culture. *The Culture of Narcissism* presents an explicit argument that characteristics hitherto linked to women have come to be considered appropriate to both sexes, while certain traditionally male-associated qualities have become culturally passé.

The particular terms in which Riesman opposes "inner-directed cowboys" to "other-directed advertising men" are quite similar to the terms in which Gilligan describes the differences between her male and female subjects. The similarity is not surprising, since it comes from the ways in which gender is used to express other kinds of cultural preoccupations. What seems to be at issue in both Riesman's and Gilligan's work is our culture's continuing attempt to deal with the relationship between individual and society, with our ambivalence about the individualism that has been institutionalized and celebrated to such an extraordinary degree in our economic and social life. Gender symbolism plays a central role in how we think about this question. While the opposition is expressed, to a certain extent, in a division of social and emotional labor between the sexes, the issue is not basically one of gender difference; on the contrary, gender takes on its meanings for us in the context of such cultural concerns as these.

A significant difference between Riesman and Gilligan concerns the moral priorities they respectively represent. Although Riesman tried to see as much value in "other-directedness" as "inner-directedness," a hierarchy between the rights of the individual and the demands of society reappeared at another level of his analysis. In his conclusions, Riesman developed an opposition between "autonomy" (from the demands of society) and "adjustment" (to the social order). As Riesman himself noted, readers tended to confound this distinction with the one between inner- and other-directedness. In his preface to the revised edition of *The Lonely Crowd*, he took pains to explain that one set of terms referred to historically-specific character types, while the other concerned the general relationship between the individual and society. What Riesman was, in fact, doing was taking a culturally embedded perspective of the human condition and treating it as a universal. Moreover, the value choice he attempted to avoid at one level was made at another, since autonomy was privileged over adjustment. The more empyrean realm of social theory, as opposed to the more empirical realm of American cultural history, now provided the setting for Riesman's defense of certain basic moral principles.

Gilligan, on the other hand, is the defender of social responsibility and of the claims relationships make upon the individual. At the same time, she makes gender, which was a silent symbolic partner in Riesman's analysis, the overt focus for an attempt to resolve the opposition between the individual and society. Once again, as in the past, women are being called upon to play their redemptive moral role.

Nature and Culture; Public and Private

The varieties of gender totemism that have been played out in specific disciplines have converged around certain general and recurrent themes. Two that have loomed large in writings on women and gender in a number of different fields are the opposition between nature and culture, and the opposition between private and public.

The notion that women are closer to "nature" than men, and that "culture" is more a creation of men than of women, has occupied a central place in our own ideologies of gender. In a well-known and often-cited article published in 1974, Sherry Ortner suggested that this ideological structure might be a universal one, and should be seen as a cornerstone in the edifice of male dominance, since the hierarchy of values that places culture above nature similarly places men above women.

The major influences in Ortner's thesis were Simone de Beauvoir, whose views on gender were shaped by existentialist formulations of human transcendence through choice and action, and Claude Lévi-Strauss, who has considered the opposition between nature and culture to be a universal human preoccupation and has seen the association with gender as relatively self-evident. It is interesting to note that the power of the totemic illusion is such that Lévi-Strauss himself, who provided the analysis that penetrated it, is nonetheless among its victims.

While Ortner argued that our concepts of maleness and femaleness did not follow directly from the inherent qualities of men and women, but were rather the result of a cultural opposition that was imposed on sexual differences and gave them their meaning, her attempt to account for *why* women should be associated with nature and men with culture led her in the direction of showing how the associations were motivated--what was "natural" about women and "cultural" about men. The focus thus shifted from what was conventional, or arbitrary, about the construct to what made it, in semiological terms, "natural," or iconic.

Ortner's analysis provoked a considerable amount of debate and criticism among anthropologists, and provided a springboard for a series of rich ethnographic studies and theoretical reflections on the subject of gender ideologies (see especially MacCormack and Strathern 1980). The major objections were that the nature/culture opposition was not a cross-cultural universal, and that within Western culture itself the meanings of this conceptual dichotomy and its relationships to gender were more complex and historically variable than Ortner had indicated. In an essay that explored both of these issues, and constituted a particularly important contribution to the theoretical and ethnographic literature, Marilyn Strathern drew upon Highland New Guinea society to show the significant differences between cultural oppositions that we might be tempted to group together under the "nature/culture" rubric (Strathern 1980). She noted that such concepts do not always enter into the constitution of gender ideologies, which are built up around a variety of

16

metaphors and cultural oppositions. She also discussed the varied uses of the nature/culture opposition in Western thought, examining contexts in which it is men who are associated with nature and women with culture.

As Strathern so clearly showed, gender serves as a symbolic operator in the articulation of oppositions significant to a particular society, the nature/culture opposition being a prime example. The process of metaphorization works both ways: sometimes gender is put to use in how we think about nature and culture; at other times, we are using the opposition between nature and culture to structure our thinking about gender.

The same analysis can be made of the opposition between public and private domains, which has commonly been viewed as a social structural universal and has figured centrally in theories of gender. Critical reexaminations of the public/private (or public/domestic) dichotomy in recent anthropological writings on kinship draw attention to the fact that the distinction between a public sphere and a private, or domestic, sphere is characteristic only of certain types of societies, notably those that have separated the workplace from the household; that the distinction can take a variety of different forms; and that it cannot be taken at face value even in societies for which it is relevant, since it should be understood more as an ideological construct that masks certain features of the social system than as a description of how that system is structured.[10]

In place of a simple parallel between public/private and male/female, we have instead a system in which the opposition between the sexes is used both to maintain and to "think" the opposition between public and private spheres. Rather than finding in the concepts "public" and "private" some universal, metacultural grid for contrasting the social lives of men and women, we see in these notions what gender differences come to be about in the particular range of societies in which the distinction is meaningful.

Feminism, Totemism, and the Discourse of Difference

Current explorations into gender differences are occurring within a wider intellectual and political context characterized by an interest in and acceptance of pluralistic approaches to knowledge, and by a relativism that seeks to separate difference from hierarchy. While the convergence between feminist theoretical concerns and other critical movements can yield forms of gender totemism similar to the ones outlined above (modernism is to post-modernism as male is to female...), it has clearly provided opportunities for major advances in feminist scholarship.

The ascendancy of hermeneutic, or interpretive, strategies in a variety of fields has fostered new approaches to what we might generally term "otherness," and has encouraged a view of knowledge as being the result of a series of open-ended encounters with worlds of experience different from our own. In such a general theoretical climate, we can be more comfortable with the idea of differences between women and men, particularly if the outcome of difference is productive dialogue.

At the same time, there are dangers in the current celebration of difference in general, and gender difference in particular. One is that differences can come to be viewed as insurmountable, which may lead not so much to despair as to giving parochialism a new lease on life. Another danger, which is the one I have been exploring here, is that we take our common sense notions of difference at face value and fail to examine them critically. In matters of gender, this can result, ironically enough, in feminists engaging in that most socially conservative of tasks-- prescribing gender roles, and telling women what counts as authentic feminine behavior.

The question, then, is how we appropriate the analytical tools currently at hand for our scholarly and political purposes. What I have attempted to argue here is that the alternative, in gender as in other domains, is between perpetuating our folklore or engaging in critical reflection that enables us to transcend it.

FOOTNOTES

Acknowledgements: This paper was first presented in April, 1984, at Carleton College, as part of a Women's Studies lecture series entitled "Rethinking the Way We Think: New Feminist Scholarship and the Curriculum." A revised version was presented later that year to the University of Pennsylvania Mid-Atlantic Seminar for the Study of Women and Society. I am most grateful to members of the seminar for their comments and criticisms, and wish particularly to acknowledge Sandra Harding's role as *agent provocateur* and partner-in-dialogue for various of the arguments developed here. Wyatt MacGaffey has been consistently helpful in pressing me to integrate a cultural symbolic analysis of gender with a political one. The most immediate inspiration for the orientation I take here comes from Marilyn Strathern's theoretical and ethnographic reflections on the symbolic uses of gender (Strathern 1976, 1980, 1987). In more general terms, I am indebted to Robert Murphy, who has consistently pointed out the arbitrariness and fragility of the most central of our social institutions, including gender.

[1] For a particularly lucid critique of cultural feminism, see Echols 1983. The term "cultural feminism" itself appears to have been coined in 1975 by the Redstockings, a radical New York feminist group critical of this orientation (Echols 1983: 456).

[2] Particularly lucid analyses of Lacan's work and its implications for feminist theory can be found in Mitchell and Rose 1983, and Gallop 1982. Representative examples of the French feminist writings referred to here, which include the work of Luce Irigaray and Héléne Cixous, can

be found in Marks and Courtivron (eds.) 1981.

[3] See, for example, Gallop's discussion of Montrelay's and Irigaray's analyses of female sexuality (Gallop 1982: 27-41).

[4] See Harding (1986a, 1986b) and the essays collected in Harding and Hintikka (1983) for examples of the positions described here; the papers by Hartsock and Keller are particularly relevant. Keller's paper also appears in her collection of essays, *Gender and Science.*

[5] I have elsewhere considered similar arguments made by feminist anthropologists, who claim that women, by view of their marginality and thus their "double-consciousness," are in a position to offer more valid ethnographic accounts than are men, whose gender-linked perspectives are dismissed as biased (Shapiro 1981: 458-463). Problems with these arguments include reliance on an analytically naive opposition between "appearance" and "reality," and a failure to make sufficient use of theoretical and empirical work on the sociology of knowledge. The result can be a rather crude double standard which, while having the charm of reversing the usual gender hierarchy, is equally untenable.

[6] Perhaps the best sources for these ideas are two essays, "A Linguistic Consideration of Thinking in Primitive Communities" and "The Relation of Habitual Thought and Behavior to Language," which were written in the 1930's and later anthropologized in Whorf's collected essays, published in 1955 under the title *Language, Thought, and Reality.* Since the time of Whorf's writing, a huge critical and experimental literature has developed around his thesis of linguistic relativity and the relationship between thought and language, which I will not even attempt to refer to here, since much of it fails to join issues with Whorf's major concerns, reducing his view instead to matters of perception and lexical reference. It is also worth pointing out, since philosophers have arguments about relativism, that the tradition of which Whorf was a part approached linguistic and cultural relativism within the context of developing satisfactory modes of cross-linguistic and cross-cultural analysis, enabling us to transcend ethnocentric projection. Relativism, in this instance, constitutes a necessary component of the comparative enterprise and not an argument for its impossibility.

[7] This tendency was nicely documented several years ago in a study of psychologists' descriptions of mental health: a correspondence was found between descriptions of what is normal in adult men and what is considered normal in adult human beings in general, whereas descriptions of the normal female included qualities that would not be considered normal or healthy in an adult when sex was not specified (Broverman et al 1970).

[8] There are, to be sure, some significant differences between Gilligan and Chodorow that reflect the divergent theoretical commitments of the cognitive-developmental and psychoanalytic orientations that they respectively represent. John Broughton has discussed some of these in his critique of Gilligan's work (Broughton 1983: 632-635). It should be noted,

however, that the major criticisms Broughton levels at Gilligan's work--notably, its tendency toward a "flat, one dimensional psychology" that is missing the characteristic depth and complexity of psychoanalysis and its concerns with illusion, conflict and contradiction--have been leveled more generally at American feminist psychologists, including those who are more psychoanalytically inclined than Gilligan (see, for example, Gallop 1982, pp. 2-4).

[9] Two particularly useful collections of critical commentaries are to be found in *Social Research* (volume 50, number 3; autumn, 1983) and *Signs* (volume 11, number 2; winter 1986). See also Auerbach et al 1985.

[10] For recent theoretical and ethnographic discussions of this issue, see the articles by Comaroff, Yanagisako, Maher, and Rapp in Collier and Yanagisako, in press, as well as Borker n.d. and Maltz n.d.

2

PHALLIC SYMBOLISM AND REPRODUCTIVE EXPROPRIATION: SEXUAL POLITICS IN CROSS CULTURAL PERSPECTIVE

Alexander Alland, Jr.
Columbia University

Introduction

When asked why they brutalize their women Baruya men reply, "They merit it!" (Godelier, personal communication). This attitude is not untypical in the New Guinea highlands (cf. Berndt 1962, Brown 1964, Meggitt 1964, Allen 1975, Langness 1967, Strathern 1972, and, of course, Godelier 1976, 1982). Coupled with this brutalization is a series of beliefs and practices that isolate men from women, but in the New Guinea context, also reinforce their economic and political dominance. These include ritualized homosexuality, the symbolic identification of males with certain aspects of female physiology, the existence of men's houses (barred to women), and strong notions of female pollution (particularly by means of menstrual blood).

All of this occurs on a background of economic relations in which men dominate women and expropriate their labor. Frequently this labor is used to fuel exchange networks, particularly those associated with ritual and the public making of big men. If, as among the Baruya, big men are made in war (and to a lesser extent in the manufacture and trading of salt), women's labor is, nonetheless expropriated by men who control practically every sphere of secular and ritual life.

Male ritual identification with female physiological and procreational functions is contradictory in the light of an ideology that devalues women. The Freudian explanation that this identification is a reflection of male envy of female genitals (Bettleheim 1962) is unacceptable for New Guinea. It does nothing as it stands to remove the contradiction unless one adopts the unfalsifiable position that male ideology merely masks male envy of women. Hage (1981) suggests that both male genital mutilation and ritualized homosexuality, as well as other traits of what he calls "rites of sexual symmetry," can best be accounted for by the natives themselves. The indigenous explanation is that such rites act to stimulate male growth. Following Douglas (1975) Hage then attempts to set these practices in a social context, one that emphasizes competition and achieved status in the arena of a big man complex.

Following Hage's advice that beliefs must be understood in their social context I think it can be shown that what has been accepted by some as the envy of males for certain female attributes has very different meanings in different social contexts. What I shall attempt to do in the rest of this paper is to expand on the notion of male dominance as it is expressed among the Baruya in their male initiation ceremonies and explain how certain women's behaviors, although directed aggressively against men, act to reinforce sexual inequality. Of key importance in this analysis shall by a myth that explains why matriarchal power was overthrown by men. In this myth the symbols of power are phallic objects, sacred flutes. I shall then compare the Baruya data to data from other societies in Australia, Lowland South America, and Africa where versions of this myth occur. My argument shall be that, in some contexts, particularly New Guinea, "growth ceremonies," including initiation, as well as the myths that support them, *are* a clear reflection of political and economic dominance by men. As such they do constitute a rationalization for, as well as the acting out of, the alienation of reproduction from women by men. In other political-economic contexts, however, such myths and practices may actually reflect male envy, not so much of the female genitals as of female reproductive powers.[1]

The Baruya

Godelier (1976, 1977, 1982) has described Baruya society as acephalous. The population is divided into thirteen patriclans, each segmented into local lineages. Villages are inhabited by members of from three to five lineage segments belonging to different clans. Patrilocality is preferred, but individuals have considerable choice in post-marital residence. Cross-cutting ties exist in the form of four male age-grades. The latter are key elements of Baruya social structure. This importance is reflected in the time and effort expended on age-grade initiation ceremonies, that occur about every other year, during which boys move from grade to grade. Young men enter the cycle about the age of nine and do not achieve full adult status until around the age of twenty when they have married and their wives have borne children. Individual initiates move up one grade every other ceremonial period, or about every four years. Ceremonies for the first stage (*Yivupmbuaya*) occur at irregular intervals and are separate from the ceremonies of the other three stages. In general boys enter the second stage (*Kawetnya*) at the age of 12, the third stage (*Chuwanya*) at the age of 16, and the final stage (*Kalave*) at the age of 20.

I now wish to examine two events that appear in the films *Toward Baruya Manhood* made under the ethnological guidance of Maurice Godelier. The first event is central and takes up the bulk of these unique documents. This is the initiation itself. The second event, apparently peripheral, is used only in an introductory segment of the first film which serves to familiarize viewers with certain general aspects of Baruya culture. This is the making of scarecrows for garden use. It is my contention that these two events, although temporally separated and of unequal importance, are two acts of the same social drama and operate together to reinforce the prevalent ideology of male dominance.

On the surface, my contention may appear paradoxical. While women are banned from participation in male initiation, the tasks of scarecrow-making falls to them and they appear to enjoy it. In fact, scarecrow-making provides women with an opportunity to engage in a mild parody of initiation. It is, therefore, an act in which women are permitted to mock openly what is to the men an event of great importance and seriousness. In male dominated Baruya society, scarecrowmaking is a unique occasion for the *public* display of derision of males by females.

Initiation

Baruya initiation is a processual event *par excellence*. Boys do not achieve full adult status until they have passed through all four stages. Each grade has its special role to play during the six week ceremony. Since these rites do not occur annually the process of becoming an adult male is a major *temporal* as well as social feature of every young man's life. In addition, the ceremony itself is preceded by a long preparatory period during which men, with the aid of women and children, construct a special ceremonial house, a *Chimya* (Womb). During the construction of this house we see an instance of overt and public female aggression against males. After a set of poles is planted in the ground and bent to form a dome, men mount the structure and the women throw roofing materials up to them. These are tough grass stalks cut so the base of the stem forms a sharp point. The women fling these stalks up to, or, more correctly, at, them like spears. Not infrequently, the men are superficially wounded, particularly in the thighs or buttocks. Judging from the film, this act on the part of women is performed with considerable fury, but also with enjoyment. There is little doubt that they intend to draw blood, and are delighted when they hit the mark.

When the house is finished, the ceremony proper begins. Young boys about to enter the initiation cycle are wrenched from their mother's company and publicly beaten. Women in the process of losing their sons, and helpless to protect them, respond with rage and bereavement. Boys and mothers will be separated for the entire ten or twelve year period of initiation. They will not be allowed to talk to one another until the entire cycle is completed. As far as mothers are concerned, boys at this period suffer a temporary, but long, social death. Sons are mourned as if they had really died.

Until initiation boys dress the same way as little girls. A major aspect of the rite is the dressing of the boys in adult men's clothes by their male relatives. As each boy passes through a particular stage of the cycle he gives up a part of female dress and adopts a part of adult male adornment. This process symbolizes a cutting of ties for boys with the world of their mothers as well as the establishment of new ties in the universe of male kinsmen. Preparatory to the ceremony men and women spend many hours making elaborate grass skirts out of ritually specialized plant materials. Layer upon layer of these skirts are worn by adult men who look very much like pregnant women as they strut around the village. A well dressed Baruya man wears about 100 of these skirts. Women's dress is rather drab in comparison and consists of a simple covering of the genital area.

During initiation special insignia of rank, marking each age-grade, are bestowed on the initiates. This process includes piercing the nasal septum for the insertion of cassowary quills. In addition, boys are rubbed with stinging nettles, and vomiting is induced by the swallowing and subsequent removal of long segments of palm leaf. These are all common events in the course of male initiation in the New Guinea Highlands. Such ordeals have both physical and symbolic significance. Boys are purged of old identities and marked with the signs of adult maleness. They are slowly transformed into men.

Scarecrow Making

Scarecrow making is an intravillage event. It does not necessarily take place at the same time as initiation. Women, girls, and uninitiated boys participate. The scarecrow figure, a practical object, always male, is made of wood and vegetable materials. Although crude in form it is realistic. The figure is equipped with a full set of male genital organs and is dressed by the women in grass skirts like an adult male. The species of grass used in the manufacture of these skirts, however, must not be the same as the one used in the manufacture of men's clothing.[2]

The scarecrow is an adult male figure complete in biological equipment *and* cultural insignia. At the same time it is clearly distinguishable from a proper representation of such a male. The materials used in the skirts signal the difference. It is reinforced by the fact that the male scarecrow is dressed by women, an event that in real life between the sexes is forbidden to them.

As can be readily seen there are both major differences and similarities between scarecrow making and male initiation. The similarities point to a unifying theme while the differences underscore Baruya male ideology. The symbolic elements in both events can be tabulated as follows:

INITIATION	SCARECROW MAKING
MALES ONLY	FEMALES AND UNINITIATED BOYS
SACRED EVENT	SECULAR EVENT
RITE OF TRANSITION	NO TRANSITION
SEXUAL HOSTILITY MANIFEST	SEXUAL HOSTILITY NOT MANIFEST
MEN DRESS BOYS	WOMEN DRESS SCARECROWS
"CORRECT" MATERIALS	"INCORRECT" MATERIALS
RULES REINFORCED	RULES BROKEN
AFFECT SERIOUS	AFFECT JOVIAL
INTERVILLAGE	INTRAVILLAGE
LONG EVENT	SHORT EVENT
PERFORMED INSIDE	PERFORMED OUTSIDE

This ordered set of resemblances and differences (the differences are differences of contrast) suggest that scarecrow making is one part of a performance: a minor act in a two act play. Together, initiation, as the major event, and scarecrow making, as the minor event, form a symbolic structure. They share a central focus having to do with adult malehood. Initiation is a powerful ceremony. It transforms everyday life, producing a condensation and heightened awareness of maleness and, at least through contrast, of femaleness. The public exclusion of women from initiation and the display of loss it represents demonstrate the powerlessness of women in the face of male dominance.

Scarecrow making involves the construction of an artificial, practical object in the context of an open social activity. As an activity, however, it is a mild parody of Baruya beliefs concerning maleness. But this, I submit, is only its surface meaning. In order to see how scarecrow making is also an aspect of male ideology we must take another look at sexual hostility from the female side.

I have already noted that the participation of Baruya women in the construction of the initiation house has a clearly hostile aspect. Women throw building materials *at* the men the way men throw spears in war.

How else do women express their hostility to men? Godlier (1976) cites the following:

1. Wives can "forget" to cook for their husbands or to save food for them.

2. Wives can refuse to take care of their husband's pigs or gardens.

3. Wives can refuse their husbands sexual access.

4. Verbal sexual abuse directed by a wife towards her husband may lead to his suicide.

5. Baruya men believe that women can kill their husbands through sorcery by gathering semen after intercourse and throwing it into the fire.

6. Wives can abort themselves or kill their newborn as an an act of revenge and spite against their husbands.

7. Wives can commit suicide (a practice that will lead the woman's lineage to take revenge against her husband's lineage).

In addition, as I have already suggested, scarecrow making and the making of initiation houses provide women with outlets for hostility on the symbolic and ceremonial level. Several of these acts have a common element. When women commit suicide, they act against men, but also against themselves. As they throw building material up at the men during the construction of the *Chimya*, they contribute to the building of a structure in which they will lose their sons. As they kill their husband's offspring they kill their own offspring. In these cases their rage is the rage of Medea. It is a fury that strikes at their own powers of reproduction. In this context I think it is fair to suggest that scarecrow making might contain a strong symbolic element that also acts against women. When women make scarecrows they give symbolic birth to a particular kind of adult male: a male that in contrast to real men, who are fierce warriors, is frightening only to birds. Thus the parody involved in scarecrow making may well mock male initiation, but it also says clearly that when women attempt to make men they can only make scarecrows.

The total public nature of scarecrow making contrasts with two forms of reproduction, one biological and the other social. For the Baruya real birth and real initiation are each, in their own ways, private events. When women are about to give birth they retire to a secret place. When a woman has a still birth or kills her new born she does so out of public view. When men "make" men they do so in a public arena, but one that is barred to females and young boys. In contrast, when a woman participates in making a scarecrow-man it is a fully public act and, like initiation, it involves group participation. Women are allowed to "fail" biologically in private (*normal* reproduction produces live babies) while failure in social reproduction is a public act. In making scarecrows women reiterate their inability to make real men. Scarecrow making is clearly not biological reproduction; as social reproduction it is a failure.

I have called male initiation and scarecrow making two acts of a single play; yet, one act, initiation, is long and involves a great deal of pre-ceremonial preparation while the other act, scarecrow making, is a temporally minor occurrence. If this is the case how can these two events be equated? In one sense, they cannot be. Scarecrow making is merely a coda to the act of initiation. To see why this *must* be the case we shall now turn to the Baruya myth that deals with male dominance.

According to Godelier, the Baruya myth tells of a former time during which women controlled ritual life. They were the keepers of sacred flutes and the performers of major ceremonials from which men were excluded. But women, like Pandora in Greek mythology, were unworthy guardians of sacred power. They sowed disorder. Men were forced to rebel against female authority and took over ritual functions. In this way they became the guardians of sacred objects and the guarantors of social order. This mythical rebellion provides the charter for present day secular domination as well. This is why the Baruya believe that knowledge and power are unequally distributed among the sexes.

...there is a general disparity between men and women regarding the possession of knowledge and power, whether ritualistic, political, or economic. Women have their own fertility magic which they pass from mother to daughter. Moreover women -- even those who become shamans and therefore maintain unusual contact with the invisible -- may never reach the highest ranks of the shaman hierarchy. Proof of this is shown when they take part in rites for disease or chasing away evil spirits; they must remain seated and cannot stand in ceremonial enclosures or join in the dance of the male shamans who are fighting the evil spirits (Godelier 1977:198-99).

Taken in the context of the myth of male dominance scarecrow-making is an important coda for it reverses a set of ritual acts: the proper initiation of boys and therefore the making of real men. Scarecrow making is a deritualized ritual, that is, it moves a set of ideological concerns back from the ritual to the secular scene. Furthermore, this must be the case since women have lost ritual power through the Baruya version of original sin. If scarecrow making were a long and solemn event it would lose its secular focus and therefore its own symbolic significance. Making a scarecrow is a minor event, but it must be so, for it involves women in symbolically breaking rules of sexual and social conduct that strike at the very fabric of Baruya order. They "repeat" the origin myth and sown disorder, but they do so only in a minor way so that Baruya culture is not terribly threatened by their act. Furthermore, this act is countered by initiation. Men take control and through initiation reestablish social order. By taking unto themselves the power to make men, men alienate an aspect of reproduction from women. The Baruya cannot escape the fact that it is women who bear children. Instead they have superimposed a social fact upon this biological reality. Only men can make men. This is a far cry from genital envy!

Male initiation does not occur every year. Scarecrow making is an event that can occur more than once during the yearly cycle. Scarecrows are made when they are needed. Because they are made within a settlement for the use of local inhabitants no intervillage participation is necessary. The forces needed to make a scarecrow are easily mobilized and need not interrupt daily life. Thus even as they "break" a set of rules women allow the rules of ordinary life to run their course. Scarecrow making is a purely pedestrian activity. Male initiation, in contrast involves the breaking of the ordinary work cycle. At the same time, warfare ceases and villages become temporarily united. In fact initiation, is the only solidifying intervillage event that occurs in Baruya culture. Men thus break the social order in order to strengthen it. Their act is dramatic and extraordinary.

In *Political Systems of Highland Burma* Edmond Leach has the following to say about Katchin agricultural activity:

> In Kachin 'customary procedure' the routines of clearing the ground, planting the seed, fencing the plot, and weeding the growing crop are all patterned according to formal conventions and interspersed with all kinds of technically superfluous frills and decorations. It is these frills and decorations which make the performance a Kachin performance and not just a simple functional act. And so it is with every kind of technical action; there is always an element which is functionally essential and another element which is simply the local custom, an aesthetic frill... . It seems to me ... that it is precisely these customary frills which provide the social anthropologist with his primary data. Logically aesthetics and ethics are identical. If we are to understand the ethical rules of a society, it is the aesthetics that we must study (Leach 1954: 12).

Scarecrows don't need genital organs that are buried under multiple layers of grass skirts. They don't have to be dressed by women in public. In fact scarecrows could just as well be made by men in a division of labor in which men do perform many agricultural tasks. Is it an accident that Baruya boys, as they become men, are dressed by men in skirts that make them look like pregnant women? It seems to me that none of these are insignificant acts. They have a common structure: a symbolic underpinning that gives a physical presence to male ideology. Scarecrow making must be a symbolic activity, but it *must also* be a secular activity: a secular ritual. It draws its special meaning from this relationship.

Alienating women from reproduction is by no means gratuitous. In Highland New Guinea women are consistently alienated from much of their production as well. It is the pigs raised by women, often with great care and affection, that are used by men to transform themselves into big men. Although this is not the case among the Baruya, where big men are successful warriors, the Baruya share the ideology of male dominance that is so prevalent in the area and they do rely on the productive activities of women to sustain themselves as they make their reputations as fighters. In wide areas of New Guinea, men take production and reproduction unto themselves one way or another. Men not only make other men, but, ultimately, if they are to become big men, they make themselves.

Reproduction and The Loss of Matriarchal Power in Comparative Perspective

So far I have attempted to show how initiation and a myth of male dominance along with a specific secular act (scarecrow making) articulate with other aspects of Baruya culture. My argument has been that ritually performed "reproductive behavior" by men is not, at least among the Baruya, an example of genital envy, but rather an expression of the alienation of reproduction from women by men in a society politically and economically dominated by men. The central myth in this belief-behavior complex explains why men have taken the sacred instruments of ritual power away from women who were their original owners. Women, the myth tells us, misused their power and broke the cultural order by sowing disorder. In the myth the instruments of power are phallic rather than vaginal in nature. This symbolic choice, of course validates the current state of male dominance with a biological fact: the phallus is a male attribute. On this background homosexual behavior, metaphorical male pregnancies (at least a possible inference from Baruya male dress), as well as the male capacity to "give birth" to men in the context of initiation, cannot be taken as examples of male envy of female genitals or of female reproductive capacities, for that matter. Expropriation is not the same thing as envy.

The "sacred flute" myth is common all over the Papua-New Guinea area (Herdt 1981). As a myth of matriarchal power loss it is also found in Australian Aboriginal mythology (Allen 1975). More striking is the fact that similar myths also occur, sometimes with, and, sometimes without, flutes, but always with appropriately phallic objects, in Lowland South American (Reichel-Dolmatoff 1971, Murphy and Murphy 1974) and Africa (Turnbull 1961, d'Azevedo 1973, Glaze 1981).[3] In what follows I shall argue that, while the control of ritual by men often requires mythic justification, and that such justification is often expressed in what might be called "Freudian" metaphors, the ultimate meaning for these metaphors is variable and dependent upon gender relations as they operate in the political-economic sphere.

Diffusion is a possible explanation for the occurrence of myths of this type in both Australia and New Guinea. Of course, because flutes do not exist in Australia, there the mythic objects are the bull roarer and sacred poles. Although ritual in Australia is generally controlled by men, economic life is relatively egalitarian in spite of an ideal division of labor in which men hunt and women gather. Survival depends upon sharing and there is no pattern of labor expropriation by one sex from the other. In this overall context, including the strong possibility that myths concerning the loss of matriarchal power from Australia and Papua-New Guinea have a common origin, it is interesting to note that in a version of this myth collected by Allen (1975) the fact that reproductive powers are exclusively female is an integral part of the story. In this version women lose their control over ceremony not because they sow disorder; rather it is stolen from them by men. The myths says:

Two Djanggawul sisters from Northern Arnhem land have control of sacred knowledge and possess the clan totems. They have two phallic objects, the *djuda* and *mawalan* poles. When the former is thrust to the ground it causes the *djuda* tree to grow, while the latter causes springs to flow. Thus both objects are associated with fertility. As the sisters journey across the country their brother continually asks them to share their powers with him. One night the brother tries to steal the totems but is discovered by his sisters and beaten by one of them. Finally three men of their clan, who have been camping nearby, manage to steal the sacred objects. The myth ends as follows:

'Let it be sister,' said Bildjiwuraroiju with resignation. 'There is nothing to be done. The men have stolen the power of our totems and will never reurn it. But all is not lost: we have the greatest power of all and it cannot be stolen. For only from our wombs can children come. All men must come from us. And we know the songs already. These we will not forget. So we will let the men keep the totems and conduct the ceremonies. From this time women will gather the yams and make palm nut bread. We will gather food to nourish the children and the men. We will comfort them, for we know we have the greater power (Allen 1975:58)

Turning to Lowland South America the loss of matriarchal power myth, in a form strikingly similar to that of the Baruya version, can be found among the Mundurucu (Murphy and Murphy 1974). Here the possibility for diffusion is remote, indeed, yet the myth contains all the major elements of the Baruya story. It says that in the past the sacred rituals were under the control of women who possessed sacred trumpets which they had found in a forest lake. Fascinated by their new powers, "The women devoted their lives to the instruments and abandoned their husbands and housework to play them" (Murphy and Murphy 1974:88). Annoyed by this the men finally tell the women, "We want the trumpets and will take them tomorrow. If you do not give them to us, then we will not go hunting, and there will be not meat to offer them." Yanyon-bori agreed, for she knew they could not hunt for the food for the trumpets or for the guests at the ceremonies" (Murphy and Murphy 1974:89). The myth recounts a clear inversion of gender power:

> The men entered the dwelling houses, and the women marched around and around the village playing the trumpets. Then they entered the men's house for the night and installed the instruments there. Then, one by one the women went to the dwelling houses and forced the men to have coitus with them. The men could not refuse, just as the women today cannot refuse the desires of men.... The next day the men took the trumpets from the women and forced them to go back to the dwelling house. The women wept at their loss (Murphy and Murphy 1974:89).

The Mundurucu are a patrilineal but matrilocal society with moieties. Men spend most of their time in the village men's house (also a common living arrangement in Papua-New Guinea), are the political leaders, and hunt as well as fish. Ritualized homosexuality does not exist here and Mundurucu men do not claim to make other men, but male power does rest, in part, on the expropriation of women's labor. The myth has a clear phallic content which is not tempered by other aspects of the culture, either ritual or secular. Women who transgress the wishes of men are subject to sanctions including gang rape. As the Murphys note:

> The myth of the karoko is a parable of phallic dominance, of male superiority symbolized in and based upon, the possession of the penis. But it is at best an uneasy overlordship, obtained only by expropriation from the original custody of the women (Murphy and Murphy 1974:95).

In this society, men must reinforce their dominant role through constant vigilance and self-assertion.

The Desana Indians (Reichel-Dolmatoff 1971) have a ceremony in which phallic objects described as trumpets and flutes are of central importance. Some of these are identified as male; others as female. A Desana myth explains the rule of these instruments in ritual. In it, the Sun Father rapes his prepubescent daughter. (Reichel-Dolmatoff notes that for the Desana such a crime is one of the highest sins, thus the event is of great mythical importance." The rape was witnessed by a praying mantis which changed into a human being and manufactured a trumpet which he used to denounce the crime. Later, after the adoption of flutes and trumpets in Desana ritual, women, for who these instruments are taboo, remove them from the lake where they had been hidden by men:

> But when they touched their own bodies with the hands that had

been touching the flutes, suddenly hair grew on their pubis, and under their armpits, places that previously had not hair. When the men returned...the women seduced them and, although they belonged to the same phatry, they cohabited with them. *Only after supernatural punishments which the myth does not describe, were the men able to establish order again.*

This fragmentary myth shows...the passage creation to chaos because of forbidden sexual acts, followed by the reestablishment of the social order in terms of exogamic law. Since then the flutes are played periodically as a reminder of this great sin (Reichel-Dolmatoff 1971:169-70, italics mine).

This myth is associated with a ceremony in which the instruments are played by men while women are forced to hide. Later it involves the distribution of fruit and meat and the beating of the women with stinging nettles. What begins as a solemn occasion turns into a sham battle between the sexes. The women, pretending to flee, actually allow the men to touch them and the ceremony ends with a feast and dancing.

Sexual union among the Desana is viewed, as it is in Highland New Guinea, with fear and anxiety. Homosexuality occurs in high frequency among both men and women, but is not institutionalized. Incest is defined as the greatest of crimes and stands for the disorder that women can sow even though the original act of incest in the myth was committed by a *male*, the Sun Father. An element of male guilt, which is not manifest in the ceremony, is embedded in the myth. In the myth, however, the incestuous male is also a god; the incestuous females are mortals. In the ceremony no gods are imitated, and the flutes (both male and female), forbidden to women are played exclusively by men. The reestablishment and maintenance of order depend upon male initiative with the cooperation of women.

There are no domestic food animals in Desana culture. The men hunt and fish while the women perform most of the horticultural tasks. Hunting accounts for about 25% of the food supply, but is the most highly valued activity of the men, and, at least in their eyes, in the society at large as well. There are no big men, no men's houses, and no important trading networks. Subsistence is essentially a family oriented cooperative venture and the accumulation of wealth is not an important element in the culture. Male dominance exists, but only in attenuated form and female claims are expressed in both myth and ritual.

Let me now turn to two African cases in which phallic objects tied to an explanatory myth are found to occur.

Colin Turnbull (1961) describes the Mbuti of the Ituri forest as one of the most egalitarian societies known to anthropologists:

The woman is not discriminated against in Bambuti society as she is in some African societies. She has a full and important role to play. There is relatively little specialization according to sex. Even the hunt is a joint effort. A man is not ashamed to pick mushrooms and nuts if he finds them, or to wash or clean a baby. A woman is free to take part in the discussions of the men if she has something relevant to say (Turnbull 1961:154).

Among the Mbuti there is no male initiation ceremony, but there is one for girls, the *elima*, which celebrates their puberty. The other major ceremony, the *molimo*, is, according to Turnbull and Godelier (1977), a unifying ritual that ties all Mbuti participants to one another and to the forest which is taken as both father *and* mother of the people. Yet the major symbol of the *molimo* is a great horn, a phallic object. The origin of the *molimo* sound is a secret kept from the women who are not supposed to know how it is made. Turnbull was surprised to find, however, that at the end of a *molimo* ceremony he witnessed, the women's former possession of the *molimo* was made evident.

> After a while the men started singing again, but gently, and then with a shock I realized that the women were singing as well, the sacred songs of the *molimo*. And they were not just joining in, they were leading the singing. Songs I thought only the men knew and were allowed to sing -- all of a sudden the women were showing that they not only knew them but could sing them with just as much intensity...(Turnbull 1961:150). All the others were in their huts, and the men seemed to be singing as though by their song they could drive the last remaining female away. They sang louder and harder, but she kept circling the *kumamolimo*, keeping in the shadows, until with surprisingly swift and agile strides she was once more in our midst. In her hands she held a log roll of *nkusa* twine. The men continued singing, and as they sang, the old woman went around knotting a loop around each man's neck, so that in the end we were all tied together (Turnbull 1961:155).

Turnbull's informants explained that the woman had bound the men, the hunt, and the *molimo* together. In order to be freed the men had to admit their bondage and give the woman something as a token of their defeat. In addition to this dramatization the Mbuti have a myth stating that the women once owned the *molimo*, and that the men had stolen it from them! In this egalitarian society the very fact that a major ritual (complete with phallic symbolism) is the exclusive property of men is questioned in the context of that very ceremony. Genital envy does not appear to play a role here. Instead the "male" gender quality of the ritual object is affirmed, as is the transfer of its custodianship from the women to men in mythic times.

The forest areas of Liberia, Guinea, Southern Sierra Leone, and the western Ivory Coast are peopled by ethnic groups that practice intensive slash-and-burn horticulture and live in relatively stable settlements.

These cultures are patrilineal and patrilocal. Big men do not exist (chiefdom is hereditary) and labor is cooperative on the lineage level. Women's labor is not expropriated by men for their exclusive benefit. Independent villages and groups of petty chiefdoms are bound together by a number of task and ritual specific secret societies that even cross ethnic boundaries. Men succeed to, and occupy, patrilineal secular political positions, but much of political life is played out and reinforced through ritual in the context of secret societies. While membership in these societies is limited by sex, both men's and women's societies exist. The most important of these are the *Sande*, for women, and the *Poro*, for men. According to d'Azevedo, who studied the secret societies of the Gola, Vai, and De in coastal Liberia, "The greatest public dramas of life are played out in the cycle of ceremonies connected with the recruitment and maintenance of membership in the all-powerful and universal male and female secret associations" (d'Azevedo 1973:127).

The myth associated with these societies states that the first use of them was the *Sand*:

> Women were the custodians of all ritual and the spiritual powers necessary for defending sacred tradition in the interests of the ancestors (d'Azevedo 1973:127).

> In the ancient days of peace and perfect social order...*Sande* was the single and all powerful sacred institution. Though men ruled, women controlled all communal intercourse with the ancestors and their spirit guardians, and men submitted to female domination in ritual matters.... But there came a time of terrible wars in which enemies attacked and tried to destroy the country. When the men of the Gola chiefdoms attempted to organize themselves for defense, the women resisted because it interfered with the activities of *Sande*....Furthermore, men learned that women cannot be trusted with the secrets of war; for though they jealously kept the secrets of *Sande* from men, they would speak out the plans of the men to their enemies (d'Azevedo 1973:129).

According to tradition it was women and war that brought the Poro society into existence. Rather than overthrow *Sande* and seize its sacred instruments the men went into the forest where they discovered and subdued a monster which became their source of power. This monster, so frightening that women cannot look at it, is the god of *Poro*. The *Poro* spirit was used by men to subdue women. The women begged for a return to the old ways, but the men refused. Instead they agreed that each society would take its turn in ritual control. A cycle was established in which the *Poro* rules for four years and the *Sande* for three.

Although the myth of *Sande's* partial fall makes no mention of phallic objects one does appear in the *Poro* ritual. While the great spirit of the *Poro* is said to be invisible, *Poro* helmet masks are topped with a small head at the end of a long thin neck. During pubic performances of *Poro* ritual a dancer wearing this mask teases the women present by running at them with his head tilted downward. The response of the crowds during this ritual leaves no doubt that the long neck and head mounted on the mask, taken together, are, in fact, a phallus. The *Sande* ritual also involves masking, but, as we might expect from what has come before, no phallic symbol is present. An interesting fact about the *Sande* mask is that it must be carved by a male sculptor who enters into a special relationship with the *Sande* group that becomes his sponsor. He is privy to information about *Sande* and has a relationship with its women that no other man can have. In a very real sense the carver is courted by the women of *Sande* as a man might court a woman whom he wishes to marry. He may even enter into a ritualized sexual relationship with a leading *Sande* woman.

When a carver finishes a mask he gives it a name, either that of some woman he has known or a name given to him by his guardian spirit. The *Sande* women, however, will have none of this. They select a male name for the mask which is to be their spiritual husband. Even after the mask is carved and delivered the carver continues to have a special relationship with the *Sande* group for which he has worked. According to d'Azevedo, they jokingly refer to one another as lovers and he, at least, in principle, can expect sexual favors from them. "This relationship is carried out with the air of a clandestine affair, with the woodcarver in the unique position of a male sharing secret knowledge and illicit intimacies with important women of *Sande*" (d'Azevedo 1973:148). D'Azevedo quotes a woodcarver's expression of delight as he sees his mask come to life in ritual performance:

I say to my self, this is what my *neme* has brought it to my mind. I say, I have made this. How can a man make such a thing? It is a fearful thing I can do. No other man can do it unless he has the right knowledge. No woman can do it. *I feel that I have borne children* (d'Azevedo 1973:148, italics mine).

Here surely, the expression of bearing children by a man does not involve the alienation of reproduction from women, but rather admiration for what women (and by identification carvers) can do. This admiration is transformed into a metaphor for what a limited number of special men do through aesthetic creation in the context of ritual. The phallic element remains in the personification of the *Poro* mask, but it is absent from the *Sande* mask and its carver who metaphorically shares with women the ability to give birth. The metaphor here is one of reproductive envy and fulfillment. It appears against the background of a social order in which women have both economic and ritual value and in which they play an active and personal role in economic and ritual life. Women alternate ritual power with the men, but they have not ceded it to them.

Conclusion

Among the Baruya, and throughout much of Highland New Guinea, myth, ritual, and even much of secular life, combine to reinforce an overriding ideology of male dominance. Women's productive activities are expropriated by men in the real world of economics and politics. In the world of myth and ritual men alienate the reproductive capacities of women by taking unto themselves the making of adult males. In these circumstances, beliefs and practices that, in other contexts might reflect masculine envy of female genitals or of female reproductive functions, are best interpreted as expressions of an ideological system that devalues women.

In Lowland South America, at least among the Mundurucu and the Desana (there are many other examples), male dominance is quite marked, but there is no real big man complex and the complicated trading networks that characterize Highland New Guinea are absent. Women are devalued by men but they fight back in different ways to maintain a near balance in social relations. Among the Mundurucu, as the Murphys tell us, matrilocality provides women with a strong base of solidarity that is absent for men. The myth dealing with the installation of patriarchy gives men a partial and shaky hold over women that is reinforced through physical threats and sanctions. There seems to be no envy of women here, either genital or reproductive. The Desana myth tells us that men held power originally; that his power was threatened by women, only to be retaken by men. The maintenance of the cultural order through the prohibition of incest was established by men. It was this act that gave them the charter to rule. On balance, the Desana myth along with its associated ritual appears to reflect an equilibrium between men and women that is reinforced by the symbolism of sacred objects some of which are designated as female, although all of them appear to have a phallic aspect.

Among the Djanggawul of Australia, where economic and social life are relatively egalitarian, even though men control major rituals, the myth that signals the loss of matriarchal power in a patrilineal society contains its own negation. Men are *allowed* by the women to believe that their totems are secret. Women are said to know that they hold the greater power which is the ability to reproduce the next generation. In addition, the myth makes it clear that totemic power was stolen by the men through no fault of the women who are nowhere characterized as sowers of disorder.

Among the egalitarian Mbuti the myth that justifies patriarchy is also negated, but this time in ritual. In the midst of a phallic rite, forbidden to women, a woman appears who takes power back from the men and reestablishes a female claim over the phallic object and the dominance of women over men.

Among the Gola, a horticultural society with relatively high productivity, economic activity is organized along lineage and family lines. Women occupy important places in both economic and ritual life. While some petty chiefdoms exist, most intervillage political power is vested in secret societies, some open to women and others to men. The male society, the *Poro*, has among its symbols a phallic mask which, judging from the associated myth, was never in the possession of women. Instead women, who were the original keepers of ritual life, had their own set of symbols. Women are valued by Gola society, among other reasons, for their ability to reproduce. This fact is clearly indicated in the rituals of *Sande* where reproduction and female initiation are celebrated. Some men express their own creative needs through the carving of *Sande* ritual masks, an act that is connected to a metaphor of female reproductive powers. Thus some Gola men are able to fulfill their reproductive needs (as women) on the symbolic level as they become mothers of their masks. Such men have a special and honored place in Gola society.

We cannot escape the fact that all through the myths examined in this paper the element of phallic imagery is very strong. Women are said to have held power and to have lost it, in many cases, because of their own inability to follow the rules of culture. The objects that stand for power (and also for culture, it should not be forgotten) are invariably phallic except in the Gola case where the celebration of power is shared between the phallus and female reproductive capacities.

It seems to me that these phallic elements represent a male claim made in the face of a truth that it is women who bear children. This claim is one of male primacy in reproductive matters as well as in the maintenance of culture. It is most prevailing in New Guinea and almost as strong among the Mundurucu. One sees it in somewhat attenuated from among the Desana, and almost, if not quite, symbolically negated among the Mbuti, the Djanggawul, and the Gola. Taken in these terms the problematic comes very close to that noted by Levi-Strauss (1963) in his search for the meaning of the Oedipus myth, for what is being questioned is whether children are the issue of one person or of two, and, if of one, which one, the male or the female. Men claim that it is they who, even if they cannot bear children, make men. The pervasiveness and authenticity of this claim in any particular culture will appear on a continuum and depend upon real gender relations in economic and political life. The continuum runs from total male power and a devaluation of women, through a kind of testy semineutrality in which myth and/or ritual reflect real ambiguities in gender relations, all the way to the appearance of reproductive envy on the part of men in societies in which women have significant economic and ritual power.

The penis on the Baruya scarecrow signals female impotence; its occurrence on the *Poro* mask and its absence on the *Sande* masks signal female strength rather than penis envy. The women of *Sande* act like men as they negotiate for their masks and they successfully force the carver to take on a female role in his dealings with them. His *own* counter claim is couched in the idiom of female reproduction. Among the Gola men make men in *Poro* ceremonies, and women make women in the *Sande* ritual, but overall symbolic life leaves reproduction in the hands of women.

The connection, first noted by Marx, between production and reproduction, and the fact that both are intertwined aspects of social relations appear to hold for traditional societies as well as our own. In both cases production and reproduction are deeply embedded in symbolic life as well as in the facts of mundane existence.

FOOTNOTES

Acknowledgements: I wish to thank Bill MacDonald for suggestions that came after his careful reading of this paper. Errors that remain are, of course, my own.

[1] It seems to me that rather than vaginal envy, it is the envy of female reproductive power that is symmetrical with "penis" envy because it is the function of organs rather than the organs themselves that are turned into symbols and envied as such. In classical Freudian theory it is the phallus that carries symbolic significance, because it is an organ ready for penetration. In any case the literature of myth is full of incidents in which males give birth, and male pregnancy wishes occur frequently in psychoanalytic records.

[2] I cannot be sure from the film material whether the use of incorrect material in skirt making for scarecrows is a male enforced rule of respect, or a conscious mocking of maleness by women. I suspect, however, that women *are* enjoined by men from using correct materials. It is certainly the case that men never allow women to dress them. This does not preclude the possibility that women are amused and satisfied by the act of breaking two cultural rules (dressing a male, and dressing a male with the wrong material) at the same time.

[3] No exhaustive attempt has been made in this paper to search the literature for myths concerning the loss of matriarchal power. The data sampled here suggest that such a laborious task would yield interesting and satisfying results. The myths referred to here were not sought out for their content. Over the years I have simply come across them in my reading of ethnographic documents.

3

OEDIPUS IN THE POLITICAL ECONOMY:
THEME AND VARIATIONS IN AMAZONIA

Orna R. Johnson and Allen Johnson
University of California, Los Angeles

Introduction

In two important works Robert and Yolanda Murphy have addressed the causes and consequences of sex antagonism in the Amazon (Murphy 1959; Murphy and Murphy 1974). In particular, their analysis concerns a complex of beliefs and behaviors that includes both unconscious projections stemming from early Oedipal experiences and social structural factors that segregate men and women and intensify sexual conflict.

In this paper we present ethnographic evidence from the Machiguenga, an Amazon community in which this complex does not occur. We intend, by examining the contexts in which two such different patterns of male-female relationships occur, to contribute to an understanding of how the political economy influences relationships between men and women both within the family and in the society as a whole.

Margaret Mead (1935) early demonstrated that different patterns of male-female relations exist cross-culturally. Later, the Whitings placed these differences in ecological context. They describe two patterns of husband-wife relations -- one of intimacy in which husbands are highly involved in domestic affairs, the other of aloofness in which the husbands are away from their families and spending most of their time with other men (Whiting and Whiting 1975). Aloofness and rooming apart has the psychological effect of producing hyperaggressive males and is associated with warfare and the presence of "a substantial capital investment that needs to be protected" (1975:194).

In pursuing this theme, we will compare the Mundurucu, as described by the Murphys, and the Machiguenga, who contrast with them by living in small family isolates scattered throughout the tropical rain forest of southeastern Peru. The essential difference between the two groups is the greater elaboration of the Mundurucu political economy. In societies like the Mundurucu the main cause of the formation of men's groups is the need for defensive alliances. Collaboration in defense is one of a set of institutionalized behaviors that we will refer to as the political economy, in which we also include multi-household food-sharing, capital investments in technology, and trade. We will show how the political economy not only brings about the need for a collectivity of men, but intensifies competition between men that reaches far beyond the subsistence economy of individual households or closely related family groups.

Men in a highly competitive male arena generally tend to exaggerate their masculine pride and fierceness through such public displays as vociferous oratory, physical contests, and other agonistic behavior. We will describe how Machiguenga men avoid such displays and, when it occurs, label it by a term we translate as "hyper-masculinity."

The plight of men in the competitive arena is shared by their sons, who must emerge from a protective mother-child household into a dangerous male sphere. Theoretically, this intensifies the normal Oedipal difficulties experienced by any boy in shifting his primary identity from his mother to his father. The real dangers attached to the competitive male role make the boy's growth toward "a joyfully entered oedipal stage" (Kohut 1984:68) a difficult and anxious process.

Two Myths

We begin somewhat inductively by examining two "Oedipal-type" myths, one Mundurucu, the other Machiguenga. It is not possible, of course, to draw any firm conclusions about individual psychology or sex roles from two myths, but it is helpful to regard these myths as windows on the ethnographic scenes we will explore momentarily. Similarities in the myths suggest the existence of a widespread, if not universal, pattern of men's ambivalence toward women and fear of violent retribution from other men (particularly from "fathers" and "in-laws"). Differences in the myths suggest how the ambivalence and fear may vary in strength and content from one cultural setting to another.

A Mundurucu Myth

It is easy to see in the following summary why Murphy and Murphy (1974:99) regard this as a "classic" Oedipal myth.

Two brothers-in-law were married to each other's sisters: Wakurumpo was of normal appearance but Karuetaouibo was very ugly, so that his wife did not want him and had intercourse with another man. In the forest unhappy at his fate, Karuetaouibo encountered the Sun and his wife, who asked what he was doing. Hearing his tale, the Sun wished to verify that Karuetaouibo was "incapable of pleasing a woman" and so had his wife test him: she found that his penis was soft and would not enter. Hearing this, the Sun made Karuetaouibo very small and placed him in his wife's womb, from which he was reborn and fashioned into a beautiful man. The Sun then gave Karuetaouibo a basket full of fish and sent him back to his village with instructions to leave his present wife for another woman who lived alone.

There, everyone gathered around to admire Karuetaouibo, and Wakurumpo, who was envious, finally extracted the story from Karuetaouibo. Wakurumpo, although he was already handsome and had a wife who loved him, went to the forest in order to find the Sun. But Karuetaouibo had failed to warn about the test of virility, and so Wakurumpo had successful intercourse with the Sun's wife. Learning of this, the Sun made Wakurumpo small and placed him in his wife's womb; but when he was reborn, the Sun made him ugly and sent him home without fish. There people stared at his ugliness and Karuetaouibo played this song on a flute:

It was your fault, Wakurumpo
It was your fault, Wakurumpo
You were curious for you mother's vagina
You were, you were.

Wakurumpo and Karuetaouibo were killed by enemies, who mounted their heads on posts. Eventually, they rose to heaven to become the visible sun, but men shot Wakurumpo's eyes out as his head was rising. Today, it is Karuetaouibo who shines on bright, sunny days, but Wakurumpo is the sun on dark days, hiding in shame behind clouds because of his ugliness.

A Machiguenga Myth

The following Machiguenga myth of Shakanari, while different in many ways from the Mundurucu myth, is also clearly of the Oedipal genre.

Shakanari lived with his father and mother. One day he went to his uncle's house to ask to marry his daughter. His uncle agreed and Shakanari went home to collect his belongings, but became angry and struck his mother. His father struck him in turn and, because he was so ill-behaved, prohibited him from leaving to get married. But the uncle decided to send his daughter to Shakanari's house anyway, and they married and built a house nearby. After a time, Shakanari's father died, and he moved back in with his mother and began treating her as a wife; that is, he gave all the meat he hunted to her rather than to his own wife.

One day his wife's father and brothers arrived to visit and learned of Shakanari's abandonment of his wife. Angrily, they beat Shakanari and left, taking Shakanari's wife with them.

Thereafter, Shakanari lived alone with his mother. Soon, he finished eating all the plantains in his garden and began stealing them from neighbors. A neighbor asked Shakanari, "Who is stealing our plantains?" Shakanari replied, "It must be a coati. Wait for him at night with a club and kill him." That night, as Shakanari sneaked in to steal plantains, he was struck and killed by the neighbor, who ran out of the dark place crying, "Shakanari! Shakanari! Shakanari! I have killed him!" But Shakanari did not answer. Next day, the neighbor discovered that Shakanari had been the thief, and buried him in the forest.

The "Oedipal" Core of the Myths

The two myths possess a number of similarities that at core constitute the Oedipal story. The focal individuals are young men who are either married or about to be married. These young men experience women ambivalently. On the one hand we find anger and rejection: Karuetaouibo's wife is unfaithful to him, then he leaves her when he becomes handsome; Shakanari strikes his mother as he prepares to leave home and later abandons his wife. On the other hand, there is a fantasy of special closeness with a mother-figure: Shakanari moves in and "marries" his mother; Wakurumpo had intercourse with the maternal figure of the Sun's wife; and both Karuetaouibo and Wakurumpo are placed in her womb and reborn.

It is relevant that food enters into these stories. Part of Shakanari's relationship with his mother is that he does not share meat with his wife, as is expected. This selfishness is reflected later in his theft of the bananas (both meat and plantains are foods produced by males among the Machiguenga, and the plantains have an obvious phallic symbolism). Karuetaouibo, the non-phallic son, receives a basketful of fish from his Sun/father, but the incestuous Wakurumpo receives none.

Likewise, and clearly as a consequence of this special closeness to mother, both myths include violent retribution by senior men. Shakanari's father strikes him, then his father-in-law (and brothers-in-law) beat him, and finally a neighbor kills him. The Sun makes Wakurumpo ugly. Both Karuetaouibo and Wakurumpo are killed and beheaded by enemies. Wakurumpo's eyes are shot out by an enemy shaman.

Both myths also represent ambivalence between in-laws. For Shakanari, an originally friendly and accommodating father-in-law becomes a violent punisher. Karuetaouibo and Wakurumpo are brothers-in-law who, although superficially companions, are fundamentally opposed as good (non-incestuous) and handsome *versus* bad (incestuous) and ugly.

In sum, the myths are similar in portraying the conflicts young men feel over their wishes for special closeness with their mothers and other women. They fantasize marriage to mother or a return to her womb, with overtones of abundance of prized food. But this creates difficulties on two levels. At the level of the group, the symbiotic absorption with mother is viewed as antisocial and something to be punished by the men (fathers and in-laws) as surrogates of society. On a more personal level, the boys' selfish wish to have their mothers to themselves generates a fear of jealous retribution by their fathers, and, when they learn that their wish cannot be achieved and must be abandoned, they come to view women as seducers and eventual betrayers.

Differences in the Myths

The Machiguenga myth of Shakanari is notable for not disguising the mother as the object of Shakanari's fantasy of special closeness. Furthermore, sexual feelings and intercourse, while apparently assumed by the story-teller, are not mentioned and it is the issue of food (keeping the meat and stealing the plantains) that holds center stage. Violence, while clearly present, appears subdued, with no mutilation and only one weapon being used, when Shakanari, mistaken for an animal, is killed by a club.

The Mundurucu myth does disguise the father and mother as the Sun and his wife, indicating perhaps a greater need to repress the unconscious meaning of the tale. The male "hero" is split into good and bad forms, which may also distance the listener from the crime. Food, while present, seems less central than sexuality: the "good" son's penis is soft and ineffective whereas the "bad" son achieves male potency and is later taunted, "you were curious for your mother's vagina, you were." Finally, the violence, although treated matter-of-factly in the story, is much more destructive than in the Machiguenga story: mutilation is found in the beheadings, the blinding of Wakurumpo, and in his being made ugly during "re-birth." Making small and ugly (unattractive to women), decapitating, and shooting the eyes out with arrows may all be symbolic forms of castration.

In our examination of men's roles among the Machiguenga and the Mundurucu, we will look for both similar circumstances leading to the standard form of the oedipus complex, as found in both myths, and differences that might explain why the Mundurucu myth 1) disguises the oedipal fantasy, 2) emphasizes sexuality rather than food (orality), and 3) includes more extreme forms of violence and mutilation than the Machiguenga myth.

The Ethnographic Evidence

The Machiguenga Case

The Machiguenga of Peru speak an Arawakan language and inhabit the mountainous *terra firme* lands of the Upper Amazon rain forest east of Cuzco. In order to minimize travel costs in procuring wild foods, including game, fish, fruits, nuts and insects, they typically live in scattered groups of single households or clusters of related households (hamlets). It is also common for a man and his wife or wives to live alone, distant from other kinsmen, for periods of several days to many weeks, even when their main residence is within a hamlet group. As a result, cooperative groups composed solely of men or women tend to be small and occasional, and a monogamous or polygynous household forms a closely bound cooperative unit with a high degree of interdependence among its members, especially the husband and wife.

Although warfare is not unknown in the Upper Amazon, it tended in the past to be concentrated along the lower rivers, where wild foods, particularly fish and game, were more abundant. The Machiguenga, living at altitudes from about 500 to 2,000 meters, experience an extreme scarcity of fish and game, a scarcity that increases with altitude until human settlement finally disappears in the Cloud Forest, a sterile, inhospitable zone intermediate between the tropical rain forest of the Machiguenga and the arid high *puna* of the Quechuas. Our best evidence is that warfare was relatively rare in this undesirable "refuge zone," and that the Machiguenga have long lived in family groups as they strive to do today. During the Inca empire the Machiguenga maintained trade relationships with the Quechuas, providing the empire with a variety of jungle products in exchange for tools and utensils. Later, the efforts of European organized rubber collectors to enslave Machiguengas for labor at lower altitudes reinforced their tendency to scatter thinly throughout the forest, hiding their trails and maintaining readiness for immediate flight whenever outsiders intruded.

A competent Machiguenga married couple master between them all the skills necessary for complete self-sufficiency in the forest. The division of labor by sex apportions work in such a way that men's and women's tasks rarely overlap, but there is a high degree of complementarity and cooperation in the production of food and manufactures (Johnson and Johnson 1975). In slash-and-burn gardens they produce a surplus that enables them to survive on their own, although exchange networks exist and households commonly share food with one another (Johnson 1983). By supplementing diverse garden produce with wild foods from the forest, a household is able to maintain a culturally appropriate standard of living with a moderate work investment, minimizing competition from other households, including those of close kinsmen.

The Machiguenga ideal is to be able to move residence more or less freely back and forth between isolated nuclear or extended households and hamlets where three to five households of close kinsmen cluster. At the time of our fieldwork in Shimaa in 1972-3, three such hamlets had come into the orbit of a new government school, but had maintained their traditional separateness by locating at intervals of a half-hour's walk by trail along the Kompiroshiato River and its tributary, the Shimaa River. In addition, most of the households kept a separate house near a garden at considerable distance (2-4 hours by trail) from their hamlet, where they would go for periods of time to escape the "crowded" conditions of the hamlets (see Johnson and Baksh 1987).

The Machiguenga hamlet is best conceived of as a grown-up family of married brothers and sisters, comprising from 20 to 35 members. Residence is typically neolocal with a strong preference for living near both the husband's and wife's relatives. This is an ideal pattern because both men and women remain close to their natal families, allowing both spouses to have parents or siblings in the vicinity -- kinsmen on whom they can rely in times of personal need. The hamlet is thus a highly inbred kin group that forms the behavioral core of each individual's personal network. Ties to individuals in other hamlets may be genealogically close, but behaviorally limited to occasional visits or participation in communal gatherings.

Within the hamlet Machiguenga women are far more likely than men to form cooperative work groups (Johnson and Johnson 1975). Women even form social work groups where no cooperation is needed, simply for the sociability, whereas men rarely do so. Men cooperate occasionally in hunting, but usually hunt alone or in company with a younger man who will serve as bearer. Cooperative fishing with poison (barbasco) is the occasion of most male cooperation, and such events occur sporadically. Otherwise, men work alone, or in the company of their wives. In any case, when Machiguenga men or women work in same-sex groups, the highest probability is that their co-workers are genealogical true siblings, first cousins, or sons or daughters.

Settlement and residence patterns thus disperse individuals in such a manner that no defined male interest groups exist. Men come together only on an *ad hoc* basis, for such purposes as beer feasts and cooperative poison fishing. These gatherings, which are sporadic and short-lived, were traditionally organized by an influential shaman who would establish himself as the center of the neighborhood of hamlets gathered together under his spiritual and physical protection. Today, local school teachers or other influential men with large households take on the role of organizing regional gatherings. Such prominent men host feasts for which their households provide beer and game. During feasts trade goods are exchanged, labor cooperation is arranged, information is shared, and a mood of camaraderie is generated among the men, who have separated from their wives, forming a men's group apart from that of the women (O. Johnson 1980). Women typically remain close to members of their own kin and residence groups, while men more readily intermingle with men from other hamlets.

On these occasions men's behavior has many of the characteristics that we will describe below for horticultural villages. At a beer feast the men, normally reserved, are uncharacteristically boisterous. Aided by the beer, the conversation inevitably tends toward cutting humor in which clever men establish momentary dominance over others. Meanwhile, individuals who leave the party to urinate in the forest may in fact complete extra-marital trysts that have been arranged earlier. Thus the beer feast commonly ends in a certain amount of bad feeling, as the objects of teasing nurse their injured feelings and husbands and wives fight over suspected infidelities.

Similarly, a cooperative poison fishing expedition is an occasion for ribald humor and boisterous interaction. It is organized by a leader who coordinates such men's activities as collecting and pounding the poisonous roots, building the dam, and introducing the poison to the water. Here, again, families have dissolved into men's and women's groups working separately. But this division is short-lived, for once the poison has been introduced to the water, individual family groups reemerge and quietly gather fish in separate, previously selected spots along the poisoned stretch of river.

Thus, a Machiguenga man, while not a stranger to competition with other men, generally lives apart from other men except for his closest genealogical kin, and this remains true today, on the eve of transition to larger communities and inevitable involvement in the Peruvian political economy (see Baksh 1984). The well-enculturated, well-behaved Machiguenga man is quiet, reserved, generous with his kin, and largely indifferent to strangers. He is an agile, skilled and persistant hunter, who can bring down dangerous animals like peccaries or jaguar with bow and arrow, and a hard-working gardener who always has a surplus of foods beyond the needs of his immediate family. He is loyal both to his family of origin and of procreation. Men typically maintain strong bonds with their mothers and sisters, and support them when they have no other men to care for them. Men likewise have affectionate relationships with their wives and children.

The father's presence in the home is particularly significant for the socialization of young boys. His association with the domestic unit provides an early role model for the son. Young boys commonly bathe with their fathers and accompany them to the garden or forest to observe. There is no formal male initiation, rather a gradual transition that allows boys to acquire masculine skills without leaving home or severing ties with their mothers.

Much of men's work in foraging, harvesting, and manufacturing is done either in cooperation with or in the company of their wives. Men also spend much leisure time at home in affectionate grooming, joking, and story-telling. Extra-marital liasons within the hamlet are extremely rare, both because there are few available non-incestuous partners, and because such liasons are highly disruptive. Men are particularly suspicious of visitors from other hamlets, because it is assumed that they have come to seek women or exploit local wild foods. While not inhospitable to an occasional visitor, the Machiguenga remain wary, unless the benefits of marriage and bride-service will follow.

A Machiguenga man is not expected to be violent or aggressive. Men who become enraged and have trouble controlling their aggression are described as "hyper-masculine" (*tovaiti iseraritake*; literally, "plenty he-male-is"). They are frightening to others and are avoided. They may be driven off or killed if they cause too much fear in the community (Johnson 1978). If a man's immediate interests are threatened, he quietly but firmly takes a stand and hopes that confrontation is not necessary.

Javier is a good example of a well-respected individual who responded to conflict by disengaging from the community when angered by pressure to work in the schoolteacher's garden. Javier's own interest was to plant a large garden for his family, which consisted of his wife, five children, his elderly mother, his widowed sister, and her daughter. Because Javier's mother was crippled, he had the added responsibility of carrying her around -- including trips to relieve herself at the edge of the forest. Rather than confront the schoolteacher by refusing to work for him, Javier picked up his entire household and moved about an hour away, leaving behind a newly constructed house and newly planted garden. His excuse was that the hamlet in the school vicinity was too crowded and that his mother was not happy there, for fish and game were scarce.

Javier is typical of many Machiguenga men who are intent on preserving their own self interest and on avoiding conflict before confrontation develops. Their primary loyalty is to their close kin and they do not seek political involvements with other men. Today, they are only minimally interested in creating the unified modern communities that are being planned under government development efforts. One can imagine the disappointment of outsiders when, having finally brought the people near Shimaa, who were well known for a lack of community spirit and unity, to hold an election for Presidente of the community, they learned that the democratic process had elected Javier! Javier represents the central ideal of a man by Machiguenga standards: he is loyal to his family, independent, has some shamanistic healing skills, behaves decorously, is honest, hardworking, and respectful of others' independence. He is not a "chief" but, in a curious way, the Machiguenga opposite of a chief, a man who has no wish to lead or to be led. He did not at all fit the mold being sought by the larger Peruvian polity, but was just the conservative, trustworthy representative the people of Shimaa wanted to stand for them in relation to the larger polity.

The Mundurucu Case

The Mundurucu, by comparison, are Tupian speakers living in the forest and savannah region along the Tapajos River in Brazil. They have a history of headhunting and long-distance raiding and live in large villages, "ideally arranged for the purpose of defense" (Murphy 1960:97). All post-pubescent married and single men are centered in the men's house, whereas women and children live apart in extended family houses at the periphery. A combination of patriliny and matrilocal residence moves men from different local groups to live with their wives while women remain in place. Thus, men from different local groups dominate the village center with its men's house and plaza, whereas a generational continuity of women constitutes the private sector.

The division of labor further segregates men and women in daily activities. Men cooperate in garden clearing and hunting but their affective ties are shallow and fraught with contradictions over competing loyalties to clan and residence group. In the past, cooperation between men was even more necessary than today because of the constant threat of warfare, and remnants of that time are still to be found in remembered rituals surrounding warfare and the treatment of successful warriors. In men's groups, the emphasis is on creating loyalties between men who are not close family members. By contrast, women's groups are transgenerational residence groups. Women cooperate in the production and processing of manioc flour in extended family groups that are united by enduring kinship and affective ties. Consequently men and women form separate collectivities, in which men exercise little real control over the activities of women.

Young boys are disassociated from both male and female groups. As infants they are exclusively cared for by women and then must progressively separate from the household and strike out on their own. Because the father is largely absent from the household, boys develop a strong primary identity with their mothers -- an identity that must be broken in order that they may assume their place among the men. Until they enter the men's house at puberty, boys mostly wander in separate play groups, forced into a marginal status of severence from the mother but not yet able to partake in male activities. Once they join the men's house, they are still subjected to a subordinate position among senior men and exposed to the factionalism of men from different kin groups -- men with whom they must eventually measure up in order to establish their own worth.

Because of conflict between residence and ties of kinship, men experience divided loyalties, as the pressures for solidarity of the men's group compete with their loyalties to their families of procreation at the periphery, and to their families of origin in other villages. In the past, warfare powerfully focused attention on the need for male solidarity, acting as a "displacement device and rallying point for social cohesion" (Murphy 1960:130). After pacification, only an explicit ideology of male supremacy remained to unite the men and give them a sense of group identity and common interest to overcome their individualistic divisiveness.

The ideology of male supremacy is manifest in the myth and ritual of the sacred trumpets, according to which the men seized the trumpets from the once dominant women. It is used to legitimize the superior status of men. The original domination by the women in the myth is comparable to the mother's domination of the male child in individual experience. Similarly, the men as a collectivity place themselves in opposition to women in order to validate their status as men.

Discussion

We have depicted two types of societies -- the Machiguenga, who represent a family level society living in scattered nuclear family households or "grown-up family" hamlets in which the domestic and political spheres are relatively undifferentiated (cf. Lamphere 1974), and the Mundurucu, who form large villages in which the sexes are segregated and the men dominate the political arena. In the former, men and women cooperate in daily activities and men's groups form only intermittently for the purpose of trade and short term labor endeavors. Boys, who remain close to their fathers, do not undergo intense rejection of their mothers in order to achieve adult masculine identity. Men commonly maintain close ties with their mothers after they marry and readily transfer nurturant and dependent feelings to their wives.

Conversely, in the latter type, men and women form distinct cooperative groups with less direct interdependence between husbands and wives. Men live apart in a men's house, while boys, who reside with their mothers, must renounce their underlying feminine identity in order to affirm their masculinity. Nevertheless, they are ambivalent and are repeatedly impelled to prove their masculine superiority (cf. Whiting and Whiting 1975).

Two lines of argument identify the conditions that inhibit men's emotional attachment to women and intensify interpersonal conflict between men. On the one hand, Murphy (1959) argues that while sex antagonism is an expression of men's ambivalence toward their mothers, it exists primarily to promote internal solidarity among men through opposition to females. On the other hand, Harris (1977) and Sanday (1981) see male supremacy as a defensive response to ecological stress that requires men to engage in warfare; in order to train men to risk their lives in combat, sex is often used as a reinforcement by allowing dominant and fearless men to monopolize wives or sexual favors from other women, making sexually charged hostility between junior and senior men inevitable (Harris 1974; 1980; see also Fromm 1948).

These theories are complementary insofar as we may consider the need for male solidarity to be a derivative of warfare. Linking them, we propose that the political economy is critical in explaining interpersonal differences among men in our two types of society. We particularly stress the importance of the defensive alliances that bring the supra-familial men's group into existence. Although there may be other factors in addition that encourage the development of men's political activities, it is primarily the constant potential for attack from outsiders that forces the men into the superordinate political arena. This happens in several ways that only make sense when we understand the nature of warfare in the Amazon, and in particular how it affects not only the men, but all members of the community.

The State of War

Our most evocative descriptions of warfare as it is actually experienced by an Amazon people are those concerning the Yanomamo by Napoleon Chagnon (1983), William Smole (1976), and Helena Valero (Biocca 1971); the following summary is based on a lengthy examination of these sources in Johnson and Earle (1987). During times of peace the large circular Yanomamo villages (*shabonos*) empty out as small extended family clusters (*teri*) move out to their gardens and forage independently in their local territories. Yanomamo clearly prefer these times and one group, the *gnaminaweteri* actually received their name ("solitary ones") from their preference for isolation. But when rumor asserts that one's group is subject to attack, small *teri* scurry together in one spot for defense. Chagnon has shown how a group of less than 100 or so members is at a great disadvantage, for it will be viewed as weak and vulnerable to attack by enemies. Thus, their very existence depends on an extended family's ability to band together with other similar groups in a defensive alliance behind the fortified walls of a large *shabono*.

Despite their exterior bravado, the Yanamamo are frightened of violence and warfare. Warfare is tremendously disruptive of their lives. Labor costs rise dramatically as palisades must be built and sentries placed on round-the-clock duty on all trails around the village. *Teri* that have moved in from distant territories must now acquire food from local *teri* and plant new gardens. Fear of ambush limits their freedom to roam widely in search of wild foods.

But, above all, warfare results in maiming and death, primarily to men and boys. The Yanomamo are loving parents and siblings, and the loss of a loved one is cause for deep and genuine mourning. The loss of a father causes boys to have nightmares for long periods after the event, and the adults mourn their lost kin for years, as the feelings are kept alive through periodic ceremonies and endocannibalism. During warfare, a general atmosphere of fear and tension pervades the *shabono*, and the overall quality of life plummets.

It is in this context that we emphasize that the role of leaders and the political unity of men exists as much to preserve peace as to wage war. Chagnon (1983) contrasts two types of leaders among the Yanomamo: the mature, wise leader, Kaobawa, who seeks through negotiation and persuasion to prevent the outbreak of hostilities, and the hotheaded, fierce Rerebawa who is admired for his bravery and has a following among the younger men. Helena Valero also records many cases of arguments between passionate men who seek violence and calm men who seek to prevent violence (Biocca 1971). The peace-keepers in these cases remind other men of the costs of war by asking them questions such as, "Who will care for your sons after you are dead?"

It is evident that the Yanomamo do everything within their power to avoid war. Chagnon has shown that the ritualized management of hostility through an escalating series of controlled confrontations -- from trading blows with closed fists to use of clubs and the flat sides of machetes and axes -- is geared entirely toward reducing the risk of homicide, and thus is "the antithesis of war" (Chagnon 1983). As the Yanomamo say, "We fight in order to become friends again." Gregor (1985:97-8) describes the male wrestling matches of the Mehinacu villagers of the Xingu in similar terms:

> "Wrestling in and of itself eliminates anger. A man with 'anger in his stomach' wrestles and finds himself at peace. The wild people beyond Mehinacu borders are violent because 'they do not know how to wrestle. All they know how to do is kill people with clubs.'"

We must be clear, then, about the bind in which the threat of warfare places men, among such groups as the Mehinacu, Mundurucu, and Yanomamo in contrast to the Machiguenga. Warfare requires men to bring their households together in large villages, so that others will be fearful of attacking. It requires them to convey a general impression of fearsomeness and strength. Whereas Machiguenga men are soft-spoken and leave the scene of potential violence, such men are viewed as weak and womanly in groups that face warfare. A respected man there must stand up to other men, pound his spear on the ground and shout his views from the village center. He must not be bullied and must glower, strut, slap himself, and gesticulate whenever he feels his willingness to defend himself and his family is in doubt.

One of the curious, and essentially tragic, implications of warfare in Amazonia is that it makes hypermasculine males, such as the *waiteri* or fierce men of the Yanomamo, attractive as group members. We have remarked already on how the Machiguenga attempt to control and then drive off or kill men who cannot control their anger and strike out against others. Lee (1984:90-96) reports that the !Kung San have on several occasions killed, "execution-style," men who could not contain their violent impulses. But in a Yanomamo village that is at war, the situation is reversed: ordinary men seek out *waiteri* males to join their groups, even offering them wives as an inducement (Biocca 1971).

The tragic irony in this is that such hypermasculine men are not only violent toward enemies, they also frequently rage out of control in their own villages, wounding their wives and close relatives in violent outbursts. The village is already a difficult enough place to live: extramarital affairs abound, the best garden lands within easy walking distance are crowded, hunting trips must range at great distances due to the local concentration of people, theft is more likely, and a multitude of small insults, frequently surrounding perceived injustice in the distribution of rare and valued foods, occur. Add to this the disruptive behavior of one or more fierce men, and the potential for violence within the village nearly matches the threat from without.

The pressures on a family man in this setting are complex. Other men in his own village covet his wife and may be jealous of his food production. His wife may be envious of another man's food production and remind him of his shortcomings. In the village center, daily events, such as speech-making, ritual celebration, or wrestling, place the man in a competitive male sphere where his mettle is constantly tested:

> A powerful wrestler, say the villagers, is frightening (*kowkapapai*). Likened to the anaconda in the quickness of his holds and the way he 'ties up' his opponents, he commands fear and respect. To the women, he is 'beautiful' (*awitsiri*), in demand as a paramour and husband. Triumphant in politics as well as in love, the champion wrestler embodies the highest qualities of manliness. Not so fortunate the vanquished! A chronic loser, no matter what his virtues, is regarded as a fool. (Gregor 1985:96)

Murphy (1959) analysed this system rather thoroughly. He took as his starting point the need for village cohesion and the solidarity of the group of men. Given the frustrations of daily life and the lack of close kin ties among men in the Mundurucu village, it was necessary for the men to unite structurally, in the men's house, and in rituals defining their separateness from and superiority to the women. The Mundurucu boys, dependent on their mothers throughout their well-nurtured youths in mother-child households, had to be forced away from the "soft" female sphere into the male world of toughness and competitive positioning. Their proclamations of hypermasculinity and superiority to women were nothing but the protests of men frightened of the seductive pull of the women and the nurturant domestic sphere. The Mehinacu village men are in a similar position:

> A man's place, when he is not out hunting or fishing, is in the men's house or on the log bench just outside it. A villager who spends too much time in the family dwellings or work areas surrounding them is antisocial and unmanly. He is belittled as a "trashyard man," as a "star" because he is said to come out only at night, or as a "seclusion boy." The barb that cuts deepest, however, is "woman." A man who does not socialize with his fellows in the men's house loses part of his claim to masculinity. (Gregor 1985:93)

Warfare and the Political Economy

We view Amazon village warfare as a major source of the multi-family interdependence that we refer to as the political economy (see Johnson and Earle 1987). Warfare requires cooperation in defense and offense. Men cannot freely chose to leave the group simply because internal disputes arise. As Murphy (1958:136) notes, the Mundurucu today can leave the village only because of pacification:

> Another alternative [to sorcery as a catharsis for aggression], withdrawal from the frustrating situation, has been made possible by the general pacification of the upper Tapajos area and the consequent possibility of flight from village life. In former times it would have been most risky for an individual or family to forsake the mutual security offered by the local group, but today it is common...

Warfare is probably among the earliest and most likely situations forcing the men of a locale into close cooperation, but it is not the only one. Other economic situations can also bring about the move from family-level autonomy to village-level interdependence. Among the Tareumiut Eskimos of the Arctic coast of Alaska (Spencer 1959), for example, whale hunting had the same effect. Whereas interior Eskimos (Nuunamiut) hunted caribou in single families or camps of related families, the coastal Eskimos formed villages with male "boat houses" based on the cooperation of men in building, maintaining, and crewing whaling boats. The political economy was further elaborated in the coordinated hunting of whales by many boats at once, and, during the extreme food scarcity of late winter and early spring, in the redistribution of whale meat and blubber stored in large ice cellars dug out of permafrost. Similar sharing of stored food supplies during the scarce season in winter villages characterized many Northwest Coast Indians as well (Johnson and Earle 1987).

It is probable that, in many areas of the Amazon, intervillage trade was another element in the political economy that required such male political activities as hosting feasts and maintaining trading partnerships. Although much of this trade acted like a market to distribute special products cost-efficiently across ecological zones, it also appears to have been created politically: that is, villages were given "franchises," as it were, to specialize in particular products, in order to have goods needed by others to trade. The resulting economic interdependence helped reduce the general level of violence in the region (Chagnon 1983: 149).

Thus, many factors -- warfare, large-scale capital (e.g., whaling boats), food storage and redistribution during a famine season, and trade -- can bring about the need for family men to abandon their precious independence and join a community of families. In so doing, they place themselves in a competitive political economy in which other men, some of them quite fierce and ruthless, are continually "elbowing" for room. A

man who does not rise to the challenge of the political sphere, to be
strong and feared, to maintain a network of reliable political and military
allies, to push back when pushed or even to push first, is a "fool" who can
count on no mercy from others. He must arouse himself to hypermasculinity and maintain that state of arousal continuously, or slip in others' esteem and be shoved aside.

The Oedipal Myths

We may now return to the two myths we presented earlier. We
found that at core both portrayed a special closeness between mother and
son, as in being married to mother or being placed in her womb and
reborn. This in turn was accompanied by a number of episodes of
violence between men. This is clearly the classic, "triadic" Oedipal structure, including both intimacy with mother and retaliatory violence from
father. We also noted, however, that the Mundurucu myth differed from
the Machiguenga myth in three ways: The parents' true identity is
camouflaged behind the Sun and his wife, whereas mother and father
appear undisguised in the Machiguenga tale; the Oedipal son's crime in
the Machiguenga myth centers on his stinginess and greed over food,
whereas in the Mundurucu myth it is his sexual potency with mother;
and the Mundurucu myth portrays greater violence, with explicit mutilation. In light of our foregoing discussion of men in the political economy, we believe these differences are explicable (or, at least, that they are
in the predictable direction).

We assume that the need to disguise the mother and father in the
Mundurucu myth arises from the greater anxiety caused to the listeners
by the mythical situation. Because the Mundurucu male has separated
with considerable difficulty, and because his masculine role is fraught
with conflicts, the return to the womb is simultaneously more highly
desired and more anxiously defended against than in the Machiguenga
case, where the degree of closeness to mother represented in the myth is
not nearly so divergent from a man's actual life experience.

The shift of emphasis from food to sex fits our sense of a basic
difference between the Machiguenga and village groups like the Mundurucu. The Machiguenga are quite modest about sex: they wear body-
covering gowns and do not play open sexual games. They were always
reluctant informants on sexual behavior, although we spoke their language
and could get them talking quite freely about many personal matters,
including who was having sex with whom. It was the details of their sexual lives, including their feelings and practices, that they were reluctant
to discuss, giving monosyllabic answers to our specific questions. In fact,
living in small familistic groups, with very few potential sex partners
around, extra-marital sex relations tended to be rather uncommon, though
by no means absent.

We do not have comparable data for the Mundurucu, but the Mehinacu, in so many respects similar to the Mundurucu, are notably sexualized: men playfully grab at one another's genitals, make broad sexual jokes at the women, and discuss openly the who, where, when, and how of sexual affairs. We suspect that at least two related processes are occuring: first, in the larger village, many more potential sex partners are available, arousing the men's desire for new partners and the women's desire for the presents of fish and other prized foods that their compliance wins them; and, second, because of the pressure on hypermasculinity, Mehinacu men have a greater need to console themselves sexually, to the degree that other avenues of intimacy, with their mothers, wives, and children, are closed. That is, we suggest that hypermasculinity closes channels for dependence that are open to Machiguenga men in their closely integrated households, and that the Mehinacu attempt to make up for the loss of such channels by emphasizing sex as the major channel for intimacy left open to them.

Finally, the greater destructiveness of the Mundurucu myth is obviously related to their past: they really were headhunters who decapitated opponents and placed their heads on the sharpened ends of poles. They might also dismember dead relatives after a battle, in order to bring home some part of the relative for ritual purposes. Thus maiming and mutilation were part of their lives. We would add, however, that in the myth the greater violence probably reflects the underlying anxiety as well. Insofar as the Mundurucu men are hypermasculine and prone to deny their dependence on women and the domestic sphere (where, after all, their food comes from and their children are reared), their anxiety over the wish to return to the womb is all the greater, and their fear of punishment for such wishes takes a more violent form of expression.

Conclusion

Myths, as tales that are told over and over again, are stories that people like to hear. Some myths, like Cinderella and the Oedipal story, are extremely widespread and have great regional and historical stability (see Dundes 1976). Although examination of myths alone is not sufficient to discern elements of individual psychology, they may be included alongside other information in order to identify patterns of meaning shared by members of a community (see Barnouw 1977). Here we have used them as "windows" on two distinct patterns of male role and identity.

The Machiguenga, oriented toward independent small families and the avoidance of direct competition or confrontation between family groups (see Steward 1959), experience a man's role as close to the family in thoroughgoing interdependence not only with his wife but his mother and sisters as well. Ideally, a man is a reliable provider and companion; only rarely is his role as defender of his family and its access to resources activated.

The Mundurucu, like many other Amazonian groups, separate men from women and children. The solidarity of men as a political unity capable of mobilizing for defense or offense, takes priority over a man's attachment to his immediate family, which is viewed as "womanly." The men elaborate symbolically their separateness from women in order to elevate themselves above the feminine domain.

This exaggerated separation of the sexes is easier to understand if we acknowledge the actual extent of the danger faced by communities living in areas of the Amazon where warfare is endemic. Men and male children are killed at every enemy's opportunity, and the immediate suffering reverberates through the community of relatives. The labor costs of defense and mobilization are also high, as are the day-to-day costs of living in multi-family villages where intense internal divisions continuously threaten the precarious unity of the alliance of men.

There is much evidence to suggest that when the conditions that have called forth a village-sized community change, the community breaks down. This was happening to the Mundurucu at the time of the Murphys' research, and it happens in some Yanomamo villages when the threat of war temporarily abates. Among the Machiguenga, where strong government pressure is being brought to bear on Machiguenga families to join large localized communities, there is a continuous struggle to keep the village from disintegrating (Baksh 1984). We conclude that it requires some extraordinary requirement of the political economy, such as need for defense, management of an essential common resource or item of technology, or dependence on intervillage trade, to maintain the solidarity of village men in the face of factionalist pressures (see Carneiro 1970).

As long as men must depend on other men who are not close family members, it appears to be inevitable that there will be competitive elbowing for position among them. Men who are less afraid than others of physical danger, or who are impulsively violent, can gain a competitive advantage over less violent men, unless the latter join with other men to control the fierce ones. Groups like the Machiguenga and the !Kung San do this, but groups at war need fierce men and, unable to dispense with them, tolerate their disruptive behavior for the sake of group security.

Where fierce men hold the competitive edge, other men must become fierce in order to hold their own. There is a general mobilization of attributes that come to be identified as masculine: bravado, physical risk-taking, reproduction with many women, and interpersonal violence (see Harris 1977). In such hyper-masculine environs, men come to view other men as competitors in the potentially violent struggle for access to valued resources, including reproductive rights to women. Men must be constantly alert to the realistice danger of physical attack by other men, which is reflected symbolically in tales of mutilation and homicide. Meanwhile, women are viewed as weak and dangerous to men's strength. Underlying this is the remembered closeness and nurturance of women and the home, which has been harshly denied and transformed into a sense of women as dangerously seductive. In ritual men seek to fight off this seductiveness and to reaffirm their male strength as individuals and as a group.

ACKNOWLEDGEMENT

We wish to thank Douglas Price-Williams and Robert Desjarlais for their comments on an earlier draft. Parts of this paper were read at the meeting, "Anthropology and Psychoanalysis," held by the Southern California Psychoanalytic Institute at Idylwild, California, May 26, 1985.

4

SEXUAL ANTAGONISM AND PLAY IN MUNDURUCU SOCIETY: THE FUN IS IN THE CHASE

S. Brian Burkhalter
University of South Florida

Sexual antagonism, like sexual desire, can be exaggerated, often with humor. In *Mundurucu Religion*, Robert F. Murphy (1958:127) relates the bawdy myth of a man who made sexual overtures to frog. After he left, the frog changed herself into a beautiful woman who seduced the man and, in the midst of coitus, transformed herself back into a frog, hopping away with his penis caught in her vagina. She stretched his organ some fifty feet before letting loose, and the man, having been long on sexual desire, was meted a long-suffering punishment by a member of the opposite sex who had been, no doubt, hopping mad. The myth illustrates revenge--penis capture--as a form of sexual reversal: the offended frog pursued her prey much as an aggressive male might a woman. From the frog's point of view, the fun was in the chase. But this was not the end of the man's troubles; his elongated penis was too awkward and heavy for him to move. Some otters came by to help and, catching and roasting a fish, applied it to his penis, which then shrank. When it reached a palm's length, he asked them to make it just a little shorter and, in dismay, discovered it had shrunk to the size of his little finger. The myth was told amid riotous laughter (Robert Murphy, personal communication), and its comical point recalls the castration complex: to abuse it may be to lose it.

Temporary inversions of sexual roles highlight sexual antagonisms in play, as can be seen among the Mundurucu Indians of central Brazil, whom Robert and Yolanda Murphy studied in 1952-1953 and whom I restudied in 1979-1981. This paper explores the powerful sexual tensions evident in Mundurucu society and how they are symbolized, relieved, and sanctioned through occasional play. Of particular interest is a game I dub "the chase" which Mundurucu men and women play before fish poisoning trips. To understand sexual reversals within their social context requires first briefly describing Mundurucu social organization and how it has changed since the Murphys' fieldwork.

Marriage among the Mundurucu entails the man simply moving his hammock and few belongings into his wife's family's house. In villages not strongly influenced by the missions, no ceremonies need occur, although some couples will journey to the Franciscan Mission to have a formal ceremony officiated at by a priest. Sometimes feasts are held; sometimes they are not. Polygyny, formerly an infrequent marriage practice (Murphy 1960:88), no longer seems to occur. Divorce is not uncommon among the Mundurucu, especially for young couples with few children. It is simple; the wife gets her husband to leave her household -- perhaps by running away with another man for a short period -- or the husband moves out and no longer brings his wife game or fish.

Formerly in traditional savannah villages, men seeking wives would stay in men's houses, where they slept and spent much time after marriage; apparently men's houses were seldom, if ever, built in riverine villages (Murphy 1960:31). At present they are found only in three of four savannah villages, but no longer serve as centers of male activities or as places where men hang their hammocks. The savannah village of Cabrua's men's house is an open shed with a sloping roof and an enclosure for the sacred trumpets on one side, but shelters only dogs and tame peccaries. There are only two sacred trumpets stored there, rather than the traditional three, and these are rarely played -- not once during my two-month stay in Cabrua.

The moiety system described by Murphy (1960) and Yolanda and Robert Murphy (1974, 1985) is still in force, although elders complain that young people pay too little attention to it nowadays. The two moieties -- marriage classes -- are the red and the white, each containing a number of clans. Both husbands and wives retain their clan names when they marry, and failure to observe moiety exogamy makes one the object of malicious gossip. Worse, still, is to marry a spouse with the same clan name, as did one couple, who then became the constant butt of jokes, their presence itself being said to provoke laughter. Such social disapproval is difficult to take for long, so perhaps it is not surprising that almost all the marriages I encountered conformed to the opposite moiety rule. Children bear the clan name and moiety affiliation of their father, and, in this sense, the kinship system is patrilineal (Murphy 1960:75-96, 150-1), although, since only some shamanistic rituals are otherwise inherited patrilineally, the term can easily mislead. There are no lineages that act as corporate groups, and a person's genealogical memory includes only those ancestors known personally, as Mundurucu do not willingly mention the names of the dead. At death, members of the opposite moiety to that of the deceased dress the body, bury it, and burn the personal effects.

A Mundurucu girl of about 13 years of age or older is considered ready for marriage, as is also true for much of rural Brazil. She awaits the appearance in her village of a suitor to her liking. For the young man, finding a wife involves visiting clansmen in different villages to look over eligible mates; often by the time he marries, he is 17 to 20 years old or more, has travelled at least some within the reservation and perhaps also outside it, and has worked enough panning gold or curing rubber to buy gifts for his new wife. Uxorilocality is the norm for post-marital residence, although there are numerous personal exceptions to the rule. A headman's sons often remain in his village, forming a powerful faction, rather than move to their wives' houses. Neolocality also occurs frequently, sometimes as a reaction to the death of a man's or a woman's parents (Murphy 1960:112,121).

Both sexes formerly underwent the painful puberty rites of having their faces and bodies tattooed. This involved pricking the skin repeatedly with a thorn dipped in genipap juice, a clear liquid that soon turns skin a blackish purple (Murphy and Murphy 1974:52-3). Pain and the risk of infection made the practice a trial, and, tied as it was to the sexual transition to social womanhood and manhood, it no doubt reinforced sexual tension already created by the strict division of labor and tough sanctions for social infractions. Tattooing is no longer practiced, although old men and women still bear these geometrical designs on their faces, chests, and arms. One tattooed woman found her markings ugly and wished she could remove them, for they embarrassed her in front of Brazilians.

From the newly married woman's point of view, her husband joins her household and should make himself fit into ongoing activities -- helping her father, her sister's husbands, and, to a lesser extent, her brothers with male chores. As the men of a household cooperate among the Mundurucu, these tasks and the expectations surrounding them are very clearly understood. The wife expects her husband to bring her game and fish and to buy her clothes, pots, pans, hammocks, and other things from the riverboat trader or from merchants in town. He should, of course, also give gifts to her family. Her position is normally very secure -- she stays in the house where she grew up and is surrounded by close kin and neighbors she has known since childhood. She is part of a tightly knit work group comprised of the women of her and nearby households and spends almost all of her time with them. Normally she bears several children, often beginning when still in her mid-teens, sharing child-care duties with her sisters and nieces and, increasingly as they grow older, with her older daughters. As she ages, she gains greater respect, for her daughters have husbands and children of their own, and she may well eventually become the head of an uxorilocal core of women.

A recently married man moves into a new household, where he feels obliged to perform bride service for his father-in-law. This obligation may exist until the father-in-law dies, although a man may persuade his wife to travel or to move to another village, thus lessening immediate expectations. The household is not always comfortable, especially for new husbands, who feel pressure to work that they did not experience during their earlier, relatively carefree lives as boys. A show of cooperation is prudent not only because it strengthens the marriage, but also because it reduces suspicions of sorcery, for sorcerers hate everybody and would likely be uncooperative. Fear of sorcerers -- almost always believed to be men -- creates tension between resident men, who usually have married in from other villages. Since sorcery suspects are routinely killed, there is a twofold reason to be careful -- a man could be a sorcerer's victim or could be falsely accused and assassinated. Young men are acutely aware of their uncomfortable status as outsiders, but, as they live in the village for longer periods and as their wives have children, they appear more at ease. A young man may have few or no kinsmen or friends in his wife's village and may keep to himself; an older man is likely to have several children to support him, especially his sons-in-law and young sons. His older sons will have normally left the village in search of wives, jobs, and adventure. By the time he is an elder, he may exert considerable sway over village affairs.

Uxorilocality and men's distrust of each other shape interaction patterns characteristic of men and of women. Mundurucu men are undemonstrative and soft spoken, tending not to display affect, although they occasionally do so toward their wives and young children. They are almost never strident, never boast or show obvious pride in their skill as hunters or fishermen, and spend much time alone -- in the forest or on the rivers. Mundurucu women interact more freely, sharing most of their time and work together, gossiping, laughing, and talking. The contrast between gatherings of men and those of women is marked, although some male gatherings are livelier than others, particularly if illegal alcohol is available.

Mundurucu women play the dominant role in preserving their culture. Because women tend to remain in their natal villages throughout their lives, their strong female cores cling more steadfastly to their traditions, their manner of behaving, and their ideas than do the men, who confront the outside world more intensively. Their low population density -- perhaps 1250 Indians in an area just less than half the size of Massachusetts, the distances between villages, and community autonomy mean that the conservative female groups stand on their own as bastions of Mundurucu culture. Should the founding of a Brazilian settlement nearby or a road disrupt life in one community, other villages need not be affected. Mundurucu society is resilient because power is diffused, customs maintained, and the effect of distant threats to stability minimalized.

The sexual division of labor among the Mundurucu is rigid. Men clear and burn gardens, hunt, fish, make basketry and necklaces, tap rubber, and pan gold. All shamans I encountered or heard about are males, as are headmen. Women harvest, process, and cook foods, care for the children, clean house, wash clothes, sew, and collect firewood. In the savannahs, processing and cooking manioc is almost always women's work, although in riverine villages, men take part as well (Murphy and Murphy 1974:138 and 192).

When away from their wives, men will cook, wash clothes, and collect firewood, but they are acutely aware that this is women's work and are sometimes embarrassed when seen doing it. It is partly this uncomfortable feeling, occasionally accompanied by light ridicule, that, along with sexual desires and the wish to have a family, hastens single men to look for wives. An unmarried woman will eat as well as everyone else, for food is shared, but will lack nice clothes, perfumes, and other finery unless her father, brothers, or brothers-in-law provide these things for her (cf. Murphy and Murphy 1974:156). These complementary roles serve to strengthen the bonds between married couples because the tasks performed are considered necessary to a full life and are clearly assigned to one or the other sex. To be without a spouse among the Mundurucu is to have to depend upon relatives of the other sex to provide one with services or to do them oneself, despite ensuing embarrassment.

Women probably do more physical labor than men, but the most strenuous tasks are assumed by males. Manioc preparation, cooking, washing, and child tending take much time, but are not as demanding physically as gold mining, now the major cash-producing activity among these Indians. Rubber tapping can require much time and is easier work than mining, so it is an exception to this general rule.

For Mundurucu still living in the savannahs, some garden clearings appear cooperative endeavors, as informants at Cabrua describe them. But, because most males there are sons or sons-in-law of Cabrua's headman, this may be more appropriately considered joint efforts of the extended family. Not all clearings are done by groups of males, for some gardens are scattered from each other, and men prepare these alone. For the riverine villages, household cooperation is the rule, and men of different households do not help each other unless there is a close kin tie involved, like a father and son, unlikely in uxorilocal residence (cf. R. Murphy 1960:105-6 and 158-9).

Their marked sexual division of labor supports a very pronounced sense of sexual opposition. This creates powerful tensions between the sexes and necessitates ways of allaying these tensions. In his article "Social Structure and Sex Antagonism," Robert Murphy (1959:93-4) described the powerful sanction of gang rape that threatened Mundurucu women who spied upon the sacred flutes carefully concealed in the men's house, who were too openly promiscuous, or who ran away from boarding school. All infractions involved women brazenly challenging male authority. The argument could be extended in another direction by observing that men are the most likely sorcery suspects and, hence, the most probable targets of assassination attempts. Although men perpetrate the violence, be it murder or rape, it is an individual's sexual identity that places him or her at risk. The result is heightened tension and a rather dire dialectics of gender.

Assassination of sorcery suspects still occurs; during the two year span of my fieldwork, two men were killed for this reason, and informants mentioned several other recent cases. Many, indeed, were fearful that too many sorcerers were about and that there was too little they could do to protect themselves. All sickness and death were believed caused by sorcerers, and shamans had to remove the poisoning magical dart before healing would take place. As shamans were prime sorcery suspects, they were in short supply. I did not hear of a single case of gang rape happening during my fieldwork or within the last few years. This could mean that it no longer occurs, that it only very rarely occurs, or that, when it occurs, Mundurucu were careful to make no mention of it to outsiders like me. But male informants agreed that it was an appropriate punishment for women who glimpsed the sacred flutes. The threat that the sanction could be applied was no doubt enough to create some female uneasiness.

But such extreme cases are not the only examples of sexual antagonism; it can be seen as a theme of sexual opposition when it emerges in play replete with sexual imagery. Two instances will suffice to make the point. One consists of aggressive displays, taunts, and role reversals during their traditional dances. The other is the women's spirited chase after men that sometimes precedes fish poisoning trips.

The Mundurucu traditional dances once performed during rainy season festivals are only very rarely held today; perhaps this has been true for several decades, as the Murphys did not observe them during their fieldwork (Robert Murphy, personal communication). The village of Sai Cinza is an exception, for the headman and some elders are enthusiastic about them. They make dance flutes -- tubes of bamboo or some soft, hollow wood two to three feet long and fitted with a reed -- and hold traditional dances to celebrate Brazilian holidays like Independence Day, National Indian Day, and Christmas. The dance flutes are obvious phallic symbols and, although smaller in diameter, resemble sacred flutes in shape and construction. Unlike the sacred flutes, men have no reluctance about letting women see dance flutes. Often young people do not take an active part, preferring to dance modern steps at rival parties a few houses away or to sit and watch; but sometimes they do participate.

The dances go on for several hours, and they represent animals doing various things. In the pirarucu fish dance, five flutists and other men line up facing the women, who form an opposing line ten feet away. Together the men take quick, aggressive steps toward the women, who retreat together. The advancing men are somewhat quicker and, just before they catch up to the women, they stop, then walk backwards, with the women now in pursuit, all in time to the regular whine of the flutes. The reversals continue for several repetitions until the two lines become so uneven that they fall apart. The pursuit of members of one sex by members of the other is a central theme, in this case showing periodic inversions.

In dances depicting fish being caught using *timbo* poison, hawks attacking monkeys, and jaguars attacking caititu, male dancers prey on women; in the latter two cases, men carry them away one by one as the women dance in two columns led by two male flutists. The "rich dance" features men chasing women with firebrands, an extremely apt depiction of sexual antagonism and also of sexual desire. The snake dance is familiar to American children; both men and women hold hands in line, one end of which stays stationary while the other end whips around at a very fast clip in a coiling motion. Participants are pressed against one another, particularly in the middle. The sexual overtones in this dance are clear, but do not rely on groups of women pitted against groups of men as in other dances. Some dances are extremely simple and rather monotonous, but others are intricate and involve both attentive dancing and improvisation.

In the tapir dance, the most popular, dancers form a large circle with women and girls comprising one part of the circle and men and boys the other. Five flutists play droning music and lock elbows; to their left are the other men, to their right, the women. The step is simple, a sideways walk that crosses one foot in front of the other and then, on the next step, behind the other. Women hold hands, and men either hold hands or lock elbows. After some time moving around the circle to the music, a man calls out something derogatory about the women such as: "Women don't know how to pan gold." This is greeted with a cheer of "Saway!" from the other men (what this means, my informants could not tell me). A woman will then answer with a like claim, perhaps: "Men cannot cook," and the other women support this with shouts of "Saway!" During the dance, such taunts are sporadically exchanged. They deal mostly with economic tasks, although perhaps once were more frankly sexual before missionary influence. One young performer claims to have yelled something about women not having penises, but the women did not respond to his taunt at all. During one dance, the headman slipped away. A few minutes later, a dumpy, rather grotesque figure, obviously pregnant and wearing a woman's dress and red scarf, joined the women's side of the circle. The figure's arms swung in the manner assumed by the women, but with an exaggerated rapidity that mimicked them. It was none other than the headman himself, and he was greeted with hilarity. When he retired to change back into his regular clothes and returned to the dance, his son and two other young men took off in the same spirit to snatch their sisters' clothes for a like performance.

This sexual banter and playful ridicule of one another emphasizes not only the latent hostility and competition between the sexes, but also their interdependence. Economic and sexual tasks require the cooperation of both sexes and make excellent topics for humor. Some rollicking fun precedes village fish-poisoning trips. Fishing with hook-and-line and, very occasionally, with bow-and-arrow is a male task, although women use woven hand-nets to catch small minnows. But during fish-poisoning trips, both sexes participate; men put the fish poison *timbo* into a small stream and stunned fish float to the surface to be gathered by men, women, and children. A similar female invasion of the male domain occurs the day before during festive chases said to bring good luck in catching fish, chases that both the Murphys (Robert F. Murphy, personal communication, 1986) and I observed. Fish themselves could easily be interpreted as male symbols, for, in Mundurucu myth, it is fish that turn into the sacred trumpets or flutes (Murphy and Murphy 1974:88) and that both cures -- and afflicts -- the man who dallied with the frog (Murphy 1958:127).

Recounting the events of one chase will illustrate its hilarious, but hostile character. It is late afternoon, and, in the shade of a mango tree, men sit and joke; the air is hot and humid and filled with ever-present blackflies. Two bundles of roots of the shrub *timbo*, cut into one and a half foot lengths, lie on the ground, and the men divide them into piles, each accompanied by a stout, short club to beat the *timbo*. In the grass near the riverbank lies a log stripped of bark, and the men, clubs in hand, squat before it to face the village with their backs to the river. The log a common anvil, they beat strands of the root to soften them enough to release their milky white, poisonous sap when placed in the stream the next morning. The sexual imagery of beating *timbo* with their clubs to bring forth sap is suggestive. The clatter signals the game's beginning. Some distance away, young women and girls have gathered and from long-necked bottles, fill their palms with a white, sticky liquid, the sap of the *sorva* tree. The white sap and the bottles' shape invite obvious comparisons, especially considering that available short-necked bottles are not used and that, during the Murphy's fieldwork (Robert Murphy, personal communication), elongated gourds -- which bear a remarkable resemblance in shape to the penis -- stored the sap.

Now the women advance together toward the men, the oldest of whom ignore them and go on pounding the timbo, but younger men flee. The men who dawdle are surrounded by women, who smear their victims' faces -- especially their eyes -- with the sticky sap. Some boys take to the trees with little girls after them. Younger men run about dodging the women and daring them. Singly or in packs, the women chase one or another man. One fleet-footed youth is caught in the alley between two wattle-and-daub houses and two packs of women, who smear his face, body and clothes; in retaliation he grabs a bottle from his pursuers and wrestles two to the ground to wipe sap on them, too. Squeals of laughter ring through the central plaza, and a spirited, good-natured battle-of-the-sexes develops, a two-hour skirmish spreading to the entire village as the older women and elders occasionally join in.

Several men, having successfully outrun the women, sit on the soccer field at the village outskirts to watch the fun and quickly dart away should a woman come near. Others flaunt their speed by running amidst the women and quickly getting away; some make a disappointing showing, for the women hot on their heels catch and anoint them to the general merriment. The setting sun draws the festivities to a close, and groups of women and men retire to the river to bathe -- cleaning the sap from their faces requires much scrubbing with soap and kerosene. Some find their eyelids stuck together. Latecomers threaten to smear bathers once again with sap or kerosene, and the banter continues a few minutes longer.

A middle-aged male informant advises on how to behave during the women's first onslaught: "When the women come to smear our faces with *sorva* milk, you keep on pounding and don't stop, no way. When a girl smears your face, you just glance at her and remember who did it. Later, you catch her and get her back." Others echo the conventional wisdom: "If you catch *sorva* milk on your face, you'll catch many fish with *timbo* poison."

The phallic symbolism is evident -- beating the timbo with clubs, white sap in long-necked bottles, and the aggressive pursuit of one sex by another. But the reversal is clear, too: women, not men, have the sap; women are pursuers; young men abandon their clubs -- symbolic penises -- to flee the women; men are symbolically "gang raped." Enacted here is men's, particularly younger men's, basic fear of women. It is the young men and boys who flee, and those who provocatively dart in and out of the plaza to flaunt their prowess are those most ruthlessly smeared with sap. The central symbol is no less than that with which these men so threaten women: gang rape. Here, too, is expression of symbolic revenge, an inversion of role and of sentiment, as women threaten those whose sanctions they fear. Like the sacred flutes, which in myth first belonged to the women before control was wrestled away by men (Murphy and Murphy 1974:88-9), the beating clubs were abandoned by men before the onslaught of the women.

The adventure that sex always offers excites adultery and infidelity, working to the detriment of marriage. This appears, too, in the chase, for women attack any and all men, without regard to moiety affiliation or marital state. What could better illustrate the dialectics of gender than this battle of the sexes, in which women defeat would-be warriors, penis capture is realized, and laughter prevails over fear? The chase is fun and funny, and, as Murphy (1959:95) notes, humor often gives clues to otherwise inaccessible data. Like many peoples, Mundurucu fear the opposite sex, but they also know sexual play can be fun.

ACKNOWLEDGMENT

This is dedicated to the Mundurucu Murphys, Robert and Yolanda, to whom I owe so much. Their fieldwork of 1952-53 provided a comparative baseline on which my own work draws, and they also read and commented on this manuscript. For their helpful suggestions, I would also like to thank Michael V. Angrosino, James H. Burkhalter, Virginia N. Burkhalter, Gilbert Kushner, Linda McCarthy, Ailon Shiloh, Nancy White, Linda Whiteford, Raymond Williams, Alvin Wolfe, and the editors, David Schneider, Richard Randolph, and May Diaz. Funding for my fieldwork was provided by the Fulbright-Hays (DHEW) Training Program, the Organization of American States, and Columbia University; none are responsible for any errors of fact or judgment in what is said here.

5

SOME CONSIDERATIONS OF MYTH AND GENDER IN A NORTHWEST AMAZON SOCIETY

Janet M. Chernela
Florida International University

Introduction

In their work on gender perception Murphy and Murphy stress the differing perspectives of males and females in Mundurucu society with regard to a Mundurucu ritual and its associated myth (1959; 1974). Murphy and Murphy point out that "The social perspectives of ... women and men are different, and [women] do not wholly identify with, nor feel bound by, that from which they are systematically excluded" (1974: 51). According to the Murphys, very different cultural realities may coexist, as they do for Mundurucu men and women, without threatening the coherence of society. Instead, they maintain social interaction as an ongoing dialectic characterized by misinterpretation, tension, intrigue, and mystery.

While the Murphys' point is convincing, we lack ethnographic data with which to evaluate their thesis as it applies to myth. In the Murphys' monograph, women's attitudes toward a Mundurucu myth were described, but no female version was supplied to counter the male version. The absence of texts from women's discourse has confounded ethnographers. Keesing recently had this to say about the paucity of materials gathered from women:

> In societies where the sexes are polarized ... women have often been relatively mute, unable or unwilling to articulate 'global' views, to talk insightfully about themselves, their life, their societies. This seeming 'muted' voice of women has for more than a decade ... posed both a theoretical/political problem in feminist anthropology and a frustration to ethnographers who would open women's lives to comparative view (1985: 27).

In the course of my fieldwork among the Uanano of the Northwest Amazon, a woman narrated a myth to a small female audience in my presence. This myth, an example of a woman speaking *as a woman* to women, provides insight into Uanano women's distinct shaping of imagination.

In this paper, the female narrator's version and a male narrator's version of the same myth are compared. The two texts offer an unusual opportunity to compare male and female vantage point in mythical discourse. They reveal that male and female perspectives do indeed differ. The male perspective, conventionally regarded as the universal one, is shown here to be as partial as the female's. The rendering of each version sheds light on the other, as the structuring and the limitations of the imaginations of each narrator oppose and complement one another.

Background

Several aspects of Uanano social organization and culture must be outlined if the tales are to be appreciated. I will introduce several features of social organization and gender ideology, then turn to the myths and discussion.

Social Organization

The Uanano are a linguistically-distinct group of the Eastern Tukanoan family, inhabiting the Uaupes basin in Brazil and Colombia. Numbering approximately 1,500, the Uanano group is one of 15-20 linguistically exogamous[1] fishing and horticultural peoples who form an integrated, intermarrying system in the Northwest Amazon.

The most inclusive category in the Uanano social universe is the *mahsa*, which encompasses the autonomous language groups of the Uaupes basin. The constituent parts of the *mahsa* are the named, exogamous descent groups -- referred to in the literature as "tribes" (Sorensen 1967) or "language groups" (Jackson 1974) -- whose villages ideally form a geographic unity. Membership in a language group is based on the sole criterion of patrilineal descent, and is exclusive. Each language group is in turn sub-divided into patrilineal descent groups which I will call sibs following Goldman (1963).

Gender Ideology

The Uanano conceive of themselves as a group of agnates descended from ancestral brothers born of the body of an anaconda. Each founding brother is the focal ancestor of a sib, whose members are spoken of as the "grandchildren of one man." One generation of brothers generates another through the name exchange. Men structure descent and generational time, linking descendant with ancestor, present and future with past. Although women participate in synchronic linkages, connecting different descent groups, they are absent from the descent model of reproduction.

The practice of virilocality furthers the solidarity of a resident male brotherhood and exacerbates the political subordination of women. A local village comprises a core of male agnates, their in-marrying wives, and their unmarried daughters. Although in-marrying wives form strong affective bonds with each other, numerous factors limit their impact as a formal, cohesive, political power. For most women, input into village-level politics takes the form of gossip and other informal social criticism.

Uanano men view women as divisive and chaotic influences, especially through their uncontrolled, critical gossip. The Uanano place extreme value on discourse style, and men distinguish between the eloquent, decorous speech of men and the undisciplined chatter of women. Women have neither authority to speak for a group nor are they considered to have the capacity of producing "correct" thought and speech.

Authority and certain types of knowledge are the exclusive domain of the head, primogeniture line. Authority is vested in the seniormost man who is referred to as "our Head" (*dahpu*); the term refers not only to his leadership role, but also to the anatomical head which "leads," "organizes," and "speaks for" the body (Chernela 1983: 145). The term also refers to the head of the ancestral anaconda, from which the descendants of the first ancestors originated. Without a "head," a group cannot "speak," and is therefore mute or powerless (Chernela 1984a; 1986).

Woman's anatomy is thought to be polluting and men feel they must protect themselves from female contamination. The literature on the Northwest Amazon mentions male purging rituals and associated strenuous mental and physical control, including control of sexual impulses. Woman's body endangers and defiles the intellectual rigor and spiritual discipline practiced by Uanano men. In short, the dominant male ideology associates men with the head and the cerebral functions of speech, intellect, and leadership. It associates women with the body and the sensate (Chernela 1984b).

The Narratives

The first account is from Yuse, who performed his rendering in the dance house before a substantial audience of men and women. The company assembled for dancing on the occasion of the visit of a brother Uanano sib. The speaker was seated, along with hosts and guests, along the four walls of the spacious house. Males and females sat separately and in order of sib seniority. From his seat near the sib seniors, Yuse recounted his tale. Because of the din of conversation he was probably heard only by men seated near him.

Yuse's Account

In the beginning there was a man called Wanari Co?amacu.[2] He had a woman. This woman didn't like her husband and lived having sex with an "Other." This other one was Dia Pino, the chief [the first ancestor] of the Arapaço tribe.

Wanari Co?amacu didn't know that his wife was lying with the river snake. The snake would transform into a man when he came to the river edge, and, like that, have sex with Wanari's woman. Wanari learned about it from his companions, who were *wicha* birds. They were often at the river edge, because of a certain fruit tree there. They were feeding on the fruit of this tree when they saw Wanari's wife having sex with River Snake. The birds told Wanari, their chief.

Hearing this, Wanari waited to see for himself. While his wife was in the garden, he went to the port. He climbed the tree and waited above, quietly, ready to observe what would happen. As he waited there, his wife returned from the garden.

She arrived at the port with a ceramic bowl (*sistu*) and a calabash (*wahaca*). She went to the port -- she didn't know her husband was in the tree. When she arrived at the port, she dipped the bowl and the calabash in the water and began to beat them together, making a sound, *curu, curu, curu*. On hearing the noise the snake surfaced. He came to the edge and became a man. Then he had sex with her.

Seeing this, Wanari became angry and prepared to kill the River Snake. He prepared his blowgun, darts, and poison. He blew a poisoned dart at the River Snake, and hit him in the buttocks. The snake became paralyzed, and lay dead on top of Wanari's wife. He couldn't get up.

When she saw that her lover was motionless, the wife told him to leave. But he was dead, and he didn't move. Not knowing what to do, she rolled him in his mat and threw him into the river. There he went rolling into the water. He rolled to the point of an island called Tunuri Nuco, Island of Rolling.

The snake stopped rolling when he got to the island. The next day Wanari went there and cut the penis from the corpse and took it home. He fished for small fishes and made two bundles to eat -- one for himself and one for his wife.

[When he got home,] he saw that his wife had returned from the garden and was arranging the fire to make manioc bread. Wanari put one of the fish packages on the fire. The other contained the penis of the River Snake but the wife didn't know this. When the first fish bundle was roasted, Wanari ate it. After, he said: "There's another one for you." And he gave her the other one. After she ate, he said this to her: "Is it that a woman who had a good husband, eats the body of her husband who isn't?" She quickly understood that she was eating the very body of the snake.

When she heard this, she said to her husband, "Did you do this?" And saying this, she took the calabash and ran to the port. There she vomited. Fish came from her mouth: an *ugu*, and a *nocohanahiro*. And this one is called *co?amacu nunu*. These fishes are from the body of the River Snake. This was the fury of Wanari toward his wife.

After some time, Wanari's wife found that she was pregnant with the child of the Snake. She regretted what happened and wanted to return to her husband. Before she didn't want to know anything about him, because she was living with the Other, the River Snake.

Wanari, in his turn, paid no attention to her. He didn't want to have anything to do with her, but she wanted him, and she was pregnant.

The Son of the Snake was inside her. He remained inside talking and calling to her. He talked, and talked. She tired of it. She thought of getting rid of him but she didn't know how.

So she planned to rid herself of her son, who was in her womb. She went to the other side of the river, and ordered him to climb a rubber (*wapu*) tree to gather the fruits. When she told him to climb up -- out came a tremendous snake!

He didn't come out completely. His tail was still in her mouth even though his head was in the trees! From far above, he took the fruits and tossed them down.

As he did this, she carefully made a leaf funnel (*sotoro*). She pulled his tail out very slowly, placed it in the funnel, and stole away. She began to cross the river but she suddenly turned her paddle. A reflection of light hit him and he realized that she was a long way from him. He understood that she was abandoning him forever.

When he saw this, he came down from the tree and went after her. But she was already home. He came after, and landed on top of the house -- right in the middle, on top of the house! He stayed on top of the house, and talked and talked, without stopping. He said this: "Send my mother out now if you don't want to die! If you don't, I will cause the river to swell and drown you all!"

Wanari Co?amacu was tired of hearing all this. "Since you are worthless, I will throw you in the river," he told her. Saying this, he painted her red [with *busio*], carried her to the river, and threw her in. There she turned into the fish *maha wa?i*. Seeing this, her son that was a snake went after her, to follow her, forever, into the river.

Nicho's Performance

The conditions of Nicho's performance were quite different than Yuse's. She presented her account to a small company of women at a house on the periphery of the village. We may regard Nicho's performance as, perhaps, an "underground" performance, no less valid than

Yuse's rendering, corresponding to the associations of male with public, and female with peripheral. However, a certain public character is rendered an otherwise peripheral performance by Nicho's special status as the highest ranked Uanano (Chernela 1985). Whereas other women who marry reside outside the Uanano area, Nicho, although married, resides in the village of her birth. The result is that Nicho is one of the few mature Uanano women living among her Uanano kinsmen.

Nicho's Account

This is woman's intelligence -- *siopuli*. *Siopuli* once belonged to Dia Pino, the River Snake, who took Wanari Co?amacu's wife. The *siopuli* are his. Even though Wanari Co?amacu treated his woman well she went with the river snake. After some time Wanari Co?amacu's woman became pregnant with Dia Pino's snake child. Wanari Co?amacu's wife was big with child when he found out. He asked her, "Is that the child of the River Snake you're carrying in your womb? Ah, then I will go to the island to collect *bacaba* to make a great exchange dance (*po?oa*). I'll make a joyful *po?oa* celebration over there in Wu?u tulia." When Wanari was gone, the River Snake came to the woman, and gave her the beautiful stones, *siopuli*. These stones are his. The snake gave her two stones: one was the color of yellow-brown wood, and shone brightly; the other was the color of green wood, and it, too, shone. The water snake gave her these things.

Wanari saw this. He prepared a strong poison, and waited at the river edge. This poison was intended to kill his enemy the River Snake. Wanari waited for the River Snake. The Snake suddenly rose up out of the water. He had come to meet his woman, Wanari's wife. When the Snake reached land Wanari raised his blowgun and shot a dart into the snake's backside. He died.

Wanari's wife was working in the garden. While she was away, Wanari gathered his companions together and said, "I know that the River Snake gave a bright stone called *siopuli* to my wife. I am going to take this *siopuli* and from now only we [men] will have the right to use *siopuli*." Wanari then went after his wife.

Wanari tricked his wife. He turned himself into an old woman. Actually, he dressed himself in the rags of an old woman in order to trick his wife. He did this only to take the valuable *siopuli*. Arriving in the garden, Wanari put on a dirty disguise and became an old woman. Arriving in the garden he said, "Look my granddaughter, I heard you say that the River Snake gave you the *siopuli*. Then, please give me this stone so that I can guard it well for you. I believe that you take pity on me. If that's true, give me this stone." The wife handed over the stone thinking that this was truly her grandmother speaking. But it was not her grandmother, it was her husband. When she gave the stone to Wanari, he didn't end his trickery. He walked away, shakily, still pretending to be an old woman, and almost falling on the ground. On his back he had a garden basken with fire wood. When he was half-way to the house he threw down the basket and hid it. He returned to the house as fast as possible. Once home, he quickly cut a vine to hang his prize. When the wife came home she saw that her husband had tied *siopuli* to both earlobes. Seeing this, she said, "Oh! my underhanded, crafty husband filched the *siopuli* from me. There's no way I can get them back!" The next day, when Wanari was cutting a new garden, she saw the light of the sun reflecting his earrings in the distance. These were her *siopuli*! So Wanari stole the *siopuli* -- and he never returned them.

After stealing the earrings, Wanari went to gather *bacaba* fruits for the *po?oa* exchange dance. Really, it was to be Wanari Co?amacu's send-off. It's sad! This Wanari had a woman that didn't get along with him. One day Wanari ordered his wife to make beer for the dance. His wife refused. Since she didn't want to make it, her young sister said, "Look, brother-in-law, since I am not like my ungrateful sister who doesn't do as she should, I'll make the beer. In turn, I want you to give me the *bacaba* at the exchange ceremony." Hearing this, Wanari happily agreed, and he went to the Waterfall of Bacaba and collected many fruits. Then he made a great exchange dance that was to be his secret send-off. And after a short time, he abandoned them. This is the end of the story of Wanari.

Discussion

1. A Husband Betrayed: Version 1

Although the two texts begin by referring to the union between Dia Pino, a supernatural water snake, and Wanari Co?amacu's wife, both quickly introduce different concerns. Yuse's version is told from the perspective of the protagonist Wanari Co?amacu, who has been wronged by his wife and exacts retribution in a variety of ways.[3]

Yuse's account opens with the statement, "In the beginning there was a man called Wanari Co?amacu. He had a woman. This woman didn't like her husband. She lived having sex with an 'Other.'" In Yuse's opening statement, the wife is the betrayor, as she is dissatisfied with her husband and cohabits with an "other." The union between Dia Pino (the river snake) and Wanari's wife is illicit on two grounds: 1) the partners are not proper in-laws, and 2) the union usurps Wanari's paternity over his wife's offspring. Since Dia Pino is "other" (that is, neither of father's nor mother's group) by rules of patrilineal reckoning, whatever offspring he fathers will also be "other." The problem posed by the wife's infidelity is a moral one. The problem posed by the ambiguous identity of the offspring is a social one. Partial resolution is accomplished when Wanari counters the sorcery (usually accomplished through breath, i.e., smoke) by blowing a dart into Dia Pino as he lies with his wife.

Wanari takes further revenge by tricking his wife into ingesting her lover's penis. Thus the sexual organ of the progenitor enters the body through an improper orifice, as the husband intensifies his wife's contamination and humiliates her. Although partial resolution to the contamination is accomplished when the wife vomits, she is not purged, for she has conceived.

2. A Wife Betrayed: Version 2

Nicho's description of Wanari's theft of the *siopuli* parallels Yuse's attention to detail in describing Wanari's assassination of Dia Pino. Her account opens with the line, "This is woman's intelligence -- *siopuli*." The *siopuli* are magical ornaments which bestow to the wearer the intellectual powers attributed to the head. Wanari's wife was given them by Dia Pino, a supernatural half-man, half-snake who inhabits the river.

The events which require resolution in Nicho's account are different from those requiring resolution in Yuse's. Nicho's central female obtains power, superior to Wanari's, from the river snake. Thus, impropriety results when woman who is "natural" receives powers which are "supernatural." The result is an inversion in the proper hierarchical relation between husband (the more powerful) and wife (the less powerful). The wife's receipt of the gift creates a dilemma, and Wanari covets his wife's prize.

In Nicho's version, the receipt of the gift is at least as offensive a transgression as the adultery. As in Yuse's version, Wanari's wife usurps her husband's prerogative as sexual initiator, since it is she who calls the snake at the water edge. Her act negates Wanari's rights to legal patrilineal succession of his offspring. Wanari avenges the infidelity by killing the paramour and corrects the injustice of the *siopuli* by stealing them.

Whereas in the male version Wanari consults with his cohorts regarding the killing, in the female version he commiserates with them regarding the magical head ornaments. "I know that the river snake gave a gem called *siopuli* to my wife," he tells them. "I am going to take the *siopuli* and from now only we [masc.] will have the right to use *siopuli*." Securing the *siopuli* would correct the imbalance of power in the man/woman relation. As a woman's freedom to go with another man is transgression, so a woman's right to own *siopuli* is a transgression: each flies in the face of male prerogative.

The jewel-like stones exchange hands several times. Initially they belong to the supernatural snake paramour, Dia Pino, who gives them to Wanari's wife. Later, Wanari disguised as a woman steals them from her. The head ornaments appear to move between conjugal pairs, suggesting a link between sexual favor and power.[4] The exchange between the illicit pair was overt and voluntary; the exchange between the legitimate pair covert and deceitful.

To secure the *siopuli* Wanari must disguise himself as woman. These events take place in the garden, women's domain, while in Yuse's version all events take place in the men's domain, at the river edge. Wanari misrepresents his husband-to-wife relation as grandmother-to-granddaughter, improperly portraying a conjugal as a kin relation and deviously usurping the powerful ornaments.

Two Betrayals Compared

Paternity is an artifact whose legitimacy depends upon woman's word. In this sense, the wife mediates relations between husband and offspring, and may at any time crosscut that relationship, as did Wanari's wife. The power inherent in woman's word to confirm or deny certain social ties is of particular importance in patrilineal systems, such as that of the Uanano, where offspring belongs to father's group.

For a man, another man's fathering his own wife's offspring is a source of potential disorder and conflict, at least in part because that offspring will be "other." This is a central problem in Yuse's account. Nicho, on the other hand, does not mention that Dia Pino is "other" (*paye masuno*, glosses as "other" or "outsider" in Uanano), nor does she mention the ambiguous identity of the offspring. As a result of patrilineal reckoning and language group exogamy, a Uanano woman is always "other," in relation to her offspring. Indeed, she is a member of a different tribe or language group. Her perception of the foreign quality attributed to members of the important Uanano category "other" necessarily differs from the perspective of her Uanano male relatives. Nicho's children, for example, are Desana, as her husband is Desana. Offspring and mother are necessarily of different groups: this is not a source of anxiety for women; it is part of their reality.

3. A Son Betrayed: Version 1, cont'd.

Deception through disguise occurs in both narratives. In Nicho's Wanari impersonates an old woman to steal the *siopuli*. In Yuse's version, a mother substitutes a leaf with spittle for the womb-mouth, so as to abandon her son.

Once again woman violates primary relationships, as now mother deserts son. The wife in Yuse's version is a perverse anti-mother. She tricks the enchanted snake offspring into emerging from her mouth so she can abandon him. However, he is careful to leave his tail in her mouth, so as not to separate himself entirely from his mother. As he climbs to the treetops, in pursuit of fruit for her, she places his tail in a moistened leaf to give him the illusion that she is still there. Then she leaves. Betrayal by mother reiterates betrayal by wife.

Several problems result. Birth through an improper orifice inverts the natural birth process. Then, mother-infant attachment by navel cord is inverted by improper attachment through mother's mouth. Finally, the mother's desertion violates the normal relation between mother and son, as does the quasi-sexual representation of the tail in the mother's mouth.

In both Yuse's and Nicho's renderings betrayal is revealed through a flash of light. A beam of light hits the snake offspring, as the dart had the snake father. When the light hits the son he understands that his mother has deserted him. In Nicho's version Wanari's wife realizes that Wanari stole the *siopuli* when, from afar, the jewels reflect the sunlight. The reflection of light, which signals mother's desertion of her son in the male version, signals the husband's betrayal of his wife in the female version. Each "blow of light" marks a betrayal and a critical transformation in the dialectical process.

The breaches of morality throughout Yuse's tale were due to the wife's misconduct: adulterous wife, carrier of inhuman fetus, and repudiating mother. Resolution is accomplished when Wanari paints his wife with red pigment and throws her in the river. A young girl is painted with the same pigment when she first menstruates. Wanari's wife is thus "remade" a virgin and tossed into the river, whence came her lover. Her snake-son follows; they will remain forever in the water realm between the natural and the supernatural.

4. A Sister Betrayed: Version 2, cont'd.

The two versions differ significantly in the structure of allies and adversaries. In Yuse's version the opposition husband/wife gives way to the opposition mother/son. In Nicho's version man and wife continue as adversaries and a new adversary-relationship is added: sisters.

In *po?oa* preparations the husband customarily gathers fruit or fish and the wife prepares beer. When Wanari's wife will not make beer her sister calls her ungrateful and makes a gesture to take her place as Wanari's wife.

As a result of a broad extension of incest rules and strongly felt preferences, the few marriageable partners available to a Uanano woman are the same as those available to her sister, placing sisters in competition for the same eligible cross-cousins. The myth suggests that one sister may capitalize on another sister's resistance with her own subservience.

When Wanari discovers that his wife is carrying Dia Pino's child, he schemes to make a celebratory *po?oa* for her, and presents her with a gift of fruit. The irony here is dramatic: a *po?oa* is an exchange ceremony, made by the husband's group for the wife's group to acknowledge a marriage or offspring. Here husband and father are not the same and the exchange ceremony is appropriately grotesque. Irony is further emphasized when the exchange, rather than cementing alliances, commemorates disorder and rupture among them.

Gifts of food appear in both narratives. In Yuse's account Wanari fishes for his wife and presents her with the fish-penis food gift. Later, as son collects fruit for mother, she abandons him. Finally, Wanari offers his wife fruit in the exchange *po?oa* marking his leave-taking. In each instance food proceeds from masculine to feminine in keeping with Uanano norms and beliefs associated with conjugal exchanges. But food, which binds and obliges, here marks a hiatus in relationship.

The accounts end differently. Yuse's narrative ends with the son continuing to pursue the mother into the realm of water; Nicho's account reaches its end when sister attempts to usurp wife's place, and wife is abandoned by husband. Yuse's rendering ends in pursuit, Nicho's in abandonment.

Conclusion

Because of their non-public status, Uanano women have little occasion to construct meaning. The rare occasions when women do tell myths signal their importance. Nicho's rendering provides us with an unusual opportunity to hear from an otherwise muted segment of the population.

Of the Uanano myths recounted here, myth 1, told by a male, calls attention to the hidden dangers of woman and myth 2, told by a female, to the treachery of men. We assume that the narrator of myth 1 was "speaking as a man," and the narrator of myth 2 "speaking as a woman." In another context, Nicho might have told the myth as a man, or neutrally. Or, more likely, she may not have told it at all. In the all-female context, however, Nicho did tell the myth as a woman and thus revealed some essential differences in the way in which women and men organize and create myth.

Yuse's version portrays woman as powerful and dangerous mediator of critical relationships. The wife in his account negates three essential relationships: 1) husband to wife, 2) father to wife's offspring, and 3) son to mother.

In Yuse's version, the woman receives a child from the snake. In Nicho's, she receives not a child, but "intelligence," an instrument of mental potency. To have the jewels is "to know"; to be without the jewels is to not know, or to forget. "Intelligence," a power which once was women's, has been alienated from them.

As woman mediates and intercedes between a man and his claim to paternity, so man stands between woman and one kind of "knowing." Each sex's relation to object (father to offspring, women to intelligence) is portrayed as indirect and precarious. In both myths, the need for contract is implicit.

Gender imagery is a subset of the larger ontological duality of self and other. Together, the two sexes constitute a totality, irreconcilably polarized by the fact that each confronts the other as object. Males are endangered by female pollution and destructive sexual powers. Females, being "others," i.e., outsiders, are potential infidels -- betraying husbands and sons. As men claim to feel endangered by women, so women feel endangered by men. Women claim that the intelligence they once possessed was lost in ancestral times when a man disguised as a woman stole the powerful head ornaments (*siopuli*) from his wife, divesting women of their control over certain types of knowledge and authority. Women say that nowadays they do not "know" but that at one time they did.

According to Uanano men, women are associated with the body and the sensate. Complementing the male image of female as body is the female image of the male as expropriator of powers associated with the head. This opposition reflects the political relation of the sexes: males dominate descent -- an ideology of reproduction -- and fear loss of their reproductive powers. Complementarily, women exercise social sanctions through gossip, fear loss of intellect and, ultimately, of political power. Each sex views the other as a dangerous usurper.

Although each sex sees itself as potential victim of the other's treachery, these negative tensions are not isolated processes. Fear is counterpoint to sexual complementarity and attraction. Tension between the sexes is but one component in a complex, complementary relationship which includes mutual nurturing, respect, and attraction.

Narratives express social tensions and contradictions, yet the contradictions on which turn the narratives of men and women may not be identical since the problematic situations of each are not the same. Vantage is critical in determining what constitutes a contradiction, a problem or a resolution. As a comparison of the narratives illustrates, women and men differ substantially when it comes to what constitutes a problem and what constitutes a solution.

If women and men are constituent parts of the same whole, who coexist intimately, they may do so despite a profound ignorance of one another. This is the consistent inconsistency from which, the Murphys tell us, culture is made.

FOOTNOTES

Acknowledgments: I wish to thank Yuse and Nicho, close friends and collaborators, who hosted my visit, encouraged and assisted my research. I also thank Eric Reed, Gertrude Dole, Mary Free, Karl Reisman and Meri-Jane Rochelson, who read earlier versions of this paper. The research on which this paper is based was carried out between 1978-81 and 1983-1985. Funding was provided by the Fulbright-Hayes Program of the U.S. Department of Education; the Social Science Research Council; the Instituto Nacional de Pesquisas da Amazonia; and the Joint Committee on Latin American Studies of the American Council with funds provided by the National Endowment for the Humanities, the Ford

Foundation, and the Andrew W. Mellon Foundation.

[1] Exceptions to this generalization exist. The Cubeo (Goldman 1963) and the Makuna (Arhem 1981) are not linguistically exogamous.

[2] The orthographic symbol ? is used here to indicate a glottal stop.

[3] I have collected many similar versions from male speakers of Uanano and other Eastern Tukanoan languages. Some patterned variation emerges. The Arapaço shift their emphasis from Wanari (called Iapo in Tukano) to Dia Pino. The Uanano consider Wanari to be Uanano, an important ancestral brother, with whom they identify. The Arapaço, who consider themselves to be descendants of Dia Pino, place their sympathies with him and his offspring. Despite this difference, greater disparity is to be found between male and female versions within the same language group than between males of different language groups. Elsewhere I have discussed an Arapaço version of the same myth.

[4] Certain equivalences here are reminiscent of Genesis: intelligence with sexual knowledge and free will with infidelity. They suggest parallels or correspondences between our culture and that of the Uanano, rather than influence or borrowing.

6

"SHE WHO IS COVERED WITH FECES:"
THE DIALECTICS OF GENDER
AMONG THE MEHINAKU OF BRAZIL

Thomas Gregor
Vanderbilt University

The Problem

In writing of the Mundurucu Indians, Yolanda and Robert Murphy wisely noted that there seemed to be almost two cultures and two worlds: one of men and the other of women. The sexes were united by the division of labor and by ties of kinship, but it was the disjunctive, oppositional character of their relationship that drew the Murphys' attention and that of their readers as well. Small wonder, since the interaction of Mundurucu men and women was charged with hostility and tension. A woman walking alone outside village was considered fair game for individual men. Collectively, the men gang-raped any woman who saw the sacred trumpets, or, as in the poignant story of Borai (Murphy 1974a), showed any sign of rebelling against the patriarchal system. The women of the village responded to the men's aggression by drawing together in cohesive groups based on kinship, residence and economic cooperation. Far from being taken in by the men and their rituals, they were openly scornful: "There they go again" was one Mundurucu woman's comment upon hearing the men play sacred trumpets (Murphy and Murphy 1974:18). Although unable to see the sacred instruments, the Mundurucu women were not mystified: "It is as if they had investigated the secret sources of the men's power -- and had found absolutely nothing" (1974: 141).

The patterns of sexual antagonism and masculine insecurity that the Murphys observed in Brazil have been reported in many other small-scale, sedentary societies in lowland South America, Oceania (especially New Guinea) and elsewhere. The psychological dynamics behind the defensive aggression towards women are probably universal, even if they are not built into religion, kinship and other institutions to the same degree in all societies (Murphy 1959). Male-female relations, the Murphys tell us, are therefore inherently ambivalent. The sexes are linked by the biology of the reproductive process and the nature of the human family. But this common destiny also suggests that there can be no escape. The result is an uneasy, bittersweet compromise.

It is the compromise that intrigues me, especially in the setting of small-scale societies with men's clubs. In their insistence on patriarchy, these groups appear to be totally uncompromising. How can they preserve the minimal tranquility needed for family relationships in the face of collective male aggression against village women? How do the men reconcile the contradiction of kinship and antagonism? What humanity is possible in a relationship that is so distorted by aggression and insecurity?

The Mehinaku and Gender Politics

My answers to these questions derive from my research among the Mehinaku, a group of 125 Arawakan-speaking Indians living in Brazil's Xingu National Park. In terms of gender relationships, the major structural difference between the Mehinaku and the Mundurucu is that the Mehinaku live in extended family households, while the Mundurucu men live separately from their wives and family in the men's house. Like the Mundurucu, however, Mehinaku men and women have a profoundly ambivalent relationship.

The positive side of this relationship is found in kinship and the division of labor. Mehinaku men and women stand united as brother and sister, husband and wife, father and daughter, and mother and son. Each of these roles is a set of economic and emotional claims that the sexes have upon one another. They constitute the fundamental obligations of Mehinaku society. Fulfilling them is onerous, but the villagers nonetheless speak positively and affectionately of their spouses and blood kin.

The most intense relationships that unite adult men and women are those of lovers. All spouses were once lovers, but it is generally recognized that passion fades with marriage. As the men put it, sex between lovers is *kaki* (salty, spicy), while sex between husbands and wives is *mana* (without taste, like water). Even after marriage, however, affairs are common. One of the young men was conducting no less than ten extra-marital liaisons during my last trip to the village. In some instances these affairs are merely routinized relationships involving the exchange of gifts for sexual services, with little joy on the part of either sex (see Gregor 1985:149-151). Ideally, however, the affair is an intense and separate relationship, in which the couple interacts on the basis of mutual affection and concern. According to the villagers they can tell when one of their comrades is engaged in such an affair: "Normally he is a sour old man," observed Kalu after her grandfather cracked a rare smile. "But now that he has a girl friend he is as jolly as can be."

The disjunctive and oppositional character of men's and women's relationship is at least as visible as the warmth and cooperation between them. A walk through the village reveals that there are separate worlds for men and women. Women are found in the houses and their immediate vicinity. A man's proper place is in the center of the village or in the men's house. This differential use of space is enforced by a pattern of sexual harassment and derogatory stereotypes. A woman feels uneasy in the center of the community. She suspects that the jokes and laughter in the men's house are intended for her. As she walks by, some of the young men who are *metalawaitsi*, or practical jokers, may shout obscene comments and jeers from inside the men's house. Even men who are more restrained agree that a woman does not belong in the public regions of the community. She is deprecated as a gossip ("woman mouth" is a term for a gossip of either sex) and laughed at when she speaks publicly. "The words of the myths," the men advised me, "do not stay in a woman's 'stomach'." If I was to use one as an informant, I was warned, all I could expect was a garbled version of Mehinaku culture. The status of "woman" is faintly ridiculous.

Mehinaku religion, as among the Mundurucu, is focused on the men's house in the center of the village. Inside is Kowka, the spirit of the sacred flutes. Any woman who sees the flutes is gang-raped by all of the men other than her closest kin. This punishment has not occurred for at least forty years among the Mehinaku, but the event and others like it in neighboring tribes live on as cautionary tales in contemporary oral culture. Typically, the woman who sees the flutes does so through no fault of her own. In the most recent instance of gang rape, the flutes were being played in the center of the plaza when a woman blundered into the community. The subsequent events are described by a villager in his forties, one of the most politically astute and powerful of the Mehinaku men:

The men whooped: "Hoooo waaaa! Kowka will have sex, Kowka will have sex, Kowka will have sex! It is not good that a woman has seen us. This is Kowka! A woman must not see Kowka! The Spirit might kill us if a woman saw Kowka and we did not have sex with her. We must have sex with her."

"Later," said the chief, "when it is dark you all may have sex with her. That has always been our tradition. It is not good to have seen Kowka. Kowka is forbidden! The women may not see it! Only the men may see it, by themselves, without the women. Even little girls do not see the flutes."

All of the women were saddened. They were not happy. "Alas for my vagina," said the woman [who had seen the flutes]. "I will be raped." Yes, she would be raped. Later the flutes would be played. The men were happy. They were waiting for her, for her vagina. The old men put medicine on their penises. Not the younger ones -- their penises were already erect and angry. The old ones put on *kaipyalu* [tiny stinging ants] to make their penises sensual. Their penises sought out the woman, with her big vagina. Their penises were angry!

They tied on their belts around their heads. That is Kowka's custom. To hide their faces from the woman. So that the woman would not see the faces of her kin. Her kin who would have sex with her. Her distant [classificatory] older brothers who would have sex with her. Her distant mother's brothers who would have sex with her.

"Aka, aka!" She shouted, she screamed... They carried her off outside, they dragged her by her hair, a little distance off and pushed her on the ground. She was sexed! She was sexed! One hundred men had sex with her. Her vagina was filled with semen. She hid her face with her hands, she cried.

All the men were delighted. "Hooo waaa!" they whooped. The chief spoke: "It is over, it is good, the tradition is good, it makes the women afraid of us, afraid of our having sex with them," he said.

Then the woman hurt, her vagina hurt her. She put *ulutaki* medicine on her vagina. She was sick, for the penises had hurt her. That is why all of the women are afraid of us. It is still that way, when Kowka is being played. "Ah," a woman will say, "is that Kowka being played? No, don't let Kowka come here." They are afraid of the men's penises! So they just stay in the houses.

Gang-rape is the most dramatic manifestation of male aggression. But rape also occurs when men casually "drag off" (*aantapai*) unmarried women for forced sexual relations. Women are most vulnerable to this form of rape when they are alone outside of the village. But numbers are not an absolute guarantee of safety. Highly aggressive men have been known to drag off women even when they are with companions. A man who does not use force may also coerce a woman into sexual relations by threatening to denounce her as having seen the sacred flutes or by hinting that he can bewitch her. The villagers generally do not approve of these forms of rape and coercion, but forced sex with an unmarried woman certainly does not arouse much male concern. As one young man explained to me, he would not go to the assistance of a woman being raped since so far as he was concerned "it was so much the better."

None of the presently living village women has ever been gang-raped, but they are acutely aware that it can happen. It is a terrible event for the many of the same reasons that it is in our own society, but there are certain facets of Mehinaku culture that make it even more traumatic. Mehinaku women, though by our standards unclothed, comport themselves modestly, so that the internal genitalia are concealed. When they are raped their legs are forced apart, exposing them to the men of the village. Even more defiling, according to the women, is that gang-rape "fills and covers" the woman with semen, which is regarded as a dangerous and contaminating bodily secretion. As one of the women explained, "the semen is disgusting. We can not make manioc flour, we can not make bread or get water. People don't come near us. You get sick, sick, sick, in a month you die. Disgust falls upon us."

What is most painful for the women is that all of this defilement has been caused by their kin. A woman who has been raped must somehow live with her tormentors. Some of the mechanisms that make it possible are suggested in the narrative. When I asked the informant if the rapists were not ashamed of what they had done to a kinswoman he replied: "No, they were not ashamed before their kinswoman. It was dark, no one could be seen. It was *very* dark when they got her. The men hid their faces so that the woman did not know who they were." In fact, I suspect that a woman would be able to identify her assailants, but the use of masks make it possible for both the victim and the rapist to pretend otherwise.

More subtly, the men equip themselves with rationalizations that justify the act. In the incident above, the village chief proclaimed: "A woman must not see Kowka! The Spirit might kill us if a woman saw Kowka and we did not have sex with her. We must have sex with her." The men thereby have a supernatural justification for rape. For those men who do not believe in Kowka's anger, rape may still make political sense. According to the narrator, gang rape "makes the women afraid of us, afraid of our having sex with them." The women thereby "stay indoors" and conform to their role. Finally, rape is justified by tradition. Raping women who see the flutes, the villagers explain, was a part of the life way of the Mehinaku grandfathers. As such, it is correct today.

Nonetheless, there is ambivalence. I have questioned most of the village men about gang rape, and even those who claimed they would participate showed little enthusiasm. They were at pains to explain that they would have to do so because of the danger of the Spirit, or because they honored Mehinaku tradition. Many of the men maintained that they would not denounce a woman who saw the flutes if they alone were aware of what she had done. Only one of the men said he would inform on a close kinswoman or participate in raping her.

'She Who is Covered with Feces' and Moral Ambivalence

The men's rationalizations and doubts suggest that they are not wholly comfortable with the culture of the men's house. Tradition and the Spirit demand that the transgressor be raped. But the victim is also the men's kin and their lover. How is the dilemma to be managed? We can approach an answer by examining a heretofore unpublished myth, "She Who is Covered with Feces." The legend is a striking one because of its sharp focus on the most intense moral dilemma of Mehinaku gender relationships. The story describes what happened when a woman dressed as a man and played Kowka's sacred flutes. The narrator is a man in his forties and the most knowledgeable and articulate of the village "masters of myth." My translation of the story, which I recorded in the Mehinaku village in August, 1985, closely follows his narration. At the outset, Yaka explains the name of the tale:

Pahikyawalu

This is a myth of a woman of ancient times. Her name is Pahikyawalu, "She Who is Covered with Feces." This is not a pretty name, it is not a name by which we greet people. It is a name from ancient times, because this woman was covered with feces, because she ate feces.

She played the flutes, she played the flutes. For five days Pahikyawalu played Kowka's flutes. Her lover looked for her but he could not find her. "Where is my girl friend?" he said. She was playing the flutes in the men's house.

She had decorated herself as a man. She tied her hair so that she looked just like us. She adorned herself as we do: She tied on this knee ligature, and that knee ligature. She tied on this arm band, and that arm band. She put on her necklace and her headdress. She put on paints, earrings and the jaguar claw necklace. She made a penis from a stick and wore it under her belt.

She wore rattles on her feet and played: Yeiyei, yei yei, yeiyeiyuyeiyu...she played the flutes! What stupidity that this worthless woman played the flutes! The men heard the flutes and the rattles: tsu...tsu...tsu. [The narrator whispers:] it was frightening and mysterious to hear her play.

"Who is that person playing?" asked all the men in their hammocks. "Who is that playing there? At dawn like this? Who is that person? Ah, what a beautiful song that is. Is it the Song Master? No, he is asleep in his hammock." And they asked the others [the next day]: "Was it you?"

"No, I was sleeping. Was it you?"

"No, I stopped earlier."

"Then who was that person?"

Pahikyawalu played and played Kowka, until five in the morning. Then she went to bathe in the stream, to wash off all of her paints and designs, to return as a woman. She untied her hair, and combed it long. Her hair was beautiful. She took off her headdress and stored and hid it. She hid her arm bands, and her knee ligatures. She hid her belts and necklace.

The next night, she played again. The men went to the men's house to see who was playing. One of them looked down very low, and saw her belt...but below that he did not see a real penis, he did not see testicles. "I think that is a woman!" he said. "Yes that one is a woman!"

Later that night her husband saw just a little *urucu* hair paint on her head and he knew! "Ah, it is so!" he said. "It is true that she is playing

Kowka." He went to the plaza and called all his friends. "Do you know that my wife is playing Kowka? That it is my wife who is misusing you?" He was jealous and angry that she was playing Kowka. He said to her, "you are like garbage, it is men who do this, not women. It is good if the men dance and play, not if you do it."

The men told the chief: "A woman is playing Kowka!" All the men were unhappy. "Oh, why is she doing that? We will have sex with her," they said. But some of the men were angry. They didn't want to have sex with her. They wanted to see her die in the grave. They wanted to bury her. They wanted her to suffer. She had misused them, she had misused their belts, their necklaces, their arm bands...she had taken Kowka. "Make her die quickly," they said.

"Yes, let her die, let her be buried," said the husband. Her real husband said that! He wanted to make her suffer. He wanted to see her misused. "Let us make a hole for her." With an ax they dug a deep hole in the men's house. But one of men was her lover. He did not want her to die, but he knew that the other men would be angry. He also dug the hole. "It is done, it is done," they all said.

A Master of Breath Magic blew towards Pahikyawalu in her hammock: "Sleep deeply! Sleep deeply! Sleep deeply!" he said. Five of the men went into her house. She was sleeping, put to sleep by the breath magic. The men untied her hammock and carefully carried her to the men's house. "Pass her down to me in the bottom of the hole," said the lover. He went down in the hole and gently laid her down.

She woke up. "Oh, what are you doing with me?" Deep in the hole, her lover said: "You must stay here. Your husband told on you, your husband said that you were playing Kowka. Your husband said that we must do it. Your husband has buried you! Your husband told everyone about you on the plaza, therefore you have been buried! But you will not die. I have put a mat above your head, to keep off the earth."

He gave her a gourd to urinate in. "So that you can drink it," he said. "It was your husband who buried you. He was the one who said that you were the song master. That is why all of the men put you in this hole." She cried. She was buried. But after they had just tossed a little earth on the grave the lover said: "That's it, she's dead."

The next day the girl's mother said: "Where is my daughter? Have you seen my daughter? Isn't my daughter here?" She asked her son: "Have you seen your older sister? Isn't my daughter here?"

The miserable, worthless husband spoke in front of the men's house: "So much the better, so much the better, it is good that she is dead!" The mother, the old mother, cried: "Ah it is true. Alas for my daughter, alas for my daughter!"

Days later, the lover went to her grave and called: "Are you there?"

"Ahhhh... I am dying...I am dying, I am not drinking porridge or water. I am drinking my urine and eating my feces. I have no fish, no monkey, no manioc. My hair has been burned out by the earth! Dig me up, dig me up!"

Later, when it was dark, he came to dig her up. He was really her lover. She was dear to him, and that is why he wanted to help. He dug down into the earth until he came to her. Oh, it was so smelly, so disgusting. She was smeared with feces all over her body, but he was not disgusted by her. She was his lover. In the middle of the night he carried her in his arms to the stream. He washed her with soap. He rinsed her with water.

"Let us go to the Waura [another Arawakan tribe], far off, far off, to my kin..." There she vomited medicines designed to make her fat and beautiful. She was so disgusting, this woman. Her arms were skinny. Her genitals were disgusting. She took the "medicine of the vulture." She took medicine to make her hair grow. After five days her hair began to come in. She grew fat, and several months later she was very beautiful, with broad strong thighs and her hair down her back.

In the village the men thought she was still in the ground. "That worthless woman is dead," they said. But [years later] they visited the Waura and saw her: Her legs were bound in cotton, she wore a twine belt, she was beautiful. "Ah, who is that beautiful one?" asked the men. They followed her to the stream. They watched her bathe: "She looks a little like the woman who played Kowka! Yes, her face, her hands, her body, her feet, they are just like that woman's!" The Waura told the truth: "Yes, her lover unburied her and brought her here. After many months she got fat and her hair grew long and beautiful."

The next day they went back to the village and told everyone. They looked in the hole and it was empty, there was no skeleton inside. The husband went to the Waura to get her. That husband, the one who had buried her, he went to get her. He arrived in the afternoon: "I am here to get my wife," he said. "Ah, there she is over there." He went to her. "You are my wife. I have come to take you home, to take you to your mother."

"Ah, that is good, I will go with you." What a lie he was told!

"Come, she said, come and make love with me. Yes, lets go, lets go far away; lets get honey, deep in the forest."

The husband was not afraid, he did not know she was lying. They went on a long path through the woods where there were trees that had honey inside them. He had an ax: Tak...tak...tak...boom! He cut down a honey tree. "Ah, there is a lot of honey in there," she said. She gave him a can, and he put the honey inside of it. He cut through the log in several places to get the honey out. "Go inside, crawl in, get in, put your head in so that we can get all of the honey-juice," she said. He went inside the log, the fool.

"It is further in, further in. Go deeper, go further, go all the way in. Go in all the way!" She took her husband's feet and pushed him all the way into the log. The honey got into his mouth and eyes! There was so much honey. He breathed in the honey: "Aka, aka, aka....!" He drowned in the honey, he died in the log! Here were his feet...here was his head... He died in there.

"So much the better, so much the better," she said. I have revenged myself, I have gotten you back! You buried me in the ground and therefore I have gotten you back. It is good that you have died, oh it is good to pay you back!"

And then she lectured her dead husband's ghost: "Don't you haunt us, don't you come back to us. You are not a spirit. When rain falls in the future [and the honey drips from the tree] say: 'uru...uru...uru.' Everyone will [know you are there] and say: 'Alas, sadness and pity for you!'"

Pahikyawalu returned alone through the woods and came to her lover: "I revenged myself." She married the lover, and went to live in his house. But the men were all so unhappy. "She played Kowka... she struck down a man, he died."

He is there now, in the trunk of honey trees. [When we gather honey] We hear the speech of this mythic person, this honey-ghost-person from ancient times: "Uru...uru...uru..."

Pahikyawalu and the Moral Dilemma of the Men's Cult

Given the context of Mehinaku culture it is difficult to imagine a more serious transgression than Pahikyawalu's. She not only violates the sanctity of the men's house, but also preempts other major symbols of male status. The narrator is at pains to list each of the items of masculine adornment that she puts on: "She tied on this arm band, and that arm band...she put on paints, earrings and the jaguar claw necklace." The wooden penis and the appropriate hair style complete the disguise.

Playing the sacred flutes in the men's house is one of the most dramatic markers of masculine status. The object of playing beautifully is to inspire a sense of fear and the uncanny. Pahikyawalu does it so well that the men comment: "Ah, what a beautiful song that is. Is it the Song Master?" The narrator adds that it was "frightening and mysterious to hear her play." So effective is the masquerade that the men must examine her primary sexual characteristics to discover that she is a woman: "One of them looked down low, very low...but he did not see a penis, he did not see testicles."

The violation of the men's house and the dress-code, and the playing of the flutes, is a direct confrontation of the patriarchal system of gender. Pahikyawalu's temporary success suggests that the differences between men and women are flimsy cultural creations. Women can assume male roles as easily as they can slip into their clothes. After all, long after the last male flute players have taken to their hammocks, the song goes on.

On learning that Pahikyawalu is playing the flutes the men respond with understandable anger. They are "misused." Pahikyawalu is "worthless" and "stupid." Her husband is "jealous" and wants to make her "suffer." The men briefly consider raping her (an idea they reject, perhaps because she has strayed so far from femininity), and decide instead to bury her alive. The matter is now raised to a community concern, with all the men and the chief engaging in the act. For his part, the husband expresses ghoulish delight: "So much the better, so much the better, it is good that she is dead." But it is at this point in the tale that we have the first hint of a moral dilemma. The mother is poignant in her grief as she questions each of the villagers regarding the whereabouts of her daughter. Knowing the truth, they are too ashamed to answer. The lover, being a "real lover" takes preliminary steps to rescue Pahikyawalu, and repeatedly tells her who is responsible: "your *husband* told on you...your *husband* has buried you!" Such a husband, the narrator tells us, is "miserable" and "worthless."

With Pahikyawalu's suffering in the pit under the men's house, the moral equation is now reversed. She is treated tenderly by her lover, who, as an indication of the depth of his affection, is "not disgusted" by her feces. In the Waura she recovers from her experience and becomes astoundingly beautiful. The narrator's emphasis on her garments ("her legs were bound in cotton, she wore a twine belt") tells us that she is once again in a feminine role.

Pahikyawalu is so successful and attractive as a woman that her husband allows himself to be led away to a distant place in the forest in the hope of having sex. Symbolically, he gets what he is looking for, in that his entrance into the log is a thinly disguised version of an act of sexual relations. Morally, he gets what the narrator thinks he deserves. Pahikyawalu is unrestrained as she gloats: "It is good that you have died, oh it is good to pay you back!"

I interpret Pahikyawalu as the resolution of a moral dilemma. The Mehinaku have established a religiously sanctioned boundary between the genders and an uncompromising tradition of punishment for any woman who would step across. Standing against the rule of tradition, there is the passion of lovers and the affection of kin. Pahikyawalu's triumph is apparently the victory of human fellowship and warmth in the face of a cruel law. A few of the village men have opted for this resolution of the dilemma as their own moral code. Hence one villager found the possibility of gang rape abhorrent in any circumstances:

> No! I don't think this is good. Only in the past was this good.
> It was those headless, faceless idiots of long ago, of mythic times,
> that did this. It was the sex fiends of ancient times. I feel
> sympathy for a woman who has seen the flutes. A man who is a

good man does not participate in raping her. If he is a good man he says to her "I am sorry that it happened; alas for you!" A man who does not feel pity is a sex fiend, an unbathed, headless fool.

The moral dilemma is thus felt by the men, and a very few entirely reject the tradition of gang rape. The majority uneasily accept the contradictions of the men's cult, and are willing to participate in rape. For them, however, the legend of Pahikyawalu is not entirely a rebuke. As is true of moral dilemmas in real life, the myth is ultimately ambivalent. The values the husband represents live on: "Oh, the men were all so unhappy: 'She played Kowka...she struck down a man, he died.'" And as for the husband himself, he will never be forgotten: "When the rain falls everyone will say 'Alas and pity for you!'"

7

HISTRIONICS IN CULTURE

C. Daniel Levy

"The perpetuation of social life depends, then, upon the placement of a veneer between its flow and its perception. Culture is an illusion, but, like other illusions, it gives life."
Robert Murphy, *The Dialectics of Social Life*, (1971: 241)

This paper deals with the notion of histrionics.[1] Its basis is the dialectics of the individual and society. It springs from the opposition of individual perceptual time and cosmic social time. It emerges from the contradiction of the Heraclitean "once" and the Platonic "deja vu," from the fact that each experiential situation is different and partial while, at the same time, it is given meaning and incorporated through its metaphorical relation with forms contained in a conceptual scheme. In this way experience is socialized. The present is made part of the past. The individual is appeased with society by taking the position of society and having the manifoldness of his/her individual perception reduced to meaning.

But because the relation between individual and society is not mechanical but dialectical, the socialization of experience is not a one way street. Every transformation from one level to another implies an impoverishment. What is left out does not vanish. It remains unaccounted for. This is the terrain where histrionics flourish. Histrionics is a phenomenon in which the opposite of socialization of experience takes place. The eternal, the past, the primeval experiences, the "forms," are made part of the present. They are presented to the individual and unfolded in front of his/her eyes, through language or action. In order to achieve this, an event which is social, either because it is past and has, hence, been socialized, or because it is part of the conceptual scheme, and hence is, as Durkheim[2] puts it, *sub species aeternitatis*, must be revived. It must be represented.

Levi-Strauss has demonstrated in his *Mythologiques* how myths expound a reality while at the same time being dressed in the garment of diachrony. The logical progressions, alternatives and explorations that the myth presents are given to the audience in the fashion of experiences and events occurring in time to the characters of the story. This mechanism rescues time for an essentially synchronic enterprise while at the same time making it more accessible to the audience. After all, the audience also reconstructs reality through experience.

Here is where a second, less explored aspect of mythology lies. Mythology is not a set of cold reasonings about reality. It is a set of emotionally engaging narratives in which the audience is transported into worlds that do not exist here and now. This ability of mythology to present realities diachronically in front of the eyes of the audience is its histrionic power. This ability is not limited to mythology. It seems to extend to the whole of narrative. For example it is also shared by the individual when he/she tells a story about his/her own past experiences. This is because past experiences are socialized experiences. They are social even before they have left the individual.

Histrionics uses the power of evocation but is quite distinct from it. Its success lies in its having the audience experience anew something they experienced before, but giving the present experience the ideological meaning that corresponds to it in the mythological reasoning. It is the ability of anchoring the mythological meaning in the individual experiences of the audience. It is the power of representation. The basis of theatre.

The Shipibo Indians, about whom this paper deals, do not have theatre in any sense of the word. They do not represent the spirits, or ancestors, or for that matter present-day characters. This does not mean that they do not have representations. They do have mechanisms by which absent events are placed in front of the audience's eyes. In this sense they have histrionic representation. But their histrionic representation is achieved totally through the power of language. It appears in two privileged situations, narrative and shamanic singing.

Narrative is performed according to prescribed rules. The narrator sits cross-legged and perfectly still. The audience sits in a circle surrounding the narrator. Throughout the performance, the narrator will not move, except for eventual minimal hand gestures. In contrast to his bodily immobility, his voice will take the qualities of all the characters he is narrating about. He will imitate the voice of different birds when they speak in human tongue or the voice of vicious spirits. The audience, on the other hand will not sit as stiff as the narrator. They, however, also follow a certain amount of bodily immobility. In contrast to this immobility, they also intervene freely in the story, asking questions, introducing comments, and so on. The narrator will normally weave their questions and comments into the thread of the narrative.[3]

Shamanic cures follow a pattern of performance that resembles somewhat that of myth narrative. They take place at night,[4] the shaman consecrates a certain area in the central patio of the village. He segregates this area from the surrounding profane area by placing mats in front of himself or simply abstractly.[5] He would sit cross-legged on the ground, his back towards the house and his face towards the river. Behind him he puts a firebrand he had brought with him from the house. On either side of him he would put a bottle of *Ayahuasca*, a gourd vessel, his shaman's pipe, his tobacco mace, and a bunch of sweet basil. Just as in the case of myth narrative, the performer sits up immobile throughout the session and allows his voice to undertake all the mobility that is called for by the performance. Unlike narrative, however, all the performance is sung. Furthermore, most of the songs used in this performance are of the same genres as those used in lay singing. There is only one type of song used in shamanic cures that is not used in lay singing. Otherwise, the same genres used in lay singing are performed in the curing sessions. The wording and imagery, however, are quite different.[6]

In contrast to shamanic singing, lay songs follow a completely different pattern. As was mentioned above, singing has a number of different genres. Some are only ritual but most are both ritual and lay. None is exclusively lay. Each genre, in its lay version has a specific dance associated with it. Performance involves both singing and dancing. Thus when a person says that he/she is "doing *maʃá*,"[7] it means that he/she is singing the genre of *maʃá* and also dancing the specific dance associated with that genre. This applies to all genres that are lay and to most of those that are exclusively ritual. The only occasions in which songs are not associated with dance are those that are performed over a reclining or laying patient in order to effect a cure or transformation. In short, they are those sung during shamanic sessions and the performance of clitoridectomy. In all other occasions, be they ritual or lay, songs are danced to. Songs performed before the actual operation of clitoridectomy are also danced to and, being a specific genre, have a special dance associated with them.

Furthermore, all songs follow the same pattern in performance. In all types of songs performers have physical contact with each other. Some songs, like *maʃá*, require the performers to form a circle holding hands. Others, like *βʷëwá*, require the performers to stand on a row of three holding hands. A third type, called *nawari*, require a line of performers holding each other by the waist. In all however, there is one performer that leads by singing the lines first. The rest immediately follow his/her wording. This pattern is very important since most of the songs are improvised and the chorus has to hear the wording before it can actually repeat it. When singing together, the leader and the chorus give the impression of a slightly disjointed choir. Seen from this perspective, shamanic songs are songs that are performed as if they were narratives.

Ideologically, however, the shamanic performance is quite different from what was just described. According to the shamans what they do is repeat, i.e., "help," the singing of a spirit. From the shaman's perspective, the shamanic performance is a succession of spirits coming down and each singing a song in front of the shaman. The shaman sees himself as sitting facing the main performer spirit, and having to his right and left a whole row of other spirits that are sitting just like the shaman himself. Shaman and the other helper spirits repeat what the main performing spirit sings. We humans, including the patient, only hear the shaman. But in reality the shaman is just the helper in a pattern of performance that, but for the fact that all the helpers are sitting down, is the same as the normal performance of lay songs. This superposing of activities in space, the crisscrossing of universes achieved by the shaman's, while in trance, partaking of both the human and spirit worlds, is complemented by a second linking of universes. During the performance, the parrot of the *Inka* relays, *m*^{w}*ëpidai*, the performance that is in progress in the human/spirit interface for the benefit of the gods in the upper world. Thus those gods see the performance in much the same way that we humans do, an oratorio by one single performer that translates what is in reality an opera of many characters in full regalia.[8]

With this background in mind, we can now proceed to describe the histrionic closure, the representation, that is achieved in shamanic songs. A description of the poetic mechanism of lay singing is also included to clarify the workings of shamanic singing.

The Narrative

Shipibos have a wide variety of myths and related narratives. The main characters in myths and odysseys are humans and spirits in human form. The odysseys are, generally, structured around one character who wanders through villages of different spirits. Trickster stories, by contrast, have only animals as their heroes and there is no interaction between humans and animals. They speak to human society in a metaphorical language, while both myths and odysseys speak to it in a metonymical vein: a universe of which humans partake.

Leaving aside the trickster stories which is a peculiar genre, offering specific problems, though to a large degree following most of the rules I will develop here, all myths and wandering stories are characterized by an original disjunction of the hero, followed by a series of adventures, and finishing in an ultimate conjunction with his people. This, of course, is seen most clearly in the wandering stories but is also present in the myths.

Keeping in mind the fact that these stories are narrated by an immobile narrator, we now pass to the content of the performance itself. I have chosen the story of the star-woman as an example.[9] I will analyze the story for both its content, i.e. what it communicates to the audience about life, and its form, the stylistic mechanisms used to express its content. The power to create images lies mainly on stylistics. But, as will become clear through the analysis, the power to engage the audience emotionally lies in the fact that the stories are disquisitions about the social and natural realities the audience lives by.

The story starts with a single man lying in his mosquito net looking at a bright star thinking that he would like to make her his wife. He falls asleep. As he is sleeping, he turns around to discover he has just embraced a woman. Wakes up and finds a very beautiful woman. She had her breast very straight and on top of it there hung a large coin that shined immensely. He asks her what she is doing there. She tells him he had asked her to come. She is the one, he had been saying he would make his wife. She is the star-woman. They make love.

This story begins, like most non-trickster narratives, with a very ordinary situation. The single man is lying in his mosquito net. He is looking at the sky observing the stars, and making a wish that is typical of single men: that he would have the company of a woman at that very moment. He falls asleep only to find himself in the confusion of the intermediate state between being asleep and awake. The man discovers a beautiful woman, and makes a detailed description of her beauty. Up to here the myth has been an essay in realistic description. At this point we have the first intromission of the non-ordinary into the story. The woman declares that she is the object of this man's wish. Furthermore, she tells him she is a celestial being. However, up to now, the non-ordinary has only manifested itself ideologically. The woman's physique and behavior are described as perfectly normal.

The next scene starts with the explanation that the man used to sleep on a pona floor just like the one we are sitting on now. Every time they would make love, the star-woman would cleanse herself with peanuts and throw them under the pona floor. In the house there also lived the mother of the man. She did not have a husband.

The narrator starts this episode by linking the story with the present, the pona floor on which the man slept was very much like the one we were sitting on. This technique of bridging story world and present is commonly used by Shipibo narrators.

In terms of content, this scene introduces new information. First, the woman starts behaving in an unusual way, she cleans herself with peanuts. Second, we are given another unusual detail. At the beginning of the story we had been introduced to an unmarried man. That situation is not unusual in Shipibo villages. Related maybe to the large quantity of polygynous marriages, there are many unmarried young adult males in Shipibo villages who live with their families of origin. Yet, if it is not abnormal to find single men, it is very unusual to find them living with their unmarried mothers. Probably also because of the polygynous situation, it is rather unusual to find marriageable women living without husbands. In the Ucayali river which is more westernized, there are more women living with their sons. However, in the Pisqui river which is more traditional, and where the rule of matrilocality is still very much in force, it would be strange to find an older woman annexed to the household of a well established son. The whole situation gives the implication of anti-sociability.[10] The man when he marries would have to leave his mother to go to live with his wife. The mother, on the other hand, could solve her isolation by taking a husband. Thus the normal resolution involves establishing links with other social units. Here, the man has not left the mother to marry into another household and the mother has not taken a husband. We are faced with a unit that refuses to establish social links.

At this point the narrator has altered the previous ordinary situation by the introduction of two highly unusual modes of behavior of the main characters, the peanut cleansing of the star-woman and the anti-sociability of the mother/son unit. The behavior he has introduced, even if highly unusual is not, however, insignificant. He has set us to expect a behavior that no well groomed Shipibo would exhibit. Indeed, he is introducing the dialectical opposite of good manners. Hence, at this point the audience is well advised that what is to come is not unknown to their experience: it is the opposite of what they know they should do.

The story continues with the admonition that the man makes to the old woman not to sweep the peanut refuse. He, however, does not explain where the refuse comes from. One day, the man went to fish "mujara" fish. The mother then saw the refuse under her son's mosquito net and decided to sweep it away. As she was sweeping under the pona floor, the star-woman spat on her from above. The old woman decided to investigate, and went into the mosquito net to find that there was a beautiful woman inside. The woman had a lip-plug that shined immensely. The old woman was upset that her son had not told her anything and was letting this woman starve. So the mother shared her fire with the woman.

One characteristic of Shipibo discourse is that indirect speech is achieved by quoting directly the person who has spoken. For example, in this scene, we are given the information that the man goes to fish for "mujara" fish by quoting the man directly as he tells his mother "I am going to fish 'mujara' in the stream." This mechanism of the language has a parallel in stylistics of storytelling. The narrator not only quotes directly the character and thus has a chance of imitating its speech characteristics, i.e. its normal pitch, its speech defects, and so on, but also assumes the perspective of the character during the narrative. Thus we saw that at the very beginning of the story the narrator described the apparition of the woman from the perspective of the man who had just awakened from a dream to find her there. Similarly, in this scene, the narrator is taking the perspective of the old woman in describing how she reached the star-woman. The whole story becomes a succession of descriptions as seen from one or another character, which are then linked by short recitatives that bridge one such description with another. This traditional artifice enlarges the characters to human size. It lowers the viewpoint to the one people are accustomed to from their own life experience as observers and, combined with other mechanisms which will be developed below, helps to account for the ability Shipibo narrative has of re-creating the scenes in front of the eyes of the audience. Of course, this constant shift of perspective by the narrator, going from character to character, also contrasts sharply with his physical immobility while narrating the story.

In terms of the semantics of this passage, we see a continuation of the aberrant behavior. To start with, the old woman decides to do precisely what her son had told her not to do. The star-woman then spits on the old woman. This is not just a simple breach of etiquette. In Shipibo society, in-laws of structurally different generations are supposed to behave towards each other with the utmost sign of respect: they are supposed to ritually avoid each other. If they want to tell each other something, they tell the linking relative, for example the wife/daughter, to transmit the information to the other. When two such in-laws are alone and need to communicate for some reason or another, they pretend that the linking relative is present and address it, requesting the absent link to inform the other. Furthermore, they are not even supposed to pronounce the name of the in-laws. This was driven home to me on one occasion when I was working with an informant when N passed with a live macaw in his hand. As he was going by I asked my informant whether N was going to kill the macaw. She looked up and shouted across the patio to R asking her whether N was going to kill his macaw. R answered that she did not know. N pretended not to hear what my informant had asked R. When I asked my informant why she had not asked N directly she told me that he was married to E who is my informant's niece, and hence he is her classificatory son-in-law.

The breach of etiquette by the star-woman was answered by the old woman by entering into her son's mosquito net, which in any event was not supposed to be down during the day, and speaking directly to the one circumstances showed was her daughter-in-law. Even the old woman's kindness in sharing her fire with the unknown woman was not without symbolic significance. Among the Shipibo, every adult woman of the house is supposed to have her own fire. Thus co-wives, in spite of the fact that they normally are sisters, are not supposed to share a fire but are supposed each to cook in her own fire. Thus all that is told in this passage is the precise opposite of what Shipibos are supposed to do in these occasions.

The story continues by having the man and the star-woman away from the house fishing.[11] The old woman again decides to sweep away the peanut refuse. As she sweeps she breaks the peanut shells. Suddenly there is wallowing and screaming. The first one to emerge was pulling the others. Farther away [one could hear a voice saying], "mother went that way, father went with mother." As he was saying that, the bigger baby was pulling the others along. The old woman tried to pick all her grandchildren from under the pona floor. She was not able. The voice continued, "Mother went that way, with her went father," pulling away at his brothers.

The star-woman hears them and tells her husband that his mother has already spoiled their children. She takes out a cloth to carry children and collects them all within it.

The star-woman became very angry. She made a heap of the peanut shells and burnt them until the smoke reached the sky. From the sky descended a large box on which the star-woman loaded her children and they left.

The man who was left on the earth started scolding his mother.

He was soon left crying alone. As he was crying, the black vulture [Coragyps atratus] came down to earth and asked him why he was crying. The man told him he was crying because his wife had just left him. The black vulture deceived him by telling him that he had just come from where his wife was and that he would take him if the man paid the black vulture. The man asked the black vulture what he could pay him with. The black vulture told him that the man should kill his mother. The man killed his mother, the black vulture ate his fill of her. The black vulture then told the man that he would take him.

The black vulture told him that he had to close his eyes. He made the man sit on him and took him to a place in front of something that looked like scissors. They got down. The black vulture told the man that he needed to rest in order to pass through the scissors. So the man got down from the black vulture. Then the black vulture told him that he was hungry and that he wanted to eat more of the man's mother before going on. As the man got off, the black vulture started to elevate and off he went. He had deceived the man.

Here again we have an escalation of misbehavior. We start with the old woman again disobeying her son and sweeping the peanut refuse. This breach has tremendous consequences that the old woman is unable to deal with. The star-woman answers by introducing the first big disjunction in the story. She and her children leave the husband. This, it must be noted, puts an end to an experiment in the myth. Shipibos are strongly matrilocal. The star-woman had come to live with her husband, thus adopting a patrilocal stance. Furthermore, she is the epitome of the wife from far away. She is of celestial origin. The myth seems to be weighing the possibility of a patrilocal marriage with a wife from far away and deciding it is not advisable. All the time the star-woman lived with her husband and his mother was characterized by continuous and pervasive breaches of etiquette. This escalation of breaches of etiquette will end up in the son scolding his mother and ultimately killing her. As we will see, in a subsequent episode the myth will consider what happens to a husband that comes from far away into a matrilocal situation.

This first disjunction brings about the introduction of a new character. This is the black vulture. The black vulture is a character that also comes from above. He, however, is aerial rather than celestial. Thus his origin is intermediate between the celestial people and the earth. He comes from the sky. He does not come from far away. He is an untrustworthy character, who does not come to marry the woman of the house. He comes to eat her. Thus in a very short passage, the myth disposes of the possibility of matrilocal marriage with a person from an intermediate distance.

As a mediator he also proves to be quite unreliable. He takes the man up to a place and faced with the first difficulty, he goes away the same way he had come. Furthermore, his price is exorbitant. He demands the man's mother as his fee.[12]

Going beyond the information provided by the myth into the architecture of providing this information, we find that this section is composed by six quite separate scenes. It starts with the old woman sweeping the house while the couple is away, next there is the scene of the wife hearing the cries of the babies, third is the scene of the burning of the shells and the lowering of the box, fourth is the scolding of the mother, fifth is the introduction of the black vulture, and sixth is the trip of the black vulture and the man to the scissors.

I will concentrate on the first two scenes in order to describe some mechanisms used to achieve the histrionic closure. The first mechanism is that of viewpoint. The first scene starts by being described from the perspective of a detached observer. The old woman is sweeping the floor. Imperceptibly however that perspective shifts to that of the old woman as the observer shares in the surprise of the emergence of the babies, to shift back once more to its detached position when he describes the old lady trying to hold them. At this moment the attention shifts abruptly to the perspective of the wife. Here we start the second scene. She tells her husband that they must go because his mother has spoiled their children. The narrator follows their perspective until they arrive to the house. In the original text it describes how on their way to the house, the wife saw the boys calling out as they walked along. The perspective shifts once more to that of a detached observer as the narrator describes how she starts collecting her children.

Beyond the issue of shifts of perspective, there are other stylistic mechanisms that help re-create the scenes in the eyes of the audience. Prominent among them is the use of aspect. Throughout the narrative there is a constant shift between the perfective and the imperfective aspects. The issue of aspect is not an easy one to describe. There have been arguments in favor and against considering the perfective as punctual, as against a continuous imperfective.[13] Yet Comrie seems to have captured the general meaning of imperfectivity when he says that "the general characterization of imperfectivity will already be apparent, namely explicit reference to the internal temporal structure of a situation, viewing a situation from within..."[14] Adequately in the unfolding of the story the narrator will use both the perfective and imperfective aspects as he shifts between the detached observer position and that of a character. Thus while describing the first scene of this section, the narrator starts with the perfective: "The old woman came sweeping... she broke the shells of the peanut." However, just as the narrator shifts imperceptibly to the viewpoint of the old woman, he changes aspects to the imperfective. Thus at that point he says, "When the shell broke, the first one came out... Farther away [another one] is wallowing and screaming..." This change of aspect is used throughout the whole narrative to emphasize the shift of perspective. It is very appropriate since the shift of detached observer to the perspective of one of the characters implies a shift into the internal temporal structure of the situation, a viewing of the situation from within.

The third characteristic I will emphasize at this point is the iterative quality of Shipibo narrative. This iterative quality gives the Shipibo narrative a very peculiar rhythm in which events are slowly unfolded in front of the eyes of the audience. Thus the full version of the quotes cited in the previous paragraph is as follows.

"The old woman was sweeping. She came sweeping. Under the pona floor she swept. They say that she swept ugh! The peanut [shell] broke. As the peanut [shell] broken was, the one made by the first copulation already the first one was. Having broken [the shell] he already came out bigger. Over there, there is [one] wallowing and screaming. The one that was made earliest, coming out, is pulling the others, 'mother went that way with mother went father.' So saying, by the arm is pulling [the others]. Over there those who were just recently made, red all over are screaming. Under the pona floor lying down [he was]. The old woman picked him up. The old woman could not manage. [She] could not manage to pick up her grandchildren. 'That way father went, with him went mother,' so saying, [he] was pulling the smaller ones, like this one [this is a reference to an actual child who was present]. Screaming for the two of them, father, mother. That way they were asking."

The iterative quality also produces the effect of anticipation. Subsequent sentences tend to echo previous ones and take them slightly forward. This anticipation coheres perfectly well with the three other types of anticipation used throughout the narrative. The first type relates to stating a rule or an intention of a character which is later either carried out or contradicted. Thus, when the story later on tells us that the man told his mother not to sweep the peanut refuse, it is anticipating the mother's subsequent sweeping of the floor. The second type of anticipation relates to thematic anticipation. As we saw at the beginning of the narrative, the narrator gives his information by stages. Thus the first paragraph introduces the theme of a non-ordinary woman. However, at that stage the theme is only at an abstract level, she has done nothing to live up to her explanation. In the second paragraph, we find that she is already acting out her non-ordinary character. We find the third type of anticipation at the still deeper level of the audience's understanding of the story. For example, by the second paragraph the story has already allowed the audience to realize that it should expect a topsy-turvy world. It then proceeds to develop it extensively in the following paragraphs.

The final point I want to emphasize about this section is that up to here the fantasy has been overdetermined. As we saw, by a process of anticipation the extraordinary had been introduced to fulfill a strictly defined role. Whatever secondary role it had to fulfill to further the semantics of the myth and the thread of the action, each piece of behavior was also characterized by being the opposite of good behavior. Extraordinary behavior was pre-defined from the beginning of the story and up to this point as the dialectical opposite of good manners. It was overdetermined. At this point, however, we are introduced the first bits of an imagination that fulfills a different role. It is represented by the box that comes from the sky and the scissors. It provides glimpses into other worlds. This is a favorite mechanism of Shipibo narrative and life and we will still see quite a bit of it in this paper. As we will see these glimpses into other worlds are closely related to the notion of histrionics. In the final analysis histrionics is the ability to create for the seer and listener what is absent. It is the ability to bring to this moment what is not, or what has not happened, here and now. This is the nature of representation. In this sense, providing glimpses into other worlds is one of the clearest ways to achieve the histrionic closure. The other typically Shipibo way is to bring the other world to the here and now. This we will develop when dealing with the shamanic sessions.

As the man had been left all alone he wandered off trying to find his wife and children. Finally, he was left crying. The hummingbird came. "Why are you crying, little brother-in-law?" he asked him. The man answered, "I am just crying because the black vulture has deceived me. He has made me kill my mother by telling me that he would take me to where my wife was. I am thinking about my wife, that is why I am crying, little brother-in-law." "What the black vulture told you is all a lie. He has deceived you and made you kill your mother. I have just come from over there and I will take you. You first have to pay me, little brother-in-law." "How will I pay you?" asked the man. "Collect all that thick pacay fruit, and give it to me to eat."

The man collected all the thick pacay. The hummingbird would stick its beak into each knot and would extract all its liquid. The man was thinking to himself, how can such a small bird carry me? The hummingbird looked up and said, "You are thinking how can such a small one carry me, little brother-in-law. I will take you. I am already full. I will now rest. I have come from where your wife is. She is harvesting peanuts. I have come from there, they have gone to harvest peanuts." Then he added, "Now come. Do not look how I carry you. Close your eyes and I will carry you, little brother-in-law." The man said, "How will you be able to support me?" "Just hop up. We will first go to the place from which you have just wandered off. There we will rest."

The hummingbird then stepped strongly on the ground and off they went. As they arrived to the place under the scissors where the black vulture abandoned the man, they stopped. "We are here already. Get off and let's rest, little brother-in-law," said the hummingbird. The man looked up and there was something like immense scissors. 'Tas, tas' it was doing. Then the hummingbird asked the man to hop up again and told him that when they go through that place quickly, to jump on top of him in order to be able to go through. Then the hummingbird elevated himself again, he entered, pssssst, and they were on the other side. "Hmm, we are here," he said.

As they got down, a big path that seemed white was seen. Then the hummingbird told the man, "When your wife asks you who brought you here, do not answer that it was the hummingbird. I will be looking at you, so do not tell her it was I who brought you. Your wife will tell you that nobody else goes around this place, that only the hummingbird is around." Then the hummingbird added, "The face of your sister-in-law is very similar to that of your wife." They went and it was true. They were harvesting peanuts. The hummingbird said, "Stay here and point to your wife with this little stick. Your wife is coming behind. Her face is very similar to that of your sisters-in-law." So said the hummingbird as he was hiding.

They were coming. It was about noon. As they were coming, the man pointed to her with the little stick that the hummingbird had given him. The hummingbird had told him to point towards her basket. As she was coming, he pointed to her. All the peanuts she was bringing fell to the ground. She told her sisters to wait because her basket had gotten untied and she had to gather the peanuts. Her sister went to assist her, but again it came untied. Then the husband came out of hiding. "Uhh," said the woman, "Who has brought you here?" "Nobody has brought me here, I have come by myself," said the man. "What about your mother," asked the woman. "I have left her, and I have come," answered the man. Then the woman said, "You have not come alone. The hummingbird has brought you. Only the hummingbird comes around these places. He has just left from here."

Then they went on. They passed through a banana plantation which was extensive and very clean. At the end of it, the woman told the man that she was going to tell her mother that she would take him in. She went and told her mother that the man that used to be her husband had come. The mother told her to bring him in, that she had been single too long. She said to bring him so they could have him. The sisters of the woman started to comment among themselves that the husband of the sister had come. Each one wanted to go to fetch him. So they all went together. As they reached him, they all wanted to embrace him. The man's wife would not permit it saying that he was all for her alone. The sisters got angry and declared that they would talk to their father when he returned.

This section introduces a new character, the hummingbird. Like the black vulture, the hummingbird is a mediator between the celestial world and the earth. The hummingbird, however, is a more successful mediator. The story itself provides the information that the only bird that is able to reach the celestial heights is the hummingbird. His fee is not exaggerated either. He only wants pacay.[15]

Sociologically, the hummingbird scene presents another interesting detail. In Shipibo, "little brother-in-law" is a normal, albeit specially friendly form of address. In this scene however, this form of address does not seem to be unmotivated. Up to now, no character has addressed another with this, or another form of address. In this scene, in every single line of conversation, both the hummingbird calls the man "little brother-in-law" and the man calls the hummingbird by the same term of address. This emphasis seems to be related to the fact that the hummingbird is being introduced as the successful in-law that comes from outside to help. The relationship between brothers-in-law, unlike that of parents-in-law/sons-in-law, is one of joking relationship, with a great deal of intimacy and banter added to it. The hummingbird in this scene has come to assume a brother-in-law position. Unlike the black vulture, however, this is a successful mediator. The myth here is commenting favorably on a matrilocal situation which an individual of an intermediate distance confronts from a different sociological perspective. The myth has effectively dissected the relationships involved in this situation and studied each separately. The emphasis is more striking by the fact that the black vulture scene and that of the hummingbird are put next to each other, and that both are made to do exactly the same actions. The hummingbird's scene, however, is harmless and successful while the black vulture's is noxious and unsuccessful.[16]

Once the hummingbird and the man enter into the terrain of the celestial wife, the myth continues in its disquisitions on the advantages of matrilocal marriage. The hummingbird points out that the face of the man's wife's sisters are very similar to that of the wife. Thus it is hinting at the sororal polygynous situation which is the norm among the Shipibo. This hint is taken up in the next scene when all the sisters of the wife want to embrace the man.

Furthermore, the matrilocal situation is characterized by returning to its right place all the elements that were in an upside-down position in the patrilocal section of the myth. Thus the man finds his wife harvesting peanuts with her sisters instead of using peanuts to clean herself and throw them away as refuse. The harvest produces food normally, instead of producing children, magically. The impolite way in which the woman appears into the world of the family in the patrilocal situation is here set aright by the very polite way in which the wife introduces her husband to her mother making him wait a certain distance away from the house. The collection of refuse under the pona floor in the patrilocal situation is contrasted by the very clean path as soon as they enter the celestial world, but more particularly, with the orderly and clean banana plantation of the wife's family. All in all, we are entering a world of normal behavior and apparently normal feelings.

> At noon the father arrived. He was thundering. He smelled and said, "You have brought here a *yoʃi* [non-human spirit]. I have come wanting to cut the neck of a Cashibo [enemy tribe epitome of savages for the Shipibo]."[17] The wife said to the man, "When he comes he is going to raise the lid of the pot. As soon as he does that you strike his eye with this stone. Be careful not to miss. This other stone is for the other eye." The woman gave the man two immense stones. Then the father finally arrived. The man was sniffing, so the daughter said, "My husband has come, father, do not eat him." As she was saying this, the old man raised the lid of the pot and took him out. The man then hit the old man with the stone and then the other eye with the other stone. Both eyes swelled. The old man said, "That is what your husband has come for." He got angry and wanted to eat him.

> At night, when it was pitch dark, the old man got up and started to go to eat the man. The man's wife said, "Father, you are stepping over your grandchildren." The old man was surprised, "Weren't you asleep?" The daughter had taken the precaution of making her husband bathe in the magic herbs of her father. Then the daughter told her father, "You should test the strength

of your voice against your son-in-law." The son-in-law then invited the father to be the first one to speak loudly. The father spoke loudly and all of the sky went *tiiiinnn*. He would raise his club and just a very thin rumbling would sound. Then the father said, "Now it is your turn. Let me see what you can do, son-in-law." Then the son-in-law took his father-in-law's club, his lightning-club. When the son-in-law held it, it shone more than the lightning. He hit the old man on the head. It almost split his head in two. The old man was tumbling back and forth. The old man asked, "Have you bathed your husband in my magic herbs? He has received my strong voice. Now I will not be able to harm your husband." That was the end of the story.

Thus we see that even though the myth favors matrilocality, it does not consider it unproblematic. The problem in matrilocality is the clash of the outsiders. Both the father of the woman and her husband are outsiders. They come from other households to marry into this matrilocal unit, the core of which is a group of women. The animosity between outsiders is inevitable. Yet it must be confronted and its final outcome must be that the in-coming male will take over the authority of the older man. The natural risk of matrilocality is, hence, not without its compensations.

Throughout this myth only two times of day are specified. There is noon and night. These have a structural role in the narrative. The conjunction of star-woman and man, be it the first conjunction or the final victory of the union, happens at night. The ordinary matrilocal family encounters of man with woman returning from garden work or with father-in-law returning from work happen at noon. Thus we have the status transforming encounters at night as against the temporary kin union at noon. Furthermore, there is a strong opposition of darkness/light.[18] This is epitomized in the requirement of the man's closing of his eyes when being transported through the air and the father-in-law's blinding in a scene that is reminiscent of *Oedipus Rex*. The closing of the eyes, or its functional equivalent, the pouring of magical herbs on the eyes, recurs in Shipibo myths whenever a man is transported to another element.

Beyond the structural implication, however, it must be remembered that myths are usually narrated at night. This story is being narrated to an audience which is physically at night. The myth starts with a scene at night and the audience is taken through a visit to diverse imaginary worlds, full of daylight, to be finally deposited again in the only other scene that occurs at night. There the story ends.

Now that we have finished analyzing the narrative we will review how the mechanisms the story has used serve to individualize the social discourse contained in the myth. We will look into how those mechanisms allowed the story to traverse the "socialization of experience" in reverse order. The most obvious first step is that the narrative, just like experience, occurs "in time." In real-life, as in the story, events happen one after the other. Yet the narrative provides the events in a pre-digested state. The individual does not have to impose structure into perceptual data, the myth already brings that order with itself.

Thus, in terms of timing and logic, we find the myth providing a simple rule. Everything is presented before it is developed. In other words, there is constant anticipation. This process pervades all levels of the narrative from merely formal rhetorics to the implicit message. Thus in terms of formal rhetorics, we saw the anticipation of enunciating one phrase and then repeating it in order to develop it. In terms of the architecture of narrative, we saw how at the beginning the story presents a woman whose extraordinary character is just announced by herself, before it plunges into a description of the extraordinary actions of this being. In terms of normative behavior, the myth explicitly states a rule, just to have the character either follow it or break it. Finally in terms of the implicit message, we saw how the story tames the chaos of the unusual by developing the precise dialectical opposites of "good manners" to allow the audience to expect the precise opposite of what they normally see.

In terms of viewpoint, the myth pre-digests a "character perspective." Just like "structuring through anticipation" becomes natural to the listener because of its repetition at every level, seeing through the eyes of the character becomes the normal viewpoint for the same reason. As we saw in the analysis this perspective emerges from its repetition at several levels. We saw how one passed from the structure of indirect speech in Shipibo language to the impersonation of characters, to the manipulation of aspect, to the actors' descriptions. This "characters' perspective" gives the myth a deceptively phenomenological quality. To the listener it evokes direct perception. Yet it is totally different because the message does not need to be processed and a structure imposed by the perceiving individual. The myth provides its own temporal and logical structure, all the individual needs to do is attune him-/herself to it.

Third, there is the "episodization" of logic. As we saw, in terms of the social code, this myth deals with alternatives to matrilocal residence. We saw how each alternative is considered in sequence and how each is provided with full consideration. Thus first we had the coming of the celestial wife into a patrilocal terrestrial situation. Next the unsuccessful intermediate matrilocal in-law, the successful matrilocal in-law, to end up with disquisitions on the problems and advantages of matrilocal residences. Each logical point is marked by a big shift in the story. Thus the patrilocal situation is marked by the arrival of the celestial wife, the unsuccessful matrilocal in-law by the arrival of the black vulture, the successful matrilocal in-law by the hummingbird and the disquisitions on matrilocality by the arrival of the man to the land of the celestial wife. Furthermore, the whole process of alternative considerations is introduced by a protracted escalation of misbehavior that proved the total unacceptability of the first alternative. Equally, the final logical resolution involves the transportation of the hero, and with him the audience, to a different realm altogether. Thus, traversing in reverse order the individual's acquisition of logic from temporal and spatial categories,[19] the myth projects into time and space its logical operators.

Finally, there are the bridges to the present. Thus the myth, as we saw, makes constant reference to the audience's present, e.g. "a pona floor like this one." It also closes upon itself by starting at night, the time at which it is being narrated, developing during day-time and ending again at night time. Through these mechanisms, the myth individualizes what is social. It makes apparently experiential what is logical. Yet the representation is quite different from perception. It is the distance from one to the other that makes narrative, like play, so pleasant.[20]

Shamanic Sessions

Having looked at the poetics of Shipibo prose narrative, we now turn to the poetic text itself. Poetry among the Shipibo comes within the context of singing. The poetic text is a sung text. The shamanic session is in a sense the most complex expression of poetic texts in that it is a whole cycle of songs that has a coherent sequence and forms a unity. In another sense, however, it is not, since what is expressed in the shamanic songs most of the time is descriptive rather than expressive of feeling. The same genres that serve as vehicles for expression of feelings in lay singing are put to the service of description in shamanic song.

The language used is the same for lay and shamanic singing. In terms of language all the genres seem to have the same basic components. A song is composed of a series of lines. Each line contains seven or eight syllables approximately, though the number of syllables is not strict for any line. Syntactically, the lines are very simple, most of the times being limited to a noun and a verb, and rarely an adjective or a complement. On some occasions, the thought started in a line is completed in the following line or lines. Normally, however, a line is a sentence.

In contrast to the simplicity of the syntax, Shipibo songs exhibit a most extraordinary complexity of figurative expression. The complexity and thoroughness of this symbolism is such that Shipibos themselves warned me that songs are very difficult to understand. The reason for this is that most of the time, the nouns used in the songs do not refer to their normal everyday referent but are used in a metaphorical sense. However, unlike contemporaneous western poetry, the extent of this metaphorization is extreme. Never will a man or a woman or a child be referred to as such in a song. Those words do not exist in the singing vocabulary. Instead there is a set of fixed metaphors that are used to replace these words. Thus women are always referred to as monkeys, men as turtles, children as small birds. This type of metaphorization I have come to call lexical metaphorization, because in the context of a song if the word monkey is used its lexical meaning will not be the hairy mammal but the human female. Thus the metaphorical meaning is attached to the word as an added lexical item. One can develop a dictionary of these metaphors and look up the referent every time the word comes up. They are objectively accepted metaphors. No great displacement of meaning happens by their introduction. Even if the real life and the metaphorical referents become linked by the use of the metaphor, the link itself is a weak one. It is somewhat like the English language idiomatic phrases, where one does not look at the metaphorical origin of the phrases. These are frozen metaphors. The mental effect on the listener is weak.

Beyond these frozen metaphors, lay singing also exhibits a profusion of personal metaphors. These are metaphors which the author him/herself has created *ad hoc* for this particular song. These are what we are accustomed to calling metaphors. The listener's action in understanding them is that of bridging the literal and the figurative meanings. What I am here calling personal metaphors, does not only include metaphors in the strict sense but also synecdoches, metonymies and so on. In some types of lay singing, there is also a complex usage of poetic images. These combinations of metaphors and images, however, are enough to obscure the meaning of the songs to those listeners who are not familiar with the language of singing.

Interestingly, even though shamanic songs use poetic images and frozen metaphors quite thoroughly, they rarely use personal metaphors. The reason for this seems to be related to their context. As we saw at the beginning of this paper, the text of the songs is supposedly derived from the actual singing of a spirit. The use of frozen metaphors is quite normal in songs. Actually, it is the lexicon of songs. Everyday referents are never used. Hence their use in shamanic singing poses no problem for the audience. Personal metaphors, on the other hand, require an effort on the part of the audience that runs counter to the transmission of the message. Even though a successful metaphor normally transmits more information that a direct phrase, its understanding poses some problems. Furthermore, the type of information that is transmitted in the shamanic session is not specially suited for transmission through metaphors. It is usually descriptions of what the spirits have seen on their way here and descriptions of the illness and of what they are doing to cure it. Of course, at times these descriptions seem metaphorical, but they are not. Thus during a shamanic song, the singer described how there was a small musician, a flute player, about 30 centimeters in height that was sitting at the tip of his tongue and was sucking the magical dart out of the patient. When I heard the expression, it was clear to me that the shaman was referring to his pipe as he was singing. When I confronted the shaman with my interpretation, he simply corrected my theory by saying that he had also seen the little character dressed in a colorful attire sitting at the tip of his mouth. I do not doubt that that is exactly what the shaman saw. It must be emphasized that he was under the influence of *Ayahuasca*. He was not creating a personal metaphor but describing what he was seeing. The metaphor appeared not as a matter of verbal expression but as a matter of perception. Its intrusion provides testimony to the depth of the metaphorizing process in the human mind.

The shamanic session starts some hour or two after dinner. It must already be dark and the shamans usually prefer the activity of the village to have died down before they take *Ayahuasca*. They say that too much movement does not allow them to concentrate. The normal progression of events on a night that a shaman is going to take *Ayahuasca* is as follows.[21] One or two hours after dinner, one would find the shaman sitting on the pona floor of his house conversing with the other members of his household. This time of the evening is usually one of slowing movement in the Pisqui villages. By then people have usually returned to their houses from their kitchens and normally visitors have either returned to their houses or get adapted to the mood of the hour. Conversations are conducted in a softer tone than during the day and people are usually reclining on the places where their mosquito nets are set.

As the whole village slowly starts to die down, the shaman takes some four straw mats down to the patio in front of his house. He forms a rectangular space with them. This is the space over which he is going to officiate. This segregation of space provides, once the session is under way, a very neat separation of sacred and profane spaces. He immediately returns to his house and spends some more time chatting. After approximately ten minutes, he comes back down to the patio bringing with him most of the necessary paraphernalia. He sits in front of the mats, facing the river across the patio and the kitchens. His back is to his house and, hence, to the whole row of houses. Just behind him, he places a live brand. On either side of him, he sets a bottle full of *Ayahuasca*, a gourd vessel, his pipe, his tobacco mace, and a bundle of basil leaves. He cuts tobacco shavings from the mace and leaves them on a plank of wood on one side. He picks up his pipe, softly whistles into it for an extended period (approximately five to ten minutes), fills up the pipe with the shavings and puts a live coal into it. He smokes and blows smoke occasionally over his own body. He sets the pipe aside and picks up the gourd vessel. He holds the vessel with both hands raised to the level of his chin, in an offering-like position, and spends a long time regarding it and meditating. He puts it down again. He ignites his pipe, smokes for a while and opening the *Ayahuasca* bottle, blows smoke into it, covering it with his hand so that the smoke does not escape. He inhales more smoke and blows it again into the bottle closing it with a cork. He repeats this procedure until the bottle is filled with smoke. He cleans the vessel, pours a small amount of *Ayahuasca* into it raises it to the level of his chin and pronounces the propitiatory words in a very soft voice.[22] Then he drinks the *Ayahuasca*.

110

By this time, there are very few people left awake in the village. Usually, there will be the shaman, the anthropologist, and maybe one or two other people. The shaman converses with those who are awake. Intermittently, the shaman fumigates himself. He also fans himself with the sweet basil. Then he stops, sits perfectly still for a long time. After approximately forty five minutes he fans himself some more with the sweet basil and starts to softly whistle. Then he is again quiet and quite still with the basil suspended in his hand. He resumes fanning himself, pours some more *Ayahuasca* in the vessel, drinks and continues to fan himself. Then, with an air of naturalness, he turns towards the live brand, puts a piece of coal into his pipe, inhales several times and fumigates his body beginning from his ankles, then his head, then his chest. He whistles for a short time and the first, a $\beta^{w}\ddot{e}w\acute{a}$ erupts from his mouth.[23]

SONG 1

I sing to heal
My body to heal
[They] come healing

My toes

5 the coldness of the water spring

revolving around the toes
revolves to untie

untying while it goes

from my body
untying it goes

10 my roof-framed body
framed as it was
[I] go untying

The coldness of the water-spring
I am finishing to untie

its yellow winds
15 cold yellow winds
my toes
that around them revolved
[I] go untying

its mist

20 the coldness of its mist,
[that rises] from the earth
[that] emanates
untying I go

All of its roof-framework
25 having untied
my toes
I am curing

From my body,
from my body
30 long time ago they entangled
entangled they did!

Untying I go,
its cold wind
the whirlwinds, to start with
35 having cut to pieces [as it passed]

untying while going
that which boils,
that which boils, to begin with,
the coldness of the water-spring

40 I will untie
those vapor, first,
the yellow vapors, first,
the cold winds that are revolving

that which revolved
45 [it] goes untying

Over there, by the side of the hill
the water boils
the coldness of the spring
[I am] finishing to untie

50 From my body
to heal well
[I am] singing well

[Even though] the body [was] framed
untying [I] go
55 from my body

I will cure it,
my body, to start with,
I am healing

Boiling water
60 that boils like this,
cold winds
on its top revolving
revolving, to start with
untying it goes

65 from my body
[they] are framing
[they] lowered the coldness
let's finish the unraveling

emerging continuously
70 let's cleanse

to sweep his body
broom to sweep
cleaning while going
untying it goes

untying it goes
75 from my body
to go healing
I sing $\beta^{w}\ddot{e}w\dot{a}$

A frame already made

[They] are descending
80 my doctors [a type of spirit-helpers]
doctors...

[The shaman asks me to fumigate him with a
cigarette]

Revolving while coming
a frame comes

We will bring to an end
85 for me to be healed
King doctors[24]

the doctors...
those that are coming down[25]

those that are coming down
90 all the windows
looking into, while passing

knowing they go
the frames go

untying [they] go
95 our king says

listen to us
do you want
our words?
Tell us!
100 Against the body itself it clinks
the clinking [he] has caught [distant past]

To know I go
it is this way
the worlds [days] of the kings
105 learning we go

Let's go looking
[how] the frames go
we go to see

Bringing to an end
110 picking up the words
only picking up

Let's go looking
it was this way [distant past]
being it that way
115 we have helped make them descend

[Without major interruption, the shaman goes
into the second song which has a different
melody. It is a *muça*. This type of
song exists only as a ritual song.]

SONG 2

The day [world] of the kings
it goes looking at

the day [world] of the kings
[it] goes looking at
5 my body to cure
to cure they go

I am going to be cured
all the machines
its days [worlds], to start with
10 knowing, let's go

the body is being caused to finish
this machine of mine
on that machine

all the numbers
15 the kings' numbers
looking at we go

looking at we go
catching the words
my body curing
my toes
20 untying [it] goes

[The shaman was fanning his feet and his
body while singing lines 19-20. After
line 20, he exhales, with his hands sweeps

the toe, then the long bone of his leg]

untying [it] goes
having sat on the machine
looking [they] go
the body, first, [they] will heal

25 doctors of the kings
doctors,
open up!

the day [world] of the people,
that which is coming down

30 with fragrant medicine of gold
cleaning [they] come
all the machines
I go sitting [under the machines]
untying I go
35 from my body

As they are coming down
let's untie

new day [world] of gold
on it sitting

40 [they] are coming down
the new day [world] comes down
day [world] of the kings

picking up words
picking up I go

45 that which comes down
the new open day [world]
picking up I go

untying [we] go
we are doing
50 listen to us!
listen swallows!

our body we cure
we are curing
saying this
55 who wants it?

from the inside of the new day [world]
our body to heal
all the machines
are making noise
60 to heal our body

such are men

[Without making any interruption whatsoever,
just by changing the rhythm, the shaman goes
into the third song which is a *maʃá*]

SONG 3

[It] goes to catch
my Mockingbird
crossing through town
happily
5 [the] parrot of the Inkas
on the branch of the tower
its cross
tower covered with designs on its top
the wind cleans
10 [it] goes to clean
to cure my body
the toes
untying [it] goes
day [world] of the kings

This goes on at the same time that the
singing is continuing]
15 [it] will untie you
we are untying
[it] is coming out
they are saying
we are untying [you]
20 my cigarette
to do [i.e. to cure] it comes
all the machines
bring them making them sing!

[At this point Alvaro, a young man
comes and sits in front of the shaman
at a 90 degree angle from him.
The shaman fans Alvaro a couple of times.

At this point, the shaman fanned Alvaro a couple of times with the
sweet basil. He commented on how much he had gotten off today, to the
extreme of having had to ask the anthropologist to blow smoke over him.
Then I offered him a cigarette and he, Alvaro and I started conversing.
Alvaro had come in the middle of this last song. His entrance had been
quite delicate. He tried to disturb as little as possible and until the shaman ended his song he and I had kept silent, and had not even looked at

each other. The rest of the village was asleep. Shipibos in general have very light sleep. Several times during the night they wake up, and sit up or stroll quietly. If someone else is awake, the two may get closer and softly whisper to each other. They wake up on very slight disturbances of the enviroment. José had awakened and walked by from his house. He also came very quietly and was standing behind me.

In these first three songs the shaman is curing himself. He suffers from rheumatism and has sung these song to get cured. The progression, however, is typical of the curing ceremonies. The first 78 verses describe the symptoms of the illness as seen under the effects of the *Ayahuasca*, the source of the illness and the actions shaman/spirits are doing to cure it. Thus lines 1-4 plainly state that the shaman is singing to cure his toes. Line 4 gives us the cause of the illness. It is the "coldness of the water spring." Throughout the next seventy verses we will get some elaborations on the cause of the illness. Thus we get in lines 19-22 that the specific cause of the illness was the cold mist that emanates from the earth. Then in lines 46-48, we get the specific location of the water spring: by the side of the mountain, where the water boils.

At the same time, we are also getting the symptoms of the illness as seen through *Ayahuasca* and the actions that the shaman is exercising. These symptoms and actions are contemporary to the singing and the actions have a direct effect in the cure. The symptoms are symptoms in the strict medical sense, signs that demonstrate the existence of the illness. We see them in lines 14-17 where the song describes the cold yellow winds that revolves around the toes. The shaman/spirit at the same time is acting upon the symptoms. Verses 5-12 describe how the spirit/shaman is untying the coldness of the spring. Untying is the method of curing in Shipibo shamanism in general. This notion of untying and cutting to pieces is repeated insistently throughout the song. See verses 18, 23, 25, 32-35, and so on. If there is a single recurrent theme in Shipibo shamanic singing it is the untying of the illness.

The object of the action of untying in this song is apparently two-fold, the winds and the roof-frame.[26] In reality this dichotomy is only apparent. The roof-frame occupies a very peculiar position in shamanic singing. It is a roof-frame that the shaman under the effects of the *Ayahuasca* actually sees descending over the patient. However, at the same time, roof-frame in Shipibo shamanism is also a frozen metaphor for songs that have an effect upon health. This duality springs from the fact that the *Ayahuasca* allows the shaman to see the true nature of the things, the "platonic form" so to speak.[27] Usually this platonic form of the object has the same shape as the object we see in everyday life, but it is more perfect, more brilliant. In the case of shamanic songs, however, the "form" is the roof-frame. As such the song can cure or cause harm. Here, the song the shaman is referring to in lines 10-11 is a song that has caused harm to him. His own body is covered by a frame that is not protective but harmful. The shaman is untying this frame.

Finally lines 70-73 present us with the second recurring theme in Shipibo shamanism. Health is associated with the cleansing of the body. The illness is cleaned away from the body through a process of sweeping. The word for curing, $\beta^w\ddot{e}\int oai$, is the same word as for cleaning. Thus in lines 27, 58, and 76 when he says he is curing himself, he is also saying he is cleansing himself. This confluence of meaning between curing and cleaning expresses itself in actual descriptions of cleaning the body throughout the sessions.

Line 78 marks the end of the first part of the first song. From line 79 onwards we have a different theme altogether. Here the song starts introducing the spirits that are coming down to sing. It must be remembered that in Shipibo ideology these songs are being sung by spirits. The shaman, along with other spirits that sit next to him, help the main singer, one spirit, by repeating what he is singing. A spirit comes down sings and departs. What the spirit sings is usually very simple. A whole string of spirits will usually be introduced with *irai namandi*, literally "are descending." Since Shipibo is an ergative language the subject is not specified. I have translated it as "[they] are descending." The spirit's song will usually start by the spirit identifying itself. At times, the spirits will also say what they have seen when coming down and at times give some more explanation of what they are about. For example here in lines 80-85, the doctors [*rokotorobo*], a type of spirit helper, state that they are coming down bringing a song [lit. a frame] with them to cure the patient. In lines, 85-94, the king doctors [*rai rokotorobo*] say they are coming down and while coming down have looked into the windows that give into the day of the spirits. Then in lines 95-115, the king [*rai*] is making a reference to the anthropologist's desire to learn their shamanic lore and is offering to teach it.

The second song is a *muça*. *Muça* songs are exclusively ritual and several of them are sung to have a direct effect upon nature. For example, for the act of propitiation later on in the evening, the spirit turns to a *muça* song. This song is taking us through a trip. In Shipibo the word for day is the same as the word for world. In shamanic singing it is used with both meanings together. The power of a shaman derives from how much he has dared to travel in the land of the spirits. The farther he has gone, the more powerful he is. Usually the determining factor is how far the shaman went on the initiatic trip. Thereafter all the spirits that he has seen have been conquered by him and are his servants. This does not mean, however, that the shaman cannot go visiting in later *Ayahuasca* sessions. Any increment in his knowledge is an increment in his power.

The day of the spirits has another meaning also. Not only is it the world that the shaman must know to be able to cure but also it is an actual day that must come. Once the shaman sees the day of the spirits dawning and fully here, then the patient has been cured. This explains lines 40-44, but the combination of concepts underlies all this *muça*.

Another interesting aspect of this song is the presence of the shaman's machine. It is a machine on which the shaman sits. Machines and quite a bit of western technology and culture in general have been incorporated into the world of the spirits. Thus I have encountered situations in which spirits are sitting in bars drinking or the shaman happens upon a land in which there are bicycles riding on the river. This does not seem to have affected the traditional ideology very much except to enrich it. Here the shaman is sitting on the machines as he "catches the words" of the spirits, i.e., as he listens to their singing and helps them sing.

A final point in the song concerns the use of frozen metaphors. Pointing them out will help one understand the song better. In line 30 the "fragrant medicine of gold" is the frozen metaphor for the sweet basil. What lines 30-31 are doing is describing the fact that the shaman has been fanning himself with the sweet basil and that its smell as well as the action of fanning helps "clean" him, i.e., cure him. In line 51, the song speaks of "swallows." Swallows is one of the frozen metaphors for human women, both in lay and shamanic singing. Its use here is a direct call on those mothers who want their children to be cured to send them. [See further lines 53-60]. In contrast to "swallows," line 61 speaks directly of "men." Never in lay or shamanic singing are human men or women referred to as such. The use of the word "men" here is a clear indication to the listener. This line is not saying the "humans are this way." It is saying the "spirits," which are the "men" referred to in this line, are this way, i.e. that they have the power to cure.

The change of rhythm after line 61, introduced a new song. Such unexpected changes of rythm as well as changes of pitch indicate that a new spirit is certainly singing. The contrary, however, is not true. A change of singing spirit does not necessarily entail a change in the rhythm or style of the song. The remarkable fact about this third song is the description of the mockingbird. The mockingbird is an apt metaphor for the shaman. The shaman, like the mockingbird, imitates the sounds he hears. The shaman is constantly repeating what the spirits are singing. He helps them sing, and is nothing more than their echo. The parrot of the Inka, as we saw in the introduction, does exactly the same for the gods. The song goes slightly farther in describing the abode of the parrot of the Inkas. However, just as in the case of the colorful flute player described in the introduction, the mockingbird is a metaphor of perception and not of language. The shaman both saw the mocking bird and the parrot of the Inka physically present themselves at the scene.

This interruption was very short, however. The shaman went to the edge of the clearing, urinated, and blew smoke onto himself. All this time, he kept repeating how much the *Ayahuasca* had gotten him off. Since this is an experienced shaman, it is quite unusual for him to comment on the effect of the *Ayahuasca*. It so happened that in this session the drug had had a particularly strong effect. The shaman calmed down slightly. He came back and retook his place. Since Alvaro had not moved all this time, he was again sitting in front of the shaman. The shaman massaged and blew smoke on him. Then the shaman blew smoke on himself for a long time, froze for a second, and abruptly started song 4 which is a $\beta^w\ddot{e}w\acute{a}$.

SONG 4

It is ending
It is ending

The frames of the sky are coming

the turtles are coming
5 those that are coming down

those that are coming down
there [they] come

Listen carefully!
so it was [distant past]
10 our very words
[he] is having [us] sing
[he] has gone to pick up the words

I went to pick up [distant past]
the words I went to pick up [distant past]
15 Listen to us
for you to take that
to take my words

the framed iron
motored frame
20 going to pick up the words

words I went to pick up [distant past]
we will tell you

did you want
our words?

the man that is wanting
25 wherefrom, maybe
does this man come out of?
He, maybe, is wanting
he, maybe, wanted [distant past]
Let's give [it] to [him]

30 The kings' tower
on top of the tower sitting
I will make [him] sing for you
this kind I have picked up [distant past]
35 untying I go
revolving around your head
hot wind revolving
revolving it was
[we] will untie you

40 on a day [world] covered with designs
a new open day [world]
sitting and doing while going
for you, [I] will untie
hot wind hat
45 on your head a cross
a cross that was
detaching we go

So doing
the wind *Jo ro ro ro*[28]

[José came up to the straw mats and
sat approximately one meter in front of
Alvaro. They are sitting in a straight line,
both 90 degrees from the shaman]

50 so it was
untying, the wind of the spirits
   [*yoŝi*]
untying
on the branch of the tree of the sun
walking [through an elevation or ridge]
55 my whistling
the wind's whistling
causing to put [into a container]
comes untying
[it] is mine
60 the hot wind machine

with that machine
revolving around your head
[I] will go untying
[I] go cleaning
65 we are also

m^wëraya people
the kings are coming
so it is
from your body
70 untying [we] go

[the sound of a boat can be heard
at a distance]

are causing to sing, first

[At this point the shaman
interrupted himself to say: "Those people
that go by, what will happen to them? That
man they have caught was thinking: 'How
will I go home.' So he was saying in his
thought. Let's listen:"]

So it was

[The shaman continues talking:
"Shit! I am a married man, he is
saying.."]

go [there] to see
you can go [i.e. can be cured]

[Elvira comes to sit next to Alvaro,
who moves backwards to allow her to sit.
Now we have Alvaro, this young
woman and José sitting in a row,
perpendicular to the shaman]

75 you are saved
so saying
I am a spirit [yoʃi]
in the depth of my eye
its depth covered with designs of gold
80 I stroll

So it was
over your body
on the other side, comes covered with
designs
I am untying [all of] you
85 cleansing I go
my toes

the gold frame comes

Once again the shaman commented on how the *Ayahuasca* has truly
gotten him off. He said that it almost made him cry. Then he chats for a
while, and laughs about what the man who had been caught told the police. As he is talking, without stopping fully from the conversation, he
launches into song 5. The beginning of a song, if it does not immediately
follow the previous one, always gives the impression that the shaman is
being picked up by the song. This time in particular, it gave the impression that he was picked up by the song without even having the chance to
finish the last word he was saying. The change in mood the shaman
experiences in passing from conversation to a song is obvious. These
changes become more abrupt as the night wears on. At the beginning of
the cures he might pre-whistle songs. Even then however, the transition
is very abrupt: the shaman is caught by the pre-whistling, the same way
he is caught by the song. It seems that the song is itching to come out of
his mouth. Song 5 is also a β^wëwá. β^wëwá songs are very common both
in lay and shamanic singing. *Maʃá* which are very common lay songs are

somewhat more rarely encountered in shamanic singing. Song 3 above is an example of that type of singing.

Song 4 starts by announcing that songs (i.e. frames) are coming down [line 3] brought by spirit people (lit. 'turtles') [lines 4-7]. Then the spirits describe how the shaman has come to pick up their words, how he is making them sing [lines 8-14]. This is the essence of the *Ayahuasca* session. The shaman in taking *Ayahuasca* is causing the spirits to come down and sing. He is going to pick up the words. It is noteworthy that when spirits sing they always use the suffix for distant past *l -nil* , even when the events have been recent. The reason is that the shamanic session does not only bridge space but also time.

It is not precise to speak of a "world of the spirits" among the Shipibo. It is not one world in which the spirits live. It would be rather many worlds, or to be more precise, many locations, village-like places quite independent one from the other, bits of mystic territories that are not easily placed in one geographic chart of the spirits, but rather that are witnessed as patches in the mystic journeys of the shamans. The description of one tier over another of geographic location of spirits is just an after-the-fact construction, a skeleton which acquires flesh only when the shaman that gives the narrative described the places to which he has been. The rest is given in some order or another, but with the obvious reservation that he has not been farther than here or there and has been told about this place by another shaman who was there. Obviously not all shamans have seen the same things, though it seems that the main features of some places are the same, e.g. the Inka's village with the parrot is remarkably similar to the Cuzco that was described by XVI Century Chroniclers.

In a historic sense spirits used to commingle with people and were fully visible to people. Nowadays, spirits can mingle with people at their own free will, or people can visit them or make them come to us by the use of the *Ayahuasca*. Through the *Ayahuasca* session not only are the spirit and human worlds brought together but also the time when the spirits normally mingled with humans is reestablished. Thus the use of the distant past suffix *l -nil*. Great distances of time are bridged through this mechanism.

Lines 15-30 refer to the anthropologist's desire to learn about their worlds. The spirits are offering to let him learn. Then lines 30-34 explain that the spirit is going to have the shaman, while sitting on top of a tower, sing for the benefit of the anthropologist. Lines 35-39 specify how the cure is done. These lines had an extraordinary effect on my relationship with the shaman. Not only did the spirits not object to my being taught the shamanic lore, but they openly approved of it. The next morning the shaman came early into my house, the same way he would visit a patient he had just cured the previous night, and started providing me with esoteric knowledge of spirit life.

It is typical of Shipibo shamanic songs to finish with one topic and go on to the next. For the audience this indicates, just as much as the changes of pitch or the changes of rhythm, that one spirit has finished and another is starting. These changes may be quite abrupt. Once I was working with another shaman in the Ucayali. He had just started one song when he suddenly changed both pitch and rhythm, while at the same time trying to overcome his own laughter. Later on when we were going over the recording, he explained that at that point one spirit was starting to sing when another one came along, pushed away the one who was singing and sang his own song.

In this song, there has been a change in topic only. This, however, is enough to indicate that another spirit is singing. Lines 40-65 are direct curing actions on the patients. Lines 40-47 describe the present situation. The spirit/shaman is sitting on the spirit day, a new open day covered with designs, and is untying the hot wind "hat" that sits on the patients's head as if it were a cross. Lines 48-65 give a more detailed description of the procedure. First it establishes that the illness is caused by the wind of the evil spirits [lines 50-51]. Then it describes how the use of his own wind machine will untie and clean the patient [lines 59-65]. He describes how he has caught the whistling wind that was walking on the branch of the tree of the sun and this is the wind he has put into the hot wind machine [lines 52-58]. This spirit wind, the one that does *ʃo ro ro ro*, is a cleansing wind that will cure, untie, the evil wind of the evil spirits [*yoʃi niwë*].

Line 66 introduces yet new spirits that are coming down. These are the m^w*ëraya* people. M^w*ëraya* is a Shipibo designation for a type of traditional healer. None of the living Shipibo healers are m^w*ëraya*. The m^w*ëraya* are remembered as being very powerful, and at least in the Pisqui, are somewhat associated with the Shetebo subdivision of the Shipibo/Conibo group. When people would describe the power of the m^w*ëraya* I always got the impression that they were a re-creation of the present rewriting the past. Somehow they fitted too well into the paradigm that the past is always better. In contrast with modern day shamans, m^w*ëraya* did not drink *Ayahuasca*. They used to drink tobacco juice. Also they did not bring down the spirits in the same way that modern shamans do. Instead of taking *Ayahuasca*, hearing and seeing the spirits and by helping them sing letting the audience hear what the spirits are singing, m^w*ëraya* used to physically present the audience with the spirits. A session with the m^w*ëraya* would start with the m^w*ëraya* sitting within his mosquito net. At one point the m^w*ëraya* would disappear, leaving the mosquito net empty. Instead of him, the audience would get the voice of spirits directly, without the mediation of the shaman and without the body of the shaman being even present. The most powerful m^w*ëraya* had the ability of bringing the spirits in body and voice. As the audience was sitting, one spirit would come down to a branch of a tree, for example, and his body would be seen and his voice heard.

The $m^w\ddot{e}raya$ referred to in line 66 is the spirit of these human healers. His presence in this song is rather short. He is only here until line 71. What he sings is just his presentation and he stops. It is interesting that in the middle of the singing the shaman is reminded of an event that happened that day and comments upon it. This had nothing to do with the shamanic session, except for the fact that they happened to be superimposed in time and space. A drug dealer had been caught below the mouth of the river and the shaman feels sorry for him.

Line 72 by introducing a new topic announces that a new spirit is singing. Alvaro has been sick of the eye. Here the spirit which identifies himself simply as a *yoʃi* says he is strolling in the depth of his own eye which is painted with gold [lines 77-80]. He then points to the fact that the whole body is sick, and that the spirit will cleanse the whole body [lines 81-86]. Line 87 announces that a new spirit is coming down to sing. Without much interruption, the shaman enters song 5.

SONG 5

We are also

We are also
we are people
$m^w\ddot{e}raya$ people
5 That king, also
over your bodies
[I] am untying
untying continuously

From your bodies
10 we are people
$m^w\ddot{e}raya$ from the Piro tribe

$m^w\ddot{e}raya$ people
we, on the other hand, also
I, on the other hand, also

15 the sick body,
so he has spoken
we also are

we will do [i.e. cure] for [all of] you
my brothers-in-law [my friends]

20 my brothers-in-law
[we] will untie you

from your bodies
we go detaching
[they] had gone by enmeshing
[$m^w\ddot{e}pidai$]
25 your framed bodies
framed by words

[I] am untying you
the wind clinks

The wind clinks
30 clinks from within
[he] has done a frame [distant past]

[he] has done a frame [distant past]
we, on the other hand, also
all the wind

35 all the wind
that revolves around [you]
that which is revolving,[I] have
picked up [distant past]

that which is revolving, [I] have
picked up [distant past]
[I] went picking up words [distant past]

[The shaman tells Alvaro: "Come
closer so I can rub your head." He
rubs/massages Alvaro for approximately
twenty seconds and continues singing]

40 words [I] went picking up [distant past]
over your bodies
[I] will untie you

[Starts fanning with sweet basil]

the fragrance of the medicine of gold
with that ventilation
45 ventilating, [we] do
over your bodies

[The shaman fans Alvaro, Elvira
and himself.]

This song is being sung by the spirit of a real living shaman who is identified in this song as $m^w\ddot{e}raya$ people. Line 4 was translated by a lay Shipibo assistant as "shaman people" [*gente medico*], meaning that most likely the audience understands $m^w\ddot{e}raya$ people within the context of this song to refer generally to people who cure rather that specifically to $m^w\ddot{e}raya$. The spirit here refers to himself and to the shaman as kings. Lines 10-14 specify that the spirit is not a Shipibo shaman but a shaman of the Piro tribe. Note also that the spirit, being a fellow human, addresses the patients as little-brothers-in-law [line18-21], a form of address that is common among Shipibos who are not relatives.

Most of the song is a disquisition on the contemporaneous actions of the spirit while curing. Lines 5-9 explain generally what the spirit is doing, i.e. untying the patient. Lines 15-42 describe in detail the cause of the sickness. It explains that the body has been enmeshed through a song (a frame) [lines 24-26]. This explanation includes another metaphor/'platonic form' for songs. They are wind that sounds. The spirit explains that the wind that clinks has done harm [lines 27-30] and that that wind is a song that somebody has sent against the patient [line 31]. Then the spirit explains that the cure for the illness is the song that he and the shaman are singing [lines 32-34] and that that song is also a wind which is beneficial [lines 35-39].

Lines 43-46 state that the fragrance of the sweet basil will also help cure the patients. The shaman had started fanning the patients just before line 43. After line 46, he stops singing and fans Alvaro, the girl and himself. Then he comments: "Why aren't ours all the things I have seen in my visions. The machines, all kinds of things, everything." Then he is quiet a long time. A long pause follows which is broken by the first line of song 6, which is a $\beta^w\ddot{e}w\acute{a}$

SONG 6

The words are finishing

[He stops and comments. "I only hear
a distant murmur, constant, constant..."
he laughs, stops and stays quiet for a
long time. Abruptly, he restarts.]

Over there where it ends,
at the end of the earth,
from the very end
5 I bring you

I bring you

We are
designed with steel
designed turtles

10 Designed turtles

[Alvaro was about to leave but the
shaman told him not to go.
The shaman continued singing.
From now until approximately verse 75,
José, Alvaro and Elvira will be
with their heads lowered, as if they
were receiving a blessing, or as if
they were deeply concentrated]

Do you want
to cure your bodies?
tell me !

We, on the other hand,
15 [are] from where the day [world] is
              covered with designs
the turtles stroll

Listen to us!

Listen to us!
The day [world] is clinking
20 under the clinking,
watches in rows,
turtles standing in rows

to wait for that
To wait for that
25 we are singing
Then

The golden frame is coming
is coming looking at
the pair groomed as if for a party

The golden frame is coming
30 the turtles are coming
he is waiting for them
we are...

we are
I am
35 on my machine
over your bodies
have come to wait

Have come to wait
over your bodies
40 untying you [I] go

We, on the other hand, are
the Christ kings

[I] bring the words
keep bringing [in]
45 my turtle's body

We sing for you
over your bodies
we make a frame [for your benefit]

We have finished
50 we will heal [you]
with my own body
your bodies to heal,
my sons of scarlet macaws
              [i.e. my grandchildren]

with all the earth [we are] healing [you]
55 with all the day [world] [we are]
              healing you
healing our body

to heal [I] stroll
listen to me!
[they are] happy
60 to heal us.

We are healed
the kings have said
with the thought of the Inka
with the thought it is

65 In the thought of the Inka
mine is the breast band
all gold

Breast band made of pure gold
let's make a breast band for you
70 I have picked up that

So that no yoʃi_ [evil spirit]
will bother you

I stroll with that
[with a] chain
75 my golden chain
I will give to you
[I am] singing
with that I am strolling

That way it was
80 [they] have said [distant past]

[They] have said [distant past]

Dove dɑoawa [i.e. woman of the
          Ayahuasca]
came to wait

The frame of the day [world] comes

85 comes the dɑoawa [type of yoʃi]
We are also
Listen to us!

People of the sound of peccary
behind us [they] come running

[The shaman stops and says:
"Peccaries are going to come. Frightened
they will come. From over there, behind
that forest they will come." {Actually
lots of peccaries were caught that very
night. Some, though, before the session}
Immediately he continues singing]

90 Make us see
so that you can catch
there we will catch

To catch from that

The kings are saying

[Here the shaman switches to muɽa
style of singing until the end of the song.
muɽa songs are magical in the sense
that they have an immediate effect]

95 bring them bring them
make them [i.e. the peccaries] eat big fruits
giving them food, bring them
make their sound come
calling they are coming
100 for you we sing muɽa
we sing muɽa.

Now the shaman throws smoke on Alvaro, massaging him with a
sweeping movement. He finishes and Alvaro leaves. Next the shaman
does the same with Elvira. She leaves. Next comes José. To José he
smoked a great deal and very attentively. Only at the very end did he
massage José. All the time there was a long conversation between José
and the shaman. José is a much older person than Alvaro or Elvira. In
this conversation the shaman was explaining to José that there was

nothing wrong with him. After this exchange José left.

Song 6 starts with the belated announcement that the spirit that was singing at the end of song 5 has already left [line 1]. Then a new spirit comes bringing the soul of the patient which had wandered off to the end of the world and, hence, the body was sick [line 2-6]. It is noteworthy that these are metallic people and all the metaphors are metallic. Thus they explain that they are groomed as if for a party [lines 29-32], but they had also explained that they were designed with steel [lines 8-16]. They announce that they have seen lots of spirits waiting to come to sing. But the metaphor they use for announcing the songs is metallic: watches for songs. Once they have introduced the metallic metaphors these will continue for the rest of the song.

Lines 41-42 announce that a new spirit is now singing. He is a Christ King. Lines 42-53 are not very exceptional. The Christ King is saying that he brings the songs in the body and that he will finish curing all those who are ill, including the shaman's grandchildren (the frozen metaphor scarlet macaws means grandchildren [line 53]). Lines 54-81, on the other hand, are quite extraordinary. The spirit here is explaining the functioning of the shamanic sessions. Much before I made the analysis of this song, I had noticed that Shipibos in general were somewhat reticent of running to a shaman for minor illnesses. This is not because they had no faith in the effectiveness of shamanic healing. On the contrary they seemed to have very strong faith in that. The real reason was that they felt it was a hassle to open up the cosmological order and bring down spirits. This is a major undertaking. It involves reestablishing the order of nature. The illness of the body continues to be the individual's business until it reaches a proportion beyond the individual's means. Once it is there, it is a matter involving cosmic proportions. It is the patient's problem but also the problem of the whole order of the cosmos. A battle between the different spiritual forces whose outcome is not necessarily preestablished. The evil forces, as often happens, may win.

Lines 54-65 is a reference to the cosmic dimension in the session. Lines 54-55 simply express that the spirit is curing the patient "with all the earth, with all the world." The reference to the Inka's thought is also a reference in the same direction. The Inka is the father of Christ. He is considered so in the cosmology, and also appears as such in one of the myths. His thought has some characteristics that make it similar to the broad God of the Judeo-Christian tradition. Inka not only appears in shamanic song but is also present in mythology and some "historic" songs. He is the central character of Shipibo cosmology. In the ideology of Shipibo shamanism he is the character for whom the parrot relays the songs that are being performed in the human/spirit interface.

Lines 65-80 are creating a protective device against intrusion by evil spirits [see lines 71-72]. Here we have again the metallic metaphors that were originally introduced by the people with the steel designs. The gold breast-band was made by Inka's thought and has been picked up by the shaman. The shaman uses it to protect himself and is lending it to the patients to also protect them [lines 73-78]. This song is a general protection against harm.

Line 83 introduces a woman spirit who explains that the spirits are advising that peccaries will come [lines 88-94] and shifts to a *muça*. This *muça* is a propitiatory song to bring peccaries. Only *muça* type songs have the power of bringing plenty of animals. After this propitiation Alvaro, Elvira and José left.

SONG 7

[The shaman has started pre-whistling
the song while he fans himself with
the sweet basil. He will continue
fanning himself sporadically throughout
the song]

The words are coming to an end

I am bringing to an end
bringing the words to an end

Over there walking on the frame
5 the words I have gone to pick up
    [distant past]
We are happy

We are happy
the day [world] is coming
the turtles are coming

10 The doves of the sky are shrieking
    let's hear the shrieks

Listen to us!
That for you to take
my voice to take
15 we sing for you
    tell me!

[The shaman calls Rurica whose son
is drunk in the house next to
where we are sitting]

We are untying you
his drunkenness, to start with,

from that body of human
20 the yellow smoke of drunkenness

I am bringing to an end
resting
for you to rest
my children of scarlet macaws

25 Circling around your bodies
    its yellow winds
    circling the body
    we are untying you
    to cure well

30 To cure you
    my children of scarlet macaw
    to cure your bodies
    think!

In the thought of the Inkas
35 in the thought it is
    your drunkenness
    circling your bodies
    the circling wind of the drunkenness

To watch [they] come
40 to watch [he] comes
    so [he] does
    untying, untying.

The words are coming to an end
my king people
45 happy they are

Walking [on a ridge]

walking on the wind

[They] come watching
my body of a turtle
50 I have come, bringing with me

Listen to me!
Over my body,
sick body,
untying they come

55 Over it
[they] come watching
the beautiful day [world] of the
dsoawa
I have come to bring

Over you
60 the wind comes to cleanse

King señoritas
señoritas
talking they come
they come looking

65 Walking on top of the frame
of the day [world]
sitting on a gold table
having sat, they bring

On the other hand, [I] have already come
[painting myself with] serpent [designs],
to start with

70 That way it was [distant past]
black fruit divided
head of the pack of doves
I have been [painted with] serpent
[designs]
[but she] has not come

75 The toes of my feet
my toes
[he] has come untying
that dios [god]

That dios

80 I will cure
my body of a turtle

All the machines
with that [they] come cleansing
the wind comes cleansing
85 over my body
untying [it] comes

It is also mine
so said
the king of the angels
90 the king Jesus Christ
[all] the Jesus Christs

Both of them sitting face to face
mine the covered with designs
boat of gold covered with designs
95 sitting on the designed boat
turning around on that
I go around picking up

My drowned body
make the yoɟi sleep first
100 massage my face
untying it comes
over my body
the sick body

We tell you
105 listen to what we say
to heal well
our body to heal
to heal with the drunkenness
of the Ayahuasca

Over there in the depth of the lake
110 people gathered together
over them standing

I bring

Words bring

Crosses in a row
115 swallows standing in a row
have come to wait

128

The same way, we,
so [he] said,
words I have brought [distant past]

[The shaman calls Sandiramba to
bring her son Orlando, a baby.
Sandiramba wakes up and brings him.
He fans over the baby.]

SONG 8

I come
my body of a turtle

My body of a turtle
For myself, on the other hand,
5 I have gone to make

Other turtles
they make
the hill of the little bird

The hill of the little bird *perico*

10 I went [distant past] with my words

The only thing they do
words only they do
his body [they] want

Having wanted, they have not made it
15 with us are the turtles...

[This very short song ended while
I was changing the tape]

The first three lines on song 7 say that the spirit who was singing has left. The shaman is walking on top of the song hunting for words [lines 4-6]. Note also that he speaks about his actions in distant past emphasizing the temporal break that occurs in his passing from profane to sacred. People are coming to sing and we, humans, are very happy about it [lines 6-9]. The bird in line 10 which has been translated as "doves of the sky" has not been identified. The shaman described it as a small yellow bird very similar to a dove; whenever it sings it brings auguries of life. Most likely however its presence in this line derives from its name. Dove is one of the frozen metaphors for women. The appearance here of the spirit of the "doves of the sky" is a perceptual pun. It is the women (doves) of the sky (i.e. spirit women) that are coming down. One is singing (i.e. shrieking) for the anthropologist to take her voice to his land [lines 10-16].

The sudden change of topic in line 17 indicates a change in singing spirit. He is singing for the grandson of the shaman [line 24] who was drunk at the moment and was starting to scream. The song is for him to get sober [lines 16-20] and get rest [lines 21-24]. The spirit describes the symptoms [lines 25-29] and again brings out the universalizing reference to the thought of the Inka [lines 34-38].

Again a change of topic announces a new spirit. Lines 39-61 announce that the spirit has come looking at the shaman [lines 39-41], that the spirits are very happy that he is getting well [lines 48-51]. Lines 46-47 give the perspective of the shaman who is walking high on the song (literally "on the wind").

Lines 55-60 announce that the day of the *Ayahuasca* women is coming and the patient will be cured. This introduces a whole series of women spirits that are coming to sing. The king *señoritas* are coming and they sit next to where the shaman is ("the gold table" [line 66]). The shaman is there through the song ("walking on top of the frame... " [line 65]). He was already there waiting for them. He is painted with designs [lines 68-69]. A woman spirit comes ("the head of the pack of doves" [line 72]) and paints him with huito fruit ("black fruit divided" [line 71]). He complains that she had not come before when he was expecting her and was well groomed, but that she is only now coming [lines 73-74]...

A change of topic introduces a change of spirit. This spirit comes to cure the rheumatism of the shaman [lines 70-86]. Jesus Christ comes [lines 87-91]. Both spirits sit next to the shaman as he is on his "boat" picking up words [lines 93-97]. During the day the spirits sleep in the sick body of the shaman [lines 98-103]. They tell him that to get cured well he will have to take *Ayahuasca* and go to the depth of the lake where evil spirits who are sending him harm are gathered [lines 104-110]. He must go there and know them to be cured [line 111], for in Shipibo shamanism domination of spirits is achieved through knowledge.

Line 112 introduces a new spirit. A spirit woman ("swallow" [line 115]) comes and brings information about the illness of a child [lines 114-119]. The shaman calls Sandiramba to bring her baby who is ill. It seems that his soul had been stolen and taken to the hill of the little bird [song 8].

SONG 9

People of the day [world] of the king

People of the day [world] of the king
there they come

with their frame they come
5 people of the day [world] of the king
the turtle come

To wait for him
I went [distant past] to wait

my body clinks
10 when it clinks
words come as frame
turtles of gold

the frame itself clinks

listen to the clinking
15 turtles of the *dsoawa*

Monkeys of the *dsoawa*
to wait for them
I do like this
from my body

20 From my body, first,
[they] come to see

Frame of gold comes down
swallows come down
I have come to bring them

25 The cross clinks
under the clinking
following the serpent

Following the serpent
dsoawa of the white flower

30 Within the body rumbles
rumbles that which is painted
with designs at the tip
that which is painted at the tip comes

My body of a turtle
I make myself pretty
35 the wind makes itself up

Listen!
catching words
Which turtle it is
this way turtles do

40 that way doing
at the tip of his tongue
that way you should not do
I screech

The day [world] circling
45 circling it I pick up

When I go by
other turtles that stand by me
do not do this way
I went [distant past] to pick up the words
50 I went [distant past] to pick up the words
head of the pack of the doves

Head of the pack of the doves
the words are waiting for
looking they come

["That is all"]

The first six lines announce that people of the world of the king are coming. Lines 7-19 explain that the shaman is singing ("my body clinks" [line 9]) in expectation of spirits ["turtles of gold" [line 12], "turtles of the *dsoawa*" [line 15]). Then the shaman specifies that what he is waiting for are the women of the *dsoawa* ("monkeys of the *dsoawa*" [lines 16-19]). These women finally come. They come to see the shaman's body [lines 20-21]. The *dsoawa* of the white flower comes following the serpent (i.e. the designs [lines 28-29]). The shaman had made himself pretty for her coming [line 33-34],the song makes itself pretty for her coming [line 35]. As an informant who was steeped in local gossip explained to me, the spirit that just came is the shaman's spirit lover. That is why he had made himself up, and was waiting for her.

Line 36 introduces a new spirit. The shaman is saying that it is only him that can sing so very well [lines 38-42]. During the session, he goes around the world of spirits picking up songs [lines 44-46]. When he is there, other shamans are also there trying to pick up songs [lines 46-47], but they are not as successful as he is [lines 48-49]. Women ("heads of the pack of the doves") listen carefully! the words are waiting for him. Looking around the words come [lines 52-54].

The session has ended. Only the shaman and I are awake. I pack up my gear and as I start walking towards my hut, the shaman reclines himself on the patio and goes to sleep under the open sky. The session is over. A number of people were cured but none saw the whole development from the start of the session to the end. Patients came up to get cured, witnessed the part that referred to them and left after it was over. This is the perspective of the audience. The shaman's perspective is slightly fuller. He experiences what we only hear. He sees the windows opening and the good open day coming. He saw the mockingbird in song 3 pass next to us and fly through the patio. In lines 50-65 of song 4, he saw the spirit of the monkey *cotocuraca* (Mycetes seniculus) come down and sing. It looked like the monkey and had a bag in which it kept the good wind. He saw the Piro m^w*ëraya* of song 5. This person had taught him and he visits sometimes when the shaman is under the effects of the *Ayahuasca*. He saw the machines and the designs, the women and the birds.

For the patients, I would venture to say that the shamanic session is effective, not only because it cures the physical effects but also because it is ritual, of which theatre is but a timid copy. This ritual is specially effective because the spirits are not acted out. If they were it would require an extraordinary performance by the actors to produce the same effect. In this ritual, however, the spirits appear in a veiled fashion. They are here through the implications of the voice. Through shifts in pitch and volume.[29] It is the audience that creates them in their imagination, basing themselves on the tradition. But Shipibo tradition does not describe most of the spirits physically. It describes them mainly in their interactions. It is a matter of description of their personality. Complemented by the knowledge of the ethology of forest animals that these hunters have, which is the other identity of some of the spirits, the mind of the audience re-creates the presence of the spirits as original social actors since they are not laden by bodies that have to be represented by masked dancers.

The shaman, on the other hand, does see the spirits in body and interaction. This is one of his personal pieces of knowledge that puts him beyond the ordinary laymen. His power derives from knowing. Knowing in turn, derives from having seen in his mystic trips the different types of spirits. Once he visits them they become his servants.

The effectiveness of this ritual lies in what I have come to call its histrionic power. Histrionics involves the re-creation of situations and characters that are not present at the time among the audience and that are considered by the audience as not their immediate reality but the intrusion of another reality into the here and now defined by the performance. Depending on the media used, the histrionic can be narrative or theatrical. It is, however, the representation that defines the histrionic. Its power derives from the two characteristics that define its nature. First, it follows the form of diachronic presentation that makes it parallel to the perception that the audience has of life: that it unfolds in time. Second, there is the intrusion of the otherness into the performance situation, brought in by the content of what is being narrated or performed. This sense of otherness is defined by the fact that in spite of the dramaturgical metaphor, people take social life seriously. They do not believe they are acting. They do distinguish between a lived-in social interaction and one that is narrated or performed in theatre. The Shipibo shamanic session takes this second aspect of the histrionic to its extreme. It physically brings the otherness, the worlds of the spirits, into the here and now of the performance. Theatre pales in comparison.

FOOTNOTES

Acknowledgements. This paper is dedicated to Robert Murphy who taught me anthropology and to Raquel Ackerman who would not accept my excuses for not writing it.

[1] The fieldwork upon which this study is based was generously supported by a grant from the National Science Foundation. Harriet Klein, Stephany Finns, Robert Murphy and Peter Roe read and commented upon an earlier version of this paper. I wish to express my gratitude to them.

[2] Durkheim, 1965:484

[3] For a description of the context of narrative in a more acculturated village, see Roe 1982:42.

[4] Traditionally narrative also took place at night. Nowadays, it still normally takes place at night, especially during warm nights of the dry season when the children do not want to got to sleep. In such nights families would sit in the patio in front of their houses and usually a grandfather would start telling a myth. Unlike shamanic songs, however, myths are also told during the day if there is rain outside and the family is congregated within the house.

[5] Shipibos nomally divide the areas abstractly. Thus we have that each house is conceptually subdivided into discrete areas. Each area is considered the legitimate place of one of the members of the household. These areas are not marked in any way during daylight. At night it is on these areas that the individual in question will hung its mosquito net. This effect of continuous space is emphasized by the absence of walls in the houses. Looking into a row of Shipibo houses from one end, the viewer will only see an expanse of pona floors bounded on the right and the left by the posts which sustain the roof.

[6] For a description of the shamanic session among the extremely closely related Conibo, see Gebhart-Sayer 1985b.

[7] In transcribing Shipibo words, I have used the following special symbols. J represents the English 'sh' sound (Palato-alveolar fricative). ç represents the 'ch' sound in English. ë is the high back unrounded vowel. A raised w is labialization. β is the bilabial voiced fricative. An accent mark is used when the words are accentuated on the last syllable. Otherwise Shipibo words are always accented in the first syllable unless the

second syllable is nasalized in which case it is accented. Underlining a vowel signifies that it is nasalized. Underlining a consonant means that it is retroflex. Except for names of tribes and geographic locations, Shipibo, Quechua and Spanish words are italicized.

[8] Angelika Gebhart-Sayer reports yet another level to the Shipibo-Conibo shamanic session. She elaborates on the relationship between the designs the shaman sees under the influence of *Ayahuasca* and the melodies of the songs the shaman and spirits sing. Gebhart-Sayer 1985b:163-64. See also Gebhart-Sayer 1984:12-13.

[9] This story was collected in the village of Charashmana in the Pisqui river from the most reputed storyteller in the village. The style in narrative will be commented upon below. It is characterized by constant repetition from different perspectives, descriptions of intentions followed by descriptions of those intentions being successfully carried out. This narrator was the most successful in using this style. His narrative had a very hypnotic quality of anticipation, that parsed the whole transference of information. He was also the most successful impersonator of characters in the village. Whenever any character appeared in his narratives, his voice would shift to the appropriate pitch (high for small birds, low for ground animals, etc.).

[10] This antisocial feeling is expressed in the explanation given in all cases of adult single women I encountered in the Pisqui. Their existence was explained as being related to a known threat by a previous husband, or a similar threat by a lover, that if anybody marries them he would harm him with witchcraft.

[11] I have tried to be rather literal in the translation of this paragraph to be able to comment upon the stylistics of the presentation of information in narrative. However, since Shipibo language tends to dispense with the reference to the actor to incorporate it into the connecting words, its translation into English becomes rather awkward. In this paragraph, I have tried to reproduce the feeling of chaos achieved by the original description. What is happening in the story is that the old woman breaks the shells of the peanuts as she is sweeping. Out of each peanut she unshells a little baby comes out crying. The one that came out of the peanut that was used after the first sexual act was bigger. Those that came out of more recent sexual acts were smaller. The old woman is not able to hold all of them, and soon they start holding hands and walking, directed by the older baby, asking where their father and their mother are and looking for them. I have only been faithful to the manner of narrating in this paragraph. Even though much of what I have come to call histrionic closure depends on the actual manner of providing the information, had I reproduced the Shipibo structure of narrative, the whole story would have become unintelligible to the English reader.

[12] As Peter Roe has pointed out to me, unattached women in Shipibo mythology are always reconnected with human society through the death

of their animal seducer husbands. Peter Roe, personal communication. See also Roe 1982:71-72. In this case we have both an unattached woman and an unattached man. Following Roe's logic, then, the structure of the Shipibo mythic thought would require the mother to be killed so that the son can be attached. Furthermore, this scene is overdetermined as it also serves to develop the character of the black vulture.

[13] For an extensive discussion of perfective and imperfective see Comrie, "Aspect: An Introduction to the Study of Verbal Aspect and Related Problems," Cambridge: Cambridge University Press, 1976.

[14] Id. at 24.

[15] I will not undertake a full analysis of the meaning of different birds in this myth. To be able to successfully carry it out, one has to study the whole range of birds in Shipibo narrative, shamanism, ritual and singing. For example there is another myth that deals almost exclusively with the visit of a man to the world of another bird of the genus Cathartidae, the condor. Shipibo ideology seems to provide a detailed accounting of the birds in the region. For a detailed study of Shipibo myth symbolism and the role of birds within it, see Roe (1982). Angelika Gebhart-Sayes presents another positive value of the hummingbird in relation to shamanic ideology. See Gebhart-Sayer 1985:162.

[16] Roe has provided an interesting argument in relation to the hummingbird/black vulture opposition. He points out that the juxtaposition of these two scenes demonstrates the victory of the inherent symbolism of the system over the syntactic position within the myth. The black vulture is negative and the hummingbird is positive even when they are doing the exact same actions. Peter Roe, personal communication (cf. Roe, 1982).

[17] For the Shipibo view of the Cashibo see Roe 1982:82-86.

[18] Roe, in his survey of Shipibo Mythology, relates the opposition night/noon to zenith/nadir. This would explain the presence of Thunder's weapon. See Roe 1982.

[19] See Piaget 1971 and 1974.

[20] Huizinga 1955.

[21] The description that follows is based on my notes on a number of shamanic sessions I recorded in the Pisqui river.

[22] The propitiatory words seem to be spoken for the benefit of the spirit of the *Ayahuasca*, the spirits in general and the shaman, since nobody else can hear it. A typical propitiation that I was able to record in another session runs: "With drunken hand this sick one, while the doctors are on this side, to the one that has continuous diarrhea to make it stop we are bring them. The fanning should not be in vain. Having fanned them, [we] want them to know how to fish. To bring them knowledge [we] sing *Ikaro*. Knowing them [i.e. the spirits], I cure you

[plural]. Having known, curing the bodies through the *Ayahuasca*, in order for her alone to untie, where the tiger of the hill sleeps, with his watch keeping the time, my wife having cured well these sick human bodies, having healed them, we are curing you [plural]. We will make all the bodies well. Having cured all, we are [emphatic] the children of God. Being so, we will cure these ones. All these boys who play football who are coming day after tomorrow, the ones of this village must win. I will take away the sickness from them. Having fanned them, following an open path those of this village [should] hit the aim [i.e. score a goal]. In the big field, so that you will understand better, listen to me! Those that come from down-river will not give the local ones a big battle. Hence, everything I tell you is good. They [i.e. the spirits] will not laugh from what I am telling you. There are already enough old people here."

[23] I have tried to keep as close as possible to the original language in translating these songs. Still much has been lost in the translation. First, the extraordinary syntactic parallelism that these songs have is totally lost. Most lines are composed by a noun phrase and a verb. Since subordination of sentences is done in Shipibo by a suffix at the end of the verb, this parallelism continues even when the song is developing a complex sentence. Second, the use of rhyme to emphasize some lines is also lost.

[24] Lines 85 and 86 were sung in a different melody

[25] This line is sung as a *maſá*

[26] After the first occurrence of the Shipibo work *kạdo* which means roof-frame, I have translated it simply as "frame" to make the verses more dynamic.

[27] The notion of a "platonic form" is not totally absent from conscious Shipibo philosophical discourse. I found that they use the word kiki to refer to something that is truly real, the quintessence. Similar uses have been reported by other authors. See Gebhart-Sayer 1985a & 1985b:161-164. For the use of the same concept among the Cashinahua (another Panoan group), see Kensinger 1975: 18-25

[28] These are sounds regarded to be related to whistling

[29] But they are here. Once early in a session there were a number of people who were awake waiting to be cured. We were all conversing among ourselves and with the shaman. Suddenly a song overtook the shaman. The jaguar spirit had come down to sing. I had never heard such a song among the Shipibo. We were all frozen. One could feel the presence of the Jaguar in the air. Nobody talked throughout that session. It was the quietest session I was to witness among the Shipibo.

8

WAR AND THE SEXES IN AMAZONIA

R. Brian Ferguson
Rutgers University

Introduction

Conflict patterns of native Amazonians have special significance in the growing anthropological literature on war. The cause of these conflicts is hotly debated, with the key issue being whether limitations on the availability of game animals are responsible for generating competition and warfare (see Chagnon 1983: 81-89; Harris 1984; Sponsel 1983). I believe that game limitations are important, but they make up only one part of the infrastructural basis for war. Moreover, the theoretical focus on the causes of war has left gaps in our understanding of several important social patterns which can strongly influence the course of hostilities.

This paper considers some of those patterns, those involving aspects of social structure, particularly post-marital residence, in relation to the organization of work and of military forces. "Social structural explanations" are sometimes contrasted to "ecological explanations" of war. No contradiction of theory is necessary, and none is implied in this analysis. The arguments to follow are fully consistent with the view that wars result from conflict over scarce critical resources. The nature of those conflicts in Amazonia, and the ramifications of political organization and the impact of Western contact on Amazonian warfare, will be considered in other articles. Study from all these perspectives can be combined to achieve a more rounded, theoretically consistent understanding of war.

The article has four sections. The first reviews existing theory on the relation of social structural patterns to war, and considers these posited relationships against Amazonian cases. The second describes the relationship of kinship and gender distinctions to the organization of work. The third argues that production and conflict patterns together determine post-marital residence patterns. The fourth proposes that residence, production, and conflict combine to influence the significance in war of men fighting over women.

The starting point is Robert Murphy's early writings about Mundurucu warfare. Murphy (1957; 1960) posits functional relationships between certain aspects of kinship systems and warfare. These hypotheses have been developed by other researchers into a major body of theory in cross-cultural statistical studies, yet they are scarcely acknowledged in recent work on Amazonian warfare (cf. Martin 1969:256).

Kinship Structures and War

Murphy's 1957 article examines the interaction of social structure and social psychology in generating war. He argues that the Mundurucu combination of patrilineal descent with matrilocal post-marital residence generates tensions which cannot be released within the society without causing major social disruption. Prior to pacification, these pent-up hostilities found release in external aggression.

The psychological elements of his argument are criticized by Wilson (1958), and defended in a rejoinder by Murphy (1958). Nevertheless, the psychological aspect is much less prominent in *Headhunter's Heritage*. Instead of being the primary motivator for war (as in 1957: 1027, 1032), pent-up hostility is portrayed as a facilitating condition in wars fought initially to gain access to trade goods, and later as mercenaries for the whites. Internal tensions were vented in these wars, but did not cause them (1960: 30, 36-38, 130, 148-150, 186). This position is consistent with the generally accepted view on the psychological relationship between external aggression and internal solidarity (Ferguson 1984a: 13). It needs no further consideration here.

Murphy's observations on kinship patterns and the organization of war have been much more influential. Drawing on Simmel and British structural-functionalism, Murphy (1957: 1029-1034; 1960: 127-131; see also 1956) argues that matrilocal residence among the Mundurucu requires suppression of conflict and facilitates cooperation among men, because men of different patriclans must live together in their wives' households. Grievances and latent factionalism persist, but their public expression is not allowed. Public harmony is maintained at all costs, since open conflict could activate patrilineal clan loyalties and oppositions, which would tear apart matrilocal households. As Mundurucu men marry outside their own village (1960: 85), the cross-cutting ties of residence and descent extend throughout their territory. That makes it possible to mobilize relatively large military forces, which can go off on long expeditions, since other men will remain at home with the female residential core to look after the warriors' interests. Murphy contrasts this with societies where patrilineality combines with patrilocality, encouraging "compartmental segmentation of the society along conjunctive lines of kinship and territory" (1960: 128). He proposes (1957: 1033) as a testable hypothesis that matrilocal societies would be internally peaceful.

This hypothesis is the starting point of a cross-cultural study by Thoden van Velzen and Van Wetering (1960). They find it supported by available data. They then expand the argument to give greater attention to male factionalism, and find that "the mere presence of power groups [of male agnates] is sufficient to make a society non-peaceful" (1960:181). Their principal diagnostic of these "fraternal interest groups" is patrilocal post-marital residence. Matrilocal residence thus contributes to internal peace by eliminating the main basis of male factionalism. Subsequent research (Otterbein 1968; 1973; 1977; 1985; Otterbein and Otterbein 1965) confirms the association of fraternal interests groups with feud and "internal warfare" (i.e., war between communities in the same culture) in politically uncentralized societies.

The researchers cited in the preceding paragraph maintain that social structural patterns lead to conflict patterns. The causal direction is reversed by other researchers (Divale 1975; Divale et al. 1976; Ember 1974; Ember and Ember 1971; see Otterbein 1977 for a review of these and other work). They elaborate and test several hypotheses regarding kinship patterns and war, and affirm that it is conflict which has causal priority over kinship structure. Conflict between local competitors favors development of localized fraternal interest groups. Conflict over longer distances and with people outside one's own culture favors development of unifying cross-cultural ties, commonly through matrilocality.

Despite disagreement over this and a few other points (see Otterbein 1977: 702), the line of research initiated by Murphy's 1957 article has produced a remarkably consistent and well-documented body of findings. So it is a puzzling fact that these findings are so rarely acknowledged in writing on Amazonian warfare. One possible reason for this neglect is that the kinship patterns of Amazonian societies resist being sorted into the categories used by cross-cultural researchers. Standard concepts of descent often seem inapplicable (Maybury-Lewis 1979a: 305; Murphy 1979: 222-223; and see Kaplan 1975: viii, 184; Morey and Metzger 1974: 43; Needham 1964), societies which were once classified as unilineal have been reclassified as cognatic (Jackson 1975: 319), and it is entirely possible to argue over whether a given society (the Yanomamo) does or does not have lineages or unilineal descent (Chagnon 1967: 142-147; 1977: 65-70; Crocker 1969a: 742; Jackson 1975: 320; Kaplan 1973; Murphy 1979: 217-222; Shapiro 1972: 99-105; 1974; 1975; Taylor and Ramos 1975). Marriage is another complicated area. Amazonian patterns vary tremendously (compare Chagnon 1977: 54-65; Harner 1973: 93-97; Henry 1964: 29-47; Jackson 1983: 124; Levi-Strauss 1967; Morey and Metzger 1974: 73-78; Riviere 1969: 188-198), and theoretical debate on the topic is correspondingly dense (Chagnon 1977: 54-65; Kaplan 1975: 183-198; Kensinger 1984; Maybury-Lewis 1979b; Riviere 1969: 272-283). Although marriage practices are too complicated to even summarize here, it must be noted that they can have important consequences for the significance of post-marital residence rules in conflicts. Post-marital residence itself also shows major variation even within single communities (Dole 1973: 295; Gregor 1977: 268-281; Hill and Moran 1983: 122-123; Kaplan 1975: 88-123; Leeds 1961: 24; Price 1981: 690-691; Wagley 1983: 94-95). (Variations in both native practices and ethnographers' terminologies lead me to disregard the distinction between uxorilocality and matrilocality proper, and to simplify this text by using "matrilocality" as a general term designating both patterns.) It is now widely recognized that an important general characteristic of Amazonian kinship systems is the ability of individuals to avoid or manipulate rules and relationships in pursuit of individual interests (Chagnon 1974: 89, 141; Dole 1983-84: 314-315; Gregor 1977: 360; Jackson 1975: 320-322; 1983: 71-72; Kaplan 1972; 1975: vii; Maybury-Lewis 1974: 168-169; Morey and Metzger 1974: 43-48). Because of this, characterizations of kinship patterns in discussions to follow should be taken to indicate dominant practices. Variations are to be expected.

Amazonian cases generally support the cross-cultural findings, although they also suggest some qualifications. On the matrilocal side, the Mundurucu of course fit expectations perfectly: matrilocality combined with external war and internal peace. So do the Tapirape (Wagley 1983: 39, 83-84, 93), the Siriono (Holmberg 1969: 157-159, 216-218) and the Tupinamba (Balée 1984b: 257). The generally matrilocal Guahibo of the Colombian-Venezuelan *llanos* make war on other Guahibo, but such conflicts are almost always between recognizable regional subdivisions, which otherwise have little contact. Within subdivisions, intermarriage, economic and military cooperation, and non-violent conflict resolution are the rule (Morey and Metzger 1974: 53-55, 99-102).

The Gê speaking peoples of the Central Brazil *cerrado* region are matrilocal (Gross 1979; Maybury-Lewis 1979b), and have extensive histories of external war against Westerners and other native groups (Frikel 1985: 360; Nimuendajú 1946: 3, 149; Maybury-Lewis 1974: 1-12). Of these peoples, the Eastern Timbira fit the hypothesized pattern exactly, with an absence of internal conflict (Nimuendajú 1946: 149), but others -- the Shavante, Sherente, and Kayapó -- are plagued by violent factionalism and internal war (Maybury-Lewis 1974: 21-27, 210, 305-309). Maybury-Lewis (1974: 306) suggests that this contrast is because the Timbira alone do not have men's houses, which among the other Gê combine with an age set system to foster a bellicose attitude which is very prominent in factional fighting. But there is reason to question the central significance of men's houses.

The Bororo, so culturally similar to their Gê speaking neighbors, have men's houses but lack internal feuding and factional conflict. The Mundurucu also have men's houses (Murphy 1960: 105). Significantly, the Bororo also have strong matrilineal tendencies and very weak agnatic ties (Crocker 1969b: 238, 256). For the Timbira, matrilocal residence has "pervasive effects ... on the organization of many of the activities of daily life," uncontested by the presence of any agnatic descent groups (Lave 1971: 342). The Shavante and Sherente, on the other hand, have patriclans despite their matrilocal residence, and it is these descent groups which act as political factions (Maybury-Lewis 1971: 382-384). The Kayapó are somewhat anomalous (although not for Maybury-Lewis' argument). They lack patrilineal descent groups, and their political factions are assembled on a more ad hoc basis (Bamberger 1979: 133; Maybury-Lewis 1974: 303, 306; Turner 1971: 366, 370). I suspect that this anomaly, as well as some discrepancies between earlier and later descriptions of social organization of other Gê groups (Lave 1971: 342; Maybury-Lewis 1971) may be related to historical changes induced by Western contact.

A few theoretical implications can be derived from the Central Brazilian cases. First, that men's houses will foster factional conflict only if distinct male factions are already present. Second, that any tendency toward internal peace inherent in the cross-cutting ties of matrilocality can be overwhelmed by other contradictory social patterns. This is consistent with recent findings on conflict among the West African Metá (Dillon 1980). A third point is suggested by comparison of the Mundurucu with the Shavante. The village exogamy of the Mundurucu (Murphy 1960: 85) disperses men of a patriclan far more than occurs among the village-endogamous Shavante (Maybury-Lewis 1974: 77-80; and see Turner 1979: 174). Shavante-style factional fighting is simply not possible under the existing distribution of Mundurucu males. This can be related to a recent analysis showing that exogamy per se is not associated with peace (Kang 1979). Elsewhere (Ferguson 1984a: 17) it is suggested that intermarriage is often "a strategy linking particular groups within a context of war." Kang (1979: 96-97) observes that exogamy is a typical pattern of fraternal interest groups, and argues that the nature of existing social groups must enter into any assessment of the peace contribution of exogamy. The point can be reversed: marriage practices can have important consequences for general patterns of military relations between variously structured social groups. The Mundurucu-Shavante contrast suggests that the tendency toward peace among matrilocal peoples will be stronger when local groups are exogamic.

On the other side of the pattern under review here, the Yanomamo groups described by Chagnon have been singled out as exemplifying the combative character of fraternal interest groups (Dillon 1980: 659; Otterbein 1973: 939). These Yanomamo are renowned for their internal conflicts and warfare, and it is true that the typical village is organized around a few groups of consanguineally related males (Chagnon 1977: 68-71). However, political conflict among the Yanomamo typically does not pit one group of classificatory brothers against another, as fraternal interest group theory suggests. The typical faction instead consists of divisions of two or more agnatic groups, bound to each other through an on-going arrangement of sister-exchange (Chagnon 1977: 70-72, 87-88; Shapiro 1972: 72, 87-90). Shapiro (cited in Jackson 1975: 322) suggests that there may be a continuum of alliance types, measured by the relative weightings of consanguineal and affinal loyalties. This is an important finding for fraternal interest group theory, because it indicates that the correlation of patrilocality with internal fighting may result from different structural patterns of conflict.

Other patrilocal peoples are found in the Northwest Amazon. In the past, they carried on internal war (Jackson 1983: 71-79, 97). Goldman (1963) provides details about one somewhat anomalous Northwestern group, the Cubeo. The Cubeo were organized into ranked patrilocal sibs, within three patrilineal phratries (1963: 24-29). Their segmentary structure was adaptable to different levels of conflict (see Sahlins 1961). Individual sibs could carry on feuds, or phratries could unite in the face of more serious threats. The Cubeo also confronted military threats from surrounding peoples, although it is not clear that they all united to fight these enemies (Goldman 1963: 34, 45, 162-163). The Northwest peoples are cited by Turner (1979: 165) as he argues that virilocality has the potential to unite wider groupings than uxorilocality. The Cubeo support his point. This does not violate fraternal interest group theory, however, since the Cubeo had a relatively hierarchical and centralized political structure, and Otterbein's research (1985) demonstrates that such structures provide a new basis of military organization.

The ten tribes of the Upper Xingú are also patrilocal. But there, despite regular conflicts and some actual fighting, the general rule has ben peace between the ten, and war against outside groups (Murphy and Quain 1955: 1-15; Villas Boas and Villas Boas 1973: 17, 28-33). It seems that in the face of constant danger from the outside, the peoples of the Upper Xingú developed an elaborate inter-tribal culture, which kept local conflicts from breaking into war and which facilitated defensive cooperation (Basso 1973: 133-153; Gregor 1977: 17-18, 309-318; Murphy and Quain 1955: 10-19; Nimuendajú 1963: 235-236; Villas Boas and Villas Boas 1973: 16). Since their defensive warfare rarely involved expeditions outside their own territory, it did not require the prolonged absence of large numbers of men, which is one of the factors argued to favor matrilocal residence in external war situations. The upper Xingú needs more study before its lessons will be clear, but it seems to suggest that, first, under the right circumstances, regional military integration of non-hierarchical societies can be achieved without matrilocality; and second, that fraternal interest groups will not lead to local war when there is a need and a structural basis for peaceful cooperation.

The Shuara Jívaro of the Andean foothills do not seem to fit either the patrilocal or the standard matrilocal pattern. There is a matrilocal residential bias, but individuals regularly move between loose neighborhoods of single households. This, combined with a flexible cognatic kin system, produces personal networks of relatives dispersed over very wide areas (Harner 1973: 78-80, 94-98, 107; Meggers 1971: 62). Other *montaña* peoples have similar patterns (Bennett Ross 1980: 49-50; 1986; Johnson

1983: 30). These networks can lead to a chain reaction of hostilities in feuds (Bennett Ross 1984: 96-105; Harner 1973: 39, 103, 180-183), but they also provide the means for mobilizing men from a wide area against a common enemy (Harner 1973: 17-25, 33, 115, 183-184). While this case is not easily classified, it does not contradict theoretical expectations. The cross-cutting ties created by the matrilocal tendency and kin dispersion aid in mobilizing large forces, but the absence of large, stable matrilocal households eliminates the need for strict suppression of conflicts between local men. The physical distance between households loosens affective ties between brothers (Harner 1973: 96), so the residence pattern certainly does not engender fraternal interest groups. But neither does it work against the formation of male factions.

Before moving on, it is worth noting that the fragmentary character of patrilocally organized societies is a relative thing. No fraternal interest group is an island. I will argue elsewhere that viable Amazonian societies (i.e., those not on a path to extinction) are characterized by crucial social relations between local communities. These are matters of functional necessity, and are patterned by political behavior. The most aggressive of fraternal interest groups typically will be constrained by a variety of ties to other local groups, and these may act to restrain some conflict. But the restraint will be *less* than with the stronger cross-cutting ties created by matrilocality, and the relative independence of the males of different groups will allow a conflict to develop between two communities without necessarily involving many other communities.

Kinship, Gender, and the Organization of Work

The cases described above support the posited relationships between aspects of kinship systems and conflict patterns, but they demonstrate that, in practice, the actual expression of these relationships is more variable and complicated than the theory indicates. Why these more complicated patterns exist is an interesting question, the answer to which may lie in the same direction as the answer to the question that divides the cross-cultural statistical studies, that is, do kin structures cause conflict patterns, or do conflict patterns create kin structures. To a degree, I will argue, both relationships exist: conflict and kinship are reciprocally conditioning. But there is also a third relationship partly responsible for the observed correlation. In this section I will argue that much of the correspondence of kin structures and conflict patterns, as well as the unexpected complications in these relationships, is because both are grounded in a more fundamental causal matrix -- both kinship and conflict are strongly conditioned by the exigencies of production and reproduction in a given ecological and social context. Ember and Ember make a similar argument using cross-cultural statistics, but the present argument differs from theirs in that they evaluate production in terms of the material significance of the product (1971: 572), and I will be looking at the organization of work effort (see Johnson and Johnson 1975; Murphy and Murphy 1980).

The economic organization of Amazonian peoples did not receive much attention in the past. Only recently have researchers produced quantitative data on time allocation and on physical production, distribution, and consumption (Aspelin 1979; Berlin and Markell 1977; Dufour 1983; Flowers et al. 1982: Hill and Hawkes 1983; Hill et al. 1984; Hill et al. 1985; Hurtado et al. 1985; Johnson 1975; Kaplan and Hill 1985; La-Point 1970; Lizot 1977; Werner et al. 1979). Despite remaining gaps in our knowledge, it is perfectly clear that Amazonian economies are thoroughly embedded in the total social structure, and that the economic aspect is "a very pivotal part" of that total structure (Murphy and Murphy 1980: 181). It is also clear from both the quantitative and non-quantitative reports (Chagnon 1977: 81-85; Goldman 1963: 58,66, 121; Holmberg 1969: 103; Jackson 1983: 182-185; Kaplan 1975: 33-45; Murphy 1960: 66-68; Riviere 1969: 42-47) that the most important economic status distinctions in these societies are those of age, generation, and above all, gender.

Yolanda and Robert Murphy (1974) discuss in penetrating detail how differences of gender and other ascriptive statuses structure the division of labor and all of social life among the Mundurucu. Siskind (1973a) provides similar information for the Sharanahua. In a later article, Siskind (1978) develops these themes into a general statement on kinship and mode of production. She argues that gender and generation determine one's position in the economic order of societies such as these; that these distinctions are reflected in kinship systems; and that, in defining categories of individuals along with their rights and obligations to each other, the basic structure of kinship *is* the relations of production. Marriage brings together a full set of productive capabilities, enabling adults to subsist and to produce and socialize the next generation. Turner (1979: 162), in a complicated analysis of Central Brazilian social structures, takes a similar idea further, arguing that the finer details of kinship systems are superstructural reinforcers of the basic mode of production.

The content of the sex-based division of labor can be summarized as follows: In Amazonia, men hunt and fish (sometimes accompanied by women), they do most "construction work" such as erecting houses, clearing gardens, and making canoes, and they carry out military actions. Women are responsible for child care, and their other duties are those compatible with this primary task of biological and social reproduction (Hurtado et al. 1985: 2; Turner 1979: 154; and see Brown 1970). Typically, those duties are domestic work and tending of gardens, although there are numerous exceptions to both. Which sex gathers wild products varies greatly by product and by society. Any aspect of the division of labor could relate to patterns of kinship and conflict, but the discussion to follow will focus on a few of the more general and important aspects.

Bitter manioc is the principal cultivated food in most Amazonian societies, again with many exceptions. (Sweet manioc is prominent in the Andean foothills; maize dominates in several areas, the most significant of which may be among the peoples of the river floodplains before contact [see Roosevelt 1980].) The processing of bitter manioc to remove toxins and its subsequent preparation as food is a multi-phase operation with substantial labor requirements (Basso 1973: 33-34; Carneiro 1983: 96-99; Hugh-Jones 1978: 49-52; Jackson 1983: 50-54; Murphy and Murphy 1974: 123-127). This encourages a degree of autonomy and cooperation in women's work, which appears to set a floor for the relative status of women. Bitter manioc processing for domestic consumption can be easily accomodated within patrilocal households, but when larger quantities are needed for feasts or for trade, there is a tendency to develop larger female work groups (Goldman 1963: 52; Hugh-Jones 1978: 49; Jackson 1983: 58-59, 97). In some instances, where local peoples regularly produce manioc products for sale to Westerners, this has encouraged a shift from patrilocality to matrilocality (Hill and Moran 1983: 124-125; Murphy 1956: 427-431; cf. Ramos 1978). Another very important characteristic of bitter manioc as a staple is its reliability. Under normal circumstances, a household can count on their own gardens to produce enough of the crop to meet their needs (Carneiro 1983: 102; Leeds 1961: 23; Moran 1983: 131; Roosevelt 1980: 121, 139; cf. Milton 1984: 17-19).

The organization of men for hunting and fishing is somewhat more variable. The most common pattern is for either to be done alone, or in groups of two to four. However, larger teams may be frequent when a group is preparing for a feast, or when the yields of solo hunting decline; and some fishing techniques, such as stream poisoning, always require larger cooperative groups (Basso 1973: 38-39; Beckerman 1983: 270; Flowers 1983: 361-369; Hames 1983: 399-401; Harner 1973: 59; Hill and Hawkes 1983: 179-182; Jackson 1983: 42-49; Morey and Metzger 1974: 34-37; Riviere 1969: 44; Saffirio and Scaglion 1982). A significant aspect of this work is its hit-or-miss character, often producing nothing or a great windfall. A single family is not a viable production unit (Chagnon 1977: 33; Flowers 1983: 365; Hames 1983: 401; Kaplan 1975: 38; Morey and Metzger 1974: 33-34; Siskind 1973a: 88; Yost and Kelly 1983: 214-215). In some areas, at least, fishing is more regularly productive than hunting (Beckerman 1980: 99; Jackson 1983: 39; Morey and Metzger 1974: 37-38). A consequence of this is the ubiquity in Amazonia of rules for sharing game and fish, often reinforced by supernatural sanctions (Chagnon 1977: 91; Clastres 1972: 168-170; Flowers 1983: 366-367; Hames 1983: 401; Harris 1984: 125; Henry 1964: 98; Hill and Hawkes 1983: 187; Jackson 1983: 47; Kaplan 1975: 38-41; Kaplan and Hill 1985: 233; Morey and Metzger 1974: 36; Murphy and Murphy 1974: 63-66; Shapiro 1972: 147-148; Siskind 1973a: 82-88; Wagley 1983: 66-67; Yost and Kelly 1983: 214-215). Hunting and meat are accorded high prestige, compared to vegetable foods (Clastres 1972: 153; Goldman 1963: 58; Jackson 1983: 47-48; Kaplan 1975: 38-39; Murphy and Murphy 1974: 62). Again, fishing is sometimes of clearly lesser status (Morey and Metzger 1974: 38; Murphy and Murphy 1974: 64). Even if hunting and fishing is done alone, the necessary pooling of the product makes male work "social," in contrast to "domestic" female manioc production. This type of inequality has been cited as contributing to male dominance in many cultures (Friedl 1975: 22), and that observation is certainly consistent with the typical Amazonian pattern of a generalized sex antagonism and an ideology of male dominance (Bamberger 1974; Hugh-Jones 1978; Jackson 1975: 317-318).

Production, Conflict, and Residence

An ideology of male supremacy related to the division of productive labor may encourage development of a male-centered residence pattern, i.e. patrilocality. But there is no *direct* functional linkage of observed hunting and fishing organization to any particular type of residence. Women's work in childcare and food production does not foster cooperation at the village level, but we have seen that commercial production of manioc flour may favor female residential cores, i.e. matrilocality. It is quite possible that trade in farina existed between native groups before contact (see Milton 1984). Other types of production arrangements may also favor matrilocality.

Matrilocality and other social institutions strengthening cross-cutting ties may be fostered by ecological conditions which lead to an annual dispersal and subsequent reunification of a population, as Gross (1979: 334-335) suggests for Central Brazilian peoples. Production or trade activities that take men away from home for extended periods may encourage matrilocality as a way of ensuring order while men are gone (Kracke 1976: 296; and see Harris 1977: 61). Another factor is a pattern in which fathers-in-law exploit and control sons-in-law residing with them, either in permanent matrilocality or temporary uxorilocal brideservice. This is reported as an important social pattern in many areas of Amazonia (Arvelo-Jimenez 1971: 104; Harner 1973: 79-80; Hill and Moran 1983: 124-125; Kracke 1978: 37-40; Maybury-Lewis 1971: 384; 1974: 97-98; Metraux 1963a: 111-112; Morey and Metzger 1974: 50; Shapiro 1972: 94; Siskind 1973a: 77-81; Turner 1979: 159-160). However, the variability and complicated political and economic interactions involved in the father-in-law/son-in-law relationship make it difficult to generalize about circumstances giving rise to it, or about its independent causal significance.

There remains to be considered one other type of male work, although it cannot be called production. Warfare requires the coordinated cooperative effort of many men. As Chagnon (1977: 40) emphasizes, in an environment of potential war, the minimum size for a village is set by the manpower requirements of fighting. He puts that at about fifteen men: ten to raid, and five to remain on guard at home. Similar or higher numbers unquestionably apply in a great many native Amazonian societies.

Divale and Harris (1976: 526-527) make a general argument that collective male dominance in war-making is the basis of a widespread "male supremacist complex." Ideologies of male superiority are reflected, they assert, in the cross-cultural predominance in non-stratified societies of male-centered patterns, such as patrilocality (see also Friedl 1975: 59-60; Harris 1979a: 57-63). It seems very plausible that warfare would reinforce ideological tendencies inherent in the male role of hunter and that these two aspects of the organization of work together would create a strong superstructural bias in favor of patrilocality. But this would be a rather weak determinancy by itself. Both activities certainly can be organized on a matrilocal basis. The Mundurucu are the prime illustration of this possibility, although the contrasting principles of organization around males *and* females may explain their pronounced sexual polarization and collective opposition. Among the Mundurucu, "the battle of the sexes is not carried on by individual gladiators, as in our society, but by armies" (Murphy ad Murphy 1974: 110).

Patrilocality is also favored, and more decisively, by the structure of conflict. One reason that conflict favors patrilocality is that patrilocality is the simplest basis of male factional organization, requiring merely that sons remain in their fathers' homes. Otterbein (1985: xxii-xxiii) suggests that the patrilocal fraternal interest group is the primordial military organization. A second and probably more significant reason is that the nature of conflict in Amazonia often renders matrilocality unworkable. It will be shown elsewhere that the general areal pattern is that competition over scarce critical resources pits local people against each other. Competition and conflict between neighboring villages or bands, or even between households in a village, can make the cross-cutting ties of matrilocality untenable from both individual and societal perspectives. The breakdown of existing ties is an early phase in the process leading to war. It is precisely this potential for destruction of matrilocal households, according to Murphy, that forces the Mundurucu to so rigidly suppress internal conflict.

Production arrangements favoring matrilocality have already been described. Where production generates matrilocality, male conflict groups will be organized through personal networks and/or more complex structures built on top of female residential cores, such as men's houses or age grades. Ritter (in Ember, Ember, and Pasternak 1974: 72) finds that age grades are cross-culturally associated with the combination of frequent warfare and oscillating group composition, which fits the Central Brazilian pattern (see Maybury-Lewis 1974: 105-164; 1979b). When matrilocality is combined with local competition and fighting, special institutional arrangements may also be needed to cope with the inevitable complications of conflict. Again, the Central Brazilian peoples illustrate this, with their development of automatic rights of refuge granted to people fleeing conflict in home villages (Bamberger 1979; Maybury-Lewis 1974: 205-

206).

Matrilocality may be based upon circumstances of production, with the organization of conflict groups adjusted to it. With or without these considerations of production, matrilocality may also be favored by external warfare. As described earlier, matrilocal post marital residence establishes cross-cutting ties in probably the simplest and most fundamental way possible, and it breaks up or at least weakens fraternal interest groups that might increase internal divisiveness. However, we have seen that internal unity against a common enemy can be attained through other means. Matrilocality is more specifically determined if external war (in politically uncentralized societies) involves making long distance strikes, because of its advantages as a means of mobilizing larger parties of warriors for prolonged absences. Where a group's strategy in external war is primarily defensive, engaging in few or no long distance raids, realization of the matrilocal tendency may depend on other economic and historical conditions.

Two cases illustrate that situation. The Tapirape rarely if ever took the offensive in external war. Their matrilocal organization was consistent with the high labor requirements of their form of bitter manioc processing (they lacked the woven manioc press used by most Amazonian peoples) (Wagley 1983: 58-59, 250) and their origin on the Central Brazilian *cerrado*, the land of the matrilocal Gê and Bororo (Wagley 1983: 26, 93-94, 124). Upper Xingú peoples were usually on the defensive, but their unification against outside attackers was built on an intertribal culture, on top of patrilocally organized local groups above.

One interesting illustration of the relationships between production, conflict, and residence is presented by the Piaroa. Piaroa men hunt, but they also rely on fishing, which we have seen may be less conducive to male solidarity. The women are engaged in commercial farina production, but the severity of the dry season limits this to a couple of months per year (Kaplan 1975: 37-39). Production, then, generates only weak and contradictory tendencies regarding post-marital residence. There is no war among the Piaroa. They are one of the many Amazonian societies reported as entirely peaceful (Kaplan 1975: 20, 26). Obviously warfare is not a factor shaping residence. What is found in the absence of both causal factors? According to Kaplan (1975: 83, 120), the Piaroa lack *any* regular residence rule.

Fighting over Women

In the preceding section, I argued that conflict patterns interacting with basic circumstances of production shape post-marital residence. The next section provides further illustrations of that, and advances the argument that established residence patterns interacting with production and conflict feed back to shape another type of conflict: fighting over women.

It has long been recognized that abduction of adult women is a prominent feature of much Amazonian warfare (Oberg 1973: 191). But it is by no means a universal practice. There is much variation, and much of that variation seems attributable to the factors already under review here, post-marital residence and the organization of female labor. These affect the feasibility of adding an abducted woman to a household, as illustrated by a range of cases running from the Mundurucu to the Yanomamo.

The Mundurucu who spoke to Robert and Yolanda Murphy (personal communication) stated that women were never captured in their long distance raids around the turn of the century. That raiding was contemporary with their commercial production of farina. The two patterns together provided a strong basis for matrilocality and female autonomy. Even after warfare ended, a man's attempt to bring an outside woman into a household would be blocked by the resident females, who would descend on the new wife "like white cells on a virus" (Murphy and Murphy 1974: 146). The capture of women, however, is reported as a main goal in Mundurucu raiding in earlier years (Metraux 1963b: 386). A change had occurred. Details of this change are not available, but one scenario can be offered which is consistent with reported facts (Horton 1963: 272-273; Metraux 1963b: 387, 393; Murphy 1956; 1960: 30-47, 79-80), and the theoretical relationships argued here (cf. Ramos 1978: 687).

Around 1850, the Mundurucu of the Upper Tapajós River area had been working for years as mercenary raiders for the whites, and capturing women on these raids. They were patrilocal. They were able to muster large forces and carry out long distance attacks by virtue of a relatively developed system of political authority (see Horton 1963: 278). Over the next fifty years, a Western presence grew on the Upper Tapajós. Along with that came commercial production of farina, and an undermining of the authority of chiefs. The former change directly favored matrilocality; the latter did so indirectly because it eliminated the alternative basis of organizing large scale long distance war. By the turn of the century, the social organization described by Murphy had evolved, and the capturing of women in war had ended. This example calls attention to the importance of a historical perspective.

Returning to the ethnographic present, the Shavante are matrilocal, but their main crop is maize, not bitter manioc, and maize processing does not require the same female cooperation. Men can take plural wives, but these usually are sisters, and the established sibling relationships are carried over to the new household. Still, there are conflicts between factions over women, and obtaining women by force does occur, even if it is considered deviant (Maybury-Lewis 1974: 47, 76-77, 87-90, 179-180). Among other Central Brazilian peoples, the Apinayé did not capture women in war (Nimuendajú 1967: 120), but the Kayapó and Carajá did, at least from the Tapirape (Wagley 1983: 30). The Carajá, however, "did not marry their female captives, but obliged them to become village prostitutes" (Metraux 1963b: 399). Along the Atlantic coast, the matrilocal Tupinamba captured some women in war, but these, like other captives, were kept for a time and then sacrificed (Metraux 1963a: 113).

The last two cases illustrate ways that even matrilocal groups can absorb a few female captives. A third way may be by taking new women into the households of political leaders and shamans, who are often polygynous and even patrilocal when no one else is (Arvelo-Jimenez 1971: 99-100; Holmberg 1969: 148; Jackson 1983: 193; Maybury-Lewis 1971: 384; Metraux 1963a: 112; Murphy 1960: 88). The social status of these men may translate into increased authority over the women of their households, perhaps through influence over a woman's kin.

The Guahibo are one case where political leaders and some other men are patrilocal despite a general matrilocal pattern. A main goal of Guahibo raiding was to capture women. Normatively, any man could take plural wives, but the anthropologists could learn of no actual case where a man brought an outside wife into a matrilocal household (Morey and Metzger 1974: 43, 76, 102).

Patrilocal peoples of the Upper Xingú and the Northwest Amazon represent another step along the continuum. Among the Trumai, bitter manioc was the principal crop, followed by maize. They also relied heavily on *piqui* fruit, the processing of which called for an annual burst of female labor. Women were regularly captured by outside raiders, and even though there was no open war among Upper Xingú groups themselves, conflict and even coerced ceding of women were common. Still, the status of women, their ability to assert themselves in their own interests, seems far above that reported for the Yanomamo (Murphy and Quain 1955: 13-14, 24, 30-31, 47-55, 94, 105; see also Basso 1973: 33-35).

The Cubeo relied on maize rather than manioc at the time of their active warfare, and the capture of women was a prominent goal in hostilities (Goldman 1963: 30, 162). Other Northwestern peoples had a war pattern, long suppressed, which is compared by Jackson to that of the Yanomamo. It is not clear if these peoples, like the Cubeo, had recently shifted from an older maize-based to their current bitter manioc-based economy. It is clear, however, that in recent years the production of farina for sale has become steadily more important. With that change, the fit of a new bride into a patrilocal household has become a delicate matter, taken into consideration in arranging marriages; disputes between men over women have become less frequent than before; and the status of women within the household and society has attained a level much higher than that found among the Yanomamo (Jackson 1983: 52, 62-63, 97, 117, 184-186, 192).

The Yanomamo stand at the opposite end of the spectrum from the Mundurucu. Besides being patrilocal (cf. Taylor and Ramos 1975), they are unusual within Amazonia for their reliance on plantains as a staple.

Plantain cultivation and processing lack the cooperative character associated with bitter manioc. Women's work tends to be very individualistic.
In polygynous unions, wives maintain separate hearths or even living
areas. The status of women seems remarkably low, with men inflicting
severe physical punishments for even trivial "offenses." So it is very possible for Yanomamo men to capture women and shift them around as
pawns (Chagnon 1977: 35-36, 81-83; Shapiro 1972: 107-108; Smole 1976:
189; see also Biocca 1971). The Kaingáng, in flight from the Brazilian
frontier, seem to be another case where women engage in little cooperative work, and where "theft" of women is a very prominent part of
conflicts between men (Henry 1964: 15-16, 59-60, 160).

Having traversed a range of cases relating to the prominence of
woman-capture in war, several general comments are in order. First, it is
difficult to be precise about the relative significance of this practice because of a dearth of quantitative data on the subject. Probably the best
data available pertains to the Yanomamo, but even there the picture is far
from clear. Helen Valero (Biocca 1971: 31-43) tells of a rout in which
almost all the women of a village were captured, "perhaps about fifty"
(1971: 38). I found no other report of such large captures among the
Yanomamo (or anywhere else in Amazonia), although taking five, six, or
seven women at a time seems to occur with some regularity (Barker 1959:
153; Chagnon 1977: 41, 125). *Keeping* captive women is another matter,
as they can flee or be retaken by their kinsmen. Chagnon (1977: 73)
presents the following information: one unusually large and militarily
powerful Yanomamo village has 38 men 35 years of age or younger. Data
on older men is not given. They have 52 wives among them. Of these, 8
fall under the heading of wives by "alliance and/or abduction," although
"most" of them are from abductions. More precise data of this sort would
be helpful. We also do not know much about how captive women are
distributed among men. Again, Chagnon (1972: 278; 1975: 105; 1977: 123)
provides some of the best information available, but still not enough to
give an adequate understanding of what occurs.

A second comment is that factors conducive to raiding for women
are more complicated than just residence and female work patterns. As
suggested above, men's organizations capable of maintaining "prostitutes,"
or political differentiation, can promote female capture. These suggest the
importance of political organization as a crucial set of variables in war.
Raiding for women may be encouraged by increasing importance of
women's work for subsistence and trade, where that work does not entail
self-directed cooperation among women. Patterns of conflict can also
have significant ramifications. Shuara Jívaro men, for instance, compete
over women among themselves, and a man might try to capture a woman
on a long distance raid. But he would usually lose the woman to another
warrior seeking to obtain a precious trophy head (Harner 1973: 80, 96,
107, 186). So the pattern of their war actually discourages the abduction
of females. On the other hand, warfare and accompanying social patterns

may generate feedback aggravating conflict over women. Raiding for women itself may further lower female status in society, thus making is even easier to bully women and so reinforcing the raiding. The use of sex as a reward for warriors would doubly reinforce this (Divale and Harris 1976: 526; and see Chagnon 1972: 274). Patrilocality generated by local conflict makes polygyny more feasible, and this can increase competition among men. Polygyny has been used as a diagnostic of fraternal interest groups (Otterbein and Otterbein 1965). Patrilocality may also be a crucial intervening variable between warfare and female infanticide (Hawkes 1981: 81-83), which can further heighten competition over women. Finally, Siskind (1973b) has argued, as will I elsewhere, that intensity of conflict over women in some circumstances is directly linked to increasing competition for critical resources.

A third comment is that the goal of woman capture is usually insufficient to initiate hostilities. The pointed difficulties and risks involved in capturing and holding women, and the more general problems of the war that an abduction might provoke, outweigh the diffuse, long-term, and somewhat uncertain benefits of adding a new woman to a household. All those cost factors are reduced or eliminated if hostilities already exist. This fits the Yanomamo case, where generally "the desire to abduct women does not lead to the initiation of hostilities between groups that have had no history of mutual raiding in the past ... Once raiding has begun between two villages, however, the raiders all hope to acquire women..." (Chagnon 1977: 123). The capture of women is a structurally determined variable which can shape and reinforce war patterns, but it is usually not a primary cause of war.

There is at least one alternative hypothesis regarding the prominence of woman capture in Amazonian warfare. Chagnon applies a sociobiological perspective to explain competition and conflict over women as a consequence of men trying to maximize their reproductive success. His hypothesis is stated most forcefully in a comparison of Amazonia and New Guinea (see also Chagnon 1979: 400-401; 1981: 507):

> Where it is relatively easy for males to assemble the material wherewithal required [to rear their offspring to adulthood], we would predict that males would attempt to have polygynous households and that competition for mates rather than competition for resources would be significant. On the other hand, where resources are relatively scarce and/or costly, energetically, to assemble, polygynous households are less likely to occur at high frequencies, for the requirements of paternal investment in that situation entail greater costs to males, and this sets limitations on their reproductive success. The contrast between Highland New Guinea and Amazonas should be obvious in this regard, especially the relationship between population densities and resources on the one hand and what the individuals seem to be fighting over on the other (Chagnon 1980: 123).

The proposition that resource scarcity and polygyny are inversely related in Highland New Guinea cannot be considered here. Within Amazonia, however, we have already seen several cases where polygyny and conflict over women are much less prominent than among the Yanomamo. To support his hypothesis, Chagnon would have to show that these others experience some resource scarcity which is not found among the Yanomamo. I doubt that this can be done. A more compelling reason to question the hypothesis, however, is Chagnon's own description of villages at the "center" and "periphery" of Yanomamo territory. The "center" is more densely inhabited and characterized by much more intensive warfare (Chagnon 1967: 113-114). The areas also differ in the degree of conflict over women.

> The attitudes about extra-marital sexual liasons differ in both areas. At the center, trysts inevitably lead to fighting and often to killing and village fissioning. At the periphery, the affairs are tolerated if not institutionalized. A corollary of this is the surprisingly high incidence of polyandry in some villages at the periphery, all of which may be summarized by concluding that there is a more equitable distribution of the sexual services of women at the periphery and, therefore, a great reduction in one of the major causes of Yanomamo disputes (Chagnon 1973: 135).

The combination of lower population density in a similar environment, negligible competition over women, and less war seems incompatible with Chagnon's hypothesis. It fits quite well, however, with the view that competition over women is, or can be, a secondary reinforcer of conflicts engendered by resource scarcity.

Finally, one cross-cultural study raises a question about the argument I have advanced. Ayres (1974) finds that "bride-theft" has a very strong negative association with matrilocality, but asserts that "raiding for wives ... occurs with equal frequency among matrilocal and patrilocal societies" (1974: 249). Unfortunately, Ayres does not present the data on the latter point. That, along with questions regarding coding and sample size (in cases of raiding for wives), prevents further consideration here.

Conclusions

The relationship between post-marital residence and conflict patterns suggested by Murphy is supported by cases throughout Amazonia, with several clarifications and modifications. Understanding the relationship, however, requires attention also to the organization of work and production. Patrilocality and fraternal interest groups are favored by an ideology of male superiority based on the social character of men's work in production and war, and by the dynamics of competition and conflict over resources. Matrilocality is favored by cooperative female production effort, by a subsistence pattern involving seasonal dispersal and regrouping, and by parents' interests in adding sons-in-law to their households.

These production considerations can lead to matrilocality even in situations of local conflict over resources, which combination produces institutional and behavioral complications. Matrilocality is also favored by longer distance war, especially offensive warfare. The strongest determination of either residence pattern is when the implications of production and conflict coincide.

In regard to the causal relationship between local conflict and fraternal interest groups -- production factors aside -- the situation in Amazonia seems to be that local competition and conflict leads to fraternal interest groups. Then, if the competition is critical and other factors not discussed here are right, those groups go to war. The presence of fraternal interest groups alone does not lead to war, although it does make it easier for wars to begin. A conflict of interest which might be resolved peaceably in a matrilocal situation may lead to war in a patrilocal situation. In this sense, fraternal interest groups can be said to be a cause of war. The varying significance of fighting over women shows another way in which structurally determined factors can have a major impact on the process of war, even in cases near a minimum level of cultural evolutionary elaboration.

The effective availability of critical resources and the actual production processes by which resources are transformed into products for human use are parts of the material base or etic infrastructure of a society. Though not the focus of this chapter, I believe that these conditions interacting with demographic factors set the basic parameters for war and peace. Within these parameters, however, structural arrangements affect the incidence and practice of war. Infrastructural determination of war patterns always operates in the context of a given social structure, of an existing family and kin organization, political system, economy, etc. (see Harris 1979b: 51-56). Despite the problems of some functional analyses of war (Ferguson 1984: 28-36), the functional interdependence of social patterns is a fact. This fact applies to war as much as any social action. To make war, men must be mobilized, and this mobilization must be compatible with the existing arrangements for carrying out other vital functions. Again, I would place infrastructural factors as the primary shaper of these structural patterns, but the latter also have independent dynamics and consequences. Only a few key structural patterns have been investigated here, mainly those related to the fundamental organizing principle of gender. The division of the sexes has still other ramifications for war in Amazonia, via the medium of politics. Political patterns constitute another set of structural variables with crucial significance for warfare, which will be investigated in another work.

Materialists commonly stress that structural and even superstructural patterns have causal significance within the more general constraints established by material base or infrastructure. They less frequently investigate those secondary causal relationships. I can illustrate this by citing my own research on Northwest Coast warfare (Ferguson 1983; 1984b), in

154

which I do consider political patterns, but rule out consideration of kinship structures (although largely because of a lack of usable data). Since, in my view, a primary strength of a materialist approach is its amenability to theory *building*, to the incorporation of insights and findings of other researchers and perspectives into more general, complete, and consistent explanations (see Ferguson 1986; Price 1982), it is important to extend materialist analyses of warfare to include causal relationships above the infrastructure.

ACKNOWLEDGEMENTS

I wish to thank the following people, who offered helpful criticism of an earlier draft of this essay: William Balee, Jane Bennett Ross, Brian Burkhalter, Marvin Harris, Robert Murphy, Keith Otterbein, and Barbara Price. Leslie Farragher offered support and suggestions throughout the research and writing.

9

THE KA'APOR INDIAN WARS
OF LOWER AMAZONIA, CA. 1825-1928

William Balée
New York Botanical Garden

Introduction

This paper presents a critical history of armed confrontations between the Ka'apor Indians and Luso-Brazilians during the period ca. 1825-1928. Using a dialectical perspective which "is critical and skeptical of received truth and established fact" (Murphy 1971:87), I suggest that Ka'apor Indian warfare reflects no aboriginal pattern of conflicts and competition, but was, rather, a consequence of neo-European colonization and political domination of lower Amazonia. I examine conflicts between the Ka'apor Indians and other groups, such as other Indian societies and runaway Afro-Brazilian slaves, also in this light. By 1825, Indians of the lower Amazon region had been subject to Luso-Brazilian domination for more than two hundred years. The colonists enslaved them, grouped them in artificial mission settlements, and incidentally introduced lethal epidemic diseases, especially smallpox, among them. After about 1825, Indian slavery in the lower Amazon region was unusual. But coercing Indian labor by other means, such as debt-peonage, to make plantations and the export of forest products profitable, was not.

I propose that the Ka'apor Indians made war during ca. 1825-1928 primarily to defend their relatively sedentary, subsistence-oriented mode of production from being undermined by the Luso-Brazilian state and its surrogates, not to conquer land, people, and resources. To comprehend the origins of Ka'apor Indian warfare, I first examine the process of pacification of lower Amazonia during the colonial period.

155

The Pacification of Lower Amazonia, 1616-ca. 1825

The capital (Belém) of the Portuguese captaincy of Grão-Pará (the eastern boundaries of which roughly approximate those of modern Pará state) was founded in 1616 by soldiers of the crown, at the site of a large Tupinambá settlement (Baena 1969:23; Cruz 1973:29). The historical records do not indicate the provenience of these Tupinambá, who occupied parts of the littoral from Belém to São Luís, Maranhão. Perhaps they had fled enslavement by the Portugese, like the Tupinambá of São Luís known to the French in 1609 (Abbeville 1945), some of the Tupi-Guarani speaking Indians in the Tocantins River basin during the mid-1600s (Berredo 1849:538-539), and the Tupinambá of Tupinambaranas Island in 1639 (Acuña 1859:119; also see Hemming 1978:235; Marchant 1942). In any case, their settlement, overlooking a major fishable water body also plentiful in crustaceans (the mouth of the Guamá River), would have borne strategic resemblance to the settlements of the coastal Tupinambá (Balée 1984b; Fernandes 1975:14).

The Portuguese soldiers quickly expelled the few French, English, and Dutch colonists whom they encountered trading with the Indians of the lower Amazon (Cruz 1973:27-28). Their next objective was to pacify the Indians, who tended to be hostile to all Portuguese. This was accomplished in three ways: through force of arms, by missionization, and by the incidental spread of epidemic disease (Sweet 1975:45-47).

The Tupinambá and the Portuguese, who quickly fortified Belém, fought intermittently between 1616 and 1621. In 1621, the *capitão-mor* (military commander of the captaincy) and his army killed perhaps as many as 30,000 Tupinambá and captured as slaves a large, unknown number of others near Belém (Almeida 1874:18; Kiemen 1954:22, n.10), neutralizing the indigenous threat to the city (cf. Sweet 1975:46). Local plantation owners purchased the captured Indians as slaves, repeating the history of coastal Bahia and Rio de Janeiro during the 16th century (Marchant 1942). In the lower Amazon, colonists forced the Indians to work on sugar plantations or *engenhos*, in the tobacco fields, and in the production of cacao, clove, guaraná, coffee, capsicum peppers, vanilla, and other spices. Colonists also compelled Indians to extract medicinal and scented oils, such as copaíba oil (from *Copaifera* spp.) and coumarin oil (from *Dipteryx odorata*), as well as to deliver dyes from the bush (Cruz 1973:67,73; Hemming 1978:319; Kiemen 1954:22; Vieira 1925:308). The captaincy exported most of its production directly to the Iberian metropolis.

By 1657, only 41 years after the founding of Belém, the Portuguese (and epidemic disease) killed perhaps 2,000,000 Indians and destroyed 500 Indian settlements "as large as cities" in the interior and coastal regions of Grão-Pará (Kiemen 1954:107-108; Vieira 1925:468). The Jesuits, who arrived in the lower Amazon in 1636 (Cruz 1973:165), continually protested the slave raids. They tried to catechize the Indians within large, artificially created settlements called *aldeias* (this term, incidentally, is also modern Brazilian Portuguese for any Indian village). During the 17th and 18th centuries, a distinction between the *indios aldeados* (i.e., those under Jesuit administration) and the *indios bravos* (i.e., those who were hostile to the state), was in common use. The Indians living in the Jesuit *aldeias* were a source of inexpensive labor for the colonists. Although the colonists were obliged to pay them, payment was evidently in kind, not money (cf. Cruz 1973:69,169). The Indians legally could not, moreover, refuse to work: the so-called "free" Indians of the *aldeias* usually served the colonists for ten months a year, as corvée laborers (Kiemen 1954:107). During the mid-to-late 17th century, many thousands of Indians were taken, as slaves in military expeditions known as *entradas* and as proselytes in Jesuit expeditions called *descidas* (whereby the Indians of the interior were encouraged to "descend" with the priests and their Indian servants to *aldeias* located near riverine towns and cities). In 1658, Portuguese soldiers took 240 Inheiguaras of the Tocantins River basin prisoner, declared them slaves, and then divided them among the soldiers (Betendorf 1909:112-116; Kiemen 1954:112; Vieira 1925:554). In 1659, the Jesuits lured many Tupinambá and 1,000 Tupi-Guarani speaking Potiguaras of the Tocantins to *aldeias* near Belém (Betendorf 1909:113-114). In 1660, the Jesuits brought 2,000 Indians under their control near Belém and elsewhere in lower Amazonia (Vieira 1925:555-556). In 1673, the *bandeirantes*, a disorderly group of gold and slave seekers who raided the lower Amazon valley from the small town of São Paulo, also took many Indian slaves in the Tocantins (Berredo 1849:539, 544).

Owners paid reward money for the return of their escaped slaves. *Escoltas* were military expeditions to capture escaped slaves and return them to their masters. In 1749, the sum of 10,000 reis or its equivalent in cloth rolls, cotton, or tobacco, was paid for each Indian and Afro-Brazilian slave who was recaptured, a sum which was more than the daily wage of the best-paid workers in the Portuguese court (Cruz 1973:67-68). As such, the intensity of slave-taking in the lower Amazon set a precedent for slave raids in the Rio Negro basin, which came under Portuguese domination by the late 1600s (Meggers 1971:122, 124; Sweet 1975:290,320).

The colonists of the lower Amazon continually complained to the Portuguese authorities that the Jesuits were harboring Indian labor. In 1758, a royal edict expelled the Jesuits from the interior and in 1759, from Brazil entirely. Jesuit missions, throughout the lower Amazon on rivers such as the Xingu, Tocantins, Acará, Capim, and Guamá, were largely abandoned. Some of the Indians who remained in some of these *aldeias* after the departure of the Jesuits became the indentured servants of the settlers on a permanent basis (Azevedo 1930:375). The army conscripted others, who were deployed in the pacification of still hostile Indians in the interior. Many formerly missionized Indians fled into zones of predominantly *terra firme* forest, far from navigable rivers (Azevedo 1930:373-374), which would also occur in Paraguay after the expulsion of the Jesuits there in 1767 (Métraux 1948:79; Watson 1952:49).

The Indians who had either avoided slavery and missionization entirely, or who had managed to escape into the forest, would probably have been less likely to contract smallpox, the disease most responsible for the massive depopulation of post-Columbian America, of which there were major epidemics that took especially heavy tolls on Indian populations in the lower Amazon during the years 1621, 1644, 1662-63, 1695, 1724, 1743-1750, 1793-1800, and 1819 (Azevedo 1930:228; Betendorf 1909:ix, 585-595; Kiemen 1954:180; Sweet 1975:79-86; Viana 1975:44,50).

From 1616 to about 1825, slave raids, corvée military and labor conscription, Jesuit missionization and demissionization, and epidemic disease were the salient features of Luso-Brazilian and Indian relations in lower Amazonia. The Indians responded in five non-mutually exclusive ways: 1) Some groups gradually submitted to the Luso-Brazilian military forces, serving as mercenaries in the pacification of still hostile tribes and of rebellious Indians, runaway Afro-Brazilian slaves, and mestiços during the civil war known as the Cabanagem (ca. 1819-1836). Lower Amazonian indigenous groups which cooperated with the state in these ways were the Mundurucu of the Tapajós River (Murphy 1960:36-38), the Turiwara of the Acará River (Rodrigues 1875:33), and the Apinayé of the Tocantins River (Nimuendaju 1983:5). In earlier times, some groups captured Indians in the interior to sell as slaves to the Portuguese. The Tapajós Indians at the mouth of the Tapajós River, for example, traded captured Indians to the Portuguese for iron tools in the 1660s (Heriarte 1874:38). A common feature of these groups was that their location was near strategic, navigable rivers. 2) Some groups adopted a permanently nomadic, non-agricultural mode of production in primarily *terra firme* forest far from navigable waterways. Formerly agricultural groups in lower Amazonia which abandoned agriculture, evidently because of Luso-Brazilian invasion and attacks by more powerful (i.e., more numerous) Indian groups who were either allied to the Luso-Brazilians or themselves fleeing the Luso-Brazilians, include the Avá-Canoeiro of the Araguaia and Tocantins River basins (cf. Rivet 1924:170,179; Toral 1985), and possibly the Guajá of the Tocantins, Gurupi, and Pindaré basins (Dodt 1939; Gomes 1980; Noronha 1856:8-9). 3) Some groups gradually became dependent on maize (a fast-producing staple) as opposed to bitter manioc (a slow-producing staple) and witnessed an overall reduction in the number of cultivated plant species, which seems to be characteristic of some of the trekking groups in the tropical forest between the lower Tocantins and lower Xingu Rivers, such as the Araweté (Viveiros de Castro 1986; also see Balée 1985 for related discussion). The maize-dependent Sirionó of the Madre de Dios basin in southwestern Amazonia represent a parallel case (Holmberg 1969). 4) Some groups resisted Luso-Brazilian domination fiercely and continuously, and thus were eventually exterminated, as with the Aruã of Marajó Island (Nimuendaju 1948:196). 5) Finally, many groups simply migrated into relatively uninhabited forest, far from navigable waterways and thus far from Luso-Brazilian armed forces and settlements. These groups continued to maintain settled villages; most of them were dependent on the cultivation of bitter manioc. Groups which responded in this way include the Wayãpi (Grenand 1982:94), the Kagwahiv (Kracke 1978:7), the Tapirapé (Wagley 1977), and the Ka´apor.

The Ka´apor vs. the Luso-Brazilians, ca. 1825-1928

The Ka´apor Indians, like many of the groups discussed above, speak a Tupi-Guarani language. At present, they inhabit a government reserve of 5,305 km² of mostly *terra firme* forest in northern Maranhão state. Although they summed only 494 people living in 17 small settlements in 1985, their population in 1928, when they were finally pacified, was probably between 2,000 and 5,000 (Balée 1984a:57; Ribeiro 1956:4-5) and distributed over a somewhat larger area than they occupy now.

The Ka´apor say that they lived at peace with the *karai* (non-Indians) in the remote past, long before their "pacification" in 1928 (also see *O Correio da Manhã* 1928). At that time, informants claim, they lived near a Luso-Brazilian settlement in the Capim River basin in what is now Pará state. One day, a headman named Tapo'õ returned home from hunting to find many *karai* as well as other Indians -- such as the *Karayá-p#tãn* -- in his house. The visitors were inebriated; they had been planning to murder Tapo'õ because he and his group refused to labor for the townsmen. The people of the Ka´apor settlement, including the two wives of Tapo'õ, hid themselves at the edge of the settlement. Sensing danger, Tapo'õ leapt to the rooftop of his house. While the *karai* and their accomplices began shooting at him with arrows and musketballs, he played long, resounding notes on the large ceremonial flute (*imi'a*, made from *Cecropia* spp.) and danced so that he dodged all the fire. His people knew he was still alive, since they could hear the flute playing. After a long time, Tapo'õ shouted to his enemies from the rooftop, "*Uruhu nde 'u ta*" ("Vultures will eat you" with the unstated implication "after I kill you"). This became the war cry of the Ka´apor; because of it, the *karai* began to call the Ka´apor the "Urubus," i.e., the "vultures." Tapo'õ then jumped to the ground and with his war club, he killed all those who had been shooting at him. He joined his people at the edge of the settlement. With them, he fled to establish a new settlement upstream.

Although this somewhat allegorical story cannot be dated, it suggests that the early Ka´apor made war originally not to conquer land, people, and resources, but to defend themselves and their way of life from forced labor. Ka´apor informants say that some of the early Ka´apor chose to live in the towns and work for the *karai*. These Ka´apor became enemies of the forest dwelling Ka´apor. When the "pacified" Ka´apor approached a Ka´apor settlement, to encourage the people to move to the town, the forest Ka´apor ambushed and killed them, according to informants. Informants describe the Ka´apor of the towns, who served the interests of the colonists, as having become *Ka´apor-rã* -- i.e., pseudo-Ka´apor. They were, no doubt, eventually assimilated into Luso-Brazilian society of lower Amazonia. These events mark the beginning of the period the Ka´apor refer to as *parahɨwá-rahã* -- "the time of rage," which also glosses as "the time of warfare."

The Ka´apor, in fact, enter history by confronting Luso-Brazilian settlers in the Capim River valley. In the 1820s (the exact year is unknown), the Ka´apor attacked the hamlet of Badajoz as well as other settlements and houses along the Capim River (see map below). In response, the settlers, who were led by a major landowner named Francisco Nunes, persuaded a *capitão* ("chief") of the riverine Turiwara Indians to help them obliterate the Ka´apor. Moreover, the governor of Pará sent a Portuguese major with 30 militiamen to aid the Turiwara in accomplishing this. Together the soldiers and Indians raided Ka´apor settlements, but casualties are unknown (J.B. Rodrigues 1875:33). In 1825, the same Portuguese major reported that about 400 Indians were attacking dwellers on the Capim, kidnapping "white daughters of citizens" as well as stealing canoes (BAP 1825). Although he mentions no tribal name, it is plausible that these Indians were the Ka´apor. Other indigenous societies of the Capim can be ruled out. The Tembé, for example, did not arrive on the Capim until the 1850s (Arnaud 1981/82; Gomes 1977). The Turiwara, who lived along the Acará, Moju, and Capim Rivers were already working as mercenaries and as peons for the settlers. The Amanajé, who were Tupi-Guarani speakers of a language evidently quite similar to Ka´apor (cf. A.D. Rodrigues 1984/85) and who were also hostile at the time, seem to be the only other possibility. But their location seems to have been between the Tocantins and Surubim Rivers, far from the location of the conflict (Baena 1969:238).

By 1861, the Ka´apor had moved east into the Guamá and Piriá basins, because of attacks by Brazilian military forces, settlers, and Indian mercenaries (Márques 1871:117; cf. J.B. Rodrigues 1875:33). The Ka´apor were described at this time as being "wild and hidden" in remote, primarily interfluvial forest (Márques 1871:117). Early in 1864, the governor of Pará ordered 25 national guardsmen to attack the Ka´apor, in apparent reprisal for Ka´apor raids on settlers in the upper Guamá. The contingent reached one settlement and because of its superior firepower, inflicted heavy casualties on the Indians, who had no guns and were taken by surprise. There were a "few" losses on the Brazilian side. The surviving Ka´apor of this settlement fled and some time later returned with reinforcements, no doubt from other settlements, to bury their dead (Muniz 1925:154). This battle was inconclusive. Later in 1864, the governor sent 150 national guardsmen against the Ka´apor. This time they reached numerous settlements. But the Ka´apor were prepared for this attack. They burned and abandoned their settlements one by one as the soldiers (which the Ka´apor call *yašipekwer*, i.e., "those whose heads are covered by tortoise shells") approached, and moved farther upstream into the headwaters of the Guamá and middle Gurupi (Muniz 1925:154).

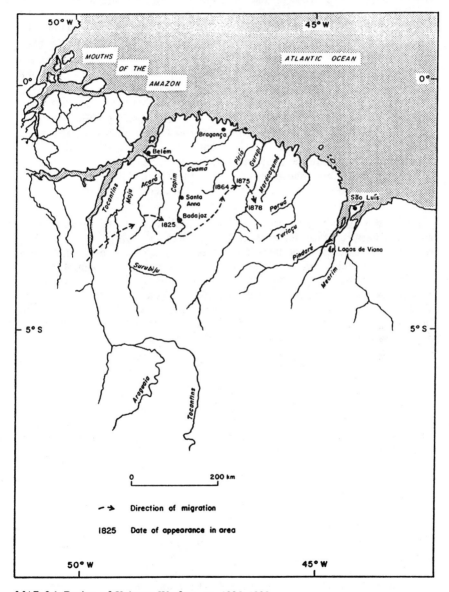

MAP 9.1 Region of Ka'apur Warfare, ca. 1825–1928

By 1872, Ka'apor settlements were situated along tiny affluents of the left bank of the middle Gurupi and Piriá Rivers in Pará (Dodt 1939:176). Some settlements remained in the Piriá in 1874 (J. B. Rodrigues 1875:33). In 1872, the Ka'apor maintained only hostile encounters with Brazilians, even though any such encounters were "quite rare" (Dodt 1939:176). The expansion of Brazilian society in eastern Pará during the 1870s pushed the Ka'apor across the largest river in the region, the Gurupi, and into the state of Maranhão, where their settlements have remained since.

In 1874, after having evidently crossed the Gurupi and Maracaçumé Rivers, some of the Ka'apor were raiding farms in the adjacent Paruá River basin, killing settlers and stealing goods (APE 1874). In 1880, they killed a woman and robbed her house in the Paruá basin (APE 1880). By 1886, all Brazilians had "abandoned" the Paruá River explicitly because of Ka'apor raids, even though the river basin had once been an important center for the production of manioc flour, rice, maize, and coffee; Ka'apor raids at this time extended from the Guamá River to the Lagos de Viana, i.e., along an arc of about 400 Kilometers [see map] (Guimarães 1887:62-63).

Ka'apor raids impeded commercial exploitation of the great tropical rainforest between the Gurupi and Turiaçu Rivers. The rubber industry, based on the extraction of latex from species of *Hevea* and *Castilloa* and which was the centerpiece of the export economy of the Amazon from the 1850s to about 1914, never assumed much importance in Maranhão, at least partly because of continuing hostility between the Ka'apor and Brazilians. In 1897, a civic leader from coastal Maranhão ascended the Turiaçu River up to the hamlet of Alto Turi, which was also an outpost of a telegraph line. Because of the risk of Ka'apor attack, he could go no farther upstream safely. He returned to São Luis with about 100 kilos of latex from rubber trees, to prove that rubber extraction could be profitable in the Turiaçu (*Diário do Maranhão* 1897:1; Domingues 1953:35). But frequent conflicts between the Ka'apor and would-be rubber gatherers greatly hindered production in this region (Fróes Abreu 1931:73). By 1912, rubber gatherers of the upper Turiaçu had largely evacuated the region, because Ka'apor Indians often "attacked" and "robbed" them (*O Correio da Tarde* 1912). In 1913, when global prices for Amazonian rubber were peaking, only one small company still exported rubber from the town of Alto Turi. But the quantity exported was minute, since Ka'apor Indians frequently burned the company's warehouses (J.P. Ribeiro 1913: 41).

The Ka'apor also obstructed communications between Belém and São Luis, the respective capital cities of the states of Pará and Maranhão. In the 1880s, the governors of these states agreed to construct a telegraph line between their capital cities. But Ka'apor Indians often raided the telegraph line workers and stole copper wire from the line itself, probably to make arrow points and the like. In 1885, the governor of Pará urged the governor of Maranhão to protect the engineer and workers in the region of the Maracaçumé River, who were the continuing targets of Ka´apor raids (APE 1885). The telegraph line was the site of frequent conflicts between the Ka´apor and workers through 1916 (Lopes 1916:184-185). It was never completed.

Brazilian settlers in the region often raided Ka´apor settlements as well (Fróes Abreu 1931:217), seeking not to plunder, but to kill. Elderly Brazilian informants from Alto Turi as well as elderly Ka´apor informants say that posses of settlers raided Ka´apor settlements. In one raid, the posse found that the men were gone hunting. They then massacred women and children, who were working at the manioc shed. I have visited the site of this settlement, which is about 55 km as the crow flies from Alto Turi, on a tiny feeder of the Turiaçu. The Ka´apor say that the survivors evacuated the settlement after the massacre. At the site, where there are many vines and spiny palms with few trees greater than 20 cm in diameter, one encounters a broken ceramic manioc griddle flush with the ground. This was one of several settlements which posses attacked. A telegraph agent at Alto Turi organized some such raids, impaling the heads of his Ka´apor victims on stakes near the telegraph post (D. Ribeiro 1970:177). According to elderly Brazilian informants, the environs of Alto Turi were kept constantly clear of weeds and secondary growth, to prevent Ka´apor Indians from having the benefit of cover in any raids (Balée 1984a:49). This tense, mutually hostile situation frustrated the Brazilian government's early attempts to pacify the Ka´apor with trade goods, as opposed to lead.

In 1911, less than a year after it was founded as a branch of the Ministry of Agriculture, the SPI (Indian Protection Service) attempted to pacify the Ka´apor. During 1911-12, an agent of the SPI left trade goods in thatched shelters in the forest near the mouth of the Igarapé Jararaca, a stream which was at the time populated by the Ka´apor, on the upper Gurupi. Some Ka´apor secretly took the trade goods, but made no moves to approach the givers (*O Correio da Tarde* 1912). In the same year, another SPI agent with a team of local workers went up the Turiaçu into Ka´apor territory. As they were unloading steel tools, cloth, and other trade goods (*brindes*) on the river bank, at a site only 5 km upstream from Alto Turi, a group of Ka´apor men ambushed them. An arrow point punctured a worker's jaw, seriously wounding him (*O Correio da Tarde* 1912).

During 1915-17, SPI funds were unavailable and no pacification work was carried out in the Ka´apor area, despite the fact that pacification of the Ka´apor was the first priority of the SPI, following the pacification of the Nambiquara of Rondania in 1914 (Ministério de Agricultura 1915:70; 1917:102).

In 1918, the Ka´apor raided settlements in the Guamá basin and near the town of Braganca, in Pará. They were reportedly after "iron tools" (*Folha do Norte* 1920). In 1920, Ka´apor men struck near Braganca, killing five settlers and carrying away many goods (*Estado do Pará* 1920). By 1919-20, the right bank of the upper Guamá had been abandoned by settlers, due to Ka´apor raids being launched out of Maranhão (Hurly 1928:32).

Meanwhile, the SPI had established an attraction post for the Ka´apor on the left bank of the Gurupi River near an islet called Canindé. This had been a crossing place for the Ka´apor into and out of Pará during the dry season, when water level is low. The post had earlier been situated on the islet itself, but since Ka´apor arrows could reach that spot from the right bank, it was moved to the left bank. The SPI team, when funds were available, left steel tools, cloth, and other goods under thatched shelters on the right bank of the Gurupi. Early in October 1928, the Ka´apor were removing these gifts. On October 16, 1928, a young headman named Pa'i (which is also the term for "priest") appeared on the right bank of the Gurupi across from the SPI post and signaled to the SPI personnel that he wanted axes, machetes, and cloth. The SPI agent sent a boat loaded with gifts and three workers across the river. Pa'i moved away from the river bank when the boat approached. He signaled to the boat's crew (led by a Tembé Indian called Caetano) to leave the gifts on the bank and to withdraw, which they did. When the boat was about 30 meters away, "Indians from all corners of the forest came out toward the gifts" (*O Paiz* 1929; *O Globo* 1929; D. Ribeiro 1970:181-182). On December 15, 1928, 94 Ka´apor Indians visited the SPI post. Some stayed for a few days (D. Ribeiro 1970:182). At the same time, some Ka´apor men in the Turiaçu basin reached the edge of the town of Alto Turi. They pointed their arrows to the ground in a gesture of peaceful intent. The people of the town invited them to stay overnight, which they did (Balée 1984:49). An elderly Ka´apor woman from a settlement in the Gurupi basin, and who would have been about 9 years old in 1928, said that when peace was achieved, the Ka´apor women became "very happy" (*huri riki*). A period of more than 100 years of intermittent warfare, with many casualties on both sides, had ended.

The Ka´apor vs. Other Egalitarian Groups

Ka´apor oral history contains references to conflicts with numerous enemies, such as the *Karaja-pitã* (perhaps the Karajá who now occupy the Island of Bananal on the Araguaia River), the *Yuruũ* (perhaps the Juruna, who once lived on the lower Xingu but who now inhabit the upper Xingu), the *Mboi-yuwar* ("snake eaters," which refers to the Eastern Timbira and perhaps the Apinayé), the *Tembé*, the *Ka´apor-rã* (Tupi-Guarani groups in the Capim and Acará River basins who attacked the Ka´apor, perhaps as mercenaries of the state), and the *Ka'apehar* (who are the Guajá and the Guajajara). Ka´apor society probably originated in the contact-induced fissioning of Tupi-Guarani speaking groups in the lower Amazon south of the Amazon River proper. It has been suggested, for example, that the Ka´apor and Turiwara were one society that split apart during the Cabanagem (*O Correio da Manhã* 1928; Nimuendaju 1948:193), although the linguistic evidence for this is scanty and there is no primary source evidence for it. Nevertheless, the Ka´apor believe that there was a schism in their society between those who favored accommodating the settlers (by working for them as debtor-peons) and those who rejected this option. Warfare between the Ka´apor and other Indians in the basins of the Acará, Capim, and Guamá can be understood in the context of hostilities between the Ka´apor and the state. When the Turiwara attacked the Ka´apor in the 1820s with Luso-Brazilian militiamen, surely this was not like warfare between aboriginal uncontacted Indian tribes. Rather, it was part of a greater war reflecting state policy in regard to the forest Indians. Make laborers of them and, if this is impossible, exterminate them. Many of the pacified tribes then--such as the Turiwara, the Mundurucu (Murphy 1960:36-38), and the Apinayé (Nimuendaju 1983:5)--were used as mercenaries in the state's policy of subjugating the forest Indians. The Ka´apor resisted the Turiwara as they would resist the militiamen, defending their perceived right to remain free from debt-peonage in the working of plantations and in the extraction of forest goods for export.

The main economic difference between the Indian societies of post-Columbian lower Amazonia was between those who occupied predominantly *terra firme* forest habitats and those who inhabited the banks of major *navigable* rivers and who were, therefore, more accessible to trade and early pacification by Luso-Brazilian forces. All the riverine Indians of the region, including the Turiwara, Anambé (Arnaud and Galvão 1969), and Tembé (Gomes 1977), became indentured to the settlers in the forest extractive industries. This distinction recalls that of riverine and/or coastal societies vs. hinterland societies in pre-Columbian and early post-Columbian times (Balée 1984b). The difference is that, in post-Columbian times, warfare was not over *natural* resources, but rather stimulated by the introduction of trade goods (cf. Ferguson 1984) and especially by the appearance of a new, export-oriented economy based on slave labor and debt-peonage.

Ka´apor warfare with other indigenous societies and escaped Afro-Brazilian slaves reflects the rise of Luso-Brazilian domination of lower Amazonia. After the Ka´apor crossed the Gurupi and settled permanently in northern Maranhão, they were in a geographical cul-de-sac, surrounded by either white settlers, escaped Afro-Brazilian slaves, or other Indian groups, who were themselves immigrants to the region. From the 1860s onward, the Ka´apor could no longer occupy their lands in the Guamá River basin. In crossing the Gurupi to escape military invasions, they had to confront the Tembé of the Gurupi who had arrived there in the 1850s and were already trading with Luso-Brazilians (Gomes 1977) and maroon settlements of runaway Afro-Brazilian slaves called *mocambos*, which from the 1830s until the manumission law of 1888 were encountered in the upper Turiaçu, upper Maracaçumé, and middle Gurupi basins (APE 1834, 1839, 1840, 1854). In 1878, while the Ka´apor were establishing settlements in Maranhão, they destroyed a maroon settlement in the Gurupi basin (Lisboa 1935:4, 51-52). Ka´apor informants claim that a site 4 km from the present settlement of Gurupiuna was a maroon settlement destroyed by their ancestors; this may be the incident Lisboa (above) referred to.

Between 1913 and 1928, the Ka´apor frequently raided Tenetehara settlements in the Pindaré River basin (Gomes 1977:123; Wagley and Galvão 1949:8-9). Along the Gurupi River, the Ka´apor raided Tembé settlements as well as Brazilian settlements (Hurly 1928, 1932a, 1932b). Tembé informants claim that in reprisal for these raids, a very large group of Tembé men surrounded a Ka´apor settlement in the Jararaca basin at dawn one day. Just as the day's activities were about to begin, they massacred the inhabitants. In another raid on a Tembé settlement, a wounded Ka´apor man was buried alive by the father of one of my Tembé informants. The Ka´apor also were at war with the Krẽ-Ye Timbira, who had migrated into the forests of the Gurupi from *cerrado* country to the south. In 1903, the Ka´apor killed "many" Timbira who were collecting copaíba oil for export along the Gurupiuna stream, one of the principal settlement locations of the Ka´apor (Nimuendaju 1946:13-14). Finally, from the 1870s at the latest (Dodt 1939:177) to 1974, the Ka´apor raided the nomadic Guajá and were in turn raided by them.

In all the above cases prior to 1928, the Ka´apor would not have been in contact with other Indian groups and runaway Afro-Brazilian slaves were it not for the fact that Luso-Brazilian military forces and their surrogates pushed the Ka´apor into regions where other sociopolitical groups were already situated. In protecting a relatively sedentary forest existence, it was less costly to go to war against other stateless sociopolitical groups than against better-armed state militiamen and national guardsmen.

Conclusions

The differences seem to override the similarities in a comparison of Ka´apor warfare and pre-Columbian tropical forest warfare. The principal similarity is a functional one: both the pre-Columbian coastal Tupinambá and the post-Columbian inland Ka´apor practiced external warfare with a basically uxorilocal residential pattern (Balée 1984a, 1984b), an association first reported for the Mundurucu by Murphy (1957) and which has been widely noted among other egalitarian peoples since (see Ferguson, this volume). *External* warfare (meaning warfare between different sociopolitical groups) seems to be the dependent part of the association (Murphy 1957). Comparative data suggest the following principle: where residence is uxorilocal and warfare occurs, warfare tends to be external. Uxorilocality in and of itself does not imply automatically any kind of warfare, as is evident in the case of the Sanumá, a sub-group of the Yanomamo (see Ramos 1972). Moreover, the sociopolitical differences between aboriginal Tupinambá warfare and Ka´apor warfare are manifest. The Tupinambá fielded between 300 and 12,000 men in their military expeditions (Balée 1948b:254); in contrast, although one source claimed that the Ka´apor in the 1880s had 3,000 "bows," i.e., men of fighting age (Guimarães 1887:63), Ka´apor informants assert that their ancestors deployed no more than about 20 or 30 men in any given raid. Although both the Tupinambá and Ka´apor were multi-settlement societies, Tupinambá settlements were, on average, 20 times larger than Ka´apor settlements (cf. Balée 1984a, 1984b). Whereas the Tupinambá were incorporated into paramount chiefdoms (Balée 1984a, 1984b), no evidence exists for ranking in Ka´apor society at any time nor for any figures more salient than headmen and shamans (Balée 1984a). The Tupinambá assembled between 3,000 and 12,000 people at cannibalistic feasts, in which their prisoners of war were consumed (Balée 1984b:257); yet Ka´apor pre and post combat rituals gathered only the participants of the raid and a few old men (women and children were excluded); there is no direct evidence for cannibalism (cf. Huxley 1957:244-264).

If the warfare of the pre-Columbian and early post-Columbian Tupinambá, Conibo, Omaguas, Tapajós, and other riverine polities involved the conquest of land, resources, and sometimes people (Balée 1984b; DeBoer 1981; Lathrap 1970; Morey and Marwitt 1975), the objectives of Ka´apor warfare were different.

It seems unlikely that the Ka´apor attempted to conquer and occupy the lands of other groups. Instead, they first defended their lands in Pará state from military invasions. Only when this defense proved futile, did they migrate and incidentally invade the territories of other stateless groups, evoking a "domino" effect. Whereas aboriginal peoples of the seacoast and Amazon River proper attempted to defend themselves against the raids of inland groups (Balée 1984b), the Ka´apor, existing in the post-Columbian period, were defending themselves against the raids of riverine groups, already subjugated to the politico-economic-military authorities of the Luso-Brazilian state. Competition was no longer for riverine zones, but for free space in the hinterlands. It is equally unlikely that natural resources alone were a stake in Ka´apor warfare. In their raids, however successful in terms of plunder, they did not tend to take over regions which were especially favored in terms of game, fish, and soil. Moreover, there was no conquest of people per se in Ka´apor warfare. Even though Ka´apor men (until recently) raided the Guajá on occasion for women, there was never slavery in Ka´apor society nor dealing in slaves. No Ka´apor wars were so conclusive as to give the Ka´apor hegemony over any group, should they have even sought such hegemony, which is unlikely, given their egalitarianism.

One might argue that the Ka´apor made war to obtain trade goods, especially steel tools. The Ka´apor used steel tools to clear forest and

make fine, lanceolate arrow points. The steel arrow points, which terror-
ized surrounding peoples, were described in the 1870s (Dodt 1939:177),
1880s (Guimarães 1887:62-63), and 1890s (Lisboa 1935:51-52). From the
1820s through the 1860s, the Ka´apor secured steel tools in raids on
Luso-Brazilian houses and settlements in Pará state. By the late 1870s
and early 1880s, they were obtaining steel in large quantities from
machinery abandoned in unproductive gold mines in the Maracaçumé
basin and from the tools abandoned by the construction crews of the telegraph line (Lisboa 1935:2; Moura 1936:17-18). Despite the salience of
steel in Ka´apor warfare and agriculture, competition for it does not
explain their wars.

The Ka´apor believe that the stone axes one finds in their habitat
are "thunder-seeds" (tupã ra'r) and that these were never used by their
ancestors for the felling of trees. In the past, the only use of these stone
axes was to impart courage in pre-battle rituals. The axe was heated on
the coals of the fire; then, each man who was to participate in the raid
took his turn by clutching the hot stone axe and placing it against his
chest for as long as he could endure the pain. Today, heated stone axes
are pressed against the chests of dogs so that they will not fear jaguars.
The Ka´apor insist that for felling trees, their ancestors always employed
only steel axes, plundered from Luso-Brazilians. This suggests that the
early Ka´apor acquired steel peacefully in the period prior to their prolonged wars against the Luso-Brazilians, perhaps from Jesuit missionaries
and/or missionized Indians. The use of steel tools, then, can be considered to have been a part of Ka´apor culture even prior to 1825. They
would only make war when they could not acquire steel by means other
than debt-peonage.

To comprehend the reasons for Ka´apor warfare, one should consider why they accepted the overtures of peace in 1928. Ka´apor informants say their ancestors did so for the steel tools--axes, machetes, and
knives. Yet the Ka´apor had been getting considerable stores of steel
through earlier raiding. The SPI offered the Ka´apor the cessation of
warfare costs with steel tools in the bargain. The SPI agents would not
indenture the Ka´apor. Moreover, obtaining steel tools from the SPI
agents involved no apparent risks. On the other hand, all Ka´apor knew
that raids on settlers frequently resulted in Ka´apor fatalities and later
gruesome reprisals. Accepting the SPI's terms seemed to mean peace
without economic subjugation to and assimilation into Brazilian society
(which is euphemistically called "integration" today--see Gross 1982).

In a dialectical spirit, I conclude that Ka´apor warfare, although
unlike aboriginal tropical forest warfare in significant ways, helped to
conserve some aspects of a basically indigenous way of life. Despite the
absence of warfare in Ka´apor society today, one could argue that in
terms of the period 1500-1986, Ka´apor warfare ceased at a relatively
auspicious time for them, i.e., after the establishment of at least nominal
federal protection for Indians. Warfare was for the Ka´apor, in

Clausewitz's words, the "extension of politics by other means." Such were the politics of cultural and economic survival, not conquest, in the post-Columbian tropical forest.

10

INVISIBLE PEOPLE:
OSTRACISM IN CASHINAHUA SOCIETY

Kenneth M. Kensinger[1]
Bennington College

Introduction

In this paper I consider two cases, both involving the use of the same sanction as a response to two quite different offenses, and why in one case the sanction was thought by my informants to have worked and in the other to have failed. The sanction is that of ostracism or shunning, a punishment exceeded in severity only by exile or death in Cashinahua society.[2] Ostracism consists of a person's being treated by his or her fellows as a non-person, i.e., as if he or she does not exist. No one speaks to persons being shunned, recognizes their presence, or interacts in any way with them. Although they are totally isolated socially, no attempt is made to restrict their movements and activities, because to do so would acknowledge their presence.

Ostracism generally works, because most Cashinahua consider it a fate just slightly less life-threatening than death. Informants invariably became uncomfortable when talking about the subject. The decision to subject a person to shunning is made formally or informally by the whole community when and if a person's misbehavior is deemed to be either (a) sufficiently grave to jeopardize the health, welfare, or safety of the community (Case I), or (b) excessively disruptive of social relationships (Case II).

Case I: The Case of the Frustrated Lover: Kadi Chapu

Kadi Chapu returned to the village from his garden about 2 PM carrying a bushmaster he had killed. He was bringing it for the visiting American zoologists to see. In the process of killing the snake he had broken its skin, thus freeing its spirit. Mothers kept their children away from the snake; various of them chided Kadi for bringing it to the village, thus making a clear trail for the snake's spirit to follow. Several men commented that he would have to go on a month-long fast, characterized by rigorous food taboos, abstinence from sex, and culminating in a purification ritual. They discussed the personal inconvenience of such rituals but noted that the entire process would make him a better hunter by clearing his system of any accumulation of *yupa*, the substance which causes a man to miss the target when he shoots his arrow. To everyone's surprise, Kadi Chapu joined the men for the evening meal and ate everything including the prohibited meat, manioc, and ripe plantain soup. Several men chided him for this misbehavior; his brother reminded him that such behavior could jeopardize the health and safety of the village, especially that of his infant nephew who was living in the same household. Kadi parried all criticism by saying he would begin the fast in the morning.

That evening he told me he had no intention of going through the rituals. He didn't mind the fasting, but he wouldn't go through the purification ritual at the end of the month because it demanded total sexual abstinence for the entire preceding 30 days. He was, he said, having affairs with three different women, one of which was particularly torrid.

During the next several days various informants told me that although Kadi was observing the food taboos in public, he was eating prohibited foods in secret -- and worse he had met and had sex with all three of his lovers, in fact, four times with the favorite. Comments expressing disapproval of such behavior were made in his presence without being aimed at him directly, and on two occasions older women tried to shame him publicly for his unseemly behavior. Unrepentant, Kadi continued to pursue his amorous adventures.

Six days after Kadi killed the snake, his nephew became sick. People openly blamed the illness on Kadi's shameless behavior. That evening when he came to the men's gathering to eat, no one acknowledged his presence. They did not prevent him from eating, but handed him nothing. As the meat dishes were finished, the man sitting to Kadi's right picked up a bowl of corn soup, took a drink and passed it to the man on his right and so on around the circle to the man sitting on Kadi's left who finished the contents of the bowl and put it on the ground empty. When Kadi spoke, no one responded. They looked past him and through him but gave no indications that they were aware of his presence.

During the next two days, Kadi went about his life as usual. He worked in his garden and went hunting. When he brought two wild pigs back to the village, everyone ignored the pigs as they had been ignoring him. When he brought me the two rear quarters of one pig, I followed the lead of others and ignored him and the proffered gift.

By the following morning, Kadi was showing signs of desperation. He went from hearth to hearth talking to everybody. People acted as if they neither saw nor heard him. He came to my house and begged me to talk with him; I continued working without acknowledging his presence.

By noon he crawled into his hammock, assumed a fetal position and began to cry quietly.

Late in the afternoon he peeled and roasted some green plantains, and brought them with him to the men's circle for the evening meal, throughout which he quietly sat and munched on his dry fare ignoring the prohibited meat and sweet gruels. By the next evening the community was convinced that he was indeed observing the required fast and so the following morning they responded to his greetings. In my interviews with him in the succeeding days I became aware of the searing emotions that had led to his capitulation.

Kadi was a normal healthy 17 year old. He lived with his two sisters and their husband and children and with his older brother, his older brother's wife and children. His father had been killed by a jaguar when he was four years old; his mother died two years later. He had grown up in the household of his married older brother and sisters.

He spoke of occasions during his childhood when his parents and siblings had responded to his misbehavior and temper tantrums by ignoring him. He recounted one particular experience when everyone was going poison fishing in a stream across the river from the village. He had been misbehaving for several days and earlier in the day his mother started to ignore him. As people waded into the river to cross, they all ignored him. Nobody picked him up to carry him across the deepest part of the channel and when he tried to swim, the current caught him and carried him downstream. After struggling back to the riverbank, he returned alone to the empty village. At first he was in a rage and broke several large cooking pots, but when he heard spirits in one of the houses his rage turned to terror. His cries for help went unanswered. He crawled up to a platform in the eaves of the house where his kinsmen found him several hours later, rigid with fear and staring blankly at his surroundings.

He had recurrent dreams about these experiences, always wakening from them bathed in perspiration. And during the shunning he had just experienced, he was afraid to fall asleep because these nightmares haunted his sleep. It was the nightmares, he said, more than the refusal of his lovers to have sex with him or even to acknowledge his amorous advances, that finally led to his decision to follow the expectations of his fellows.

Case II: The Case of the Red Hot Lover: Dinis

[In the following event, the central figure, Dinis, is largely off-stage. However, it was his behavior during the preceding months which precipitated the drama. For nearly a year, Dinis, an immigrant to Xumuya, had systematically attempted to seduce most of the women with no little success.]

About 9 PM the peace and quiet of the village was shattered by raised voices and then screaming from Usirin's house. His wife, Dasiu, fled the house sobbing, and ran across the plaza to the house of her classificatory father. For a short while the murmur of voices and sobbing could be heard before quiet returned to the village. My informant told me that Usirin had beaten his wife because she refused to have sex with him and angered him by saying that he was a lousy hunter and a lousy lover. Why should she give him sexual favors for nothing when a real hunter was glad to give her meat in exchange for sex? Such flaunting of an affair rightly angered Usirin, justifying the beating, according to my informant. The following morning Dasiu returned to her home after Usirin left to go hunting. Except for some quiet gossiping about the event, life in the village went on as before.

About a week later, the quiet of the village was broken again by yelling and screaming from Usirin's house. When Dasiu rushed out of the house, Usirin followed, striking her repeatedly with a tapir-hide whip. When she tripped and fell, he stood over her and continued the beating. At that point two of her classificatory brothers rushed from their house, threw Usirin to the ground and kicked him. Dasiu ran to her classificatory father's house. After a few minutes her brothers and Usirin returned to their houses, but the murmur of conversations, some evincing agitation, could be heard throughout the village. It continued for almost an hour.

The following morning, the atmosphere of the village was charged; the previous evening's events were the major topic of conversation. Late that afternoon after the men had returned from hunting and had bathed, they gathered as usual near the headman's house to eat. Each man brought bowls of manioc or plantains and meat, their wives brought them bowls of corn or ripe plantain gruel. The conversation was subdued and somewhat strained. When nothing but gruel remained to be consumed, Uxasa, one of Dasiu's brothers, berated Usirin for beating his wife. Although he had a right to beat her and she probably deserved it, he should not have pursued her when she fled and clearly should not have struck her with the whip after she fell.

Usirin responded that he had been angry, that she had taunted him with her affair with Dinis, about having made love in his, Usirin's, hammock that afternoon. Her brothers responded that she was having an affair because her lover provided her with game animals, and a woman has a right to do so if her husband doesn't provide sufficient meat. Usirin's brother Dapida joined the argument saying that perhaps Usirin wasn't the best hunter, but that he was the best turtle tracker in the village. What other woman had more turtles tied under her house waiting to be butchered and eaten? In addition, her husband had provided her with large gardens so that she had an abundance of vegetables.

At this point everybody got into the discussion. Charges and counter-charges were made. At various points women, eating in another circle nearby, added additional input to the rapidly heating argument. Just as it seemed that tempers would explode, the old headman cleared his throat, stretched, scratched his groin and said, "Now in the days of the ancestors there was a young tapir." The audience subsided. "He was an over-sexed tapir who propositioned everything that moved. If a leaf blew across his path, he suggested they have sex. One day he encountered a turtle. pecker.' 'I've never had sex with a beauty like you,' he said. When he was at the height of his passion, *Chun*! her jaws clamped shut; she had her dinner. The tapir crawled off in the bushes and died."

The audience responded enthusiastically throughout the story, giggling, making ribald comments, grimacing, clutching their groins, moaning, and laughing. Yes, it was good.

When the headman finished, Dasiu's classificatory father told another story about a deer married to an agouti who failed to provide for his wife, because the food he brought was food which deer ate but not agouti. Again comments from the audience formed a counterpoint to the storyteller. Four other traditional stories followed, each adding new nuances to this once removed discussion of the dispute. Throughout, the audience expressed its opinions of each story.

Finally, the old headman again cleared his throat, scratched his groin and said, "Now, as the ancestors told us ... " and launched into a new story. This was not one of the traditional stories although it was in the same form. It contained some of the cast of characters of the preceding six stories. People listened carefully to his speech, after which they commented freely. "It was a good story," "That's what I think," "*Habiaskaki*, -- that's the way it is," etc. The group quickly disbanded, each family returning to its hearths and hammocks.

As I was informed the following day, the story contained a series of recommendations, but without ever naming any of the parties to the dispute. First, Usirin should agree to the marriage of his young daughter to a suitor who had been seeking Usirin's approval of the match, thus bringing a successful young hunter and perhaps a more varied meat supply into the household. Second, Dasiu owed her husband respect as a good provider, and should she continue to have affairs she should carry them out with discretion, and without flaunting them in her husband's face, and that since she was eating food he provided, she should accept the conjugal obligation implied by that acceptance. Third, Dinis should be ostracized until he mended his ways because his amorous behavior was causing so much disruption within the community.

Throughout the story telling, Dinis had been silent. It was his indecorous behavior which provoked the dispute and for him was reserved the harshest judgment, ostracism, until he gave evidence that his amorous predation would cease or at least be carried on with discretion.

The following day no one spoke with Dinis. He went from house to house only to be ignored, even by his wife and former sexual partners. He came to my house, and although I studiously ignored him, he talked at length. He didn't mind the shunning, he said. Why should he care if they would not talk to him. They envied his penis. If he left the village, they would miss the game animals he always brought back from the hunt. He could go to Pipi's village. They would welcome him there. No, he wasn't going to be chased away like a capybara from his gardens and hunting trails. His resolve lasted two days. He packed his possessions into his canoe and went downriver -- *alone*.

Informants were in complete agreement about why shunning or ostracism failed in this case. [Note that from the Cashinahua perspective, ostracism had failed both because it did not produce the desired effect, i.e., it did not produce a change in Dinis' behavior, and because it cost the village a successful hunter.] Dinis was a shameless misfit who never learned how to behave, they argued. He was an orphan. His mother died when he was about two years old. An older sister cared for him for about two years until her husband died and her new husband did not want him around. He then lived with his aged, widowed and husbandless maternal grandmother who was loosely attached to the household of a distant kinsman where she did much of the labor in exchange for the food they ate and a place to hang her hammock. Their presence was tolerated by their housemates; neither was especially wanted. When his behavior became intolerable around the house, his grandmother would take him to the garden or forest where he would play or work with her, free from the scowls and demands of their housemates. He and his grandmother would occasionally hike downriver to another village to visit his classificatory mother's brother and other distant kinsmen. Dinis bullied his grandmother, who in turn doted on him. She cuddled and coddled him, protected him from disapproval of any sort. In short, she spoiled him. Shortly after his initiation at about age 10, his grandmother died leaving him at the mercy of the housemates from whom she had protected him for 6 years. Soon after her death, he fled to the village of his classificatory mother's brother, whose son, a boy about 3 years older than Dinis, befriended him, taught him to hunt and make gardens. These were good years, he had a friend. His behavior apparently was normal for a boy his age.

This period ended abruptly when Dinis' cross cousin married and, burdened with the obligations of being a son-in-law, could no longer spend his time leisurely working and playing with Dinis. Furthermore, the new wife's mother disliked Dinis, probably with some justification. From her point-of-view, he was boisterous, rude, shameless and apparently a threat to the tranquility of her household.

At 13, Dinis ran off to live with a Brazilian family where he worked for three years. These were hard years. Disobedience was punished by kicks, slaps, and beatings. Why he stayed is unclear. He spoke often about the threats made by his Brazilian "father" to hang him up by his thumbs, to sell him to downriver traders, or to castrate him. After a particularly severe beating for insolence, he fled back to a Cashinahua village where he was taken in and cared for by his cross-cousin. All of his kinsmen were outraged by the visible proof of the severe beating he had received, so that when his Brazilian "father" came searching for him they smuggled Dinis out of the village, claimed that he had died from infected wounds and threatened to report the "murder" to the priest on his next visit to the village. Several axes and machetes bought their promises of silence.

Dinis was delighted to be back with "his" people. He was a hard worker and a good hunter. He was charming, witty, disarming, handsome and horny. Lovers were readily available in exchange for the game he brought back to the village. His sexual escapades would have been tolerated and perhaps even considered amusing had they been carried out with discretion, but they were not.

Dinis' cross cousin arranged for him to marry his, the cousin's, prepubescent sister, in hopes that the marriage would curtail his sexual exploits. His efforts were in vain. Dinis continued his campaign to cuckold every male in the village regardless of age or relationship to him. He told me of this with glee and in considerable detail. When his position in that village became untenable he fled to another village, then another, and finally four years and two marriages later to Peru -- and we are back to where we started an examination of his case.

Ostracism had failed because Dinis never learned how to behave. During the crucial years from 3 to 10 he was sheltered from most disapproval by a grandmother who, because of her emotional dependence on him, failed to train him or allow others to do so; he was never properly socialized. During his three years with the Brazilians he felt isolated and alienated; he was treated as a servant or slave, slept under the house with the pigs and dogs, and was never able to play with children his own age, and ate alone in the cookhouse. Thus, the threat of ostracism did not strike terror in him. He knew he could survive -- he had for 3 years.

Discussion and Conclusions

In his discussion of ostracism as a mechanism of social control, Robert Murphy has argued that "Ostracism, whether voluntary or imposed, is one of the worst penalties society can exact, for it inflicts a social death while the person is still alive (Murphy 1979:139)." He continues, "Social ostracism in smalltown America has sent many people to seek refuge in the anonymity of the city, but in primitive societies there are no alternatives to life in tight little communities (Idem:139)."

In light of Murphy's argument, what conclusions can we draw about the nature of social controls in egalitarian societies like the Cashinahua based on these two cases I have described, particularly as they relate to ostracism?

First, sanctions against anti-social or asocial behavior are effective to the degree that the individuals subjected to them have been socialized to feel those sanctions as a threat to their well-being. By threatened, I do not mean that they see the sanction against them as a warning of potential physical violence. Rather, they perceive it as a warning of the loss of their social persona. The effectiveness of ostracism as a form of social control is predicated, at least in Cashinahua society, on childhood reactions to the practice of "looking-through" a child as a means of inducing proper behavior. It is the psychic trauma of early childhood experiences, where recognition of one's existence is withheld, that motivates the adult to mend his ways. Dinis, because his grandmother protected him from such experiences, seemed immune to shunning.

Second, in the absence of a single authority or agency with coercive powers there must be (1) agreement among the members of the society that the violation poses a threat to the health, welfare, or safety of the community or one of its members or threatens to rip the social fabric; and (2) a willingness of the members of the group to act in concert. A corollary of this point is that egalitarian societies appear to be concerned not with protecting the perpetrator of an offense from the consequences of his misdeeds but with protecting society. Thus, the socialization process is more concerned with the development of a social conscience than with building strong egos. Notice that although Dinis' grandmother's behavior -- which screened him from social disapproval, and thus helped to protect his ego from the trauma of shunning experienced by most Cashinahua children -- may have been useful preparation for the three years he spent with the Brazilians, it ill prepared him for living in his own society.

Third, in a society where physical coercion is rejected as a means of social control, the socialization process must include mechanisms that make effective use of psychological pressures. The reference in Dinis' case to the emasculation of the horny tapir was not a threat of physical violence but a reminder that just as the loss of the genitalia leads to a death of sexuality, the loss of personhood leads to social death. In Kadi Chapu's case, behavior which causes actual or potential physical harm to another is balanced by the withdrawal of recognition of one's social persona.

Finally, I suggest that social control, or at least the illusion thereof, can be sustained in egalitarian societies only so long as the ultimate sanctions leave no desirable alternatives for the miscreant. For Kadi Chapu, the loss of his social persona threatened his self-identity. Dinis, on the other hand, was convinced that *he* did not need the approval of others, that he could go elsewhere and be himself -- to another Cashinahua village or if need be a Peruvian or Brazilian town. I last saw Dinis in the jail of a small Peruvian border town. He had been caught in bed with the commandante's wife.

FOOTNOTES

[1]This paper was first written for presentation to the Columbia University South American Indian Caucus and in its present form has benefitted from comments from the Caucus, from members of Professor Charles Wagley's South American Indian Seminar at the University of Florida, and from the Montclair State College Anthropology Club. The paper has also benefitted from criticisms and suggestions from Mike Brown, Trudie Dole, Tom Gregor, Emmi Ireland and Nat Heiner, Harriet Klein, Waud Kracke, Jim Loriot, Pat Lyon, Luis Monguio and Alicia Colombi, and Sally Sugarman. I am deeply indebted to Bob and Yo Murphy for writing about Waru (Murphy 1974b) and Borai (Murphy 1974a; Murphy and Murphy 1974) and thus providing me with the inspiration for this essay. My greatest debt is to Kadi Chapu, Dinis, and all my Cashinahua informants who permitted me to live with them and shared with me some of their memories, experiences, and hopes.

[2] The Peruvian Cashinahua live in several villages along the banks of the Curanja River in the southeastern part of the Departamento de Loreto. Each village comprises 20-100 inhabitants, 80 being the optimal size. For most of my fieldwork I lived in the villages of Maneya and Xumuya. This paper reports on the only two cases of "full" ostracism I observed during my 84 months in the field between 1955 and 1968; milder forms, in which the person was not shunned by the entire community, were applied with some regularity, especially to children. I became interested in this form of sanction after feeling its effects for having broken a taboo and failing to start the required month-long fast. I have never felt so totally isolated; the fast and the purification ritual, although most unpleasant, were a small price to pay in order to be restored to their good graces. I learned the language monolingually and all discussions with informants were in Cashinahua.

11

CONFLICT, CONTRADICTION,
AND THE STUDY OF RELIGION

Seth Leacock
University of Connecticut

Introduction

One of the most enduring legacies of British social anthropology is the notion that the way to study religion is to relate it to the social structure. Although this approach has been much criticized, it had the great advantage of focusing on behavior, and it effectively rescued the study of religion from an obsessive concern with belief. The British perspective dominated the anthropological study of religion for fifty years and became less prominent only when many anthropologists abandoned the study of social structure and returned to the study of culture.

In *Dialectics of Social Life*, Robert Murphy presents an incisive critique of British social anthropology, then concludes:

Society, as we have depicted it, is not as tidy and transparent as it is to the structural functionalists, but it is not chaotic either. Its order only lies at a deeper level (Murphy 1971: 240).

By order at a deeper level, Murphy is of course referring to the pattern of oppositions that structuralists suppose lies behind the obvious features of society, oppositions that Murphy and other dialecticians prefer to call "contradictions." One of the crucial issues in anthropology today is whether the search for an underlying order is improving our understanding of observable human behavior. Rather than debate this issue in the abstract, I will deal with a body of specific ethnographic data and consider some of the ways in which a search for "order at a deeper level" advances or retards an understanding of the behavior involved.

The ethnography to be considered deals with a possession religion, the Batuque, that I studied in Belém, Brazil in the 60s and 70s (Leacock and Leacock 1972). One striking feature of this religion is that it is filled with conflict. In effect, it is a religion of shamans, each claiming control over certain spirits and each attempting to sell supernatural services to clients. Although a variety of factors forces most members of the religion to serve as mediums in fairly stable congregations, the possibility of eventually becoming the leader of a congregation, and obtaining income from a number of clients, produces competition at every level of interaction. It is not very productive to approach the Batuque with the British assumptions that religions are orderly and are usually a major source of social solidarity. It is more useful to assume that all human institutions show only minimal order (just enough for inefficient functioning), that values and norms are always highly variable, and that conflict and ambiguity are the stuff of social life. Given these assumptions, the issue is whether it is still possible to make sense of the present organization of the Batuque by using a modified version of the British structuralist approach, or whether, if the Batuque is to be saved from appearing chaotic, an appeal must be made to some hidden, underlying order.

In the city of Belém, in northern Brazil, where the Batuque is practiced, there are several hundred Batuque centers. Each is headed by a man or woman who has usually founded the center and who is considered to be in complete control of it. The superordinate position of the leader is symbolized by the title assumed: *pai de santo* for males, *mãe de santo* for females. *Pai* and *mãe* mean "father" and "mother" in Portugese. *Santo* is a polysemic term that can mean "saint" or "spirit," but in the context of leadership is essentially meaningless. What is significant is that the leader of the congregation is called "father" or "mother," and the members of the congregation are called "son" and "daughter" (*filho* and *filha de santo*). As the terms suggest, at least ideally the leader of the group is expected to take a parental interest in the members, and if necessary to apply parental discipline.

One of the most obvious features of the Batuque is the competition among centers, or better, the competition among the leaders of each congregation. The basis of this competition is in large part economic. Since the people who participate in the Batuque as mediums are ordinarily much too poor to maintain the centers, the leaders must obtain income from outside sources in order to support themselves and the ceremonial activities of the group. Essentially, leaders perform services for clients, who respond by giving the leader presents of cash or goods. The services, of course, are based on control of the supernatural, and range from curing disease to bringing success in business ventures. Although there are large numbers of people from all walks of life who seek supernatural assistance from Batuque leaders, the fact is that clients are in short supply, and all Batuque leaders are in direct competition in attempting to attract them. Of course not all leaders are equally competitive, and the extent of antagonism between leaders varies greatly, but most leaders constantly criticize their rivals, spread malicious gossip about them, and make more or less strenuous efforts to enhance their own position vis-a-vis all other leaders.

Clients are attracted to a particular center in part by the reputation of the leader, but also by the reputation of the mediums who participate in the ceremonies. It therefore behooves a leader to encourage his or her followers to develop their mediumistic skills, and also, if possible, to attract mediums with experience and ability who may be attached to other centers. The attempt by one leader to lure away the mediums of another is the source of some of the most intense acrimony that occurs among rival leaders.

In addition to this conflict between leaders, there is also conflict within each congregation between the leader and some of the mediums. The possibility that a medium abandon one leader and join another is a constant source of friction between leader and follower, and this friction increases as a medium gains experience. In the beginning, as a medium has his or her first trance experiences, it is the leader who identifies the spirit and explains to the person what the obligations to the spirit are. But once the relationship between a person and a spirit is set up, the leader no longer has a role to play. The medium becomes completely independent, being possessed by the spirit on a regular basis and being perfectly able to carry out almost all necessary obligations. In time the medium usually begins "receiving" additional spirits, and in such cases usually identifies them without any outside assistance--it is the spirit itself that now defines the obligations that it expects. In most respects the equal of the leader, the medium may now decide to join another center, or, if endowed with the necessary ambition and resources, may attempt to found a new center.

One problem facing a leader, then, is how to ensure that the developed mediums remain loyal to the center. Needless to say, the medium must be shown consideration at all times, and the leader will often sponsor important ceremonies on the medium's behalf. Even so, disagreements frequently occur, and developed mediums often do change centers. When mediums remain in the same center for long periods, the leader is faced with the problem of how to inspire them to behave in ways that will enhance the reputaton of the center. This means essentially that the mediums must attend ceremonies, must purchase new costumes periodically, must endure long involved rituals, and most importanly, must rapidly develop their mediumistic abilities. But the leader has few sanctions that can be applied, and even beginning mediums may desert the center if too much pressure is put on them. Leaders constantly complain about how recalcitrant their followers are, and it seems clear that their frustration arises in large part from their helplessness.

If leaders frequently complain about their followers, the reverse is also true. Leaders are usually charged with exploiting their followers, or being inconsiderate of them. Exploitation occurs in the form of exorbitant charges for initiation and other rituals, although this would occur only in a large, established center--a beginning leader would not dare raise funds in this way. Leaders are considered to be inconsiderate if they require the mediums to purchase new costumes too frequently, or demand their participation in too many ceremonies.

In addition to competition among leaders, and to conflict between leaders and followers, there is also both competition and conflict among the mediums attached to the same center. However, in this case the range of variation is much greater. The most intense competition is among developed mediums, especially those who are on the verge of attempting to found their own centers. Such mediums are constantly attempting to enhance their reputations, and they often try to do so by denigrating the ability of others. Beginning mediums, on the other hand, who have only a confused idea of what is happening to them, are hardly in a position to compete. Then there is a middle group. Many mediums, even after years of experience, find it difficult to take the role of a spirit. They may be able to dance to some extent, to sing a few songs, or even to give mumbled and inarticulate consultations. But they never gain the expertise that characterizes the developed medium, and they never escape dependence on a leader (who is often considered to be responsible for their inability to perform because of a botched initiation). Such mediums are considered to be full-fledged members of the religion, and they take part in all important rituals, but since they cannot take the role of the spirit well enough to do services for clients, they have no real prospects as far as becoming a leader is concerned. Depending on the center, perhaps one-half to two-thirds of the mediums are either beginners or they have learning disabilities of the sort just described. Competition is relatively limited among this part of the membership.

During public ceremonies there are few signs of overt conflict among the mediums, but the status hierarchy in the center is readily discernable. The leader, whether man or woman, is always shown the greatest deference, usually goes into trance first, and is expected to receive the most important spirits. But as the ceremony continues it becomes apparent that there are other mediums present whose prestige rivals that of the leader. When such mediums go into trance, everyone lines up to greet their spirit, just as they do for the leader. When the leader is absent temporarily, it is the mediums whose spirits have received the most deference who lead the singing and direct the dancing. It sometimes happens that two mediums with high prestige will engage in a kind of contest to see who will lead. The contest is decided by the drummers and other mediums, who follow the lead of one medium, and drown out the other.

In contrast, when a medium with low prestige goes into trance, no one may pay any attention. Such mediums may actually fall on the floor as they enter trance because no one bothers to catch them (when entering trance most mediums fall backward, but they are either caught by other mediums or manage to regain their balance). If no one notices the medium go into trance, the ceremony continues without the customary pause to allow the spirit to identify itself. Although the person in trance may be so dissociated that he or she does not realize that a snub has occurred, women sometimes burst into tears when they go into trance and are completely ignored by the other mediums.

Outside the ceremonial context, developed mediums frequently criticize one another and often express doubts about the trance experiences of their friends as well as their rivals. Only very rarely is it suggested that a medium pretends to be possessed; the more common and insidious assertion is that the medium was actually possessed by a spirit other than the one supposedly present. This kind of attack is often made by a medium who claims to be the only member of the group to receive a particular spirit. To maintain her exclusivity, she claims that her rival was possessed by an imposter--a lower status spirit or even a demon. In making this kind of interpretation, a medium is assuming the position of a leader, since it is usually the prerogative of the leader to identify spirits. Such conflicts sometimes come into focus when two mediums claim to be possessed by the same spirit during a ceremony. Supposedly the issue of which medium is really possessed by the spirit is resolved by an ordeal-- the women are said to put their hands in boiling oil and the one with the spirit is not harmed.

Competition among mediums is directly related to the aspirations which most mediums have of someday becoming the leader of their own center, and competition is most acute among those mediums with realistic aspirations. Most mediums, however, while wistfully expressing the hope that someday, somehow, they might have their own center, do very little to turn this hope into reality. Almost all developed mediums do make the services of their spirit available to their family, friends, and neighbors. Usually one day a week is set aside for the medium to go into trance in the home, and anyone in the neighborhood may bring a problem for the spirit to solve. If a medium is unusually successful in solving problems and begins to attract a regular following, the stage is set for larger and larger gatherings and eventually the opening of a center. Most mediums however, even the most developed, never get beyond the weekly service and a few impoverished neighbors as clients. Only a few ever open their own center, and fewer still manage to attract enough clients to support themselves completely from their religious activities.

In this litany of conflict and competition, we come finally to the lowest possible level--the competition that is sometimes thought to take place between the several spirits that a medium is thought to receives. In the ordinary course of events, as a medium has more and more experience, he or she is expected to receive more and more spirits. As will be pointed out shortly, the spirits that are thought to possess people are of two kinds--serious and playful. An experienced medium usually claims to receive at least two spirits, one of each kind. During public ceremonies the serious spirit comes first, takes part in serious rituals, then departs. For the remainder of the ceremony the medium is possessed by a playful spirit and usually smokes cigars, drinks rum and has a good

184

time. Now it sometimes happens that the relationship between these spirits is conceptualized as including a certain amount of competition. When a woman is possessed by her playful spirit, for example, it may make derogatory remarks about her serious spirit. Moreover, since any present given to a medium is always specifically intended for a certain spirit, one of the spirits may become upset if the other spirit monopolizes all the presents. Some mediums have the problem that one spirit hogs the spotlight during public ceremonies. In other words, every time the medium goes into trance, the same spirit appears. This is an undesirable situation, because such spirits are usually playful spirits, and they are thought to be usurping the position of other more powerful spirits that the medium has received in the past and ought to receive again as part of the human-spirit contract. Again the medium's body is seen as the arena in which a struggle between spirits takes place.

As this brief summary indicates, the Batuque is a religion in which conflict and competition occur at every level--between leaders, between leaders and followers, between mediums generally, and sometimes even between spirits. There is another kind of conflict as well, which can be conceptualized as a conflict between women and men. Traditionally, although probably never actually, the Batuque was a religion of women. Today the proportion of women to men is approximately three to one. The tension between female mediums and male mediums does not arise, however, from the mere presence of men, but from the widespread belief that male mediums are homosexual. Since homosexuality is considered to be immoral, many women resent the presence of immoral men in the religion. The husbands of these women resent it even more and often pressure their wives to choose centers where few men are involved, and where the leaders are women. Leaders of either sex must be concerned with the number of men associated with their centers, because too many men gives a center a bad reputation as a hangout for homosexuals, and this may drive away clients.

In spite of the conflicts that have just been described, the Batuque is flourishing. Moreover, there is no indication that the conflicts are declining in intensity, nor that some kind of new synthesis is about to appear. Given the existence of these conflicts, some overt, some less so, the question arises as to whether any of them might be considered to be the kind of "contradiction" that Murphy would have us look for as part of the dialectical approach. This is not an easy question to answer, since, as one of the arch-critics of dialectics puts it, "The central weakness of dialectical epistemology is the lack of operational instructions for identifying causally decisive negations" (Harris 1979b: 145). Using one of Murphy's definitions, none of the above mentioned conflicts would be considered contradictions, since the opposed entities ". . .do not generate each other, they do not cut against each other, they do not clash, nor do they pass into each other in the process of being transformed into something else" (Murphy 1971: 175). On the other hand, in terms of a much looser definition that Murphy uses repeatedly, namely, that a contradiction exists when behavior and norms are not congruent, several of the conflicts found in the Batuque might qualify, especially the conflict between leader and follower, and the conflict between women and men. A major difficulty in considering the conflicts described as "contradictions" might be that they are part of the superficial, observable aspects of social life and not part of an underlying, deeper reality. On the other hand, since the boundary between "superficial" and "underlying" is not easy to locate, rather than argue fruitlessly about how best to conceptualize the conflicts I have identified, I will arbitrarily identify the two conflicts listed above as "contradictions." I will then argue that it is simpler to explain them in terms of observable factors outside the Batuque rather than in terms of some hidden, internal dynamic. Before proceeding with the argument, however, I need to describe in more detail some features of the Batuque belief system.

One point to be stressed at the outset is that most of the conflicts in the Batuque seem to be completely divorced from the ideology[1]. In fact, Batuque ideology recognizes only one likely conflict, the confrontation between spirit and human in those cases when a person refuses to become a medium. The basic belief about spirits is that there are a group of non-Christian spirits, the *encantados*, that like to possess the human body and participate in ceremonies. These spirits are part of the same supernatural universe as the Christian supernaturals, but unlike God, the Virgin, and the saints, who are thought of as being very distant and difficult to contact, the *encantados* are expected to constantly interfere in human life. Moreover, the spirit always makes the first move, and if a person has fainting fits, or sees visions, or even has a long series of misfortunes, the interpretation is that a spirit is seeking contact but is being rebuffed. If a Batuque leader is consulted, the ready advice is for the person to join the cult center and be prepared as a medium. If the potential medium resists, it is expected that the spirit will not only make life intolerable but will eventually kill the person involved.

Once a person has agreed to become a medium, i.e., to allow the spirit to enter his or her body and participate in ceremonies, most of the person's difficulties are thought to be over. The spirit is expected to look out for the medium's welfare and to take care of health and financial problems. However, Batuque ideology is strictly this-worldly and provides a ready explanation for the fact that mediums never lead carefree lives, regardless of how many spirits are supposedly looking out for them. Illness, accidents, unemployment, desertion, are all explained as punishment by the spirit for failing to properly carry out certain ritual obligations. Essentially, a perspective develops in which mediums attribute any good thing that happens to them to the support of the spirits, and any bad thing that happens to them to punishment by the same spirits.

Once a medium has joined a center, the expected relationships with other mediums are not clearly defined. Members of the congregation are considered to be "brothers" and "sisters," as might be expected (and in some centers are urged to avoid romantic relationships with one another), but this particular use of kinship terms has very little significance, and generally among mediums attached to the same center only the common courtesy of the mundane world is expected, except in cases where friendships develop.

As was noted above, one possible "contradiction" in the Batuque relates to the relationship between the leader of a Batuque center and the mediums that make up the congregation. When discussing the relationship, Batuque members will insist that leaders should be concerned with their followers' welfare, and that followers should be loyal and obedient to their leader. At the same time, leaders are accused of exploiting their followers, and followers are constantly asserting their independence. And there are also several widely held beliefs that seem to indicate a hostile relationship rather that a supportive one. For example, it is often remarked that leaders never teach their followers very much, and certainly not everything they know. Above all, they do not teach their followers any sorcery, for fear that they will be the target of their pupils' new found skill. There is another belief to the effect that if a leader is forewarned of impending death, one of the mediums of the center can be substituted to die in the leader's place--this means that a leader who lives to an advanced age is assumed to have achieved such longevity only at the expense of several followers. It would seem, therefore, that the conflict between leaders and followers is at least implicitly recognized in certain beliefs, even though the generally accepted norms emphasize support and obedience. In any case, as far as leaders and followers are concerned, the ideology is largely contrary to observed patterns of interaction, and we seem to have a "contradiction," at least in terms of Murphy's definition.

It is quite striking that Batuque ideology in effect denies the possibility of the conflict between women and men that arises because of the stigma attached to homosexuality. In the first place, it should be clear from the earlier discussion of beliefs about how spirits approach people that if a man is chosen by a spirit to be its medium, the man obviously has no choice but to become a medium. Since being a medium requires participation in public ceremonies, a man clearly must be allowed to dance alongside the women mediums. In the second place, whether or not a man is homosexual is thought to be a matter of indifference to the spirits. As long as a medium, whether male or female, fulfills his or her obligations to the spirit, the other aspects of the medium's life are considered to be irrelevant. The spirit is therefore thought to be unconcerned with the sex life of a male medium, as long as the medium observes the usual taboos regarding sexual activities before public ceremonies. If there are negative attitudes toward male mediums, then, or homosexuality, such attitudes must come from outside the Batuque, not from inside. And again there would seem to be a contradiction between the norms which specify how male mediums should be treated, and how in fact they are treated.

A possible source of insights into the underlying structure of the Batuque is the pantheon. There are hundreds of spirits, organized in several different ways. It should be noted, however, that the way the spirits are organized does not seem to reflect some basic logic of the human mind, but rather reflects certain features of Brazilian society. There are, for example, male spirits and female spirits, with twice as many male spirits as female. This majority of male spirits would seem to be expectable in a male dominated society in which most of the Christian supernaturals are male. There are high status spirits, the *senhores*, of both sexes, and low status spirits, the *caboclos*, of both sexes. As was noted earlier, these two kinds of spirits may sometimes be conceived of as being in competition within the same medium, but the primary significance of the distinction is that the high status spirits are expected to perform important services for the medium, and for clients, while the low status spirits are primarily hedonists and possess the medium in order to dance, drink rum, and enjoy themselves. This basic dichotomy of spirits in terms of status seems to be a direct reflection of the Brazilian class system, and indeed the terms *senhor* and *caboclo* are commonly used to refer to members of the upper and lower classes, respectively. The spirits are also organized into families, most families consisting of spirits of both statuses and both sexes. There are also a number of evil spirits, the *exus*, but these are significant only in certain ritual situations and in the practice of sorcery. These also come male and female, but they are not part of the status system.[2]

The one obvious opposition in the pantheon is that between high status spirits and low status spirits. However, even in this case these spirits are complementary, as well as opposed, since they come at different times, take part in different activities, and in effect serve different functions. There is no emphasis on the opposition of good and evil spirits, and sorcery is associated with some of the low status spirits as well as with the demons. There is no obvious opposition between male spirits and female spirits, nor between the heads of families and their children (although the family head is always a high status spirit, while the children are often low status). Except for the oppositions noted, I am unable to find any other dichotomies that might give clues to an underlying order.

Although both male and female mediums, at least those with some experience, receive spirits of all kinds--male, female, high status, low status, etc.--the relationship between gender of medium and gender of spirit is not completely random. There is good evidence, for example, that women are more commonly possesed by male spirits, and that they prefer to receive male spirits. This can be in part inferred from the fact that for a large majority of female mediums, the "chief" spirit (the spirit thought to be most responsibe for the medium's well-being) is a high status male spirit. Although the ways in which chief spirits are chosen is quite complex, and often involves the intervention of a leader, it is certainly not surprising that in a male dominated society in which the major Christian supernaturals are male, women would feel that being possessed by a high status male spirit would maximize their status with reference to other mediums and clients.[3] On the other hand, although the data are less extensive, it would appear that women receive female playful spirits about as frequently as male ones.

There is also apparently an affinity between some homosexual male mediums and female spirits, but the evidence is somewhat limited. Of 34 male mediums that I interviewed, 25 said that their chief spirit was male, not female. However, I did not determine which of these men were homosexual. A later study by Fry (1982), during which he interviewed some of the same men that I did and in the process determined that a number of them were avowed homosexuals, suggests that in fact homosexual male mediums feel a much closer affinity with female spirits, regardless of who their chief spirit may be. Being possessed by a female spirit was described by the men involved as being more satisfying because it gave the medium a chance to express feminine tendencies, to show off in front of other homosexual mediums, and sometimes to attract sexual partners (Fry 1982: 72). It might be noted in passing that the relationships between gender of medium and gender of spirit do not contain any surprises, nor do they suggest any underlying oppositions.

As this brief survey indicates, there do not seem to be any major oppositions in Batuque ideology that would serve as templates for the conflicts that are found in the behavior patterns of Batuque members. In any case, it is much simpler to relate the conflicts based on economic competition and homosexuality to factors outside the ideology than to attempt to find an underlying set of oppositions within it. The possibility that an indiviual can derive income from performing supernatural services would seem to be dependent on a set of beliefs found in the larger community in which the Batuque is practiced, and the major source of competition, a shortage of clients, is completely unrelated to Batuque beliefs. It is difficult to imagine how a structuralist analysis, or at least one that was limited to Batuque ideology, could ever produce a meaningful interpretation of the behavior of Batuque mediums.

The attitudes centering around homosexuality represent the best example of the significance of external values in influencing the behavior of Batuque members. Although in some respects the general Brazilian attitude toward homosexuals is relatively liberal, and male transvestites have a prominent role in Carnaval, in Belém the activities of male homosexuals are still considered to be immoral, sinful, and basically ridiculous. Since it is widely believed that all male Batuque mediums are homosexual, a Batuque center in which there are a large number of men is assumed to be a gathering place for homosexuals, and it will be avoided by both mediums and clients who may have strong feelings regarding homosexual behavior.

The belief that all male mediums are homosexual is undoubtedly based in part on the observation of some male mediums in trance, since it is not uncommon for men to ostentatiously adopt feminine mannerisms when they impersonate female spirits. But the mere participation of men in the public ceremony raises questions, since after all the men wear costumes, dance with a large group of women, and wait passively for a spirit to enter their bodies. This is not appropriate behavior for a Brazilian heterosexual male, who is expected to conform to the basic Latin *macho* ideal.

Although female Batuque mediums share most of the values of the larger community regarding homosexuality, they must constantly interact with reputed homosexuals, since one-fourth of all mediums are male, and one-half of all leaders are male. Women frequently express contempt for homosexual men and constantly complain that too many men participate in ceremonies. At the same time they readily interact with male mediums during public performances and some seek out known homosexuals to be their religious leaders. In the latter case the women are apparently attracted by the personality, leadership qualities, and supernatural potency of the men involved--although it is also possible that some women appreciate a homosexual leader because he does not represent the sexual threat that Brazilian males in positions of authority sometimes become. What is involved, then, as far as female mediums are concerned, is the holding of contradictory values, without undue strain and without any apparent resolution, as part of the perpetual series of compromises that characterizes all social life.

The number of male mediums participating in ceremonies varies greatly among centers. In a few centers no men at all participate, but it seems likely that this is a temporary condition due to special circumstances. In a few centers the number of men approaches the number of women. In all centers, however, the basic conflict remains unresolved. Whereas male mediums must be allowed to receive their spirits in public, the presence of male mediums gives the center a bad reputation. When speaking to outsiders, leaders always play down the number of male mediums associated with their centers and often insist that the men involved are of good character. In any case, the number of male mediums is clearly limited by the stigma attached to male mediumship, and it is apparently this stigma as well which accounts for the fact that most male mediums are relatively young. Most men who become Batuque mediums either become leaders, or they abandon the religion before they reach middle age.

In spite of the prominence of homosexual males, especially as leaders, it should not be supposed that heterosexual males are excluded from participation in the Batuque. Two large centers in Belém were headed by men who were not only married, but who had a reputation for having affairs with women attached to their center. There are several ways to avoid the stigma attached to male mediumship. Some men never wear a costume or dance during the beginning phases of a ceremony, but serve as drummers or simply sit in the audience until they are "seized" by their spirit. Another role available to men that carries no implication of homosexuality is that of curer. Although curing as a specialty is considered to be peripheral to the Batuque, it involves the same kind of behavior--going into trance and taking the role of a spirit. For men who find trance congenial, who believe that being a medium will benefit their lives, but who are put off by the prospect of associating with or being identified with the homosexual men found in the centers, being a curer is one solution.

Although there are female homosexuals in the Batuque, they attract much less attention than male homosexuals, and there is no general conception in the surrounding community that all female mediums are homosexual. The fact that most female mediums have husbands (or male companions) and children clearly promotes the assumption that they are not sexually abnormal. Moreover, there is clearly a double standard operating, since no significance is attached to the obvious affinity between female mediums and male spirits, nor to the way in which women in trance very often speak in a deep voice, act in a brusque, assertive and pompous manner, and in other ways take a masculine role. No stigma whatsoever is attached to such behavior, which is seen as quite appropriate. Women are assumed to be homosexual only if they seem to have female sexual partners. The reputation of a center does not seem to suffer, regardless of how many female homosexuals are associated with it.

The other values from the outside community that influence the behavior of Batuque members are derived from the Catholic Church and deal essentially with the definition of "religion." Although the differences between the Catholic Mass and a Batuque ceremony, in which mediums are supposedly possessed by non-Christian spirits, drink rum, and dance all night, do not have to be labored, in a number of ways the influence of Catholic ritual is obvious. And this is not surprising, because most of the Batuque mediums have grown up in the Catholic Church, and many remain active members all their lives. In fact, the only teaching of the Church that Batuque members do not accept is the assertion by the priests that Batuque spirits are evil spirits and it is sinful to contact them. Moreover, a direct link is made between Batuque spirits and the Catholic saints by associating each spirit with a saint, maintaining that the spirit "adores" the saint, and using the image of the saint to represent both the Christian and the Batuque supernatural. The influence of Catholic models is quite prominent in Batuque ceremonies. In most centers the public ceremony begins with a Catholic prayer in honor of the saint associated with the spirit being feted. The dancing begins in front of an altar decked with images of saints, and burning candles and incense are a part of every ritual.

In a more general way overall structure of the Batuque ceremony is modeled after a Brazilian Catholic festival, especially a rural Saints' Day celebration, which typically contains two phases--a religious ritual and a largely secular period of festivity. In the ideal Batuque ceremony the first few hours are devoted to the serious, high status spirits, and to well-organized rituals under the tight control of the leader, while after midnight the playful spirits arrive and a party-like atmosphere develops. Moreover, just as the rural Catholic dance is not expected to degenerate into a drunken brawl, so there are limits to the kind of behavior that is acceptable during a Batuque ceremony.

According to Batuque theology, it is the spirit that drinks and not the medium, and mediums are not expected to show signs of intoxication (or have a hangover the next day). The "religious" character of the ceremony is seriously compromised if too many of the mediums are drinking heavily. Most leaders readily admit that excessive drinking is a serious problem, and perhaps the most common way for a leader to attack his rivals is to claim that too much drinking occurs in the other centers.

In these various ways community pressures draw boundaries which define the acceptable ceremony and "religious" behavior. However, community pressures are largely negative, condemning behavior that is considered immoral, like homosexuality, or non-religious, like drunken frivolity. There are other factors which have a more positive effect in molding the particular features of the Batuque. One of these is competition, especially the intense competiton that occurs among beginning leaders, which seems clearly to promote orthodoxy. In order to attract a following, and eventually clients, the aspiring leader must demonstrate that he or she is competent in handling mediums, and in conducting ceremonies. In order to be accepted as knowledgeable, the aspiring leader has no choice but to adopt the practices of the established leaders.[4]

Among other factors influencing orthodoxy, one of the most important is the nature of the trance experience itself. As was noted earlier, mediums in trance seem rarely to be completely dissociated. Mediums watch one another very closely and are always ready to seize upon some unexpected (i.e., unorthodox) behavior as a sign that some fraudulent spirit has arrived under an assumed name. If a medium in trance does behave in an unorthodox fashion, doing or saying things that are not appropriate to the spirit supposedly present, the medium is apparently never enough dissociated that he or she does not realize that the other mediums are expressing disapproval. For most mediums, certainly, the sense of being the chosen vehicle of a supernatural being does not sustain them in aberrant behavior. The result is that trance behavior, at least among developed mediums, tends to be remarkably similar.

Most of the factors that favor orthodoxy are effective because in spite of its shamanistic ideology, the Batuque is a religion in which great stress is placed on being a shaman in public. The basic contract between a spirit and a human requires that the spirit be allowed to use the human body in front of an audience--and the larger the better. Although there are hundreds of very small centers in Belém where beginning leaders shepherd a handful of mediums through the intricacies of trance, this is always considered a stepping stone to something bigger and more dramatic. Almost all developed mediums receive their spirits in their homes, often on a regular basis, but it is generally accepted that every medium must periodically participate in a public ceremony. There is a common convention, in fact, that if a medium does not allow his or her spirits to dance in public every two weeks or so, the spirits will make the medium ill. This means that even those mediums who have become independent of any leader must maintain ties with some center in order to be welcome to participate in ceremonies. Thus at any given point in time almost all mediums are associated with one center or another, and although membership may be temporary, ties develop that convert a gaggle of shamans into some kind of congregation. And it is within this congregation, and during the cycle of public ceremonies, that enough beliefs and values come to be shared that we can identify something that can reasonably be called the Batuque religion.

Conclusions

In this paper I have questioned the usefulness of either a structuralist or a dialectical approach in explaining the observed features of a specific religion, the Batuque. In particular, I have suggested that anyone undertaking a structuralist analysis that concentrated on Batuque ideology would be hard put to account for most of the conflicts that characterize interaction in this religion and would be completely nonplussed by the relative absence of men. Assuming that the goal of anthropology is to explain human behavior, it is difficult not to agree with Murphy that "The study of the structure of signs or mental images independent of human activity leads to sterility" (Murphy 1971: 205).

In taking issue with the usefulness of the notion of "contradiction" and the conception that there is an internal dynamic operating that resolves contradictions and transforms them into something new, I have argued essentially that several contradictions that can be identified in the Batuque can more easily be explained in terms of outside factors than in terms of some internal process.[5] The conflict between Batuque leaders and some of the mediums in their congregations seems to be based on the possibility of economic gain and an ultimate shortage of clients, while it is a set of values from the outside community relating to homosexuality that results in conflict between female and male mediums. There is also no evidence, as far as I can determine, that any of the conflicts in the Batuque are being resolved by some inevitable process of transformation.

A more traditional analysis of the Batuque, based in part on British structuralism, which situates the religion in a specific community, considers its history, and even takes into account some psychological variables, seems to provide a better understanding of its characteristics. The conflicts that are found at every level of interaction can readily be traced to a social context in which large numbers of desperately poor people have the prospect of converting control over the supernatural into cash. Since only a few individuals ever make a living as mediums, however, the conflicts are perhaps best attributed to competition for prestige, status, and finally income. The Batuque is also practiced in a community where negative attitudes toward homosexuality are widespread, and the resultant stigma attached to male mediumship has had an important role in restricting the number of males in the religion, as well as creating additional conflicts. Another external source of influence is the Catholic Church, which has provided models for rituals and the basic organization of ceremonies.

Although many early studies of Afro-Brazilian religions like the Batuque stressed historical background and African roots, the Batuque is essentially a modern religion that is well adapted to Brazilian society. Some of the basic beliefs about spirits, including the crucial conception that spirits like to dance in public spectacles, are probably of African origin, but the pantheon itself has been greatly modified, and as was noted, now faithfully reflects the Brazilian class system. In the melange of old and new, it might also be suspected that whatever underlying structures there might once have been in the belief system would have been considerably garbled.

There are also features in the Batuque that can only be explained in terms of certain psychological variables. The Batuque is a possession religion, and there is no question that trance is more congenial to some individuals than to others. This limits the number of potential leaders, since only some individuals can perform well enough while in trance to take the role of leader. Moreover, the organization of the religion into congregations is affected, since congregations are composed in large part of mediums who because of psychological and other disabilities are never likely to open centers of their own.

To return to the quote from Murphy with which I began, it seems clear that the Batuque religion, filled with conflict, composed of evanescent congregations, and headed by entrepreneurs, is not a "tidy and transparent" institution, but it is also not chaotic. I would contend that the analysis I have presented makes the basic organization (structure) of the religion reasonably understandable, and that an assumption of "order at a deeper level" is neither necessary nor desirable.

FOOTNOTES

[1] The beliefs held by Batuque members are extremely varied, but certainly a solid majority of Batuque members would subscribe to the beliefs that I call their "ideology."

[2] A more detailed description of the Batuque pantheon can be found in S. and R. Leacock (1972).

[3] This association of female mediums and male spirits would seem to support Lewis' (1971) interpretation of religions like the Batuque as being based on a desire by downtrodden women for enhanced status. However, merely being possessed by a spirit, any spirit, does very little for a woman's status. Shy and diffident women tend to be shy and diffident as spirits, whereas those women who run their households, dominate their spouses, and have the respect of their neighbors are the most successful mediums. In other words, women bring their status to the religion as much as deriving their status from it.

[4] A similar relationship between competition and orthodoxy was found by Glazier (1983) in his study of the Spiritual Baptists in Trinidad.

In order to make this paper of manageable length, I have of course greatly oversimplified the concept of "contradiction" and have simply ignored the point stressed by E. Leacock (1972), among others, that if a question arises about whether a variable is external or internal, all the dialectician has to do is raise the level of abstraction until everything is internal. This procedure obviously makes the distinction meaningless.

12

FEMALE CIRCUMCISION IN AFRICA:
THE DIALECTICS OF EQUALITY

Elliott P. Skinner
Columbia University

> Culture and society must, of course, always take account of
> human biology, but they do so in complex ways. The distinctive
> characteristics of culture is that it transcends nature; but this does
> not mean that it has left it behind -- rather, it has turned it
> upside down.
>
> Robert F. Murphy (1977)

Female circumcision or clitoridectomy, called by the Mossi, the
Bongo, is another of the not too subtle mechanism of Mossi women to
challenge the superiority of men. This was the thought that flashed
through my mind, as I watched with amazement, the quiet pride of the
women and girls performing the rituals of the graduation ceremonies of
their own Bongo. Here were women doing things that they usually never
did, and more importantly, should not have been doing. They had pro-
cured the drums from men and, much to my surprise and their amuse-
ment, were beating them. Where had they learned? Oh yes! They must
have practiced these rhythms while pounding millet and sorghum in their
mortars. Inexplicable was the source of their knowledge of the songs and
dances of the Bongo which were allegedly the sole province of males, but
which they performed equally well. True, I had learned both the dances
and songs of the Bongo during my numerous visits to the circumcision
lodge, but these female graduates did them better than I ever did. Surely
some Delilah had tricked a Samson who had then revealed the secrets of
arrogant men. During the Bongo ceremony, Mossi women were showing
to the men publicly, that they knew male secrets, and moreover, these
were not important after all.

The dialectics of social life, especially those involved in the
endeavor of women to assert their equality with men, has been a major
theme in the anthropology of Robert F. Murphy. In his now classic article, "Social Distance and the Veil," he suggested that one of "the great

human dilemmas ... derives from the premise that the concept of the self is bestowed upon us by society, and through social interaction." (1964b:1259) According to him, the well-mannered Tuareg man wears the veil almost all the time. Importantly, "*it is brought up to the eyes before women or prestigeful persons, while it is a sign of familiarity when it is lowered.*" (italics his) Significantly, the highly egalitarian Tuareg women do not normally veil themselves. We are told that "in fact, women only pull their shawls across the lower parts of their faces when expressing reserve and modesty." (*Ibid.*:1264)[1]

In view of the practice of male veiling among the Tuareg, what should one make of the charges that the veiling seen among Middle Eastern women is largely due to males' jealously guarding the beauty and purity of females? Those who believe that Middle Eastern men could ever have restrained the will of the women, have never read *The Book of the Thousand Nights and a Night*, or speculated on what took place in the perfumed garden of Allah! Is it not possible that the women themselves were responsible for initiating the use of the veil? No one knows for sure why Tuareg men veil and why North African and Middle Eastern women do, and whether there is any historical relationship between the two customs. Why Tuareg women did not use the veil in the same way as did the men may well have been due to their having a great deal of equality with males in this society. In most societies however, women have been relegated to an inferior position beneath men, and in many cases have used all types of stratagems in the attempt to overcome what they considered to be grave social disabilities. Therefore, female activities have often carried the added socio-psychological baggage of being used to assert their equality with males. In a number of cases, their premise of equality has involved attempting to become as male as possible, and they often did not care whether this pleased the males or not. The dialectic here is that women or other subordinate groups, faced with the often calculated indifference of their social superiors at attempts to gain equality, often accused the latter of being responsible for their behavior in the first place. In social structural terms this is often correct.

Both Robert and Yolanda dropped the veil in *Women of the Forest*, to reveal that among the Mundurucu the women were often the original dialecticians. Here they pointed out that women never really lost the knowledge about the *karoko*, the sacred and now secret trumpets, the supposed symbols of wisdom and male ascendancy, which men bragged about having purloined from them (Murphy & Murphy 1974:87ff). Through the employment of elaborate myths and symbols, Mundurucu males assert their superiority over the female. The woman who openly challenges male superiority is gang-raped, a vicious use of the collective male phallus to keep women in line. Yet the Murphys assert that the vaunted superiority of the Mundurucu male is fragile, and that the men are highly vulnerable. The one universal and existential flaw that Mundurucu males share with other men is that "they are born of women, nurtured and loved by women, protected and dominated by women, yet must become men." (*Ibid.*:226) Robert and Yolanda did acknowledge, and stress that "the fundamental ontological differences between the sexes -- conditions of simple *being* -- based in the first instance on anatomical distinctions [are] ... not immediately a part of them." (*Ibid.*:232) Nevertheless, it is a fact that when either males or females attempt to acquire the status of the other, they often attempt to manipulate biology in order to do so.

The subject of male circumcision and female clitoridectomy and infibulation in African societies has been the source of great speculation and controversy, primarily because it involves the "fundamental ontological differences between the sexes -- conditions of simple *being* -- based in the first instance on anatomical distinctions" and what flows from these. Questions raised have been: 1. Are these operations cruel? 2. Do they have anything to do with sex? 3. Do they reveal anything about the relative merits of various cultures' sexual sensibilities? and 4. Do male and female versions of the operations differ with regard to the answers to questions 1 and 2? Some anthropologists and some non-anthropologists have already strong views on these questions.

Fran P. Hosken discussing "Genital Mutilation in Africa," severely criticized those "Anthropologists (mostly men) who have studied African traditions have done no service to women by utterly disregarding women's health while they attribute 'cultural values' to such damaging traditions as excision and infibulation." Considering these practices "deleterious to health and indeed dangerous," Hosken lamented that many African groups "subject their female children to genital mutilation for a multitude of 'reasons,' many of which conflict and all of which are based on total ignorance concerning reproduction." She wondered aloud whether it was really in the interest of such populations "that such damaging myths are perpetuated under the cloak of silence and are praised as 'culture' in the literature? I think not. The time has come to face the facts." (Hoskin 1976:6). Hosken is tired of, and angry about those "explanations" of men and of what she calls "brain-washed women" who attribute clitoridectomy "to the fear of female sexuality," and the need to "prevent adultery." (*Ibid.*)

Simon D. Messing, an applied anthropologist, feels that he and his colleagues "cannot evade the issue of such a serious and widespread problem as genital mutilation of females, if they are concerned with public health ... they should not leave the burden of this task entirely on the shoulders of radical feminists -- and the latter in turn should welcome our cooperation." (Messing 1980:296)

Neither the radical feminists nor the anthropologists have considered the possibility that in the frequent dialectics that we find in social life, female circumcision might well be one of the numerous ways in which women challenge the vaunted superiority of men. In an article dealing with women as spirit mediums in East Africa, entitled: "Rebels or Status Seekers?" Iris Berger cited innumerable cases of women who take over the status of men during important rituals.[2] She cites the case of female initiates among the Buha "who dress as their spirits say that they are no longer men, and they allow themselves many insults and even dishonest actions that they would not permit themselves in a normal state." (1976:172) Robin Horton reporting on this phenomenon among the Kalabari of Eastern Nigeria remarked:

> The fully-developed complex of possession roles typically figures a man: not just an ordinary man, but a man of wealth, power, and status. In adopting this complex of roles a woman is enabled, from time to time, really to 'be' what she has always yearned to be but never can be in ordinary normal life. (Horton 1969)

The origin of the practice of circumcision among human beings is lost to us. It is allegedly portrayed on the walls of the tombs of dead Pharaohs, but whether the Nefretitis or the Ikhnatons of the past practiced this ritual is unknown. These women may have done so since they participated jointly with their consorts in the governance of ancient Egypt during many dynasties. On the other hand, their equality or near equality with men, might have made this ritual unnecessary, that is, if it served the function of gaining them equality to the men. Understandably the frescoes do not reveal this secret. Also unknown is whether circumcision is an ancient pan-African trait-complex or whether it diffused to other African societies from ancient Egypt. Its distribution is fairly widespread in the northern part of the African continent, and parts of the east and west, but not too common in central and southern Africa.

Given the contemporary controversy surrounding "female" circumcision (really an interesting misnomer), it is generally ignored that circumcision is predominantly a "male" ritual. Many well-known ancient peoples, such as the Hebrews (who probably adopted this ritual in ancient Egypt as they borrowed other interesting aspects of that culture) limited circumcision to males. The same thing is true for many African populations. As far as I can ascertain, there is not a single African society in which female circumcision exists without its male counterpart. The reasons for this are as intriguing as they are germane to this article.

Since the controversy concerning circumcision and clitoridectomy is usually linked to sexual activities and, according to Gray, these rituals are usually performed at about puberty, (1924) it is important to note that the time of circumcision for males is variable. Judging from the Hebraic practice, infant male circumcision may also have been characteristic of the early Egyptians. Due in part to the influence of contemporary Jews, this practice is now common among white Christians and other ethnic groups in the United States of America. In contrast, circumcision in most of Africa is part of the initiation rituals of puberty. One of the few exceptions is among the Galla people of Ethiopia where circumcision is part of the rituals in the last grade of their complicated Gada age-grade system. Instead of being a preparation for marriage and the begetting of children, circumcision comes at a point where Galla men have abandoned sexual relations, and prepare themselves for the roles of priests and ancestors.

Initiation ceremonies preparatory to marriage, sexual relations, and the creation of families, are widespread in African societies, but are not necessarily linked to either circumcision or clitoridectomy. Mbiti is substantially correct when he tells us that: "The initiation of the young is one of the key moments in the rhythm of individual life, which is also the rhythm of the corporate group of which the individual is a part. What happens to the single youth happens corporately to the parents, the relatives, the neighbors and the living-dead." (1970:158) Characteristic of this *rite de passage* is the customary withdrawal of the initiates from the world of people; their education into the knowledge and lore of their societies; and their subjection to a great deal of physical pain and other hardships.

In the case of the Nuer, that classic African people, there was no circumcision, but according to Evans-Pritchard almost all young boys are "initiated from boyhood to manhood by a very severe operation (*gar*). Their brows are cut to the bone with a small knife, in six long cuts from ear to ear. The scars remain for life, and it is said that marks can be detected on the skulls of dead men." Despite this ordeal, however, young boys whose fathers refused them permission to be initiated, "would run away to the home of a kinsman and the father would be humiliated." (1940:249) As far as it is known, Nuer females were not initiated and subjected to the *gar*, but "by analogy" were incorporated into the age-sets of the males of their generation.

The Mossi initiated and subjected their pre-pubescent youth to both circumcision and clitoridectomy. In the Manga-Nobere districts of Burkina Faso (formerly Upper Volta) in southern Mossi country, every three or four years, during December, the coldest part of the year, and depending upon the food supply, the Mossi opened the "Bongo" or the initiation ceremony for boys, in a secluded area in the woods. Here were gathered about twenty to thirty boys, age seven or eight to twelve years old, from the surrounding villages and their helpers. Known as Bankousse, these youths built a camp called the *Keogo*, placing barriers on the paths leading to it so as to warn off uncircumcised children and women. The mothers of the boys brought food daily to the barrier, but did not cross it.

The Mossi considered circumcision to be a simple surgical act which was only incidental to the Bongo -- a veritable initiation to life involving a great many hardships. Almost immediately after arriving at the Keogo the boys were circumcised by the head of the camp, known as the *Nane* who used a harp razor for the operation. As in other parts of Africa, the initiates were not expected to cry, and their wounds were cared for by the Nane. Then came the important post operation period called *komtogo* or "bitter water" by the Bankousse because of the pain involved. Despite the cold nights, they had use of only a small fire and were not permitted to use any covers. Every morning they were forced to bathe in a cold pool, and when they returned, they had lessons to learn involving history, nature study, and life.

The Bongo had its own mystery language whose words turned out on analysis to be synonyms for ordinary More (the language of the Mossi) with the prefix "na." The camp had its own rules on which rank was based, not on those on the outside, but on the order in which the youths were circumcised. What the Nane attempted to do was to forge a link between the boys in opposition to himself, who acted like a veritable ogre. Walking about the camp with a long stick, he whipped the youngsters into line, threw sand in the food brought by the women, and made the Bankousse dance and sing until they were exhausted (Cf. Pacere 1979:105-109).

Graduation ceremonies of the Bongo involved going into the woods, cutting grass for the horses of the chiefs, and wood for their fires. Then on the appointed day, the mothers brought new clothes for their sons, hoping that none of them had died during the ordeal of the Bongo. Then on the appointed day the graduates dressed in their new clothing marched through the market place, and visited the chief. Then they engaged in dancing and singing at a public place just outside the market place.

As usual in almost all parts of Africa, the Mossi women were in complete charge of their Bongo from which they excluded all men. Their *Keogo* was not in the woods, but was in the compound of a woman who lived by herself. But as usual for males, I could find out nothing about the nature of the excision that took place. I did hear the drumming and singing that took place there all night until the wee hours of the morning, and did observe the young girls going backward and forward to their homes. Invariably they carried a tufted staff, said to have been given to them by their prospective husbands. The women would say nothing about the symbolism involved, considering the information specific to women alone. The most that they would say about what went on in the female Bongo was that the males have their secrets and so did the women.

Like the graduation exercises of the Male Bankousse, the female ritual was a village-wide affair, but strictly within the province of the women. Market days before, the relatives and prospective husbands of the graduates, shopped for the clothes and headties, and makeup for them. Then on the day of the exercise, the young girls went to the home of the female Nane and accompanied by their mothers and sisters who were beating drums and singing, went to the village square where the Bankousse danced and sang the traditional airs of the Bongo. From time to time, male relatives and husbands would detach themselves from the line of spectators and approach the dancers, giving them presents of money. To all intents and purposes, the female Bongo was structurally and functionally quite similar to that of the males. This ceremony demonstrated to all that the Mossi women were just as capable as the men in performing an initiation ceremony whose function was to transform girls into women, as the male version transformed boys into men. Moreover, they had more effectively kept men from knowing their secrets than did the males, whose secrets they had obviously shared.

Thanks in part to the fieldwork of Janice Boddy in rural Northern Sudan, something is known about female "pharaonic circumcision." Significantly, she apparently learned as little about the male ritual here as I learned about the female one among the Mossi, but our data appear to be complementary. Boddy reported that whereas there was great "pomp and ceremony" associated with the circumcision of male children, the circumcision for females "is celebrated by the briefest and most subdued of ceremonial feasts: morning tea. There are no religious festivities associated with the event, as there are for boys. The operation, however, renders her marriageable; undergoing it is a necessary condition of becoming a woman, of being enabled to use her one great gift, fertility." (1982:683)

What is important about Boddy's report is the seeming simplicity of the operation. There is none of the pain, suffering and retreat from the world, that is characteristic of initiations in most African societies. She wrote:

> The girl is lying on an *angareeb* (native bed), her body supported by several adult kinswomen. Two of these hold her legs apart. Then she is administered a local anesthetic by injection. In the silence of the next few moments Miriam takes a pair of what look to me like a children's paper scissors and quickly cuts away the girls' clitoris and labia minora. She tells me this is the *lahma djewa* (inside flesh). I am surprised that there is so little blood. Then she takes a surgical needle from her midwife's kit, threads it with suture, and sews together the labia majora, leaving a small opening at the vulva. After a liberal application of antiseptic, it is all over.

> The young girl seems to be experiencing more shock than pain and I wonder if the anesthetic has finally taken effect. The women briefly trill their joyous ululation (*zagharuda*), and we adjourn to the courtyard for tea. While we wait, the sisters receive the ritual ornaments (*jurtig*) that will protect them from harm as they recuperate (*Ibid.*:863-4).

In direct contrast to the puberty ritual among the Northern Sudanese, involving as it does a surgical pharaonic circumcision, but without an elaborate initiation, is the *Marmo* ritual among the Iraqw. The Marmo ritual did not involve any mutilation of the female's sexual organ, but was abandoned in the 1930s because of "horrible stories of women dying during the Marmo rite, and of their bodies being discarded in the bush or left in an isolated hut." (Wada 1984:187) The reasons for the horrible stories of deaths or even of the deaths themselves are unknown since this was "a secret heavily guarded by the women." What is known about the Marmo appears to be rather benign, involving as it did the female initiates changing their hairstyles, applying different types of cosmetics, embroidering skirts and capes with beads, being taught sexual manners, and learning folk songs, word games, and the like. In the words of the ethnographer, "From the foregoing, which represents what is known of the content of the training, it is hard to understand why there might have been deaths. But it is true that during the period of the *Marmo* parents had absolutely no knowledge of what was happening to their daughters. Even when a girl had the misfortune to fall ill, she was not returned to her home." (*Ibid*.:190) Parents would only discover the death of their daughter when the body was discovered, but they did not protest for fear that the mother would be accused of sorcery.

What is intriguing about the *Marmo* ritual is that like many puberty initiation rituals, whether accompanied by genital mutilation or not, it symbolized the death of the children and their rebirth as adults. In the case of this ritual the girls were said to have been "eaten by hyenas" and their return to their parents was interpreted as a rebirth. More important perhaps, was that the Marmo "was not simply a ritual to celebrate female maturation. It functioned also as an association manifesting women's dignity, and was effected on the basis of the belief in death and resurrection held by the Iraqw as a whole." (*Ibid*.:187) Here then, among the Iraqw, was an initiation without genital mutilation or even the terrible cuts experienced by the Nuer males, but whose participants were believed to have endured horrible suffering. Judged in the light of Boddy's report from the Northern Sudan, does it mean that many of the stories about death and burial in the clitoridectomy lodges may be of the same order as those reported for male circumcision lodges?

What is important about the puberty rituals in African societies, whether they involved painful initiation, and whether they involved genital mutilation with recognizable pain, are the emic and etic features involved. The Africans do have their own views of their rituals even though others have ignored these views and insist upon their own interpretations. This is perhaps par for human beings involving as it does relative power. There is no doubt that had they the requisite power, Africans would insist that the world accept their interpretation of their own rituals, as well as their views of the rituals of others. Anthropologists would do well to keep this in mind.

The Mossi are not much given to speculating on the imponderables of social life, or the world in general, judging such ratiocinations quixotic. To them the Bongo for men and for women have the same meaning and serve the same function for both men and women: preparation for marriage and rearing families. Indicative of this equality is that the two genders control their own initiation rituals, even though women have to borrow drums from the males. When badgered about the sexual features involved in genital mutilation, an admittedly chauvinist Mossi male might suggest that since females are inferior to males they are not permitted to touch the male organ during sexual congress, and that clitoridectomy makes sexual congress easier. This may be as good a rationalization as any other, but flies in the face of the anxiety of Mossi men over the conduct of their wives, and their stated axiom: "Women are so important that if a man receives as a wife, either a blind woman or a leper, he should close his eyes, close his mouth, and close his ears, and keep her."

The equally male chauvinist Dogon explicitly associate both circumcision and clitoridectomy with elaborate myths concerning creation and cosmology. Both operations are said to have been instituted as punishments and are indicative of the incomplete state of human beings resulting from the primordial crime of a godling. There is the removal of the opposite sex complement with which all human beings were originally intended to be equipped. Thus for the Dogon there is complementarity in the operation. Mary Daly criticizes the Dogon for what she considered an emic patriarchal obfuscation of the true purposes of the operation, namely the intimidation and humiliation of women. What she conveniently ignores is the fact that the Dogon forbid men to have intercourse with their wives against their will and that the sexual responses of wives are in large part conditioned by the treatment they generally receive from their husbands.[3]

Somewhat like the Dogon, both the Egyptians and the Northern Sudanese stress the complementarity of circumcision and clitoridectomy. Referring specifically to the Sudanese, Boddy asserted that

> Through their own operation, performed at roughly the same age as when girls are circumcised (sic) (between five and ten years), boys become less like women: while the female reproductive organs are covered, that of the male is uncovered, or, as one Sudanese author states, of a child's sex ... by removing physical characteristics deemed appropriate to his or her opposite: the clitoris and other external genitalia, in the case of females, the prepuce of the penis, in the case of males. This last is emphasized by a custom now lapsed in Hofriyat wherein one of the newly circumcised boys' grandmothers would wear his foreskin as a ring on the day of the operation (Boddy 1982:687-8).

Paying special attention to the widespread African emic notion of complementarity in the rituals of circumcision and clitoridectomy, Boddy insists that

> By removing their external genitalia, women are not so much preventing their own sexual pleasure (though obviously this is an

effect) as enhancing their femininity. Circumcision as a symbolic act brings sharply into focus the fertility potential of women by dramatically de-emphasizing their inherent sexuality. By insisting on circumcision for their daughters, women assert their social indispensibility, an importance that is not as the sexual partners of their husbands, nor in this highly segregated, male-authoritative society, as their servants, sexual or otherwise, but as the mothers of men. *The ultimate social goal of a woman is to become, with her husband, the cofounder of a lineage section. As a respected* haboba *she is "listened to," she may be sent on the* hadj (*pilgrimage to Mecca*) *by her husbands or her sons, and her name is remembered in village genealogies for several generations* (italics supplied) (*Ibid*.:687).

Although Boddy had her own etic views of female genital mutilation among the Sudanese, her ethnographic data support the etic argument of this paper, namely that in this instance of the dialectics of social life, clitoridectomy rather than a ritual performed by women, to demean their already low status in many African societies, is a declaration of equality. What is interesting is that there are few, if any, cases in the ethnographic record where African women (as contrasted to the normally sexist African men) see this ritual as reducing their status. Feminists may consider the African women who defend this practice as "brain-washed," but should be aware that many African women, as well as men, take the same jaundiced view of many rituals of Western Christendom. True, some contemporary African women object to clitoridectomy, but few had dared to confront their mothers and grandmothers over the issue for fear of being taken for "black" white women. The implication here is that these women have failed to assert that cultural equality for which Africans have fought long and hard.

What is important about the controversy about clitoridectomy in Africa is that African women were never part of it. The issue grew out of a Judeo-Christian concern over human sexuality, involved Christian missionaries in Africa, and was used by African men in their struggle for cultural autonomy from Europeans, and ultimately for political independence.

The relationship between circumcision and male sexuality was the subject of great speculation among the early Jewish scholars and their Christian counterparts for centuries. There were as many arguments that this operation increased sexuality as that it curbed that passion. Moreover, circumcision among Jews became the plaything of many anti-Semites who railed against presumed Jewish male sexuality (Lyons 1981:505ff). Historically, female sexuality was the cause of even more speculation and fear because, as Robert Murphy indicated,

Culture creates an artificial and untrue shortage of female sexuality, whereas in nature, the supply of female sex far exceeds any possible demand that males can make upon it. It is the male whose sexual potential is limited, and it is limited by virtue of the fact that nature makes a different demand upon him in the sexual act (Murphy 1977:21).

While the Europeans who went to Africa could and did view male circumcision within a now old and hallowed tradition, they were deeply troubled by clitoridectomy. We are told that there was a "late nineteenth- and twentieth-century vogue in Europe and America for clitoridectomy as a cure for female masturbation or even excessive interest in sexual inter- course ..." (Lyons 1981:506).[4] Reflecting the sexist views of the period, Sir Richard Burton declared:

> The moral effect of clitoridectomy is peculiar. While it diminishes the heat of passion it increases licentiousness, breeds a debauchery of mind far worse than bodily unchastity, because accompanied by a peculiar cold cruelty and a taste for artificial stimulants to 'luxury.' It is the sexlessness of a spayed canine imitated by the suggestive brain of humanity (Burton 1885:279).

Whether the missionaries who opposed clitoridectomy for African women held the same views of it as did Richard Burton is unknown, especially since much of the subsequent writing about this subject criti- cized the lack of female pleasure as a result of the operation. That the early missionaries subscribed to the notion of excessive sexuality among African women is well known. They opposed the manipulation and extending the labia and sometimes the clitorises of young women in Cen- tral and South Africa, practices they interpreted as "gross invitation to sexual indulgence" or worse (Bryk 1934). Pious European missionaries frowned on many aspects of African culture which they held to be sexu- ally suggestive, especially the dances which while often emphasized exag- gerated pelvic movements, seldom involved bodily contact.

Missionary opposition to clitoridectomy among the Kikuyu was very much linked to their opposition to all aspects of African culture that could frustrate their attempts to impose Western Christendom. We are told that

> The missionaries recognized the significance of the initiatory rites, of which circumcision was the outward physical symbol, and they were appalled at what they saw in them. The physical operation they considered brutal and unhygenic and in the case of girls a barbaric mutilation with permanent ill-effects. *But the atmosphere in which the ceremonies were carried out seemed to them even more evil, with what they took to be the sexual innuendo of the dances and songs, the licentiousness of the old men and women and the gloating cruelty of the operators and their attendants. They taught against the practices and prayed that the people might forego them altogether* (Italics added) (Murray-

Brown 1972:50-51).

It was as much the desire of the missionaries to get control of African women, as the opposition to both circumcision and clitoridectomy, that made for conflict with the Kikuyu. Much to their chagrin, the "missionaries found their hardest task was to convert girls, but once they succeeded, the possibilities existed of Christian marriages between Africans. Only in this way, in effect, could a new, native church be born." The Europeans viewed this problem as one of a struggle over the status of the African woman. Leading the fight for the Scottish mission were "two outstanding women, Mrs. Watson and Marion Stevenson, who first taught against female circumcision." An attempt was made by the missionaries to "give a positive lead, as they did with the initiation of boys, by providing proper medical supervision and ensuring that the girls' sponsors were Christians. In this way, at least, they could prevent much of the dancing and sexual 'instruction' to which they objected almost as much as to the physical operation." (*Ibid.*:134-5) This was actually attempted by mission doctors, and was welcomed by "leading native Christians" upon whom the exposition by these doctors of the harmful effects of clitoridectomy "made a devastating impression." (*Ibid.*)

What is not generally known is that African Christians in Kenya, meeting at a conference in March 1929, put forward resolutions concerning clitoridectomy, debated the issue among themselves, "in other words, were taking their rejection of female circumcision one stage further by seeking for a uniform approach in all their churches." (*Ibid.*:135-6) This initial positive response of the Kikuyu Christians about clitoridectomy was changed when all the churches (with the exception of the "Roman Catholics [who] were not concerned about it"), and the colonial government sought to use this issue to impose all sorts of restrictions on those persons who hesitated to ban the practice. Inevitably the issue got involved in the first nationalist rumblings. The nascent Kikuyu Central Association (KCA) which had started to protest white seizure of Kikuyu lands "made it (clitoridectomy) a political matter by including it among several tribal customs for which they canvassed support in the reserves. Their argument was that the culture of the tribe was threatened and its traditional structure in danger of being broken up." (*Ibid.*:137)

Much to their subsequent regret, but then fully understandable given their involvement in what George Balandier has termed "the Colonial Situation" (1965), the mission demanded that the teachers on its payroll declare their acceptance of the "church ruling on clitoridectomy and to repudiate membership of the KCA 'until that body should cease from its anti-Christian propaganda.'" Twelve of the fifty-three teachers refused the order and were dismissed. When the church's African elders were confronted with the same demands, especially since they themselves had drawn up the church law against clitoridectomy, one-third of them refused stating that membership or non-membership in the KCA was "a matter of individual conscience." When the mission asked its rank and file for a "simple declaration" of their acceptance of the church's ruling, a full nine-tenths of the body of the church was lost. The mood of the people was soon reflected when "a scurrilous dance song swept through the villages to add to the dismay of the missionaries. It was supposed to be derived from a Swahili tune, but the Kikuyu ... invented any number of verses, most of which Europeans regarded as "quite unprintable." (Murray-Brown 1972:137-8)

What had started out as an issue over clitoridectomy, and a practice which many African Christians were prepared to change, became a cause célèbre over the issue of African cultural and political freedom. Much to the alarm of the colonial government, it became known locally in October 1919 that "John [Jomo] Kenyatta" who had gone to Britain to protest settler colonialism, had been to Moscow and was "in close touch with Communists and Communist Organizations." Songs praising Kenyatta and ridiculing the governor were outlawed as seditious, creating anger among anti-mission Kikuyu. Some of these performed "evil" dances, disrupted church services, boycotted and raided schools, and abused the parents of school children. These incidents culminated in the murder in January 1930 of Hilda Stumpf, an elderly American missionary of the African Inland Mission. The post-mortem revealed that she had been "sexually mutilated in a brutal fashion. Her attackers had smothered her face with a pillow to stifle her cries and she had died from suffocation. Behind this outrage lay the drama of the female circumcision controversy." (*Ibid.*:134)

As one would expect, the crisis in Kenya reverberated throughout Britain and the colonial world.

In London, female circumcision, or clitoridectomy as the fastidious called it, became the talk of advanced circles and Kenyatta was sought after by hostesses at tea-time discussions. A powerful group, headed by the Duchess of Atholl, a Unionist Member of Parliament and protagonist of women's rights, was well briefed by the Scottish Church. They called female circumcision barbarous mutilation and pressed for its outlawing by government action ... Was not this one of the objects of the civilizing mission? (*Ibid.*:139)

The Duchess, who chaired a special Committee for the Protection of Coloured Women in the Crown Colonies, held hearings on clitoridectomy in December 1929 and again in May 1930, to which she invited persons such as Jomo Kenyatta to give testimony.

Kenyatta was caught in a dilemma. Both the KCA and the Christians, and both Kikuyu and European attempted to use him. As a young convert of the Scottish missionaries, he and a group of boys had been taken by a missionary teacher to a stream to be circumcised by an operator who used a surgical knife from the mission hospital. All the boys "had their 'sponsors,' or circumcision fathers, who stood behind them during the ceremony and acted as guardians on behalf of the tribe." By so doing the young John could take his place as "a true heir to ancestral tradition. At the same time he continued with his catechumen classes." (*Ibid.*:52) The young Kenyatta had therefore accepted the modifications suggested by the missionaries.

The problem now was that clitoridectomy had become inextricably linked to the Kikuyu desire for equality in their homeland. The missionaries were insisting that Kenyatta "should tell his people to obey government officers, Kikuyu chiefs, and missions in control of schools." As one of the new group of leaders, Kenyatta could not accept this advice, but he decided once again to compromise. He took the position that the KCA was not against the church, suggesting that it could not be since so many Kikuyu were Christian. It was the church, he said, and not the KCA, which had produced the row, and that he, like the KCA, felt that it was wrong for the church to attempt to legislate against clitoridectomy. He suggested that the abolition of this ritual "could only be achieved through education, perhaps by sending doctors like Dr. Philip ... around the reserves." Kenyatta warned that "any attempt to coerce my people by 'force majeure' will have the very opposite of the desired effect as it causes my people to attach accentuated importance to the maintenance of this custom." He concluded that as the Kikuyu saw it, "the way of gradual conviction is to be preferred to that of a direct attack by means of spear and shield." (*Ibid.*:140-1)

There was, however, little give on the part of the missionaries. They refused to separate the spiritual from the secular, and to permit the Africans to chart their own course. One missionary declared that "First of all I could not agree that school and church could be separated ... it would be worse for them [the children] to receive education without Christianity than no education at all." Kenyatta would later lament that in traditional African societies with all their evils, people had the liberty to exercise their own will in concert with those of their fellows. But today an African, no matter what his station in life, is like a horse which moves only in the direction that the rider pulls the rein." (Kenyatta 1962:40ff)

Kenyatta's subsequent defense of clitoridectomy as an operation in which the operator had "the dexterity of a Harley Street surgeon ... with a stroke she cuts off the tip of the clitoris ... the girl hardly feels any pain" (Jomo Kenyatta 1962) is only understandable in light of the role that clitoridectomy had played in the drive of the Kikuyu to achieve equality for their institutions in the face of Europe's arrogance. Like Bob Murphy, Kenyatta was very aware of the dialectics of social life. For him colonial tutelage was oppressive and alien. He wrote:

> In our opinion, the African can only advance to a 'higher level' if he is free to express himself, to organize economically,

politically, socially, and to take part in the government of his own country. In this way he will be able to develop his creative mind, initiative, and personality, which hitherto have been hindered by the multiplicity of incomprehensible laws and ordinances. (*Ibid*.:192)

What the conflict over clitoridectomy did was to bring to "an abrupt close the paternalistic phase of missionary activity; henceforth the emphasis would be on the growth of native churches. The high noon of imperialism ... [and the attempt] to extend white dominion over all of East Africa, was over." (*Ibid*.:151)

Kenyatta has been pilloried by many female scholars and feminists, for defending a practice (which he was prepared to see abolished), in the greater interest of political equality for Africans. Few noted, as did Harriet Lyons, that Kenyatta had suggested, perhaps as an after thought, that clitoridectomy may have been practiced to prevent masturbation, a practice condemned in both Kikuyu boys and girls, and that his major emphasis was "largely on social structure." (1981:510)[5] Moreover, he was fully prepared to use education to abolish it. A more intemperate view of Kenyatta's action is that of Fran Hosken who declared that

An international feminist observer cannot help but wonder why the male African leadership does not speak out about the mutilation of women, a custom that was reinforced by Kenyatta in Kenya and is also supported by the independence movement under his leadership ... It clearly affects the status of women in political affairs. (Hosken 1976:6)

Understandably, there are some African feminists who agree with Hosken. Nevertheless, it should be noted that "the resistance of African feminists to anti-clitoridectomy agitation-evident at the United Nations World Conference on women held in Copenhagen in 1980" (New York Times 1980; B4) accords fully with the demand of Kenyatta for African cultural autonomy. Like him, these women realize that African practices must be brought into line with those characteristics of the emerging global civilization. What they insist upon is respect, and the end of European arrogance.

The problem with blaming Kenyatta and other African men for clitoridectomy misses the important point that African women have always been in control of this ritual (until now when male doctors may perform it in modern hospitals), and probably used it, to declare their equality with men. Faced with discrimination for not possessing those characteristics with which dominant social strata have linked their dominance, African women, like other women, and subordinate groups, have striven to acquire the traits viewed as valuable. These practices vary cross-culturally in time and space, and can be as different as Japanese females surgically operating on their eyes to approximate those of American males during the occupation of their country; to certain American females bobbing their noses; other Americans bleaching or darkening their skins; and still others dressing like males, and creating female counterparts of such organizations as Masonic lodges, veteran groups, and institutions of higher learning. In many of these cases, the males or dominant groups whose characteristics were being imitated, were not aware of the attempts to achieve equality with them, or to win their favor. That they were responsible for the behavior in the first place may well have been true, but a dialectician like Robert Murphy, whose eyes were probably opened by his wife, Yolanda, would smile at the irony of it all.

FOOTNOTES

[1] Referring to the widespread pattern of avoidance between a woman and her father-in-law, Murphy states that Tuareg brides pull their shawl across the lower parts of their faces in the presences of their fathers-in-law. "This," he asserted, "is the nearest any Tuareg woman comes to the Near Eastern purdah, one aspect of which entails the veiling of the woman's face in compliance with Sura 4 of the Koran, which says of good women: They guard their unseen parts because Allah has guarded them." The question remains as to whether this really refers to the face, which in contrast to other parts of the body, is usually quite open.

[2] See Lewis (1971) for an extended treatment of this phenomenon.

[3] cf. Marcel Griaule, *Conversations with Ogotemmeli* (1965); Genevieve Calame-Griaule, *Ethnologie et langage* (1965); Marcel Griaule and Germaine Dieterlen, *Le Renard Pale* (1965); Mary Daly, *Gyn/Ecology: The Metaethics of Radical Feminism*, (1978); Harriet Lyons (1981).

[4] See Marie Bonaparte, *Female Sexuality* (*1953*).

[5] *cf. Kenyatta, op. cit.,* pp. 129-130; 154-156.

13

ABIDING WOMEN:
SEXUALITY AND CONTROL IN MODERN TESO

Joan Vincent
Columbia University

Introduction

Robert Murphy once remarked that exogamic patrilineal societies have a relatively easy time "abiding women." Among the Iteso, he observed, "some of the most important economic and residential ties between families are established through their women." This he attributed to the processes of social change in eastern Uganda whereby agnatic units have been undercut by Western economy. He speculates further that "when the corporate ties of patrilineality are subject to attrition, the negative side of the descent system is left... Women are not just 'exchanged,' as in Levi-Strauss; they are the connective tissue of the social whole" (1971: 219-220). This paper explores the implications of this structural attrition for the dialectics of gender with particular attention to the control of women's sexuality.

After a brief characterization of the colonial construction of modern Teso, three questions are raised. First, what was the place of women in Iteso society: how public were their activities; how was their sociability controlled; and how were they able, in turn, to exert control in this patrilineal society? Second, how did the gender dialectic operate during different phases in an Iteso woman's life: in premarital sexual relations; in marriage, and after marriage? Third, what were the personal and social costs of the changes in gender relations that came about with the attrition of the patrilineage and the emergence of the nuclear household; to what extent were these borne equally or unequally by women and men?

Answers to these questions are based upon (a) observations of interactions between the sexes systematically coded during a field inquiry between February 1967 and May 1968; (b) inquiries into premarital sexual alliances, patterned relations between lovers; and (c) an analysis of homicide records collected for a five year period from February 1962 to

211

February 1967.[1] This data relates to Iteso experience in the early 1960s and so is the end-product of fifty years of colonial rule. As Etienne and Leacock have noted the impact of colonization "on the quality of personal relations between women and men, between parents and children, and among people in general is perhaps most striking in egalitarian societies" (1980: 3) such as that of the Iteso.

Modern Teso

Both Claude Meillassoux's explicit model of a domestic community set out in *Maiden, Meal, and Money* (1983) and Jack Goody's schema of a bridewealth economy in his exegesis on the development of the modern western family (1983) would generate the social organization of the Iteso of eastern Uganda. The Iteso live in what both would call a Simple Agrarian Society which, in spite of colonial conquest and the introduction of capitalist agriculture, is still characterized by a high degree of communalism. Thus the Iteso population "(a) practices self-sustaining agriculture; (b) produces and consumes together, on common land, access to which is subordinated to membership in the community, and (c) is linked together by unequal ties of personal dependence" (Meillassoux 1983: 3).

Colonial rule, between 1912 and 1962, introduced several features of economic and social change that greatly affected the dialectics of gender in the exogamic patrilineal society. The taxation of all adult males as individuals and the introduction of cotton as a cash crop fostered both male residential stability (within an administrative parish) and individuation (at the expense of the corporate patrilineage). Residence in large patrilineal homesteads gave way to small nucleated settlements dispersed throughout the countryside. This was made possible and encouraged by the establishment of "law and order" in a society which, on the eve of conquest at least, was prone to cattle raiding and internecine feuding. Further individuation of both men and women was encouraged by Christian missionaries whose goal it was to replace the polygamous ideal of the Iteso with monogamy.

Through all these changes Iteso society remained characterized by what Meillassoux has called gynecomobility (1983). The movement of women on marriage away from their own patrilineal kinsmen and a neighborhood of known affines was, in the early colonial period, contractually underpinned by the exchange of valued bridewealth and the continued legal interest of their natal lineages in their well being. By the 1960s, however, as Murphy's remark indicates, the communalism that had kept agnatic kinsmen together as close, cooperative neighbors had given way to the organization of small clusters of homesteads (*atutuben*) in which ties through women were increasingly important. Where this occurred one would assume the status of women would be enhanced. This being so, the situation was fraught with tension. As this paper will show, as the interstitial structural role of women as wives becomes more prominent in Iteso society, and as the egalitarian gender relations of their premarital state give way to the demanding asymmetry of conjugality, so wives become more vulnerable to subjugation and physical abuse. The contradictions and conflicts of capitalist society are encapsulated in their modern, largely autonomous, nuclear households.

Women in Their Place: Interaction Observed

The status of women in simple agrarian societies, and hence the dialectic of gender, has often been linked with their participation in the public arena, a formulation which has been shown to be overly simplistic (Engels 1884, Kuhn and Wolpe 1978, Murphy and Murphy 1974, Rogers 1978, Sacks 1974, Sanday 1974, Stoler 1980). Yet an exploratory analysis of visible women in the public domain may still be suggestive.

Women in Iteso society are not domesticated. In this tropical agricultural setting life is lived out-of-doors for twelve hours a day and women are prominent in public places. They work in the fields alongside men and in gardens and bush in large visible groups. Women as well as men engage in the heavy work of clearing the bush in addition to performing the "nimble fingers" tasks of weeding and picking cotton. In the ritually restricted domain of cattle-keeping women may own cattle in their own names (though this is rare) and they engage in ox-ploughing. Men and women work together in communal work parties (*eitai*) and a woman may be "sent" to take the place of a man. No task seems beyond them. In the early days of colonial rule, Iteso men often sent their "womenfolk" to work on road building in their place and it is unlikely that they appreciated why their Edwardian administrators frowned on the practice.

By and large studies of gender relations suffer from a surfeit of cultural generalization and the secondary analysis of received ethnography which is one dimensional (Murphy and Murphy 1974: x-xi). Field research in Gondo, a small town in western Teso, involved the daily observation and recording of "situations" or "public occurrences." These were then subjected to analysis in order to address several specific questions of social organization. Here data are abstracted from 141 recorded cases (out of a total of 500) in which women were involved in public activities. The observations were made between February 25, 1967 and May 31, 1968.

In almost one third of the situations the women were working at agricultural tasks: ploughing, sowing millet, harvesting, and digging sweet potatoes. In some cases their tasks were interchangeable with those of men but in most women did not control the technology, simple as it was. Thus men dug for sweet potatoes while women scrabbled with their hands for those they unearthed. Men tended to plough while women broadcast the millet seeds. Men shaped and plastered the mud and wattle houses while women fetched grasses and thatched. There was, indeed, a clear ideology of "women's tasks" in agriculture, the most tedious being seen to be those for which they were best qualified. Quite often, however, old men and children of both sexes worked alongside the women. Only the ploughing operation appeared, for a moment, to yield gender symbolism: men guided the ox-drawn plough while their beaters walked alongside, the women always on the left hand side of the ploughman. Sociological imagination was curbed when, later in the morning, the wife was seen driving the plough while her husband broadcast seeds. As might be expected, in a long ploughing session, the tasks were rotated.

Work in the fields began soon after sunrise and continued until around one o'clock in the afternoon, sometimes to be taken up again in the cool of the evening. The afternoons were spent around the beer pot. In most cases (43 out of 45) men and women drank together, sitting in a circle around a beer pot on the ground out of which protruded the long reed through which they drank. Kin, affinity, age and, above all, gender relations were expressed in their spatial positioning. There were also rules: men might sit on chairs, women must not: "to show a woman is under a man," as one respondent put it. Exceptions were observed but they were few and could be accounted for by the prestige of wealth or great age overiding gender. A wife had to sit next to her husband even when her father or brother was a member of the group, particularly then, perhaps. Her placement reflected the primacy of the conjugal tie and the control of wives in this society in which the corporate patrilineage had suffered attrition.

Women exercised a more subtle control over the beer drinking situation. Only women brewed beer, adding boiling water to the pot as the afternoon drew on. It was men, however, who called for a fresh brew when the beer became too insipid. Sometimes the women heard them, sometimes they did not. In the public arena some chose to flaunt disobedience, encouraged, perhaps, to do so by other women. Since the prestigious authority of the husband required the deference of the wife, women were empowered to shape men's public demeanor. In the preparation of beer, and of food in general, women controlled and could thwart the appetites of men.

Folklore and popular songs about food were all pervasive in this agrarian society which had long suffered dearth and still knew "hungry months." Women's control of food was feared by men even as it was valued by women. Among the Iteso deaths were seldom attributed to natural causes, poison inevitably being suspected. Even more to the point, the major danger posed by women was seen to be their manipulation of male virility through charms and potions they might add to the food they cooked. Thus, by means of food, in a small way women controlled a public as well as a domestic world -- and some, as will be seen, were struck down fatally when they dared to exert this petty power.

Since work in the fields lasted throughout the morning and beer throughout the afternoon, there was little time when men and women were not together in public. Simple agricultural production breeds the equality of women and, among the Iteso, it also bred women who were physically as strong as their husbands (as Llewellyn-Davies also found in another East African agrarian society, 1978) and who could and did resist unwelcome sexual advances -- a matter to which we will return. First it is necessary to consider the institutionalization of pleasurable sexual relations in Iteso society.

The Context of Marriage: Sexual Relations at Large

The cultural dialectics of gender require the recognition of sequence and continuity: for this reason Iteso equate women with wives and with human reproduction. This androcentric focus on women in their child-bearing years is here placed in the analytical context of premarital sexual relations on the one hand, and the developing autonomy and freedom from gender restraints of the divorced and "deserted" woman on the other. The "solitary" as she has come to be known in historical literature which deals with a similar phase in the development of capitalism in Europe, is an emergent social phenomenon in Teso.

The Papero Relationship

The sexuality of unmarried men and women is given virtually free rein in Iteso society. Even the breaking of incest rules can be socially rectified with a quite small and inexpensive ritual. There are many cultural possibilities, a wide range of pre- and extra-marital expressions of sexuality. Some are interrelated with and provide the context for marriage as an institution. On the one hand, marriage as an event may be seen to crystallize out of a salty concoction of illicit sexual relationships. On the other, it may be argued -- as indeed some Iteso wives do argue -- that polygamous marriage as an institution would not endure without sexual alternatives to the conjugal role.

Dyadic and spontaneous sexual transactions between friends, lovers, the affianced, and prostitutes are no less structured, if less ceremonially recognized, than those of marriage partners. We might emulate Murphy's dialectic and call them the negative side of marriage within the patrilineal, patriarchal society. We might even go further: if, indeed, sexism holds a functional value for capital (Stoler 1980) pre-marital sexual relations, which are essentially egalitarian, are shared by the relatively propertyless and powerless women and youths. Their silences speak to both protest and resistance, not necessarily to capitalism itself, but to their exclusion from its spoils.

A relationship between lovers begins when a young man asks a girl if she will become his *apapero*. The girl may refuse outright in which case the youth will not ask her again. If, however, she refuses him in such a manner as to encourage him, he will court her with small gifts. This he will do three times and no more. If the girl lives close by he will pay such attention to her daily; if she lives further away, he may visit her once a week or so. If the girl finally says no, the young man looks for another *apapero*. If she says yes, she goes with him to his house where they will have intercourse. This is done secretly without the knowledge of the girl's father. Should he learn where his daughter is spending the night, he pretends not to know. The function of selective knowledge and rumour is critical since, while the reputation of a girl is enhanced by her sexual prowess, her father must remain in formal ignorance of her doings. Within the women's sphere (which includes the mother of the *apapero*) gossip made bedfellows of all.

The girl visits her *epapero* (boyfriend) at night once or twice a week and their trysts might go on for several months. It will be ended when one partner becomes tired of the other or when they decide that they are well matched and will marry. In most cases, the *papero* relationship is one of sexuality only and does not lead to marriage even when it leads to conception. If the couple intends to marry the girl begins to cook simple meals at the young man's home -- a task that involves a certain amount of visibility. Lovers who marry usually do so five or six months after pregnancy is evident.

A man usually has his first *apapero* when he is about nineteen and living in a separate homestead away from his parents. It is unlikely to be his first sexual experience. My most reliable respondent considered that most girls would have their first lovers at fourteen and would anticipate being married by sixteen. Both partners will probably have three or four *apaperi* before settling down to marriage. Should a girl become pregnant during the affair and should there be no inclination to marry, the young man is fined. This fine, sanctioned by local government by-law is paid to the girl's father who is usually quite content to accept it as compensation. The compensation is not for violation of the patrilineage's control over a member's sexuality but for its loss of the bridewealth that would be paid under a marriage contract. If the fine is paid and the girl married, a child born of the *papero* relationship belongs to the patrigroup of its genitor; if no fine is paid, the child belongs to the patrigroup of its mother.

Conspiracy binds together all women and youths within the *papero* institution. The women of a neighborhood wish a young girl well in the freedom of her pre-marital sexual rights and conspire with her and her lovers against the men of the older generation, the beneficiaries of patrilineal privilege. The domestic married state is not a very happy one for many Iteso women and, for some, domestic violence is a frequent occurrence. The daily line-up of women with black eyes and bruises at the judicial headquarters, and the records of medical treatment for such injuries at the dispensary, attest to the commonplace nature of wife-battering. (To be sure, a few battered husbands were also in evidence). This was particularly the case when the husband was young and making his first marriage. Within the *papero* institution while sexual relations were initiated by men they were maintained by women who thus retained control over their own sexuality. This state of affairs was ended by marriage. The prevalence of wife-beating in the households of newlywed youths testified to the recalcitrance of women to accept the authority of males of their own generation and so cooperate in their own subjugation.

The Solitary Woman

The greatest freedom from corporate patrilineal control was experienced not by nubile young women since they were nominally under the control of their fathers, nor by wives in autonomous nuclear households, where control was contested, but by mature women who lived alone. Historians of Europe have seen the emergence of such women, "solitaries," as a phenomenon related to the spread of capitalism and the development of modern society and, indeed, the relatively slight extent to which capitalism had penetrated the communal kinship fabric of Iteso society might be measured by the comparatively few widows who remained uninherited and the few more women who chose to live alone, independent of male authority.

Such women, in Teso, certainly *chose* to live alone. All seven women living alone in Gondo were interviewed. Some, like one entrepreneurial widow, were wealthy enough to be independent of male control. Forty-five years old, she had lived alone for five years following the death of her husband because, as she put it, she was "old enough not to be inherited" and her husband died leaving her with riches in the form of 69 head of cattle, 8 head of goats, 5 sheep and fifteen hundred shillings so that she was "able to look after (her) own life." At his death she returned to Gondo where she had lived as a child, building a house close to her elder brother. She was a large-scale employer of farming labor, including groups made up entirely of women. Another Iteso woman, aged forty nine, similarly chose (after three divorces) not to be inherited and remained alone in Gondo, the home of her last husband, living alone, kinless but close to ex-affines, farming. Clearly, freedom from male control was possible for such women past child bearing. Frequently, however, they chose to live close by, if apart from, male relatives and among neighbors on whose protection and support they could count.

Yet the social costs of such independence were high. The Teso homicide files, to be considered next, record the deaths of nine such women living alone: thus of 88 women killed in the district over a five year period, almost one tenth lived alone.

Conflicts of the Hearth: The Social Costs of Sexuality

Between February 1962 and February 1967, 359 homicides called for police investigation in Teso. Of these almost one third arose out of quarrels between spouses in nuclear families. Thus the paradox that, in a society where the domestic unit founded on monogamous marriage was becoming more commonplace and a husband's dependence on his wife increasing with every season that passed, more women have become the visible targets of societal stress. In the long run, Iteso women have become more vulnerable. The daughter and sister so privileged and protected within the patrilineal structure has become the subjugated, individuated, and vulnerable wife. For this reason many Iteso women who had experienced polygamous marriage expressed a preference for it: the solidarity of co-wives made up for the loss of support of patrikin.

As it has become less corporately patrilineal, Iteso society has, in Murphy's words, found it less easy to abide women. An attempt may be made to document this outrageous statement. Of the 359 homicides that occurred in Teso between 1962 and 1967, one hundred involved cases in which women were involved or in which control over women's sexuality was an issue. Three categories may be recognized:

Husband kills wife	53 cases
Wife kills husband	12 cases
Sexuality related killings by other than spouses	35 cases

Each category will be discussed in turn.

The Killing of Wives

In almost every one of the 53 cases in which a man killed his wife, beating was involved. This was usually done with a stick (a familiar accoutrement of the Iteso farmer) but, upon occasions, iron bars and hoes were used. In one rather dreadful instance a wife was stomped to death. Ten of the 53 killings took place after a beer party and two at a beer party. The very rules of spatial propinquity required by patrilineal propriety rendered the wife vulnerable. She was both under the eye and within easy reach of her husband and as the drink took over anger flared over real or imagined jealousies. The layering of shared neighborhood experience in work and play (for *apaperi*, as we have seen, were usually neighbors or from contiguous neighborhoods) and the social importance attached to neighborly conviviality around the beer pot, made it very hard, indeed, for wives not to become the foci of quarrels among men. Most of these homicides were over sexual advances being made to other men's wives. This was particularly destructive of the social fabric when it occurred at the neighborhood beer parties given by each household in turn when millet was exceptionally plentiful. There is, indeed, a seasonality to wife-killing which reflects this.

Other causes of quarrels between the spouses appeared with some regularity. In 39 cases in which motive was unambiguously stated in the police record, a husband's loss of control over his wife's sexuality and her disobedience in this and other domains of domestic life were the main reasons for his anger and violence. Adultery and suspected adultery were cited in nine cases; a wife's refusal to have sexual intercourse in six. Other forms of disobedience may seem petty without an appreciation of their cultural meanings within the Iteso code of gender relations. A refusal to bring a husband food or water epitomized, as we have seen, the defense of the world that women controlled. Their potential for autonomy and independence within the cash economy was reflected in refusals to hand over money to their husbands or in borrowing tools and household goods from neighbors without his permission. "In those cases of monogamous marriage with a rebellious wife, Engels says, 'we have a picture in miniature of the very antagonisms and contradictions in which society . . . moves, without being able to resolve and overcome them'" (Delmar 1976: 280). We also have the ongoing struggle over the rights of men and women over themselves.

In several cases in which monogamous marriages were at risk, the husband's authority and right to control his wife's activities was being challenged. For example:

Case 63. Husband beats wife who picked vegetables from his mother's garden without permission.

Case 109. Husband kills wife when she refuses to hand over keys.

Case 111. Husband kills wife who refuses to fetch his bicycle from inside the house for him.

Case 155. Man kicks wife to death for refusing to leave another man's house where he found her eating.

Case 334. Husband kills wife in a quarrel over her leaving his house to fetch fire from a neighbor without his consent.

Even these few cases suggest the interwoven threads of changing kin, gender and neighborly relations in which the small domestic unit is held.

One extreme case of an assertion of a husband's right to subjugate his wife contains also the elements of traditional principles governing the relations of kin and affines. Thus

Case 219. Man beats his wife to death after she has been escorted back to him after two weeks at her parents' home. She had no permission to go.

The wife's parents had honored the bridewealth transaction and acknowledged conceding jural control over their daughter to her husband. The husband, feeling that he was within his conjugal rights, himself reported the death to the authorities.

The most striking feature of the Teso homicide statistics and the killing of wives is how frequently their deaths came about through beatings. Wife-beating, as Levinson has intimated, is part of a cultural configuration and a full analysis (which cannot be made here) would delineate at least two sets of values in Iteso society upon which it rests. There is, on the one hand, the value complex that surrounds property, bridewealth and wives (the jural aspect so well discussed in the classical literature on patrilineal societies). There is also an associated set of values surrounding authority and subjugation. In Teso this was expressed not only in the beating of wives but in the beating of recalcitrant taxpayers by chiefs, of sons by elders, and of laborers by employers.

The beating of males by those in authority over them does not appear to have worried colonial authorities very much but the beating of women, which was believed to be both prevalent and increasing in Teso by 1926, caused much concern. An evolutionary explanation was given: the status of women varied according to the social evolution of the various Uganda districts. In the centralized kingdom of Buganda "native public opinion did not support the beating of women since the tribe had advanced beyond the stage when this form of government is regarded as suitable." In Teso, where not even traditional chiefs had been developed, "growing licence" had been observed among women. "Unfaithfulness on the part of wives is definitely on the increase and cases of ill-treatment of women by their husbands have become more frequent." Worst of all, in Teso "the women are showing a growing tendency to neglect their cultivation -- an important consideration for this agricultural tribe." Tribes such as the Iteso were believed to be passing through a dangerous transitional phase.

Native courts found it difficult to "preserve the reasonable authority of the husband over the wife" while at the same time providing the wife with immunity "from brutal assaults by the husband." A long term solution to the problem was envisaged in 1926. Education and the spread of religion, it was hoped, would "evolve a sense of proper responsibility and public opinion to replace the old tribal sanctions and safeguards which are bound to be loosened by the impact of western ideas and ideals." The inevitability of the attrition of the corporate patrilineage seemed assured. Only a short term conclusion was reached and that was no solution: "the control of women must be left to the husbands" (C0536. 147/14386). It was in this context that the disobedient wife could be beaten to death with some degree of impunity even in the enlightened 1960s. The punishment for most of these homicides was short term imprisonment or a fine.

The Killing of Husbands

In striking contrast to the number of wives killed by their husbands, only eleven out of 359 homicides involved the killing of a husband by his wife. In contrast, too, was the form taken by the police record. When a husband killed his wife the reason for his grievance was provided in some detail; when a wife killed her husband the curt "domestic quarrel" was entered in the blotter. The triggering event was often similar: eight of the killings occurred after a beer party. Since women, unlike their husbands, did not carry sticks they had greater recourse to iron bars, hoes, and even stools which might suggest a greater element of self-defense. Yet some of the killings would appear to be very deliberate.

Case 92. After a beer party a man assaults his wife. She kills him with a hoe, striking him twice across the throat as he sleeps.

Case 200. A husband refuses to let his wife back into the house after a beer party. She waits outside and when later he opens the door to urinate, she beats him over the head with a stick.

Sometimes neighbors or the wife's kinsmen are involved in the killings. In one case, for example, a husband and wife quarrel after a Christmas Day beer party. A neighbor hears and joins the wife in beating the husband to death. In another, a man and wife quarrel and she runs away into the bush. He goes to find her. Two nights later he is found beaten to death by his wife, her father, and brother.

Although a wife's killing of her husband was rare in Teso between 1962 and 1967, it is noteworthy that *all* the recorded instances took place in the more economically and educationally advanced regions of the district. Here the "breakdown of traditional patrilineal system was most evident and young women enjoyed the greatest economic independence."

Sexually-motivated Killings by Other than Spouses

It is virtually a truism that capitalist agricultural development is characterized by uneven regional development and it would convey a false impression of Iteso society to suggest that the corporate ties of patrilineality are everywhere experiencing attrition to the same degree. In those parts of Teso where kinship and communalism remain strong violence related to women's sexuality usually involved more individuals that spouses alone. Kin and neighbors were still important.

Five quarrels involving a woman's sexuality may be used to document this. They have been selected to illustrate those features of jural control over women in patrilineal societies that are vested in kin and affines.

Case 16. A woman's first husband is killed by her second husband and her father when it is discovered that she has returned to have sexual intercourse with him. The second husband had paid bridewealth, notes the police blotter.

Here we see in operation rights to control the sexuality of a woman granted by the bridewealth transaction. In Iteso society a portion of the bridewealth is returned upon divorce and is usually used again to transact a new marriage. The partners in this transaction, the woman's father and his agnates and the second husband and his patrilineage, are defending their rights.

Several cases support most strongly the patrilineal principle of sibling solidarity and jural rights and responsibility of a brother in the control of his sister's sexuality. Two cases involving nubile girls follow.

Case 45. A man beats to death his sister because she has sat on a man's lap at a beer party.

Case 45. A brother beats to death a man to whom his sister has given beads, an indication of her sexual interest in him.

In both cases, the brother sees in jeopardy the bridewealth that his patrilineage will receive on the occasion of his sister's marriage. Threatened, therefore, is the prospect of his own marriage using the same cattle. (The principles and practices of such marriage transactions have been fully described elsewhere (Vincent 1971)).

For a woman, return of bridewealth cattle upon divorce returns, in principle, the control of her sexuality to her agnates. This may, nevertheless, be contested as the following case shows:

Case 57. A man meets his ex-wife at a Christmas Day beer party at the home of a neighbor. She refuses to have sexual intercourse with him and he kills her.

Finally, there is the mutual interest of husband and agnates in maintaining a reputable marriage established by the transfer of bridewealth:

Case 175. On coming out of prison a man kills the kinsman in whose charge he has left his wife when he finds that she is pregnant.

The reproductive rights in the woman, acquired by the payment of bridewealth, have been transgressed. For this he holds his kinsman responsible.

In all these cases, the act of homicide is, of course, one event in a series of events, each enmeshed in a matrix of cultural understandings, rules and practices. Each case cited above contains nuances and intricacies that cannot be explored here. They are presented simply to document the type of situation in which non-marital sexuality brought about criminal homicide in Teso. In that they reflect a lack of effective jural control over women by their spouses and kinsmen, they support Robert Murphy's observations on the attrition of the corporate patrilineage among the Iteso. They also, like the other cases cited in the previous sections, reflect the cost to women in Iteso society of their assertion of rights over their own sexuality.

FOOTNOTES

[1] Field research in Teso between 1966 and 1970 was funded by the Ministry of Overseas Development of the United Kingdom and by Barnard College. The doctoral dissertation that resulted from my first field trip was sponsored by Robert Murphy who insisted that I state clearly that the Iteso of Uganda in no way resemble the Mundurucú. I take the occasion to do so here. I would also like to express my gratitude to Joan Scott and George Bond whose comments on a longer and somewhat incoherent ethnography of Iteso gender relations helped me arrive at this essay.

14

WAGE CONTRACTS AND WAGE CONFLICT
IN NORTHERN NIGERIAN AGRICULTURE:
TOWARD A DIALECTICAL UNDERSTANDING OF
THE CHANGING SOCIAL ORGANIZATION OF WORK

Louise D. Lennihan
Hunter College

Introduction

A large literature has grown up concerning the nature of change among the Hausa in rural northern Nigeria focusing on the organization of work, a central empirical and methodological commitment of the Murphys' research (Murphy and Murphy 1974, 1980; Murphy and Steward 1956; Murphy, 1970, 1971). Following M.G. and Mary Smith's (1955; 1954) groundbreaking work on the Hausa in the late 1940s, the 1960s and 1970s have seen agricultural economists (Norman, 1972), sociologists (Williams 1983), geographers (Watts 1983), historians (Shenton, 1985), and anthropologists (Hill 1972, 1977; Lennihan 1983) all take their turn at documenting the organization of work among the Hausa. In the 1980s, differing interpretations of these data have led to considerable disagreement as to whether incipient class formation and the development of agrarian capitalism is taking place (Hill 1972, 1977; Williams 1983; Shenton 1985; Shenton and Lennihan 1981; Lennihan 1983; Watts 1983; Clough and Williams nd).

The emergence of agricultural wage labor, as one aspect of the changing organization of work in northern Nigeria, is key to understanding the development of agrarian capitalism. This process requires a special sort of scrutiny for two reasons. One is that the emergence of wage labor is taking place in a context where for the most part laborers are not landless.[1] The other is because the "change" involved is constituted both by the emergence of new social relations as well as the persistence of old pre-existing ones (Murphy 1971: 95; Thompson 1974, 1976; Marx and Engels 1974: 27). Nowhere is the complexity of this historical process more evident than in the consideration of present-day agricultural wage contracts and the labor conflict they engender.

In contemporary Hausaland, there are three basic agricultural wage contracts. Examination of these contracts reveals a continuum along which capital, or wages, increasingly replace non-monetary rights and obligations of employers and laborers. While capital is the basis of all three contracts, along this continuum employer-worker relations become increasingly objectified. I shall argue, however, that the progression of this objectification is not a simple linear one through time. For one thing, all three contracts exist simultaneously. The most highly objectified contract has recently emerged as an option, not a replacement, to earlier contract forms with their ensnaring social rights and obligations. The point of my analysis is not to argue that capital has replaced ties of community, patron-clientage or kinship. Rather, capital has supplanted the hegemony of these non-capitalist relations in production and has entered into a phase of dialectical alternation with them. This alternation is one reason why some claim that the development of capitalist production relations is taking place (Shenton and Lennihan 1981; Shenton 1985; Watts 1983; Lennihan 1983, 1986) and others insist it is not (Williams 1983; Hill 1972, 1977; Norman 1972).

Background

My interest in the emergence of wage labor I owe to having been among those schooled by Robert Murphy in the method of cultural ecology shortly after he wrote "Basic Ethnography and Ecological Theory" (1970). This article was especially influential for three reasons. The first was its treatment of the trinity of environment, technology, and work in Julian Steward's theory of cultural ecology. Murphy left no doubt as to the primacy of work. As he put it, "Quite simply, the theory of cultural ecology is concerned with the process of work, its organization, its cycles and rhythm and its situational modalities. This is not at all the sole determinant of the fabric of social life, but it is always the point at which Steward starts" (1970:155). Second, Murphy pointed out the applicability of cultural ecology to the analysis of social change, not just social structure. In "Tappers and Trappers" (Murphy and Steward 1956), for example, he and Steward had undertaken an examination of two societies in which social change resulted from the commercialization of subsistence and exchange activities following exposure to similar European mercantile systems. This historical analysis had great appeal. By the 1970s, the statement of the problem of "culture change" was different (and grossly obscured by such terms as "the commoditization of social reproduction," according to Murphy, once it became clear that we were talking about the same thing). Nevertheless, twenty years after "Tappers and Trappers," there was still great interest in how the increased production of commodities for the world market, often under the aegis of European merchant capital, was affecting the nature of social reproduction in a range of societies. Regardless of differing terminology, Murphy and Steward had been there first. (And as Murphy points out so had Steward's Puerto Rico project (1956), not to mention Robert Lowie!)

There was, however, one problem. Murphy and Steward dealt with change in two simple societies. Therefore a third important point in "Basin Ethnography" (1970) was that cultural ecology was equally applicable to the analysis of complex societies. According to Steward, the determinative effect of nature on society was greatest in societies having rudimentary technology and low social complexity. "In complex societies certain components of the social superstructure rather than ecology seem to be determinative of further developments" (Steward 1938: 262, quoted in Murphy 1970: 159). Murphy agreed to the extent that the term ecology refers to the natural environment. But for Murphy, the most important ingredient of ecology was not the natural environment but the organization of work. Thus he concluded, "I would question whether the course of history is influenced less by work in complex societies. Rather it would be more accurate to say that work is decreasingly conditioned by nature as human artifice increases" (1970: 159).

Many probably underestimate the impact of "Basin Ethnography and Ecology Theory" (1970). The publication the following year of *The Dialectics of Social Life* (1971) undoubtedly overshadowed it. But it is important to consider "Basin Ethnography" (1970) in light of the great interest in ecological anthropology at that time. Given the dominance of the ecosystem approach, Murphy's reintroduction of Steward's cultural ecology was significant. For many students, Murphy's interpretation of Steward was extremely attractive. It was distinctly materialist. It was suited to the analysis of historical process. It was applicable to complex as well as simple societies. But first and foremost, it focused on the social organization of work.

This background framed my research on wage labor. That these data make most sense when one notes their dialectical nature is a testament to Murphy the dialectician. It also confirms his view that data influence one's theoretical analysis as much as one's theoretical orientation defines one's research; i.e., data and theory interact dialectically as they proceed toward explanation.

Agricultural Wage Contracts in Northern Nigeria Today

The use of capital to mobilize labor in northern Nigeria must be discussed in the context of several facts concerning labor in relation to land and technology. As for the latter, while the odd tractor is seen in the countryside, the hand plow and hoe are ubiquitous. Also, as noted earlier, most producers have not been separated from the land. While there are landless laborers, both local villagers and wandering men, a large proletariat laboring for the landed rich has not emerged. The household (*gandu*, pl. *gandaye*) is the primary unit of agricultural production. Of varied composition, the unit includes any combination of a senior male, along with his married and unmarried sons and brothers, their sons, and clients. In the past, it also might include slaves, and before the spread of wife seclusion, women of the household (Smith 1954). It is this production unit which recruits extra-household labor. The following discussion of agricultural wage labor, or *kwadago*[2], is based on research I conducted in a small town of 5,000 in Kaduna State from 1977-79.[3]

Agricultural wage contracts take three basic forms in Hausaland. One is *jinga* which people say is the oldest. An employer negotiates with one or more men a piece-wage for a set task, say, weeding a field of maize.[4] While the employer is concerned with the task's timely completion, the number of days the laborer toils is not the specified basis of the wage. Nevertheless, laborers expect small payments as the job progresses. Significantly, they are called *kudin abinci*, literally "money for food." In the past, an employer also sent a noonday meal of porridge to the field where *jinga* men were working. While this practice has withered away in most locales, numerous other social rights and obligations continue to tie employer and *jinga* workers. A loyal worker who guarantees his services to an employer and who works in a careful and timely fashion expects to be rewarded for more than delivering his labor power. Requests for loans of food or money are common. Employers wishing to insure loyalty not only entertain such requests, they also provide generous gifts on religious and ceremonial occasions. In some instances, long-term patron-client relationships grow to the point where an employer may assist a loyal laborer in obtaining land, a wife, even setting him up with a secondary trade. Recipients of such assistance of course take on varied obligations, many of them typical of clientage relationships (see Scott 1972).

To understand fully the nature of *jinga* contracts, particularly their non-monetary aspects, it is useful to consider the pre-existing social rights and obligations that once constituted an earlier form of extra-household labor recruitment. This is the now defunct institution of *sarkin noma* (lit. "the chief of farming"). In the past, a wealthy large farmer called *sarkin noma* was expected to help his neighbors in times of hardship. Should a village be struck by famine or a poor harvest, the customary expectation was that the *sarkin noma* would respond in a number of ways. First, he was expected to open his grain stores to the less fortunate. Second, in lesser calamities, such as harvest shortfalls, he might pay the tax of individuals or even of the entire village. While the repayment of these "gifts," as well as other incidental loans made in times of personal and community crisis, might not be calculated directly, repayment in the form of labor service was customary. Confronted by a maize harvest threatened by rains, a *sarkin noma* could and did call on the labor of fellow villagers to help him. As such the institution of *sarkin noma* was a system of redistribution where extra-household labor was provided to large farmers facing production crises in exchange for assistance to small farmers facing crises of simple reproduction.

Informants disagree as to the date of the death of the last *sarkin noma*. While some say twenty to thirty years ago, all agree that the institution is dead. A big farmer still may be called a *sarkin noma*, but the term now refers to the size of his harvest, not his generosity. Nevertheless, the nature of *jinga* contracts is such that they allow laborers to continue to press people to whom they supply labor for aid, loans, and gifts. It is true that *jinga* contracts are based on a negotiated wage for a set task. Still, it is extremely difficult for an employer not to make a gift on ceremonial occasions to a fellow townsman who labors for him. Similarly, employers squirm under social pressure when approached for loans of food or money for food, the sort of aid typically expected from a *sarkin noma* in the past.

The second wage form in contemporary Hausaland is one contracted on the basis of a time wage. In fact, there are several time-wage contracts which vary according to the length of the working day. The first is *wuni-wuni* (in other locales called *uni*.)[5] Informants hold that *wuni-wuni* arose about five years prior to the famine known as *Yar Gusau*, in 1942-43. It is a payment for a day's work, starting at about 7:00 A.M. and ending with the afternoon prayer at 5:00 P.M. Payments do not vary with the task, nor are they subject to negotiation, which is most significant.[6] The wage, however, does vary seasonally, dipping at points in the agricultural season when labor demand drops.

While Marx points out that "wages by piece are nothing else than a converted form of wages by time, just as wages by time are a converted form of the value or price of labour-power" (Marx 1967: 551), one must still note the advantages and disadvantages to employer and laborer of time- and piece-wage rates. The onset of *wuni-wuni*, for example, is attributed to an increase in the number of strangers arriving in town seeking work. While small daily advances could be gotten with a *jinga* contract, strangers wanted to be paid in full at day's end so that they could leave town when they wanted. Local employers obliged, because with the advent of an increased number of strangers -- many of them laid-off workers from the nearby Jos tin fields -- *jinga* became a less secure contract. Strangers were more likely than fellow townsmen to run away with daily advances, without completing the job.

At some point, *wuni-wuni* gave way to a second time-wage, *sha biu*. In the past on market or mosque day, workers employed to work *wuni-wuni* only worked until *sha biu*, which literally means twelve, or noon in this case. In time, *sha biu* became the predominant time-related labor contract. It is possible to view this change as a shortening of the working day from 5:00 P.M. to twelve noon, but its introduction allowed for a second shift of afternoon time-rated work, *yammaci* (lit. "to eat the west," e.g., the direction of the setting sun). *Yammaci* workers labor from about 2:00 P.M. until 5:00 P.M. In the past, *sha biu* and *wuni-wuni* workers received a meal while laboring, just as *jinga* workers did. Hill (1972) reports this is still so where she worked, but this custom has withered in my research locale.

The most recent innovation in labor contracts is *farashi*, a third contract form that has not reached many areas of Hausaland.[7] *Farashi*, like *jinga*, involves a piece-wage. The difference is that while *jinga* contracts are negotiated for a job -- such as weeding a field -- *farashi* is negotiated by the ridge. A worker may complete as many ridges as he chooses. The number of workers on a field may vary throughout the day. Often employers do not even know how many men are involved or their names. Not surprisingly, such customary fringes as a noonday meal, a kola nut, or a cigarette do not figure. Even more to the employer's liking, their impersonal relationship to *farashi* workers means that other customary expectations drop away. Few see their employers as sources of loans or gifts, or as patrons.

Accounts of the origins of *farashi* are conflicting, dating it anywhere from five to fifteen years ago. Some claim that laborers initiated *farashi*, wanting the option to intensify their effort and to be paid immediately a sum based on output. Others claim that employers pushed for *farashi* because *sha biu* workers increasingly required careful supervision, or they slacked off during the day.

Whatever its origins, *farashi* is popular with employers. First, it does away with requests for loans and gifts. Second, there are no daily cash advances, which removes the risk of disappearing *jinga* workers. However, like *jinga*, it guarantees the relation between wage and output. *Sha biu* as a time-wage subjects the employer to the variation in employees' work speed, especially if they are unsupervised. *Farashi* shifts the burden of this variation back onto the laborer. *Farashi* is also preferred among certain laborers: itinerants, those seeking fast cash, the young and strapping. The old and tired do not do well with this new wage form. Nor do employers who are concerned with the quality or specifications of the work done by hasty *farashi* workers trying to maximize their wage by working as quickly as possible.

The emergence of these contracts points to the increased commoditization of labor. The order of their emergence suggests a continuum along which capital, or wages, increasingly replace non-monetary rights and obligations of employers and laborers. While capital is the basis of all three contracts, along this continuum employer-worker relations become more narrow, more individualized and ultimately more objectified. But this tendency is checked by another. All three contracts exist simultaneously. Each one emerges as an option to an earlier contract form, but it does not replace it. The effect is that the progression toward increased objectification is not a simple linear one through time.

Jinga, first to emerge, initially coexists with the institution of *sarkin noma*. Both involve extremely similar, if not identical, patron-client rights and obligations. But when it comes to these rights and obligations, *jinga* differs in one crucial way. It frees the patron from those rights and obligations that tied a *sarkin noma* and the community as a whole. As such, *jinga* dismantles a system of redistribution where a patron's assistance to a community in times of crisis was repaid in the form of community-wide labor service. Neither the assistance or repayment was calculated with the precision of a market transaction -- i.e., they were not commodities. What *jinga* preserves, and then modifies, is the relationship of the *sarkin noma*, or patron, to the individual in times of personal crisis. Gifts, loans, influence, lodging, food, and so forth pass from the employer to individuals he has engaged in a *jinga* contract. And just as these items of patronage are not viewed as commodities, neither is the worker loyalty that is expected in return.

While a positivist might note that *jinga* adds a wage to the patron-client relationship involving a *sarkin noma*, a dialectician would also see *jinga* for what it is not: a set of rights and obligations that links a patron to a community as a whole. These rights and obligations are narrowed under *jinga*. *Jinga* maintains only the set of *sarkin noma* rights and obligations that pertains to individuals. After all, under *jinga* labor becomes for the first time a commodity which is purchased and sold for a precise price. Associated with the specificity of this new market transaction is the fact that it is contracted on an individual rather than community-wide basis.

Wuni-wuni (and its later variants, *sha biu* and *yammaci*) goes considerably further toward severing patron-client rights and obligations. It acknowledges that labor is a commodity that is purchased not only from individual community members, but also from individuals who are strangers. On the surface it changes the basis of payment from piece work to time. Most significant, however, is what does *not* happen in this arrangement. There is no explicit obligation on the part of the employer to extend gifts, credit, or food to his employees, nor is he subject to *jinga's* other ensnaring obligations. The other side of the coin is that there is nothing binding the worker. At the end of the work day, he can leave, free of obligation or further expectations, his wages paid in full. This arrangement clearly responds to changes in the organization of labor that increasingly find strangers contracting with one another.

Farashi, the latest form, is a response to a heightened level of estrangement between employer and employee. It is based, once again, on piece work rather than time. This returns to the employer a measure of control over the relation between wage and output, like *jinga*, but does so under conditions where the social relations of work are impersonal and temporary. What *farashi* does not do is reactivate the unwaged social rights and obligations that accompany *jinga*. From the employee's point of view, *farashi* provides the option to intensify his effort for immediate reward. What is absent here is the confidence previously held by employers implicit in a time wage. In other words, the employer no longer trusts the employee to do the work. He must structurally guarantee it by tying payment to a complete job. To date, *farashi* is the last point on the continuum which moves toward the increased objectification and estrangement of extra-household labor relations.

Along this continuum, however, something is not happening. *Sha biu* and *yammaci* have not replaced *jinga*, nor has *farashi*, the most objectified of the three, wiped out its predecessors. Each successor is indeed born of its previous form. But it is only *sarkin noma*, the unwaged, uncommoditized social relation that, after an initial period of co-existence with *jinga* and *wuni-wuni*, finally has been laid to rest. Meanwhile the three new wage forms, although differing in the degree to which they objectify labor, co-exist.

Given the temporal arrangement of these contracts and the increasing preeminence of capital, one might be led to expect the capitalists always to favor the more objectified contract, and conversely, the employee always to favor the older forms, hence their coexistence. But this is far from always true.

The Organization of Work and Contract Types

The realities of the organization of work on the ground create interests on the part of both employee and employer that lead to different contractual arrangements and preferences. The pure commoditization of labor is not in every instance in the best interest of the employer, nor are the rights and obligations of clientage always most attractive to the worker. While history may be favoring the objectification of employer-employee relations, the agents of history, in this case those negotiating the terms on which labor is bought and sold, act differently.

The Agricultural Cycle and Changing Labor Demand

When examining factors of the organization of work that lead to the choice of one contract over another, one of the most important is the changing demand for labor over the course of the agricultural season, which runs from May to December. The terms of employment shift dramatically during this period. For example, labor bottlenecks occur during May and June when new ridging and planting take place, favoring the worker (Lennihan 1983: 236). Because late planting can sharply reduce yields, employers go to great lengths to insure that they will not be caught short of labor during this crucial period (Lennihan 1983: 223). As might be expected, many enter into *farashi* contracts. For one thing, it insures the work will be done quickly by men wishing to maximize output because they are being paid piece-rate. Another good thing about *farashi* is that because it is contracted by the ridge rather than by the whole job, an employer can increase his total labor supply with miscellaneous laborers interested in very brief periods of employment. For example, a local man interested in extra cash can do a little *farashi* work after returning from his own farm. But it also is at this period of peak labor demand that employers may enter into *jinga* contracts. Acts of patronage on top of a wage can help to secure labor from men in need of credit, housing, food and so forth.

There are, however, also times when labor demand drops off, favoring the employer. There are several periods in the agricultural cycle when it is common to hear workers complain, "*ba aiki*" ("no work"). This area's bimodal rainfall distribution means that a short period of inconsistent rains in May, during which labor demand for ridging and planting is great, is followed by a dry period of several weeks (Lennihan 1983: 244). During May and June there are typically numerous periods when the soil is so sun-baked as to make work impossible. Again, in August and September, the demand for labor drops off. For one thing, it rains almost every day, often all day, making it hard to work. Also, by this time most crops are maturing, requiring less attention. During this time, the terms of employment shift in favor of the employer. One might expect then that *farashi* would predominate, being the least ensnaring contract from the employer's point of view. *Jinga* contracts, however, are also common at this time. After all, a wise employer tempers his labor arrangements knowing that shortly there will be a gradual upsurge in labor demand as different crops become ready to harvest from October through December. There is also the ridging season of the next year to keep in mind. Contract negotiations reflect the supply and demand for labor at the specific moment a contract is negotiated, but they may also be influenced by anticipation of supply-demand relations over the length of the entire cycle, or even subsequent cycles.

Skill

Not all workers possess the skills required for certain tasks and crops. Strangers from areas of the far north where soils are sandy and ridging is uncommon may lack the skill for this task -- demand for which constitutes a major labor bottleneck in May and June. Those from other areas of the north where there is ridging, but with a different sort of hand plow, often are unskilled in handling the local tool. An employer's approach to such men is tricky. While they may be slow and awkward at ridging, there is no such problem with their weeding skills. Furthermore, when it comes to weeding, they are extremely hard workers. They claim this is because of the shorter rainy season in the north. They extend cultivation time by working far longer days than are commonly worked locally. True or not, because of their speed and endurance they prefer piece work. And, as it turns out, they prefer *farashi* to *jinga*. For one thing many such northerners have no intention of settling. Many have their own farms in the north and are only looking for brief employment. In some instances this is due to harvest shortfalls following inadequate rainfall, often a more severe problem in the northerly region of their origin. More typically, it is because rains in the north arrive later. As a result, the patronage associated with *jinga* lacks appeal, although many employers would love to find a way to have first call on these hard workers, even if they do not know how to ridge.

Ridging is not the only operation some workers do not know how to do. Weeding upland rice is particularly difficult because blades of young rice and grass are difficult to distinguish. Until recently in this area rice was a relatively uncommon luxury crop. Because of this many laborers lack experience with it. Nevertheless some unskilled workers take the job *farashi*, do a hasty job, at best leaving many weeds and at worst trampling the rice. Only the most skilled worker is able to make good enough time to undertake such a task *farashi*. A conscientious worker with only limited experience with the task might well prefer to be paid a time wage, of *sha biu*.

Care

Other factors that impinge on contract choice include the care and thoroughness which is required to different degrees for different crops. Take ridging. Ridges can be prematurely inundated by weeds because grassy topsoil has not been turned deeply or thoroughly enough. Obviously this concerns an employer, but how much will it affect the sort of contract he negotiates? It is true that hasty *farashi* workers may create ridges that will shortly turn into a weeding nightmare. The question is whether an employer would rather negotiate a *sha biu* or *jinga* contract. After all, a worker being paid the time-rated *sha biu* wage might be more likely to work in a painstaking manner. So might a *jinga* client if he is hoping for extra gifts and loans. In actuality, many employers nevertheless choose *farashi* and risk the possibility of sloppy work. It is not just that *farashi* frees the employer of social obligations to his employees. In addition he knows that *farashi* workers have incentive to get the job done quickly. As noted earlier, this is a very important consideration when it comes to ridging, especially for the early-planted grains which suffer yield declines from delayed planting. In the last analysis, care and thoroughness in ridging is a worry, but there are other concerns as well which affect the organization of this work.

This, however, is not the case when it comes to transplanting delicate seedlings which requires extreme care. As it happens, those crops that grow from transplanted seedlings are in almost every instance high value cash crops -- tobacco, tomatoes, and peppers, to name a few. The prices these crops fetch make the exercise of care more essential than in the case of ridging. As a result, an employer would be unlikely to hire a stranger in a *farashi* contract to transplant tomatoes. Not only do *farashi* workers work fast to maximize their wages, but the *farashi* arrangement involves the lowest degree of employer-employee contact and the smallest amount of employee obligation.

The Stranger versus Local Question

Another characteristic of labor that affects the organization of work and is reflected in the contract is whether the worker is a stranger or a fellow townsman. One survey I conducted showed the town's labor pool to be constituted of almost equal numbers of strangers and townsmen (Lennihan 1983: 236). There are advantages and disadvantages to hiring from both categories.

What are some of the advantages of hiring strangers? First, unlike townsmen, strangers do not have local farms and therefore are a potential source of regular labor. Secondly, because employers may be seen as a source of patronage, there is another reason for hiring a stranger. Many transient strangers depart before those religious holidays that require gift-giving. Similarly, because strangers traveling afar in search of work usually do not bring their families or are bachelors, their employers escape requests for large gifts and loans either for the general maintenance of the worker's family or for special ceremonial occasions.

There are disadvantages related to the transiency of strangers, however. Foremost is the fact that it mitigates their potential to provide an employer with a constant labor supply. For example, as mentioned earlier, there are men who come from the north where the rains arrive later or are inadequate who practice a brief southerly labor migration. With farms of their own, their stay is necessarily brief.

A second category of transient laborer is the *gardi*. His attractiveness to the employer is greater because he does not have a farm. While no research has been done on the *gardi*, it seems he is a middle-aged man who travels to the country from a large urban area. He is considered to be so serious a Koranic student that he denies himself wives or children, regarding them as distractions from his true calling. The fact that he supports himself by doing agricultural wage labor, and not merely by collecting alms, distinguishes the *gardi* from other Koranic scholars, as does his permanent bachelorhood. While employers attempt to win over the *gardi* with accommodation and food, most arrive in town, take on a large single job requiring several weeks for completion, collect their pay and leave.

The most numerous category of laboring strangers are called *yan duniya* (sing. *dan duniya*, lit. "son of the earth"). These are men who disappear from their hometown under the cover of night, usually leaving their families and their possessions behind. Some are running from the law or have been released from jail. They are said to have adopted the world as their mother (*ya tafi uwa duniya*) (Hill 1977: 143). Alternatively such men are called *yan dandi*. *Dandi* in this context applies to someone thought to have disappeared to "live a profligate life in a big city; those whose whereabouts are unknown and are presumed to be wrongdoers" (Hill 1977: 143). A less derogatory term is *yan iska*, literally "sons of the wind."

Relations between such wandering men of the countryside and their employers naturally take account of the laborers' unknown past as well as of their potential future mobility. Typically, a *dan duniya* arrives in town and begins inquiring about work. Nobody knows anything about him. He may arrive penniless. He requires lodging. Usually he does not bring a hoe, so he must be lent one, which may disappear when he does. He may be a careless worker. There is no assurance of how long he will stay. He may vanish in the middle of a job, after taking an advance.

Such are the risks. Nevertheless, many employers take a chance. In fact, when coming across a man who seems to be a good and reliable worker, employers may set out to develop ties of loyalty. While strangers often sleep in rented rooms and eat in the marketplace, employers may seek to win over a good worker with lodging and an evening meal. There develops the unspoken assumption that the employer has the first right to the worker's labor service.

As for the hiring of locals, there are also advantages and disadvantages. Foremost among the disadvantages of hiring a townsman is that his own farm competes for his time, if not always successfully, and may make him less available for wage-laboring than a stranger. A second, previously mentioned liability is that fellow townsmen see their employers as a traditional source of loans, advances, and outright gifts.

Foremost among the advantages of hiring a local is a public reputation. Townsmen who are lazy, slow, or careless workers are well-known. Similarly, townsmen have their own tools, which does away with the fear of loaned implements being stolen. Unlike strangers, locals do not require lodging or a place to take their evening meal. Finally, townsmen are not likely to vanish from town altogether, taking with them advances for an uncompleted job. This does not mean hiring a local man is risk-free. While less likely to act in a downright dishonest fashion, many local men prove unreliable.

Two Cases

The following cases are examples of how the variables just discussed come into play.

Musa is a twenty-two year old *dan duniya*. He claims to have left Karen Namoda in Sokoto State two years ago to greet his dead father's brother in Zaria. Musa's best friend and constant companion, a native of the town, says he does not know the real reason Musa left home even though he has known him for two years. Musa told him it was because of trouble in his house with his mother since his father died. Musa says he will go home this year before his wife divorces him. His friend doubts he has a wife. He also doubts Musa will go home.

In Zaria, Musa began doing *aikin kasa* (soil preparation for making adobe building blocks). At that time one Alhaji Isiaku, living in Zaria, received a contract to build a primary school in Kulle, a small village near my research locale. Musa and four others came to Kulle as laborers to work on the school. Through a friend he made in the village who did farm labor, Musa met Alhaji Sule, a man from the town where I worked. He moved to town and rented a room in a house with another wage laborer. At the end of the dry-season, Musa met Alhaji Sule's brother, Alhaji Yahaya. Musa worked for Alhaji Yahaya continually throughout the rainy season. He also worked for Audu Kosai for one day weeding his peanuts with one other man. Musa says he only did this because Alhaji Yahaya had no money until he sold a cow in Zaria. Musa also worked for Tanko making new ridges for tomatoes in the rain. Musa held that he only worked for Tanko because Alhaji Yahaya would not work in the rain. Musa says that he is loyal to Alhaji Yahaya because he gives Musa money when he has none. The Alhaji makes these loans without interest and on the days when Musa is working off the debt, the Alhaji "dashes" him fifty kobo (one-half a naira; in 1976 N1=$1.56). Similarly, when Alhaji Yahaya tires and dismisses Musa early, Musa still gets paid for a full day's work. Alhaji Yahaya lent Musa the *galma* (hand-plow) he uses as he did not travel from Sokoto with one. Alhaji Yahaya, however, never pays Musa *farashi*, that is, by the ridge, but rather by the day, *sha biu*, or by the job, *jinga*. Being young and strong Musa could make more money being paid *farashi*.

By the end of the rainy season, however, when employment was scarce, Musa became disgruntled. The Alhaji had offered him and two others a *jinga* contract for N15 to weed a very grassy farm. They refused, insisting on being paid by the day *sha biu* or a larger sum, *jinga*. The Alhaji refused. Musa said he knew he would end up doing the work eventually. If the Alhaji approached him first, it would be *sha biu*; if Musa approached the Alhaji it would be for the N15 *jinga*. Musa claimed he would not do the work because the other two laborers refused. At the same time he said, "But how can I take work from someone else when Alhaji Yahaya still has work?"

After four days Malam Ibrahim asked Musa to make new ridges for beans and cotton. Offering to pay Musa *farashi*, the price was fifty kobo a ridge for nine ridges, or N4.50. Musa had worked once before for Ibrahim during the period of fasting when Alhaji Yahaya found going to the farm too tiring. Ibrahim explained to Musa where he had hidden a *galma* (hand-plow) on the farm since it would be inappropriate for Musa to borrow Alhaji Yahaya's. When Musa went he could not find it. Claiming that he would drop the work should Alhaji Yahaya approach him, it took Musa seven days to track down Ibrahim in order to clarify the location of the *galma*. A young bachelor, he passed his idle days in one of the town's eight houses of ill-repute. Upon renegotiation with Malam Ibrahim, the lucrative ridging job had vanished, and a weeding job had replaced it. Two days of weeding forty ridges *jinga* brought Musa N5.50.

There are two ends to Musa's story. One day he disappeared from town. His friend says that his mother came from Sokoto and took him home. Others say he entered a transit van heading for Jos.

As a young man, Musa might have been expected to seek *farashi* labor which would enable him to capitalize on his own physical strength. Similarly, a *farashi* contract would expedite the mobility often sought by strangers because it provides them with their wages at day's end. Instead, a *jinga* contract with Alhaji Yahaya is attractive to him. Associated with this is a patron-client relationship that gives him a line of credit at favorable terms with the Alhaji and the possibility of permanence a wandering man might desire. Alhaji Yahaya, for his part, is acting in such a way as to suggest that Musa has something to offer him beyond simple labor. Perhaps Musa's youth and strength or his apparent willingness to settle down induce the Alhaji to offer Musa *jinga* contracts. Certainly the Alhaji is hoping that loyalty will insure him of Musa's labor in the period of highest demand. A dilemma emerges, however, during the slack period when the demand for labor has fallen off. The Alhaji has to decide whether his desire to turn Musa into a client and a source of guaranteed labor is such that he is willing to back this up with a generous wage when labor is abundant. As it turns out, Musa shows great ambivalence when it comes to Alhaji's expectations during this period and ends up being seduced by the offer of *farashi* elsewhere. When Musa leaves town it is clear that he has been a bad investment for Alhaji Yahaya. Maybe the Alhaji anticipated this possibility, because he had never increased the benefits of patronage beyond the use of his hand plow and small loans for spending money. He never, for example, offered Musa lodging or food in his own home. Perhaps the Alhaji will be reluctant in the future to hire a stranger in a *jinga* contract.

Dan Kaka is a fifty-five-year old farmer who farms together with his thirty-year old married son, Haruna. Haruna is married to the daughter of his father's senior brother, by whom he has a young child. They live and eat with Dan Kaka's family. In addition to farming together, they both take in laundry to wash and press. Dan Kaka does not hire labor, nor does he sell it. His household lives modestly, is self-supporting, and appears stable. By the middle of July, however, Haruna was no longer working with his father. In fact he had run away. It turns out he wants to take as a second wife a forty-year old prostitute with whom he has been in love for three years. Dan Kaka is adamant in his refusal to allow his son to marry this woman.

The upshot in this rift between father and son is that Dan Kaka is for the first time confronted with the necessity of hiring labor. As it happens, shortly after Haruna's departure Ramadan began, requiring Dan Kaka to begin fasting. By August his fasting has taken its toll and he finds it increasingly difficult to do the farm work, especially without Haruna. In particular, he is extremely concerned about his rice crop, which Haruna helped him plant, but is now becoming choked with weeds.

He realizes he must hire labor. His neighbor, whose farm needs little attention at this point in the agricultural cycle, has a reliable son Dan Kaka has known since his birth. Dan Kaka hires him to do the painstaking and skilled job of weeding his rice. The contract is *farashi*.

The choice of contract is unusual considering the dangers to a rice crop that hasty work represents. What is more, at this point in the agricultural cycle when there is a labor glut, it would appear that Dan Kaka could surely find a worker happy to work *sha biu*. This is especially true given that the need for cash has been heightened by the forthcoming celebration of the end of Ramadan at which time gifts, new clothes, and fancy foods are purchased. It is no mystery, therefore, that his neighbor's son had a burning desire to work and to work hard, a propensity which favors his desire for *farashi*. Dan Kaka is willing to go along with this for two reasons. One is because he is sure of his neighbor's son's reliability. The other is that he plans to sit there and watch to make sure the young man works carefully.

Conclusion

A dialectical approach to agricultural wage contracts in Hausaland reveals forms that emerge from earlier forms that differ as much in their noncontents as their positive attributes. Each later form contains both the persistence of attributes of its predecessor an the contradiction, or negation, of other attributes. Using this point of view, largely indebted to Murphy's formulation, I have been able to demonstrate a trend toward commoditization of labor that is supported by, but is not wholly defined by, the linear arrangement of this emergence through time.

The fact that such a trend remains largely unacknowledged by proponents of both classical (Hill 1972, 1977; Norman 1972) and radical (Williams 1983) persuasions is attributable to the fact that both regard the nonexistence of a large landless laboring class as justification for their neglect of the compelling topic of Hausa wage labor. Perhaps they would find further justification for their positions in the fact that, of the wage contract forms, none has completely supplanted its predecessors. I can only suggest that even in modern industrial states different degrees of objectification can be found in contracts for wage labor; few would argue that, owing to this variety, labor has not emerged as a commodity.

The organization of work itself, the Murphys remind us, is at the base of the cultural pyramid, and it is in these particulars -- the crops, the tasks, the seasons, the characteristics of labor -- that we can find the dynamic tensions that elevate one form of contract over another in one situation, and favor another contract under other conditions. These particulars show us that "capitalists" do not always opt for objectified forms, while workers seek more broadly encumbering personal ties. The explanations, both for persistence and change, are far more complex. The

Murphys would not be surprised.

FOOTNOTES

[1] There are exceptions in the densely settled zones surrounding the cities of Kano and Sokoto, but others as well (see Hill 1977, Ch. 3; Mortimore and Wilson 1965). How the 1978 Land Use Decree, which for the first time allows for the registration of private title to land outside of urban areas, will affect the question of landlessness is not yet certain.

[2] The term *kwadago* is used here to refer to agricultural wage labor in general. Hill (1972) and Norman (1972) make a distinction between *kwadago*, hired labor calculated and rewarded in terms of time, and *jinga*, contract labor employed for the completion of a fixed task. Where I worked, however, *kwadago* describes agricultural wage labor without reference to the nature of the contract. *Sha biu*, which I describe below, is used to refer to what Hill calls *kwadago*, a time rate for a morning's work of five or six hours.

[3] I have dealt elsewhere with the historical factors affecting the increased importance of agricultural wage labor in the colonial period (Lennihan 1983: Ch. 3; Shenton and Lennihan 1981), and also with the frequency and purposes of such labor transactions in a contemporary Hausa community (Lennihan 1986, forthcoming).

[4] Hill's (1972: 105) discussion of wage labor holds that *jinga* is a relatively unimportant system of contract labor. This is very surprising, for *jinga* is the most frequent form of labor payment where I worked. In the area of her research, the predominant labor contract involves a day wage. A laborer is paid a "standard" wage, which varies somewhat seasonally, for some five to six hours' work. While Hill does not name it, in my research locale this contract is called *sha biu*. In this area, no noonday meal is expected by a man working *sha biu*. In Hill's area a man is served "free porridge" (*fura*) while at work (Ibid.).

[5] It is known as *uni* in Kano (Paul Ross, personal communication), and *aikin rana-rana* in southern Katsina (Tukur Ingawa, personal communication).

[6] Reddy (1984: 63-64) and Hobsbawn (1964: 8) draw attention to important differences between wages which are fixed by customary expectation and wages which involve bargaining in the context of some degree of market calculations.

[7] Hill does not mention it (1972: 105). Watts confirms its absence in northern Katsina (personal communication). It does, however, occur in southern Katsina where it is called *aikin kuyya* (lit., "the work of ridges") (Ingawa, personal communication).

15

FAMILY, RELIGION AND STATE: MIDDLE EASTERN MODELS

Suad Joseph
University of California, Davis

Introduction

The resurgence of Islamic fundamentalism in the Middle East has spurred a rapid growth in the literature on women, family and Islam (Esposito 1982, Rahman 1980, Al-Hibri 1982a, Al-Sayyid-1983, Smith 1980). An expanding scholarship on women, family, and the state in the Middle East is also emerging (Sanasarian 1982, Nashat 1983a, Soffan 1980). This latter literature is mainly in articles (Tekeli 1981, Halila 1984, White 1978, Tessler 1978, Hussein 1985, Attir 1985, Hatem forthcoming) or in conference papers (Kandiyoti 1984, Charrad 1984, Paige 1985, Joseph 1984, 1985a, b, Lazreg 1985, Hatem 1985).

Because of the historic close connection between Islam and Middle Eastern states, the issues raised in these studies are of direct relevance to each other. However, given the recency of the research on the relationships between gender, family, religion, and state in the region, the linkages have yet to be developed. Empirical studies are often relatively sketchy. And, given the state of empirical research, theoretical work is speculative and schematic.

In this paper, I will outline the beginnings of an investigation into the relationships between women, family, religion, and state in two Middle Eastern societies for which little literature exists linking these issues -- Lebanon and Iraq. My purpose is to expand the available case studies in order to enhance the possibilities for comparisons and theory-building. A more thorough understanding of these questions, however, requires an historical anthropology of Middle Eastern family systems. I will follow the case studies with a discussion of a provocative model for such an undertaking -- Jack Goody's historical anthropology of the European family. I will conclude with a research agenda for an historical anthropology of the relationships between gender, family, religion, and the state in the Middle East.

The State of Research

While the literature on women, family, and Islam is expanding, relatively little of it is concerned with the state as a central question. The literature on women, family, and the state, however, often does consider Islam. That is, scholars are more likely to treat Islam as a system apart from Middle Eastern states in discussions of women and family than they are likely to treat the state as a system apart from Islam. This is perhaps based on assumptions of the unity and continuity of Islam and the temporalness of states. It is, however, probably more useful to see both in their diversities and historical specificities. As Leila Ahmed (1984) has argued, the hegemony of an orthodoxy should not prevent scholars from recognizing the multiplicities of Islams that have and continue to thrive.

Much of the literature on women, family, and Islam is concerned with the question of whether early Islam constituted an advance in women's status vis-a-vis men, either in the intent of the Prophet or in the lived early practice (Al-Hibri 1982b, El Saadawi 1980), 1982, Smith and Haddad 1982, Smith 1985, Rahman 1983, Ferdows and Ferdows 1983). For Al-Hibri (1982b) and El Saadawi (1982), the pre-Islamic Arabian peninsula was matriarchal. Women continued to play key roles in early Islamic society, and even in later periods in mystical Islam (Schimmel 1982, Ahmed 1984). It was the rise of patriarchal Islam (Al-Hibri 1982b) or the combination of patriarchal Islam and class society based on private property, reinforced later by capitalism and imperialism (El Saadawi 1982) that has led to the oppression of women in Muslim societies. Some scholars (Soffan 1980, Esposito 1982, Rahman 1983) contend that early Islam improved the status of women. It is only later corruptions brought about by state formation, the rigidification of tradition, or outside influences that have resulted in women's reduced status. A return to an earlier, purer form of Islam (Soffan 1980) or revitalization of Islam's earlier potential for self-reform would improve women's position vis-a-vis men (Esposito 1982, Rahman 1980). For other scholars (Sabbah 1984), oppression is a fundamental process in Islamic practice -- for both men and women, although doubly so for women. Islam is seen, by some scholars, as a possible avenue to improved status for some classes of women who find in it protection and mobility, in the context of current social, political and economic turmoil (Haddad 1985, Ahmed 1985). For believers in the faith, Islam is the true path to women's liberation (Khomeini 1982, Taleghani 1982, Tabatabai 1982).

The debates on the "true" meaning of Islam in regards to women are often exegetical. They tend to take the form of new readings of the Qur'an, interpretations of hadith or decodings of formal (legal) and informal (non-theological) discourse. As in earlier debates on whether Islam fostered or prevented the rise of capitalism (Rodinson 1973, Gran 1979), the textual analysis must be linked to the social practices of particular historical periods. For this, an historical anthropology of Islam is needed.

More particularly, the study of the meanings of Islam for women needs to be linked to analyses of the practices and institutions of Islamic states. While an historical anthropology of the relationships between women and Islamic states also has to be developed, there is the beginnings of a scholarship on women and contemporary Middle Eastern states. This literature falls into several topical foci: political movements and/or state formation; state legal reforms, particularly in the area of personal status laws; state extension of social services which affect women; and state creation of jobs or regulation of work conditions. It is in the coverage of the first two problems that scholars tend to discuss the relationships between gender, Islam and the state.

Scholars interested in the impact of state formation on women tend to be concerned with the conditions which affect women's political participation, who and how women come to be defined as political actors, the benefits and limitations of state programs for women, the connections between nationalism, feminism, Islam and the state -- among other questions (Joseph 1986a).

A number of scholars have argued that there is a close connection, in a number of Middle Eastern societies, between women's issues, nationalism, religion, and state formation. Kandiyoti (1984) argues that feminism was an integral part of nationalism in Turkey from the 19th century, disagreeing with Tekeli (1981) who contends that the nationalists' position on women emulated and aimed to win over Western approval. Pahlevi Iran, however, Sanasarian (1982) argues, was emulating Turkey and presenting a modern face to the West. In Iran, as in Iraq (Joseph 1982), Tunisia (Charrad 1984), and Turkey (Tekeli 1981) the agenda of the political leaders in their program for women has been primarily state construction. Similarly, nationalism and not feminism was the priority of political movements among Palestinians (Peteet 1986), Iranians (Sanasarian 1983, Bauer 1983), Algerians (Minces 1978).

Given that women's participation in programs organized by state agencies or state-forming political movements is often not seen to be about women by either the women or those who mobilized them (Peteet 1986, Bauer 1983, Minces 1978), scholars have sought to evaluate what women have gained. Despite disappointments and costs, some women appear to have benefited to some degree from state building in Algeria (Lazreg 1985), Pahlevi Iran (Mirani 1983), Iraq (Joseph 1982), United Arab Emirates (Soffan 1980), Turkey (Abadan-Unat 1981), and Tunisia (Tessler 1978). Other scholars find that women's participation brought about little improvement in their status in post-revolutionary Iran (Hegland 1986) or Algeria (Minces 1978).

The arena in which states are perhaps most put to the test concerning their stance on women is legal reform, particularly in personal status laws. Personal status laws are one of the most contested areas between modern states and religious institutions. The study of personal status laws therefore is a rich domain for investigating the linkages between Islam (and other religions) and Middle Eastern states in regards to women and family.

The conclusion of most scholars has been that most Middle Eastern states have been cautious in their approach to legal reform, desiring to remain primarily within the domain of Shari'a (Islamic law) (Mueller 1985, Esposito 1982, Rahman 1980) or fearing to challenge clerics and religious fundamentalists (White 1978, Hussein 1985, Lazreg 1985). The most progressive have been Turkey and Tunisia, but even there, scholars have found that personal status laws continued to be contested between "traditionalists" and modernists, circumscribing the achievements of the more secular ruling elites (Kandiyoti 1984, Charrad 1984, Halila 1984, Tessler 1978). In Algeria, Lazreg (1985) finds that the political leadership has sacrificed women in order to make a bid for the support of the Islamic clergy. Hatem (forthcoming) argues that in Egypt there has been an enduring alliance of nationalism and patriarchy in the domain of personal status laws, while Hussein (1985) argues the regime was careful to forestall confrontation with religious elements. Similarly the Ba'th in Iraq (Ismael 1980) and the Pahlevis in Iran (Sanasarian 1982, Pakizegi 1978) were cautious in their reform of personal status laws. The Lebanese state has also been reluctant to change personal status laws.

The growing scholarship on women, family, religion, and the state in the Middle East is raising critical questions and laying the basis for cross-cultural comparisons and theoretical work. Towards that end, it is useful to discuss in more detail two societies for which little work has been done to investigate the linkages between these issues.

Iraq: Women, Family, Religion, and State

Iraq is a heterogeneous country with a population of about 13 million. While the majority of Iraqis are Muslim, divided equally between Sunnis and Shi'ites, about 25 percent of the population is non-Arab, including Sunni Kurds, Sunni Turcomans, Christian Armenians, Assyrians and Indians (Gotlieb 1981).

Despite the religious, ethnic, and linguistic heterogeneity, the Iraqi state has been ruled primarily by Sunnis. For over the past decade and a half (since 1968), the Arab Ba'th Socialist Party has been consolidating its control over the state. The party is run by a rather homogeneous ruling elite of petty bourgeois origins, many of whom are from the northern Sunni town of Takrit. A number of the key figures in the party are consanguineal or affinal relatives (Batatu 1979).

The party is highly centralized, relatively disciplined and organized around an ideology of Arab socialism and pan-Arab nationalism. The party controls the leadership of public formal agencies and penetrates activities in many arenas outside the state, in a rather repressive and authoritarian manner. Given that the same leadership controls the party and the state, there is a degree of coherence in the programs and policies of the party and the state.

There is some controversy as to whether the Iraqi ruling elite can be called a class. Regardless of their current sociological status, the elite appears to be using their control of the state to create or consolidate their class position (Stork 1982). The wealth of the state, since the nationalization of oil in 1972, has made available to them considerable resources for state building. Women have been important to the Ba'th agenda for state construction, for two key reasons: their need to wrest allegiance of the population from the large family/tribe/ethnic groups and their need for labor for economic development.

The Iraqi state was created by the European powers after World War I from three former provinces of the Ottoman Empire (Baghdad, Basra and Mosul). The peoples of these provinces had never lived together as an autonomous political entity and had little allegiance to the newly created state. In the rural areas, where the majority of the population resided at the time of the formation of the state, large tribal groups organized and claimed the loyalties of the different ethnic, religious, and linguistic groups.

When the Ba'th took control of the state, they embarked on an extensive program of economic growth, focusing on industry and services. Agriculture, which had begun to deteriorate before the Ba'thist take over, appeared to offer less to the masses than the expanding industrial and service sectors. As a result a large percentage of the population is becoming urbanized -- 51.1 percent in 1965, growing to 63.5 percent in 1977 (Iraq, Ministry of Planning 1978:11), giving an annual urban growth rate of 5.3 percent during that period. Despite the growth in the urban areas coming from rural migration and natural population growth, Iraq continued to be labor short. Some of the shortage was covered by the importation of labor from other Arab countries, from India, Pakistan, Korea and South East Asia. However, to the Ba'th, importing non-nationals was not a politically acceptable long-term solution to their labor requirements. Offering Iraqi citizenship to Arabs (other than Palestinians) from other states has not increased their population or labor force significantly, either.

In the context of labor shortage and their desire to win over the allegiance of citizenry, the Ba'th have developed a rather complex set of programs, a number of which are aimed at women. The objective of the programs appears to be the mobilization of women into state-controlled agencies where they are resocialized into the "new Iraqi women." The resocialization process entails general, vocational and political education for participation in the formal economy and the polity. In addition, the Ba'th has extended services and rights to women apparently to increase their autonomy vis-a-vis the large family groups.

The resocialization process has been many-pronged. Perhaps the strongest aspect of the Ba'th program has been the campaign for formal education. Article 45 of the Ba'th party constitution proclaimed education an exclusive function of the state, abolishing foreign and private educational institutions. Article 46 made primary and secondary education compulsory and education at all levels free to citizens. In their concern to retain ideological control over the socialization of the young, the Ba'th, in Article 48 of their constitution, barred non-Arab citizens from teaching in primary and secondary schools (T.Y. Ismael, 1976:135-7).

They rapidly built or expanded public schools, recruiting young females and males into the state run curriculum. Prior to the Ba'th Revolution, of the almost 4 million females in the population only 23,000 had achieved secondary certificates or their equivalents; 8,000 college or institute certificates; 200 graduate degrees or diplomas; and 90 Phd.'s. Sixty-seven percent of the females were illiterate (Iraq, General Population Census 1965:341). A decade after the Ba'th take-over, females constituted 43 percent of the children in primary schools, 30 percent of those in intermediate and preparatory schools, 45 percent of university students, 25 percent of those in vocational schools (General Federation of Iraqi Women 1980:13). In the decade of the 1970s, female enrollment in primary schools increased 366 percent, in secondary schools 314 percent and in universities 310 percent (Sharqi 1982:80).

School expansion helped to reach the youth, but not the adults. To educate the adults, the Ba'th embarked on a literacy campaign in 1978. They promulgated a law requiring illiterate adults, female and male, from the age of 15-45 to participate for a two year period in one of the many literacy programs which the government established. Literacy centers were built across the country, particularly in the rural areas where illiteracy was highest. Penalties were to be imposed on those who did not attend or those who barred others from attending.

While I do not have evidence of whether penalties were imposed, I did interview women in both rural and urban areas, who attended these centers, as well as some who did not -- apparently without penalty. The Illiteracy Secretariat of the General Federation of Iraqi Women (1980) claimed that in one year alone 2.5 million women attended various literacy classes -- a number exceeding those between 15-59 considered illiterate.

Perhaps one of the most interesting of the ruling elite's strategies for resocialization and mobilization of women is the General Federation of Iraqi Women (GFIW). The GFIW was created by the Ba'th in 1968, immediately after their take-over of the state, as a female arm of the party. The leadership of the GFIW are party members appointed by the Ba'th. Their programs are coordinated by the party and their generous budget comes directly from the state.

The party outlined the goals of the GFIW in the Revolutionary Command Council's law No. 139 of December 9, 1972: 1.) to work for and fight the enemies of a socialist, democratic Arab society; 2.) to ensure the equality of Iraqi women with men in rights, in the economy and in the state; 3.) to contribute to the economic and social development of Iraq by cooperating with other Iraqi organizations and by raising the national consciousness of women; 4.) to support mothers and children within the family structure.

Towards that end, the GFIW had, by 1980, established 256 centers around the country organized in a bureaucratized structure that claimed over 177,000 active members, or 7 percent of Iraqi women aged 15-59 (Al-Alusi 1980). GFIW staff worked closely with the state run industries to train women for factory work and to trouble-shoot when incidents arose on the job. They collaborated with the trade unions in educational and service programs. They worked with the peasant cooperatives in the rural areas where women formed a significant segment of the labor force. The GFIW also was given, by the ruling elite, an important role in the implementation of the changes in the laws of personal status.

In the spring of 1980, I attended the annual meeting of the GFIW held in Baghdad. Activist women from all over the world had been invited, at Iraqi state expense, to attend the meeting. The objective was apparently to showcase the GFIW to the Iraqi population and to create networks between the leadership of the GFIW and women from other countries. The conference received a tremendous amount of publicity in Iraq, covered daily on the state-run television, radio, newspapers and magazines.

The visitors were given a controlled view of the organization, allowed into only certain sessions. The lobbying of several of the visitors with close Ba'th connections eventually resulted in increasing the access of a small number of us to the non-public sessions. What I observed in those sessions was later born out in more detailed research on the organization the following summer.

The structure of decision making in the organization was quite hierarchical. Programs and policies were decided at the executive level as were all candidates for office. One slate of officers (as with all other organizations I observed in Iraq) was presented for elections, with few members knowing precisely how the slate was chosen. I gathered that the slates, like the programs and policies, were determined in conjunction with the Ba'th party. Members were considered cadres and were expected to be leaders. Above all, members were taught that they must serve and be loyal to the party and the state. In particular, GFIW staff spend considerable time evoking, among the membership, affection and loyalty to the head of the party and state, Saddam Husein, who made frequent pronouncements and public appearances lauding the work and leaders of the GFIW.

In addition to the GFIW, the Iraqi ruling elite have created numerous other organizations into which women are mobilized. Trade unions attempted to recruit women, although in 1977 only 4 percent of the membership and administrative leaders of the unions were female (Iraq, Annual Abstract of Statistics 1977:258). Young girls, along with boys, from elementary schools to college were organized, through the school system into paramilitary organizations. Sports groups, music and art groups, literary clubs, scientific and professional associations, student organizations, hobby clubs, service groups, youth hostels were organized by the party and subsidized by the state. With the backing and legitimacy of the party and the state, women were encouraged to participate in an expanding public domain of social, cultural, political and economic activities. The women received experience in organization, hierarchy, discipline, service. Commitment to the party, state, ruling elite and the ideology they proclaim of Arab socialism and pan-Arab nationalism was taught in all these contexts. The organizational incorporation of women into state and party run agencies also offered women an alternative to kinship for participation in the political community (J. Ismael 1980:243).

The Ba'th have sought to win the allegiance of women away from the large family/tribal/ethnic groups not only by providing them organizational alternatives but also by extending rights and services to them that would presumably assist in freeing them from the controls of the primordial groups. This has entailed legislative reform as well as subsidization of programs of immediate relevance to women.

In the area of legislative reform, the Ba'th in 1978 made some modest, but important, changes in the personal status laws. Interestingly, members of the GFIW explained to me that the Ba'th made a strategic stand to placate the religious conservatives in the population. Rather than secularizing personal status laws directly, which might have been too severe a challenge to the clerics, they merged more "progressive" aspects of Sunni and Shi'a law and modified both, thus staying with Shari'a. For example, in cases of divorce, mothers were given custody of their children until the age of 10 (previously 7 for boys and 9 for girls) at which time, at the discretion of the state-employed judge, custody can be extended to 15. At that age the child can choose with which parent to stay. The code widened the conditions underwhich a woman may seek divorce. While the law does not prohibit polygyny (considered too controversial to challenge), it does make the permission of state-employed judges necessary for a second marriage. The law also prohibits family members from forcing women into marriage.

In other areas of legislation, the Ba'th have legally extended the same rights in the work place to women as to men including areas of pay, pension, training, advancement, retirement, compensation and medical care. Women were given the right to vote and run for office in national elections.

I witnessed the first national election in 1980, finding that women did turn out at the polls in large numbers. Often their men folk accompanied them into the open polling booths telling them how to vote or marking their ballots for them. The party put 19 women on their slate of candidates for the parliament -- all of them were elected. Considerable publicity was given to the women candidates during the campaign -- primarily an educational event since there were few opposing candidates. Saddam Husein was frequently seen with the women candidates, particularly the president of the GFIW and the two other members of the GFIW executive board who ran. Government officials assisted the illiterate in voting in the polling centers. In an interesting twist, I noticed at a couple of the centers, the women reading off the list of candidates to the voters would periodically not read the entire list, but simply ask, "Do you want Manal," (the president of the GFIW).

The Ba'th also extended services of vital importance to women, particularly women working in the wage labor force. Among the services was the provision of free child care to working women, often adjacent to the place of work. Nursing mothers were given time in the morning and afternoon off from work to attend to their infants. Since the Ba'th have been attempting to encourage women to have more children to increase the population, they have also offered women rather generous maternity leaves -- one month prior to delivery and 6 weeks after at full pay followed by 6 months leave at half pay. Women, like men, can qualify for child allowances -- increases in their pay for each additional child they have. The government also gives free meals to school children during school hours. In addition, the state subsidizes low-income housing to workers which women workers can apply for independently of their male kin. Free transportation to and from work is available at many of the state-run industries. And medical care is either free or subsidized.

The record of achievement and limitations of the Ba'th program is rather mixed. While it is too soon to evaluate the long-term implications of these programs for women and families, some changes are evident. There has been an increase in female labor force participation: an increase from 2.5 percent of the total labor force in 1957 to 12 percent in 1977 according to one report (Al-Hassan 1980: 230) or an increase from 7 percent in 1968 to 19 percent in 1980 according to another report (Sharqi 1982). There is an increase in women's education and literacy. Women are participating in public organizations in larger numbers, including military and government agencies. There is clearly a sector of the female population, particularly petty bourgeois and some recent urban immigrants, for whom the Ba'th program has brought some not inconsiderable advantages.

The limitations of the Ba'th program can partly be seen in the resistance of the population to participation. For example, while some working class women found the day care centers useful, many of them and many more middle class women refused to put their children in them, preferring instead to leave them in the care of family members. With rapid urbanization, there continues to be a housing pressure which is often resolved by younger couples building on to the homes of their parents. Resistance is often seen in absenteeism in places of work and what appeared to me to be rather extensive work sabotage or considerable wastefulness and inefficiency. Further, there has been extensive documentation of the on-going resistance to Ba'th rule that organized particularly, though not exclusively on the basis of religious-ethnic groups, especially among the Shi'ites and the Sunni Kurds (Batatu 1981). These groups and the secular political opposition have been rather brutally suppressed by the Ba'th, as they try to consolidate their control over the population.

Their attempts to reorganize the family have also had mixed results. Jacqueline Ismael (1980) argues that the Ba'th have merely strengthened the defunctionalization of the family and the undermining of the family as a unit of production that was already underway prior to 1968. The Ba'th, she contends, have attempted to subordinate family to the state by taking over family functions (child socialization, health care and social control), transforming the family from a unit of production to a unit of consumption and subsidizing the nuclear family in order to win allegiance away from kin/tribal groups to the state.

Despite the attempts of the Ba'th to undermine the allegiance of the population to the large family/tribal/ethnic groups, these primordial groups, at least in the short run, still claim the loyalties of a significant sector of the population. One reason for this is the repressive political atmosphere. The repression in the regime and the lack of legal political alternatives to the Ba'th has driven opposition to the state into an underground or into silence. I noticed in 1980, a general state of fear. Individuals rarely talked politics, even to friends, since they were afraid of state informants. The on-going mistrust of the state generated by this political repression, has made family an important arena of trust and security.

The family groups continue to be strong also because the Ba'th indirectly subsidize them. The pro-natalism of the Ba'th and the stress on marriage and producing large numbers of children has resulted in an idealization of the family on the one hand. The nation is seen to be a large family with the president being the father. Article 38 of the Ba'th party constitution asserts that the state is responsible for protecting and developing the family which is considered to be the basic cell of the nation. The Article continues that the state must encourage, facilitate and supervise marriage which is a national duty. And finally, that offspring are entrusted to the state immediately after the family (T.Y. Ismael 1976:134).

Economic and political realities also affirm the dependence of individuals on their families. The assistance of the extended family is necessary to support young couples as they work and try to produce children.

Additionally, since the Ba'th leaders have relied on members of their Takriti clan to rule, they provide implicit legitimacy for maintaining the solidarity of the large family group.

Lebanon: Women, Family, Religion and State

While small in territory and population, Lebanon has been historically one of the most heterogeneous of the Middle Eastern states. The Lebanese state formally recognizes the participation of 17 religious sects in the polity. Officially, the Christians and Muslims are in a ratio of 6 to 5, with the Christian Maronites ranked the largest group (30 percent of the population), followed by the Sunnis (20 percent), Shi'ites (18 percent), Greek Orthodox (10 percent), Greek Catholics (6 percent), Druze (6 percent), Armenian Orthodox (5 percent) and others collectively making up the rest (about 5 percent). However, an official census has not been undertaken since 1932. As the current war has made apparent, the official figures do not represent the reality. The Muslims probably account for 55-60 percent of the population, with the Shi'ites now the largest sect in Lebanon.

Such heterogeneity in a population of about 3 million is remarkable in that, while there has been some sectarian territorial concentrations historically, the different sects were found residentially mixed throughout the country. Lebanon also was, by Arab standards, rather densely populated in both urban and rural areas. It was, however, more urbanized than most Arab countries. Seventy percent of the population lived in cities in 1975, with the capital, Beirut accounting for about 40 percent of the population (UNDIESA 1982:326).

Unlike Iraq, the Lebanese state incorporated the religious/ethnic heterogeneity into the formal structure of the state. Lebanon did not spawn a revolutionary movement or party capable of taking over the reshaping the state, as did Iraq. The structure of governance, now violently contested, remained relatively unchanged from 1943, the ending of the French mandate period until the beginning of the current war.

Article 95 of the Lebanese constitution requires formal representation of the 17 recognized religious sects in government. This has been implemented through an informal agreement, the national Pact, designed by the ruling elite at the time of independence. As a result of these formal and informal strictures, since 1943, the president has been a Maronite, the prime minister a Sunni, the speaker of parliament a Shi'ite and his deputy a Greek Orthodox. Seats in parliament and positions in formal government offices are allocated according to a formal definition (based on the 1932 census) of the proportions of the sects in the population.

The formal definition of sect demography in a politically sectarian state, combined with the extensive powers of the presidency in the hands of one sect, has produced imbalances in power and allocation of state resources. The Christians, especially the Maronites, have been over-represented in the state, controlling key ministerial and military posts and receiving disproportional amounts of benefits from the state. Among the Muslims, the Shi'ites in particular were underrepresented and disadvantaged.

While scholars have evaluated at length various aspects of Lebanon's formal political pluralism, little systematic investigation of the dynamics of the relationships between the state and sectarianism, on the one hand, and women and family on the other has been carried out. Control over matters relating to women and family have been central issues in Lebanon, although the processes and outcomes have been quite different from those in Iraq.

Questions of women and family may have eluded most scholars concerned with Lebanon's pluralism because these issues are, in large part, delegated to the authority of the private sector -- in particular to the authority of the religious sects. The state does not intervene directly in legalities of family codes. The apparent absence of the state, however, does not imply an indifference or neutrality on the part of the ruling elite vis-a-vis women and family. It is, rather, a concerted stance of the Lebanese state to place control over these matters in the hands of the private sector.

Women and family are vital to the reproduction of the social basis of sectarianism on which the ruling elite have relied to reproduce the basis of their legitimacy and dominance. I would argue that the ruling elite has allocated control over issues related to women and family to the private sector as a part of a strategy of maintaining the balance of sectarian power in the state.

The Lebanese ruling elite, since independence, has maintained a relatively minimalist state. Key social, economic, and political matters have been left to the private sector, with the state often subsidizing programs undertaken by private agencies. For example, unlike the Ba'th which has attempted to build a cohesive system of national education, the Lebanese ruling elite extensively subsidized private education. In 1968-69, 68 percent of Lebanese primary, intermediate and secondary level students were in private schools and 32 percent in public. By 1972-73, the percentage of students in public schools had increased (45 percent), but was still less than those in private schools (55 percent) (Lebanon, Ministry of Planning 1969, 1973). The tuition of many of the students in private schools was paid by the state. Not only was there no national curriculum, but also, many of the schools, including those considered to be the best, were run by foreign agencies, often with a primarily foreign teaching staff.

The structure of the school system helped to fragment the population on a sectarian basis. Most of the private schools were organized by religious sects serving their own membership. Private schools run by non-religious organizations often, nevertheless, served one sect or were predominantly Muslim or Christian. To the degree that residential sectarian segregation occurred, public schools were often mainly Muslim or Christian. This was particularly important in that the public schools were attended primarily by rural and urban working and lower middle classes. The middle and upper classes generally sent their children to private schools.

The schools contributed to social fragmentation in other ways. A large part of the curriculum focused on language instruction. Each school was known for its primary language of instruction, usually French or English, but also Italian, German and a few others (depending on the cultural orientation of the directors). Few of the private schools used Arabic as their primary language. School curriculums varied tremendously, including what days they closed (Fridays, Saturdays or Sundays and other holidays), which affected whether children were available to play with each other. The impact was profound. The citizenry was systematically were being socialized in different social, cultural, linguistic, religious, and political orientations.

The school system was only one aspect of the social fragmentation process. Rather than building a system of public social services, the state, to the degree that it offered a social program, tended to encourage activities in the private sector. Most hospitals, clinics, social work agencies, projects to assist the rural or urban poor and the like were carried out by private, mainly sectarian, agencies. Many of these received state funds. Youth groups, men's groups, women's groups, cultural institutions, sports clubs were also mainly privately organized, which meant they were mainly sectarian. While the government ran some social services and a few programs for youth, these were minimal and designed to not compete with the private sector (Joseph 1986b). Most of the religious sects were relatively well organized in terms of offering social and cultural services to their membership. Most individuals looking for these services, therefore, tended to turn to agencies within their own religious sects.

Perhaps one of the most significant domains left to the private sector by the state was that of personal status laws. Lebanon, unlike Iraq, did not legislate a national family code. Rather, all matters of personal status were left in the domain of religious law. Marriage, divorce, inheritance, child custody were regulated by the 17 formally recognized religious sects. Given the absence of civil marriage, mixed marriages usually took place within the church of the man, with the woman often converting and the children raised in the religion of the father.

The impact of this legal fragmentation was to create as many different legal realities as there were sects. The difference in legal realities tended to produce different social experiences. Muslim and Christian men and women I interviewed in the early 1970s in an urban working class neighborhood of Greater Beirut often indicated that their circumstances were fundamentally different because of the different laws they followed. Muslim women sometimes envied Christian women because divorce was harder among them, while sometimes Christian men envied Muslim men for the same reason.

Whatever their feelings about their own religious laws, the men and women recognized that the laws helped to create or maintain differences. The absence of the state in this arena affirmed the power of the religious sects over these critical matters concerning women and family. Commonalities of social experience often, therefore, were clouded by the legal differences. As Yolla Sharara, a Lebanese feminist, noted, women in Lebanon did not feel the presence of the state in their lives. Rather they felt more the effects of the men of their sectarian communities (Sharara 1978).

Leaving personal status laws to the religious authorities was consistent with the ruling elite's strategy of maintaining a minimalist state. It was part of a strategy of reproducing the basis of their own political leadership. Like the Iraqi elite, the Lebanese elite did not comprise a class. The elite was made up of members of some old ruling landed families, some petty bourgeois families, merchants, compradores. Highly factionalized, they organized their power bases to a large degree through their own family groups and through vertical and horizontal alliances with other families.

The zu'ama (political leaders) established vertical alliances on the basis of patron-client relationships, some of which were with individuals, but most of which were on a family basis. That is, a za'im (sing.) usually courted heads of families on the assumption that family patriarchs could deliver their kin into the following of the patron. Patriarchs, for their part, tried to control their kin because they were then in a better bargaining position with the zu'ama.

The zu'ama offered their clients protection and access to state resources and services, while the clients gave the zu'ama votes, labor and loyalty. Given the minimalism and weakness of the Lebanese state, it was, in fact, prudent for individuals and families to be allied in a face-to-face personal relationship with a za'im. Individuals additionally integrated into a cohesive family stood a better chance of gaining the protection of a za'im. Access to most services in Lebanon required wasta -- contact, brokerage. Jobs, housing, medical and social services, legal procedures and the like were obtained more easily if doors were opened by zu'ama. Many of the zu'ama maintained private militias, which collectively, prior to the outbreak of the 1975 war, outnumbered the volunteer Lebanese national army. The militias were used against the state as well as against competing factions to protect the position and following of the zu'ama. Few Lebanese considered the state legal or law enforcement systems as ultimate protections. Ultimate protection, most Lebanese felt, came from families and zu'ama.

In addition to being organized on a family basis, most patron-client relationships tended to be within the same religious sect. This reinforced the link between family, politics, and sects. Families, in general, could more effectively take care of their needs if they acted collectively. Further, they tended to have greater leverage if they acted as a bargaining unit in relationship to political and religious leaders of their own sects. Zu'ama were similarly more powerful if their families were cohesively organized and if they could control large numbers of people by contact with a few patriarchs. In a politically sectarian state, claims of legitimacy tended to speak loudest when they appeared to have religious sanction. Religious sanction came from the support of the clerics as well as the assumptions (or myth) of commonality of culture within sects that underwrote the sectarian organization of leadership.

The ruling elite won the support of the clerics, in part, by respecting their domain of power over personal status laws -- a key to the power the clerics had over their membership -- and their control over a number of important social services. It was in the interests of most of the ruling elite to encourage social fragmentation on a sectarian basis among the population. Political, legal, religious and social fragmentation fed into each other.

Thus an alliance between the political and religious leaders and key family patriarchs was carved out, in which issues of fundamental relevance to women and family were the bargaining chips. Women were important in this arrangement because of their fundamental role in reproduction of the young. In a patrilineal system (characteristic of both Muslims and Christians in Lebanon), lineages lose membership primarily when women marry out. The Muslim pattern has been to encourage lineage endogamy, expressed in the preferred marriage choice of parallel cousins. Christians, influenced by Muslim practices, often married within their lineages as well. Lineage endogamy became ipso facto, sect endogamy. The fact that legal authority over marriage, divorce, child custody and inheritance was in the hands of sectarian institutions affirmed the practice and ideology of endogamy. Thus family and sect affiliation often reinforced one another in their control over women and children.

Paradoxically, while the Lebanese ruling elite was quite directly encouraging the cohesiveness of the large family groups, the economic and social transformations in Lebanon had offered individuals social alternatives outside family groups perhaps to a greater degree than was the case in Iraq. Because of a rather open market economy Lebanon, prior to the war, was, despite the efforts of the leadership, moving toward a more secular society. The economic and political openness, in a period of relative economic growth and prosperity, allowed some individuals a degree of autonomy and mobility out of family control. Additionally, Lebanese, unlike Iraqis, turned to their families less for protection from an oppressive state rather than for support in the face of a weak state.

However, the challenge to the ruling elite of the increasing secularism, I have argued elsewhere (Joseph 1978), contributed to the events leading to the war in 1975. One of the outcomes of the war has been an increased politicization of religious identity, and an increase in the importance of family. With the collapse of the state, individuals had to rely on their families for support. In addition individuals and families have had to forge even closer personal relationships with the political leaders who, through their control over militias, control political, economic and social life. Finally, the militias, in their efforts to mobilize the populace have relied heavily on the support of the churches to gain legitimacy. Thus, the war has more deeply enmeshed family, religion and politics in Lebanon.

Iraq and Lebanon: Comparisons

Family, religion and the state are fundamentally interconnected in Iraq and Lebanon. There are important differences in the relationships of these variables in the two elites who also control a disciplined political party able to penetrate most institutions of the society. The Lebanese state is controlled by a heterogeneous, factionalized, and highly competitive ruling elite, few of whom have established disciplined political parties. The ruling elite of Iraq has organized a relatively systematic ideology on the basis of which they have attempted to moralize and legitimate their rule. The ruling elite of Lebanon has lacked ideological coherence. As individuals or factions, members of the elite, with the possible exception of the Kataib (the Maronite right wing party founded by Pierre Gamayel), have not produced systematic ideologies to legitimate their rule. While personalism and individual charisma is a moralizing force in both states, in Lebanon it is the primary agency of legitimacy, while in Iraq it is organized within an ideological frame.

Women and family have been important in the dynamics of state and religion in both countries. In Iraq, the ruling elite pursued a program for state construction that entailed winning the allegiance of the populace away from the large family/ethnic/tribal groups. In Lebanon, the ruling elite's strategy subsidized primordial affiliations at the expense of national loyalties. The Iraqi strategy for control of the populace entailed extensive state programs in education, social services, and development of the economy. Given the nationalization of oil, the elite had extensive public monies available for their programs. The Lebanese strategy entailed elaboration of basic social and economic programs in the private sector where zu'ama maintained more direct control of their individual followings. The Lebanese state had fewer resources available than the Iraqi and much of what could have been public resources was funneled by the elite into the private sector. The Iraqi elite used the state as an agency of legal reform, attempting to change the position of women and the family structure. The Lebanese elite shied away from legal reform, affirming the authority of religious institutions over women and family. The state was the center of action in Iraq; in Lebanon it was the private sector.

Iraq and Lebanon represent different strategies of state building. Each required processes for controlling the populace, mobilizing followings and gaining legitimacy. Each of the ruling elites developed programs with important consequences for women and family. In one, it was to attempt to draw women into the state, away from families/tribes/ethnic groups. In the other, it was to draw women into families/tribes/ethnic groups. In both cases, strategies of the elites, whether coherent or less developed, were significantly affected by other variables such as market conditions and interpersonal political processes. Both sets of elites have been in power for too short a period of time to have been able to affect enduring structural changes in family structure. It remains to be seen what the long-term consequences of these programs and practices will be. However, what can be undertaken is a more systematic analysis of the processes that brought Iraq and Lebanon into the contemporary configuration of family, religion and state dynamics. An intriguing model for this kind of historical anthropology is available in the recent work of Jack Goody.

Goody, in his recent study, The Development of Family and Marriage in Europe (1983), argues that the development of the European family was significantly affected by church and state formation. He contends that family forms in the Middle East and Europe were more alike than different in the pre-Christian period. The change in the European family, he contends, was linked to the rise of the Catholic church into a state power.

Goody outlines P. Guichard's comparison of the occidental and oriental family. The occidental family is typically considered to be bilineal. Because of monogamy and weak extended groups, it produces strong conjugal pairs and kindreds. Wife givers are considered superior to wife takers in this exogamous system. The sexes are not rigidly separated and honor is attributed to titles, ranks, or riches which can be inherited. The oriental family, on the other hand, is patrilineal. Because of patrilineality, polygyny and the ease of divorce, the conjugal pair is weak with agnatic lineages, organized around tribal solidarity ('asabiyya) being strong. Wife-takers are considered superior to wife givers in this endogamous system. Women are separated and secluded from men and honor, attributed to being rather than to having, cannot be inherited.

In the pre-Christian period, Goody argues, European and Middle Eastern families were significantly similar (especially when compared to sub-Saharan Africa) in their systems of filiation, the conjugal pair, kin group form, the position of women, and the notions of honor. The solidarity of the kin group in the Middle East, he notes, was always weaker in urban areas than in tribal and peasant areas. The pre-Christian European clan was also stronger in the hills than in the plains where feudal landlords organized production and the state exerted control. All the major societies of the period shared the ancient Mediterranean dowry system in which women acquired property from males as well as from females.

This system of diverging devolution, shared by both northern and southern Mediterranean societies, was more significant than the differences caused by patrilineality and bilineality. He adds that the differences in the position of women were not as great as might be expected given monogamy in the northern Mediterranean and polygamy in the southern. Polygamy was always rare in the Middle East and women occupied favorable positions in ancient Egypt, among the Turks and in other Middle Eastern societies. Finally, honor as attached to being and to titles is found in all societies and is therefore not an important differentiating feature.

The key difference between the northern and southern Mediterranean, for Goody, is the form of matrimonial alliance -- exogamy in the north and endogamy in the south. However, in this regard, contemporary Europe differs not only from the Middle East, but also from pre-Christian Europe.

Goody observes that by the 6-7th centuries a new kinship system was emerging in Europe which included the following elements: divorce was more difficult; ecclesiastic kinship (godkinship) was encouraged over consanguinity; consent and affection between the marrying parties was encouraged. This kinship system originated in the 4th century, developed between the 8-12th centuries, but remained contested until the 18th-20th centuries. Central to the development of this new kinship system in Europe was the rise of the Catholic church.

As Christianity moved from a sect to a church between the first and fourth centuries, Goody explains, it attracted middle and upper class members and increasingly became the hegemonic religion. As the church consolidated, centralized and bureaucratized it came to need places of assembly, residential organizations for the clergy, land, funds -- in short, it came to need wealth.

It was during this period and under pressure of these new needs, Goody discovers, that the church began prohibiting certain marriage and family practices prevalent throughout the Mediterranean and endorsing others which increasingly differentiated the northern and southern rims. The church condemned or prohibited close cousin marriage, adoption, polygyny, concubinage, divorce, widow/er remarriage, and wet-nursing.

These practices involve the provision of heirs to lineages and the maintenance of family wealth and status in a stratified society. Goody contends that the elimination of these practices resulted in the elimination of male heirs to almost half of the families. Families left without heirs were encouraged to will their properties and wealth to the church.

To become one of the largest property owners in Europe, the church began encouraging ecclesiastic kinship, mutual consent for marriage, affection between marrying couples, monogamy. In controlling heirship, the church also subsidized the individualization of choice, the reduction of male authority and the authority of the family, and the development of the child-oriented "elementary" family.

The development of this family form was neither smooth nor lineal. In what he calls the hidden economy of kinship, Goody describes resistance to the church's prescriptions, particularly among the peasantry. Concubinage persisted through the 18th century; in areas of France cousin marriage was practiced in significant percentages until the 20th century; wet-nursing proscriptions and consent prescriptions were also resisted. The consolidation of the European family system -- including exogamy, the child-oriented elementary family, the individualization of choice, affectionate conjugal relationships -- was therefore quite recent.

Towards an Historical Anthropology of Middle Eastern Families

Goody's study raises a number of questions for the analysis of relationships between women, family, religion and state in the Middle East. Family, religion, and state are competitive forms of social organization in many respects. While at times they may reinforce one another, they often contest each other for control over membership. Control over women and their progeny are often central to the contest between families, religions, and states. Research into questions concerning these relationships could lay the basis for an historical anthropology of Middle Eastern family forms.

The Middle East has apparently not produced strong centralizing institutions such as the Catholic Church or the modern European nation-states. It would be useful to investigate why the Islamic clergy did not aggrandize, centralize, bureaucratize, and claim land and wealth as the Catholic church did. It is possible that control over land and heirship was not as important a strategy of rule for either the Islamic clergy or the Islamic states. Tribute levied on trade appears to have been a more important source of state revenues in the Middle East than in Europe. Middle Eastern states often did not or could not collect taxes from peasants and tribes.

A number of questions present themselves: Why were Middle Eastern peasants and tribes more able to resist the control of states than were their European counterparts? Why were the Middle Eastern states not able to break the control of large tribal groups over their members until quite recently? Historically, were there institutions or agencies which attempted to undermine endogamy and lineage solidarity?

The Islamic clergy was perhaps more enmeshed in the Islamic states than was the Catholic church in the European states. The clergy had access to state funds and were less bureaucratically organized than the Catholic church. Given the clergy's closer proximity to Islamic states, they may have had less need to control family wealth. The claims of Islam may also have been more compatible with extended family forms.

To understand the relationship of Islam to Middle Eastern women and family, however, requires research into pre-Islamic domestic arrangements. It would be necessary to study how early Islam changed these social practices and how early Islam differed in its stance on women and family from later Islam. It is important to recognize the plurality of Islamic practices over different historical periods and in different cultural contexts.

An historical anthropology needs to be developed to answer these questions. The results of such research can fruitfully be compared to the lived experience of family life in contemporary Middle Eastern states. This kind of historical and current empirical work can then lay the foundation for building theory to explain the similarities and differences of the dynamic relationships between women, family, religion and the state in the Middle East, Europe and other areas of the world.

16

THE BENI MEKLAAB OVER THE HORIZON:
MALES AND FEMALES, DOGS AND BEDOUIN

Richard R. Randolph
University of California, Santa Cruz

The word (I almost wish to say theory) *haraam* is a powerful Arabic symbol, as is its twinned opposite, *halaal*. Haraam, whose triliteral root is H R M, gets this entry in Wehr's dictionary (1961):

HaRaaM, HuRuM (pl.): forbidden, interdicted, prohibited, unlawful, something forbidden, offense, sin; inviolable, taboo; sacred, sacrosanct, cursed, accursed. ibn HaRaaM: illegitimate son, bastard. il-bait il-HaRaaM: the sacred house, i.e., The Kaaba. aš-šahr al-HaRaaM: the holy month, i.e., Muharram. al-masjid al-HaRaaM: the holy mosque in Mecca. HaRaaM 'alayk: you mustn't do (say) that. bilHaRaaM: illicitly, illegally, unlawfully.

Another form rising from the same root appears on the same page:

HuRMah: holiness, sacredness, sanctity, sacrosanctity, inviolability; reverence, veneration, esteem, deference, respect; that which is holy, sacred, etc.; woman, lady; wife.

Woman, whose very name is *hurmah*, is one embodiment of the status *haraam*. The place of woman, *muharram*, is forbidden and sacred as is the woman herself.

Wehr's dictionary under the triliteral root H L L lists the following:

HaLaaL: that which is allowed, permitted, or permissible; allowed, permitted, permissible, allowable, admissible, lawful, legal, licit, legitimate; lawful possession. ibn HaLaaL: legitimate son; respectable man, decent fellow.

Other words arising from the H L L root have to do with untying, unpacking, solving, being free, and available.

Haraam, in its various forms defines spheres of life and marks them with a warning sign which says: Access Prohibited! No Entry! Permission

Denied!; for instance, women and holy places are "off limits" and not to be "entered" without the proper entitlements (*daxal*, to enter, is of course the common Arabic euphemism for sexual intercourse and also is used when sanctuary is being sought, as will be explained below). Entry to a holy shrine is a high good which only a consecrated person can attain; entry to a woman is a high good to which only a proper husband *haliil* should attain. Sanctuary and protection, however, can be had by all, as we shall see.

One can also "enter" sacred times: the month of Muharram, or the month of the pilgrimage (*Hajj*) or the month of fasting, Ramadhan, in which normal eating is *haraam*. Tension between the mundane world of close family members and the forbidden and consecrated people, places and times is the fundamental dialectic in Bedouin life.

The root, H L L, ramifies from the simple sense of untying and unraveling into complex notions of unpacking, settling down, occupying a position and holding possessions, and doing all of this legally, properly, and freely. The H R M words stand over and against the H L L forms and set up a dialectic between what is forbidden and what is permitted -- *haraam* and *halaal*.

Places, people, periods of time, certain activities and the possessions of this world, are variously *haraam* or *halaal* and some of those that are forbidden may, by proper ritual and legal activity, become permitted, available and open. A wedding is such a ritual activity. What is mine is *halaal* to me but *haraam* to you and vice versa. God's holiest places are *halaal* to a submitting Muslim, but forbidden, *haraam*, to all others. Killing is *haraam*, but a ritual sacrifice is *halaal*, if it is done "in the face of God." Haraam and *halaal*, then, are not absolutes but they are always opposites.

We can now take a closer look at the architecture of Bedouin culture whose medium is the Arabic language. The nomad's tent is the best place to start.

The tent is the one human artifact visible on the desert landscape; in it all matters of importance are concluded and all moral and significant social life takes place. The tent physically embodies the main themes in Bedouin culture, and is sacred in any number of circumstances. Its roof is made of goat hair, twisted into yarn and woven into cloth by women; the panels of cloth are stitched together, again by women, and finally supported by poles of wood and secured by ropes and pegs.

It is called simply *beyt*, or house, and when compared to other kinds of houses it is called a "house of hair." The walls are made of goat hair and wool in the same manner as the roof, and they are fastened with wooden pins to the edges of the roof. The earthen floor is partially carpeted. The spaces thus enclosed, covered and divided by the handmade and homemade textile serve all -- or nearly all -- the purposes of social life that the house, meeting hall, school, law court, coffee shop and church serve in more architecturally and socially differentiated societies.

The tent's roof protects from the sun and the rain, and its sides from the wind. Its one internal wall divides the world of men from that of the tent-making women, with profound implications for the total way of life of the Arabs. In each half a fire pit is the focus of sitting people, women and children on the left and men and older boys on the right. It is not an imposing structure, yet it concretizes the major divisions within Bedouin culture as surely as if it were built of stone. Because the tent is such a powerful source of metaphor in Bedouin life, one easily moves away from the object itself into the further reaches of Bedouin folk philosophy.

On the right hand (north) is the *šiqq*, hereinafter spelled "shigg," where any man may enter uninvited and expect protection and hospitality from the owner of the tent. It is the arena of male culture where decorum, decency, diffidence, etiquette, openness and liberality are the values that govern sociability. It is, in short, supremely *halaal*.

The left (south) side of the tent is *haraam*, covered, private, protected, sacred, domestic and closed to any but members of the family. Separating the shigg from the *muharram* is a curtain of woven stuff called the *ma'nad*. It extends several feet in front of the tent so that one who enters the shigg may not see into the *muharram*.

Women are thus associated with the world of *haraam*; a woman is a *hurmah* who lives in a *muharram*, a harem. Her face is covered as is her half of the tent. This isomorphism: the covered face and the covered space, is an important aspect of Bedouin values, and men are responsible for covering, i.e., protecting, women (cf. Meeker, 1979:94). A woman wears black clothing and covers her head with a black shawl -- when she is inside her black tent she may use a white shawl. Her body is covered with clothing, a veil and tattoos, and from her neck, ears, nose, wrists and fingers hangs the jewelry of coral, amber, gold and silver that her father and/or her husband have given her. She is covered and she is also adorned, and she is considered to be one of life's adornments.

Men, on the other hand, are not tattooed, do not wear jewelry, do not cover their faces (except against the weather) and do dress primarily in white. They move about with extreme freedom and represent what is *halaal* right, public, white, adult, and open in the world. Their faces are open to others; in Bedouin language, their faces may be "entered," by those seeking protection, as may their half of the tent. Their faces are liable to the threats of "blackening" which they experience if they do not uphold the obligations of their culture. The word, duty (*waajib*), is often on their lips and minds.

Almost as if they had been reading the works of Claude Levi-Strauss, the Bedouin have erected a set of binary distinctions which separate the halves of the tent into the worlds of *haraam* and *halaal* with such a rigid and logically consistent set of polarities that one may marvel at the tidiness of it all. After writing and thinking about the clusters of dichotomies in Bedouin culture for many years, I have come to the conclusion that there is no *a priori* reason to accord gender or sex first place in these distinctions and then to stack on further oppositions as accretions to the "basic" distinction between male and female. I now believe that the fact of polarity is the logical beginning point. *Haraam* and *halaal* express this polarity better, I think, than other pairs. In this view, Bedouin cultural conceptions are organized in a binary manner and gender is obviously one of the most "natural" kinds of cultural distinctions that can be made, rather than the primary difference from which all others flow.

haraam	*halaal*
female	male
left	right
black	white
covered	open
private	public
access forbidden	access permitted

In the Negev, tents always face east, towards the rising sun and away from the prevailing westerly wind. The men's section is thus the northern or right half, and the women's is the southern or left. I was surprized, therefore, when once we visited a shigg of the Abu _____, and on approaching the front we entered the left or south side. Here were the men of the family seated in what should have been the women's half. We stayed for the mandatory coffee and tea, and completed whatever business had brought us there. On leaving I asked my Hawaashleh friends what on earth was going on. They explained the situation with the following logic. The Abu _____ had become increasingly pious, and the senior man had urged all of his family to pray five times each day as the religion formally requires. Given the usual orientation of the Bedouin tent, and the fact that Mecca lies to the south of the Negev, they found themselves in an intolerable position at prayer times: the women were in front of the men, between them and the direction of prayer (*qibleh*). Given the new necessity of prayer and the ancient priority of men over women, there was no other solution but to reverse the normal living arrangement and declare the *muharram* the shigg and *vice versa*, i.e., the men and women changed places. My Hawaashleh friends found the whole situation risible, but had no logical alternative except the obvious one adopted by most Bedouin: not to worry about the formal prayers.[1]

Tents come in four basic designs. A young couple may live in a small one-room tent which is pitched near the larger, two-chambered tent of a senior man. This one-room tent is only half a house, the left and forbidden half, and it is not a place where guests can be entertained. The basic tent is the house of two rooms which has been referred to above. The third type is the larger, winter tent of three chambers. The left or south chamber is used to shelter the newborn small stock from rain and wind. Significantly, the animal section is to the left of and adjacent to the muḥarram and farthest from the shigg. Nowadays summer tents are often made of burlap sacking because of its cheapness and lightness, and because the summer sun can damage the oily goat hair roof of the traditional tent which can be stored away for use in the winter.

The fourth type of tent is that erected for weddings, circumcisions and other major feasts and festivals. It is itself a visible announcement that its owner is planning a major celebration, a faraḥ. The festival tent is simply a much larger version of the normal tent of two chambers. Bedouin distinguish the size of these tents by the number of rows of tent poles.

A tent can be taken up, moved and relocated as climate, pasture, economics, and politics may dictate. Certainly it is the major Bedouin artifact. Pitching a tent immediately establishes a moral milieu in the desert.

The tent is the center of a precinct whose owner's face (wejh) is always on guard, and always involved. Entering the tent puts one "in the face of" the owner, implicating his honor in all that goes on under his roof. Thus, the tent is not an institution in the abstract sense; it is always someone's house, and it matters a good deal just whose it is. First, it is the place where one man's family resides and where that man will display his own unique character to outsiders. If he is an important man, people will come to him for aid and advice, and to reaffirm their affection toward him and their good relations with him. The paraphernalia and activities of domestic life are used there, in an elaborate code of hospitality and honor, to accomplish ends and form relationships that are not strictly domestic in their nature. The symbols of public life, then, are taken from the private and domestic realm of the tent and the family. If the tent is primarily the private home of a man and his family, it is also open to others and the homely activities of eating together and sleeping in the house are shared with visitors. It is the arena of that great pattern of hospitality which so impresses the stranger in the Bedouin world. Eating together, sitting together, drinking coffee together, are elaborated into formal events and become the practices and occasions that take the place of full-blown institutions in more differentiated societies. Between the informality of close kinsmen and neighbors and the hostility of enemies lies the middle ground of formal hospitality: the personalized, but highly structured relationship of the guest and the host.

A visitor approaches from the north end of the shigg. Typically, dogs bark and someone comes out to fend them off. The visitor enters to a round of greetings and shakes hands with each man present, giving the greeting to each in turn and receiving the greeting from each. He will be offered a seat with his back to the *ma'nad*, the curtain that divides the men's and women's halves of the house. As he is seated and takes off his sandals, the fire will be stirred up, the teapot put on to boil and the coffee pots placed in the fire. While sweet tea is served in small glasses, someone roasts the coffee beans. As they are tossed in a frying pan and the water is heating, one of the hosts says, "God give you good morning." The guest's response is "God give you good morning in prosperity." This interchange is repeated between each of those present and the newcomer. The formula is changed appropriately after midday.

The coffee beans, now roasted, are carefully poured into the mouth of the mortar and pounded rhythmically with a pestle of stone, wood, or steel until they are pulverized. The coffee is brewed first in one pot, then another, and as it is nearly done the host crushes some cardamom and adds it to the coffee before it is served in diminutive cups. But I am not describing how to make coffee; I am stressing that each step in the process, from the entrance of the guest through the greetings and until his departure, is stylized, familiar and formal, as structured by the rules of etiquette as any English tea party and as formally toned.

The preparing of tea and coffee is a daily affair. It is the first thing done in the morning, and is done as many times during the day as is necessary, surely at least once in the mid-afternoon whether strangers are present or not. The coffee and tea drinking is a part of life of the family extended and elaborated for the guest. Men camped near each other assemble in one of their tents for coffee in the afternoon every day of their lives. If a visitor is not a close member of the family, an animal will be killed shortly after his arrival, and people from the host camp will butcher the victim and boil it in a large metal pot. To accompany the special meal of meat, one of the women will make the same unleavened bread she makes every day for her family. One of the host's men, using a pitcher and a basin, pours water over the outstretched right hand (or both hands) of each guest, and this is the signal that the meal is about to be served. The meal is eaten quickly, politely and ritualistically. The host may eat with his guests, but he also makes a point of selecting particular morsels for the guest and hands them to him; he urges people to continue eating. When the men have finished, their hands are washed again and, commonly, they wipe their greasy hands on the north, outside wall of the tent. A greasy north wall is a sign of the munificence of the tent's owner, as well as a fine case of Bedouin metonymy.

Many times I have had to eat my share of a goat I did not want, from a host who probably did not want to sacrifice it. It was not a matter of my hunger or his economy. Nutritionally the meal was supererogatory, but culturally it was absolutely necessary. Happily, a chicken could often be substituted, and the code technically upheld. Face, reputation, duty and decorum are public affairs, and a meal is one medium by which they are upheld and validated. At the highest levels feasting, and fasting (which is but another form of feasting) are central features of Islamic ritual. In ordinary times, eating together also has a strong ritual component. The relatively unimportant contingency of whether the guest is actually hungry takes second place to the constraints of the culture of hospitality. The sense of obligation to participate formally and to conform to the rules and duties animates a good deal of Bedouin social life. The supererogatory nature of eating, probably in all cultures but certainly among the Bedouin, is revealed here. It is a truism to note that man must eat to live. He need not share his food with others to stay alive, but he must do so if he is to amount to anything in this world.

The guest-host relationship and the sharing of food are extended into the sphere of stateless politics, and the symbols from the homely meal are the main elements in peace-making and peace-keeping. Indeed, the visit and the shared meal, including the immolation of an animal, mark every significant social affair in Bedouin life. The shared meal ratifies and makes public and binding the actions and agreements of persons at all levels. Marriage, circumcision, death, a new house, a visit from a stranger, a compact with a saint, the purchase of a mare, the Feast of the Sacrifice the end of fasting, and many other occasions are solemnized by the entertainment of visitors and the sacrifice of an animal.

After the meal and the hand-washing, coffee is poured one last time and guests leave in the afternoon after the familiar and formulaic farewells. Or, a guest may stay the night. He will be provided with cushions and bedding and will sleep in the same place he has eaten.

Politely toned talk, dignified behavior, a sincere effort to make the guest feel welcome, open-handed generosity, interested questioning and expressions of personal concern for the guest's health, his family and his affairs -- these are the ingredients of Arab hospitality, and they have never failed to make a strong impression on any Westerner who has experienced them. These patterns are also impressive to the Bedouin themselves, and are one of the main themes in Bedouin poetry and song. A famous poem, versions of which were collected by Musil in North Arabia, by Bailey (1972) in Sinai, and Alwaya (1977) in the Negev, contains these lines (Musil 1928: 467-69):

> O Kleb, light the fire, O Kleb, light it!
> To light it is thy duty; the fuel will be brought
> To prepare cardamom and coffee beans is my duty,
> Thine to have the tarnished pots ready.
> * * *
> The mortar's voice will be heard at the night's end,
> And a rap on its brim will sound like the howl of a wolf.
> Mayest thou, when thou lightest the fire and its flame flares up,
> Mayest thou, O Kleb, bring us night pilgrims from far away,

* * *

Oh, how many fat wethers' heads have we thrown away,
And besmeared the necks of she-camels from the wound made
   by the knife.
A pure heart seeks no gossip,
And should those heroes refuse to salute me (I shall salute them).
For both the chief and the herdsman should walk the path of love,
as Allah keeps the account of each being.
A guest is Allah's guest and must not be insulted,
And this one we shall protect against wrong.

Through the proper execution of the acts of hospitality, people show themselves to be civilized, honor-bearing, altruistic and self-controlled. Other forces in Bedouin society are atomizing, anarchic, individualistic, and centrifugal. Weakly institutionalized public structures are balanced by strongly ritualized patterns of hospitality, but hospitality is not an institution of differentiated social roles and offices. It is always a particular host and particular guest who are cementing ties and creating obligations in the acts of drinking coffee, breaking bread and eating meat.

The bond of the meal is conceptualized concretely. There is a rule that a host must shelter an enemy if that enemy seeks his hospitality and protection, and the protection lasts for three and one-third days, that is, the time it is thought the food remains in the guest's belly. The highest value in Bedouin life may well be the rule that the host must protect his guest.

Sliim il-Hawaashleh was entertaining a guest in his shigg when Mhammad, an enemy of the guest appeared unexpectedly. He was greeted and admitted to the company of men awaiting the meal. When the newcomer saw his enemy, he threatened him. Freyj, Sliim's younger brother, snatched one of the poles from a corner of the tent and stood with it poised over Mhammad's head. The food was brought and Freyj commanded Mhammad to eat: *"Kul!"* As Mhammad took his first mouthful, Freyj replaced the tent pole and squatted near one of the basins of food to eat with the others. No further incidents occurred to interrupt the meal. The guests ate, drank coffee, said their farewells and left separately. Honor, face, hospitality and commensality worked together here to save a social occasion, and to keep the peace, at least temporarily. Mhammad was bound by his honor to be aggressive, but he was also bound by the code of hospitality to commit no wrong in his host's tent, especially after he had eaten his host's food. That he ate under duress was immaterial. The food in his belly was a substantial and material bond between the guest and host. Had he injured Sliim's guest he would have been under a powerful double jeopardy: the threat of revenge from his enemy and liable for heavy damages for having harmed his host's other guest.

Here the guest-host relationship and eating together are sacred social events transcending private interest and vitiating anarchic tendencies. That Freyj used a tent pole to support the "law of the tent" is perhaps fortuitous, but it is the kind of metaphor a Bedouin would appreciate.

The Beni Meklaab

Against the context supplied in this paper thus far, I now wish to juxtapose a minor bit of Bedouin lore that has no great importance on its own but may illuminate certain of the themes I have adumbrated above.[2] Early in my fieldwork in 1961 I encountered a bit of folk geography, a very brief "text" that is neither folk tale nor myth yet it can be interpreted rather easily because of its scantiness, or so I thought for over twenty years. The item came to me in the form of a question I was asked several times by Bedouin in the Negev. They wondered if I had come across a place they called the land of the Beni Meklaab. Protesting real ignorance, I turned the question back on them and they indicated there was a place, probably in the south, where women mated with dogs and the issue of these matings were baby girls and male puppies. Furthermore, the women could converse with the dogs. Nothing more was known of the place although all had heard of it and were genuinely curious about it. Similar questions were asked during my trips in 1966 and 1984 by members of the Hawaashleh tribe. I remembered that Murray had reported a similar belief from the Sinai in *Sons of Ishmael.*

> There are almost as many strains in the dog tribes of Egypt as among the Bedouins, their masters. Indeed if their traditions be true, the stocks must have coalesced! For the Desert 'Ababda all firmly believe in the existence somewhere to the south of them of a race called Beni Kelb, whose males are all dogs but able to talk, while the females are normal women. This fairy tale was told to Doughty in Arabia and Hamilton in North Africa, and is widespread elsewhere as far as China (1935:97).

Checking Hamilton I found a similarly sparse report, evidently told to the traveler by an Italian sea captain and mate on the way to Tripoli. They seem to have learned it from Arabs.

> I much enjoyed one of their stories, which they told with the greatest gravity, assuring me that they had heard it from the most respectable natives. In the interior of Africa, beyond the black hills, is a race of people whose men are dogs, their women being like those of other nations. The husbands spend their days in hunting, and at night bring home to their wives the game they have killed; these cook and eat the meat, and give the bones to their dog-husbands. They were both intelligent men, able to give a satisfactory account of their trade; but they made no difficulty in believing this story, and other tales not less marvellous

(Hamilton 1856:4).

And finally, Doughty gives his inimitable but brief account of this unlikely tribe.

> Wonders are told also in Arabia of the *Beny Kelb*, a tribe of human hounds. Kelb, "a dog," now an injury was formerly an hounourable name in the Semitic tribes. They say "The Kelb housewives and daughters are like fair women, but the male kind, a span in stature and without speech, are white hounds. When they have sight of any guest approaching, the hospitable men-dogs spring forth to meet him, and holding the lap of his mantle between their teeth, they towse him gently to their nomad booths." Some will have it "they dwell not in a land of Arabia but inhabit a country beyond the flood; they devour their old folk so soon as their beards be hoary" (Doughty 1926:130).

Dogs, women, talking, eating, and mating are the five elements in this fragmentary Erewhon. With these processes and these inhabitants, a society is believed to exist and reproduce itself. An examination of the five elements should help us interpret the text.

Dogs. Dogs are unclean beings living as close to the tent as they can but never allowed inside. Their eating habits, sexual license, and inhospitable behavior to strangers are the exact opposites of proper human conduct. They are never touched or petted; indeed, they are often the targets of rocks thrown by people within. They would like to enter the tent, and especially at meal time they come as close as they possibly can. They survive on the boundaries on scraps of food, offal and garbage. They are domesticated animals living symbiotically in human society but they certainly are not pets. Dogs are also closely associated with blackness. To call a man a dog is certain to provoke violence. The formula used to blacken the face of a man, i.e., to publically dishonor him is to say in front of others, "You blackness, blacker than a dog."

Women. Women, as we have seen, are also associated with left and black, and they are closer to the animal world than are men; they also are more magical and mysterious, veiled and forbidden as they are. Islam endorses this view of women and has continued to see the proper sequestering and protecting of women as central to the faith. Let me quote from a tract written in defense of the veil by Hajji Sheykh Yusif in 1926. He writes from another part of the Islamic world, Iran, but is apposite here. He was a literate and traditional spokesman for the fundamentalist attitude toward the female sex. While his views cross over the line into misogyny, their clarity is helpful:

> *The Creation of Woman.* The expositors have said that the creation of woman from a rib taken from the left side of man, as stated in the traditions, suggests that the physical and animal side in woman is stronger than in man, and that the spiritual and

angelic is greater in man than in woman, since the right side is the symbol of the spiritual and the left the symbol of the physical nature. (Rivlin and Szyliowicz 1965:356)

Mating, Talking[3], *and Eating*. In the mythical geography of the Beni Meklaab three forms of unnatural (I really mean uncultural) intercourse are taking place. It is precisely talking honestly, mating legally and endogamously, and eating properly that distinguish human beings, Beni Adam, from sons of dogs, Beni Meklaab. Doughty's version has it that the male dogs do not talk but they are hospitable, sharing their food. On the other hand they are cannibals, eating their elderly at the first signs of age. Murray says the male dogs "are able to talk." He is silent about their hospitality. The Hawaashleh of the Negev whom I interviewed knew none of these details.

The hospitality code, the separation of the sexes and the protection of women from themselves and men, and the importance of honest speech are certainly three of the most powerful complexes in which Bedouin culture, or humanity, finds its expression and its realization. The related set of rules about blood revenge would be a fourth. All of the versions feature the element of canine males marrying and mating with human females. While Bedouin have no objection to some hypergamy, for instance they will marry peasant women, they are fierce in their belief that none of their daughters should marry inferiors. The land of the Beni Meklaab, then, images the least endogamous and most hypogamous form of marriage. Yet in other details, its inhabitants seem to live like other Bedouin.

In 1984 when the subject came up again among the Hawaashleh, a number of the men argued that no such place existed, because, they said, the whole world has now been explored and if there were a land of the Beni Meklaab, we would know about it. Never have I heard Bedouin dismiss the possibility of such a place on biological grounds.

Is there more to be made of the Beni Meklaab world? It should be clear that the mystery of the land of the Beni Meklaab gains its power by virtue of its missing element. Here there are no men to uphold the cultural standards, to keep separate what is permitted and what is forbidden. And women, alone, albeit with their fertility and magical powers intact, are left to commit the most heinous of indecencies. Yet they survive with dogs for husbands -- afterall, women weave tents and cook food.

Without men, one would think, there would be no hospitality, no protection, no whiteness of face, no sacrifice, no duty or shame, *waajib* or *hismeh*. Only the animal and the female exist. But Doughty argues that the white dogs were hospitable.

While it may be that most problems in the real world come from the antagonisms between men, in the fantasy world without them, unspeakable chaos of another sort prevails. The belief in the Beni Meklaab is a paradigm without syntax. It is not a "once upon a time" story, meaning nowhere, and at no time. It is a place that may exist now in this world, somewhere vaguely to the south and its presence over the horizon means that the world of Bedouin culture is threatened by the power of female and animal nature; or does it mean that men are not really necessary?

In 1984 during a three month field trip to the Negev I became a bit more dogged in my pursuit of the Beni Meklaab. I began asking more aggressively about the existence of such a place. Finally, Hajj Musa Abu Sa'ad, a client of a Bedouin tribe in the Northern Negev but himself of peasant backgound, told me the following story:

A sailor was shipwrecked on the shores of the Black Sea. The sole survivor of the wreck, he was rescued by some women who took him to their tents. The women were all married to dogs. Their male children were dogs and their female children were human girls. The women ate cooked meat and the males ate raw meat. Because the sailor was of human form he was sent to eat cooked meat with the women instead of eating with the males.[4] While eating with the women, the sailor met and fell in love with a young woman and they decided to flee the land of the Beni Meklaab so that they could marry. They knew that the dogs would pursue them as they attempted to flee so they decided to escape across the broad Valley of Thistles, reasoning that the dogs would finally have to stop pursuing them because of thorns in their feet. One night, wearing their shoes, the sailor and the girl fled across the Valley of Thistles. When the dogs noticed their absence in the morning they began to track them. One by one the dogs abandoned the chase because of the thorns in their feet. Only the brother of the girl continued despite the pain, finally overtaking the couple, whereupon he killed them both.

As we left the Hajj, his nephew told me the story meant that even a dog will protect his sister and his family honor. Now that the paradigm has syntax, does it change the analysis I had been giving above and in lectures for some years? Certainly the story contains many of the same themes present in the fragments: women married to dogs (all versions), raw food and cooked food (Hamilton), canine hospitality (Doughty). But it also contains a new element. Dogs are now enforcing their own kind of endogamy (no pun intended). While their tribe contains two biological species, marriage outside the tribe even though within the same species, is a breach in the honor code, 'ird. In addition the dogs are incensed by the breach in the code of hospitality displayed by the shipwrecked sailor. He abused the freedom given him as a guest and had to pay with his life. The dog who was brother to the young woman was only acting as any good Bedouin brother or father should act (cf. Antoun 1968). In the end the cultural and technological superiority of the humans, i.e., their shoes, was no match for the committed dedication of the dog whose honor was blackened.

Still, in the land of the Beni Meklaab, things have gone terribly wrong. No proper men are present to enforce the values of *ḥaraam* and *ḥalaal* and yet life goes on.

FOOTNOTES

Acknowledgements. Robert Murphy first taught me about the Bedouin. May Diaz, David Schneider, Carolyn Clark, Andrew Castro, Steven Caton, and Elaine Combs-Schilling, have all read versions of this paper and it is better for their reading than it was before. They, of course, are not responsible for any errors. Fieldwork in the Negev desert was sponsored by the Social Science Research Council and by grants from the Academic Senate Faculty Research Committee at the University of California at Santa Cruz.

[1] This was the case in 1961-2 but by 1984 the Hawaashleh had become very observant and the vast majority of them were faithful about their prayers. Needless to say they did not switch places with their women. Emannuel Marx has another version of why the Abu _____ switched places with their women (personal communication). The *qibleh* is not directly towards the south but a bit southeast.

[2] The belief in, or more correctly, question about, the Beni Meklaab no more characterizes Bedouin culture than Little Red Ridinghood characterizes the thought and culture of the West. I suspect that it is seldom on the minds of the Bedouin and probably then only when they are confronted by a stranger who has traveled widely, an anthropologist perhaps.

[3] There is a Bedouin saying that "All the trouble in the world is caused by the tongue and the penis."

[4] The dogs are showing double hospitality here as they permit a relaxation of the separation of the sexes in favor of giving hospitality. Bedouin do this and boast that if there are no men in camp they will allow their women to sit with a male guest and make and serve him coffee and food. They rank the rules of hospitality higher than the rules about the separation of the sexes.

17

BED POSTS AND BROAD SWORDS: TWAREG WOMEN'S WORK PARTIES AND THE DIALECTICS OF SEXUAL CONFLICT

Barbara A. Worley
Columbia University

Robert F. Murphy was the first American anthropologist to undertake field work among the Tᵉmajᵉq-speaking Twareg pastoral nomads. His research in Niger (1959-1960) and observations (1964a, 1964b, 1967) bring to light, for the first time in the anthropological literature on Twaregs, some of the more important kinship-related and economic concomitants of Twareg women's high social position.

Murphy notes that, while cultural norms mediate basic contradictions in nature, in doing so "they set up a series of subcontradictions" (Murphy 1971:211). Basic biological oppositions of what Murphy (1977:17) has termed male "initiative" and female "restraint" are resolved through culture, resulting in a normative situation where, among Twaregs, men may be characterized as aloof and distant, and women as independent and assertive. While tension on the biological level is altered, it in turn produces new *angst* over cultural sex roles. Beneath the surface of the happiest of situations, where Twareg women enjoy social privilege about equal to that of men, simmers "the procrustean and deadly struggle of the sexes" (Murphy 1971:212). How this ongoing dialectic reaches temporary dissolution through a "ritual of rebellion," to borrow a term from Max Gluckman (1963 [1954]:110-136), is the subject of this paper.

Twareg pastoral nomads inhabit the Central Sahara and contiguous areas of the Sahel. They herd camels, sheep, goats, and, in Sahelian regions, cattle. They are Muslims of Berber origin, and most Twaregs in the Agadez region and to the south, including the Kel Gress Twaregs studied by Murphy, originated in the Fezzan and other areas of Libya.

As a Muslim people, Twaregs are unusual in regard to women's rights and privileges. Twareg women are not sequestered, do not veil their faces (although Twareg men do),[1] and have considerable independence and freedom of movement. The separation of the sexes is relatively minimal. Men and women regularly meet and socialize in public.

Women are the organizers of all social events, such as the drum playing gathering (*tende*), where women devise an impromptu drum by stretching a wet hide across the top of the wooden millet mortar (*tende*). Women are the singers and drummers at these events, which are attended by men and women kin and neighbors from camps nearby. While the women drum and sing, the men circle around them on their camels, pulling slightly on the reins so that the camels' long necks arch back. During the rainy season, when Twareg camping groups from all over the pastoral zone in Niger converge in a large drainage valley known as the Ęghazer, young people between about 10 and 35 years of age, married and unmarried, gather in an open sandy area between camps nearly every evening to sing, dance, play courting games, and sometimes even sleep together at a distance from camps.

The *tende* gathering often gives way to dancing later in the evening. Women stand in a circle open on one side, clapping and singing, and receive groups of men who enter the circle dancing, two, three, and four at a time. The men dance in a chorus line, arms around one another's shoulders, each man stomping one foot forcefully outward to dash sand at the women. Men wearing their swords (*takoba*), the epitome of Twareg maleness, press them to their sides to keep them from swinging, or they may brandish their swords while dancing. Although Twaregs no longer hold military dominance in the Sahara, the men continue to wear Medieval type broad swords as part of their attire, and may spend many hours polishing the blades of their swords, discussing their swords' genealogies, and admiring one another's weapons. The men's dancing has a sensual and highly charged vocal accompaniment produced by the dancers, which consists in a rhythmic groaning cadence. The women ululate as each group of men enters the circle. They laugh and shriek, jumping out of the way as jets of sand assault them.

Throughout their lives, Twareg women enjoy freedom of choice in sexual involvement and actively pursue romantic preferences (King 1903:280, Rodd 1926:174-175). They may regularly have male visitors when their husbands are absent (Ibn Batutah, *Travels*, French edition Vol. IV:388-390, cited in Rodd 1926:175; Nicolas 1946:225). According to Lhote (1955:335), they may continue to see former lovers and engage in flirtatious behavior at social gatherings after they marry without fear of reprisal from their husbands.

Twareg women prefer monogamous unions, and polygyny is a rare occurrence. Divorce, however, is frequent, and my data indicate that roughly one-third of men and women among Ighalgawan nobles have been divorced and remarried, about one-tenth of them for the third time. The divorce rate is even higher in other Twareg groups. Murphy (1964a:13) reported that the number of unions may even exceed seven or eight during the lifetime of an individual. Candelario Saenz' (personal communication) genealogies demonstrate that Twareg smiths (*inadan*) married as many as nine times. The Ighalgawan nobles seem conservative by comparison, but this may be due to later first marriages (average age 22 for women, 29 for men), their stated preference for political marriages within the Ighalgawan tribe and the short supply of appropriate noble spouses to choose from. In most instances, relations between former spouses are cordial and sometimes even friendly.

The ideal in Twareg marriage is an enduring relationship based on romantic love. Twaregs often say they prefer to marry cross-cousins because the joking relationship that ordinarily obtains between them is conducive to a strong marital bond (Bernus 1981:149). As the marriage solidifies, the joking relationship becomes a more serious relationship of mutual respect, with some aspects of an avoidance relationship.

Name avoidance, which is practiced after marriage (and between persons of a number of other social categories as well), does not entail wife-to-husband deference among the Twareg as Alice Schlegel (1975:167-168) inferred from the incomplete information available on Twaregs through the HRAF. The use of teknonyms and "pet" names applies equally to both sexes. One of the most common terms used in speaking to one's new spouse is *eméd ji* and *teméd jit*, the masculine and feminine forms respectively of 'friend.' The same terms are used during courting (*enilkam*) to denote 'boyfriend' and 'girlfriend.' Mature spouses may refer to one another as simply 'wife' (*tamtut*) or 'husband' (*elés*).

Wife-to-husband deference is not a feature of Twareg society, as it is among Hausas, for example, where a wife ritually kneels when serving her husband. Twareg women do not ritually kneel, bow their heads, or engage in any other extreme gestures of subservience to their husbands. In Twareg society, husbands regularly "defer" to their wives' wishes about as much as wives do to husbands. It is a mutual respect relationship.

Women often take the initiative in setting a divorce into motion. Women's lack of a legal basis under Quranic law for obtaining the divorce themselves is recognized, but as Murphy has observed, "if a woman indicates that she wishes to terminate the marriage, her mate has no choice but to intone the divorce and make public notice of it" (Murphy 1964a:14).

A woman may show her contempt for her husband's behavior by returning to her mother's camp, taking the children and bed with her but leaving the tent behind. The vacant tent serves as an embarrassment to the husband. The husband must seek out other relatives to share meals with, and must sleep elsewhere, usually on a mat next to another relative's tent, to escape the evil influence of the bush spirits (*kel ésuf*) upon solitary people. If the husband does not come to his wife and either make amends or divorce her, she may increase his embarrassment by removing the tent and its contents, which belong to her by custom, leaving the man entirely without a shelter. There are normally no heated words or violence on the husband's part, since a show of anger is considered dishonorable, and often there is no exchange of words at all. The couple may later make amends and the wife will return with her tent, or the husband will come to realize that no amends can be made and get a divorce. To impress upon the husband the seriousness of her intent to obtain a divorce, a wife may scoop up some dirt in each of her hands and toss it at the man. This is a signal to the husband that he is expected to formalize the divorce. It is a matter of ongoing social embarrassment for him until he returns to her tent with two or three witnesses and says, "I give you your head" (*ǝffe-q-am eghaf-nam*) three times, which makes the divorce final.

Twareg women frequently retain custody of their children after divorce, contrary to Muslim tradition which holds that the husband alone has custody rights after a child's infancy (Bernus 1981:117, Murphy 1964a:22,28-29). Most Kel Fadey Twaregs say that, in principle, after children are weaned they must go to live with their father. However, most Kel Fadey I have questioned argue that if a woman shows an emotional attachment to her children or cries when the husband tries to take them away, the husband should not take them and would be considered 'not human' (*wǝr ge awiden*) by other Twaregs if he did so. Fathers who took older children after a divorce had difficulty keeping them because the children would walk back to the mother's camp. Among Twaregs, children are the financial responsibility of their fathers, but they are considered by nature and by custom as belonging to their mothers (Murphy 1964a:22). Murphy expresses the Twareg thinking best:

> One [Twareg] put the question to me succinctly: "If you had a cow camel and another person's stud mounted her, to whom would the calf belong?" Informed by the American cowboy tradition, I answered, "To the owner of the cow camel." "So you see," my informant replied, "the child always belongs to the mother's people." (Murphy 1964a:22)

Twareg political structure is male dominated. The camping group (*ǝghiwan*) is an extended family headed by a male elder (*amghar*). A number of camping groups related through kinship comprise a named group (*tawshet*) headed by a male leader (*amghar* or *gantu*, a Hausa loan term) chosen by consensus from among their numbers. Allied named groups comprise a drum group or confederation (*tobol*) under the power of a drum chief (*ǝttǝbǝl*), a legitimate male successor from the dominant noble group. The confederation is socially stratified into noble and vassal named groups. Several rare cases in which women have served as temporary political leaders have been noted (Rodd 1926:169, King 1903:280). A legend exists in another Berber culture of a queen named Kahena who led men in battle (Lhote 1955:188, Rodd 1926:170). Twaregs have no "Amazon" myths that feature women as military leaders, but Rodd (1926:129) recorded an isolated story concerning an Ikazkazkan Twareg woman named Barkasho who wore male garments and a sword after she married, engaged in a series of livestock raids, and singlehandedly took seven camels from three men who were guarding them.

Although Twareg women do not figure in formal political structure or military power, women are central to Twareg founder myths. The Ighalgawan nobles have a founder myth concerning two Twareg women who "came from the East" or who came from Djanet, on the Algerian-Libyan border. One woman was clever and competent (*tẹla teytti*, literally 'had brains,' and *tẹla eghaf*, 'had her head about her'), the other woman was neither. The first woman was believed to have been a descendant of the Prophet (*tẹsherift*) and is the ancestress of the noble Ighalgawan; the second woman is thought to be the ancestress of the Ibẹrgẹlan, recognized as the earliest vassal tribe of the Kel Fadey. By some accounts it was two sisters who came from the east. One sister had no children; the other sister had several, and her offspring were the first Ighalgawan. By some accounts, the second sister was Tẹsiggelet, a woman five generations removed from the current drum chief, who is said to be the mother of the Ighalgawan. She is acknowledged as having originally possessed the Ighalgawan's great kettle drum (*ẹttẹbẹl*) which is the symbol of the chief's authority, and having brought her vassals, slaves, and livestock with her which became the basis for the Kel Fadey confederation.

Twareg women's opinions are highly valued, and they are normally consulted by men on decisions that affect the life of the camp (Bernus 1981:146-147, Rodd 1926:168-169). While Twareg women do not as a rule hold formal positions of command, they do participate in public discussions over matters of concern to the group (Bernus 1981:146, Nicolas 1946:220, Rodd 1926:168-169), and they exert great influence in the public sphere.

In the domestic realm, Twareg women have a great degree of control. The hub of Twareg family life is the tent, although many of Twareg women's domestic and social activities take place outside the tent and beyond the camp, which represents a departure from the Middle Eastern norm in Cynthia Nelson's (1973) discussion of public and domestic spheres among Bedouin women in general. The tents and their furnishings are the personal property of the women, and each woman does the work of setting up and dismantling her equipment and packing it onto camels and donkeys during camp moves. Subsistence work regularly takes women outside the camp for the collection of firewood, wild grain, berries, and other plants, and the daily drawing of water at a well which may be several miles from the camp. In addition, Twareg women regularly herd small livestock, donkeys and, on occasion, camels when men are absent. Women milk the small livestock and process the milk into cheese and butter. Women's subsistence work is considered critical in Twareg pastoral production, and they must be capable of taking over some of the men's work on occasion when men are absent for warfare and raiding (in the past), on supply trips, or away looking for lost animals or scouting out new pasture.

Domestic work takes a minimum of women's time. Older children usually watch small children and toddlers. Infants may be carried on the mother's back while she is working. There is little house cleaning to contend with. The tent needs to have the wall mats (*éghelli*) adjusted several times a day as the direction of the wind changes, and it is swept out occasionally. Only three or four pots and bowls are dirtied at mealtimes, since Twaregs prefer to eat together from one or two bowls, depending on the size of the family. Also Twaregs keep practically no material goods that need constant cleaning and organizing. Clothing, blankets and pillows are kept in leather bags and left in a pile in a wooden rack. Each person does his own laundry, and children do not wear clothing often until they are old enough to launder it themselves. Most things are covered with sand and dust, and this is considered normal. Grinding and sifting millet and sorghum is the most exhausting work that women do, and it may take as much as two hours a day. But children often do this work, and help with preparing foods for cooking. The actual cooking, which involves building a fire, takes about an hour per meal, depending on the type of food cooked and the weather conditions. During sand storms, which occur nearly every day during the rainy season, and frequently during the cold winter months, the work of grinding the grain, building the fire, and cooking amid gusts of sand requires a major effort and this, Twareg women say, is the hardest work of all. Men contribute to the family meal by making bread, which is baked under a bed of hot sand and fine cinders.

Twareg women enjoy a high degree of economic independence, since they own significant property in livestock (Bernus 1981, Keenan 1977, Lhote 1955, Murphy 1964a, Nicolaisen 1963, Nicolas 1946, Rodd 1926). Murphy was the first to document and point to the importance of a custom among the Twareg that allows women to acquire more property in livestock than they would normally have right to under Islamic law. This practice, known as *élkhabus* or *akh idderan*, allows an individual to make a premortem gift of livestock to female relatives, which they then own and control corporately. This custom serves to redress the inequalities of the Islamic inheritance rules, whereby females receive only half the portion of males. Twareg *élkhabus* is a special adaptation of the Qur'anic institution *al habus*, also known as *waqf*, a trust providing support for the needy or for a public institution such as a mosque. Among Twaregs, *élkhabus* serves to draw off wealth before the death of an individual, so that women will not get short-shrift in the devolution of property according to Muslim law.

Additionally, Twareg women accumulate livestock through important gifts from both parents and other relatives after birth (*alkhalal*) which form the basis of their own herds. Women may receive outright gifts of livestock from consanguine kin throughout their lives, and in all marriages after the first, it is usually the wife herself who accepts the brideprice (*taggalt*). As a result of these gift and pre-mortem inheritance practices Twareg women may become quite wealthy in livestock (Lhote 1955: 332), and it is not uncommon for a woman to be wealthier than her husband (Murphy 1964a:26). "In fact," says Murphy (1964a:26), "[Twareg men's] wry reference to the greater wealth of the women sounded almost American at times."

Twareg women maintain direct control over the use and sale of their herds, even after marriage (Bernus 1981:163). A husband has no right whatsoever over his wife's property (Rodd 1926:168) either jurally or by custom and, apart from the sale of a wife's livestock at her request, he is permitted to sell only animals belonging to himself (Bernus 1981:170). A husband is not likely to sell a wife's livestock without her consent because he runs a serious risk of his wife leaving him and taking her belongings, which include her livestock, the tent and its furnishings, and the bed.

The Twareg bed (tedǝbut) more resembles a wheeled conveyance than it does a piece of furniture. It is shaped with an adze by Twareg artisans (inadan), from pieces of wood whose ends are burnished and decorated with linear designs using a burning iron.

The larger and smaller ends of the bed (tabataqqat tǝzawǝrat and tabataqqat tǝmaccikkat) are massive barbell-shaped pieces, having enormous flared ends like wheels. The sleeping platform rests upon these; it consists of six straight cross members (afasas), running from the head to the foot of the bed, which are topped by three woven mats (tesabart, tedǝmbǝrut, and tesǝlǝlt, in lowest to highest order) to soften the sleeping surface. The Twareg bed is for Westerners a most uncomfortable place to sleep, as it is not only bumpy and hard but also shorter than the standard American bed. Many Twareg adults must sleep on the bed in a near-fetal position.

The bed is held up by four pillars, or bed posts (tesǝtkǝlt, sg.). These vertical supports are short, stout, columns that flare at the ends, their bottom ends having broad, round, flattened bases, their top ends having a smaller, elongated, delicately carved concave surface that serves as a saddle to accommodate the heavy head and foot members. The ritual use of these bedposts will be elaborated below.

The twelve pieces of wood which make up the bed are separate units, so that the bed can be dismantled easily and packed on camels or donkeys by the women for camp moves. The tent too, is portable, consisting of wooden supports and six to eight large woven mats bound tightly against the framework by rope.

The bed is purchased usually before, sometimes shortly after, the woman's first marriage, with some of the money from the sale of the brideprice camels. The large end of the bed and the six cross-members are carved by Kel Gress artisans in the Tanout area, from the wood of a tree called koriya that is imported from Nigeria. These pieces are brought up by camel caravan and are sold at the In Gall market during the transhumance season when most weddings occur. The smaller end of the bed and the bed posts are carved by local artisans from the wood of the *tirza* tree (*Calotropus procera*) in the Agadez region and from the *adaras* tree (*Commiphora africana*) in the Tadarast area south of Agadez.

After the tent, the bed is the largest, one of the most expensive, and perhaps the most well-used item in a Twareg household. The bed occupies about a third of the tent and is set up in the very center of it. Much of family and social life revolves about it, since it is also used as a place to sit, relax, and talk. The concepts of "home" and "marriage" are more fundamentally related to the Twareg bed than the tent (*ehan*) itself. The most common way of expressing "she got married" is *tega ehan* ('she made a tent'). The the word *ehan* connotes 'marriage.' But as one older male informant put it, "there's no house/marriage (*ehan*) without a bed (*tedebut*)." The bed is the focal symbol of the domestic domain.

The tent and most of its furnishings are the property of the woman; she takes them with her when she becomes separated from her husband, divorces, or remarries. The removal of the bed is first and foremost in a woman's show of contempt for her husband's behavior. One day in June 1985, I returned to my camp at Chimumenen and noticed that the bed was missing from the tent owned by Miriama, who had been married for nearly two years to Zuher, the son of my camp's *amghar*. No one said a word, and when I asked I was told that Miriama was at her mother's. Zuher slept on a blanket next to his mother's tent, and never went near his wife's empty tent. The wife slept on her bed at her mother's camp after that, and the two saw one another publicly at *tende* gatherings nearly every night. In September, the couple's problems were still unresolved, and one afternoon Zuher's mother and I were sitting in front of the family's tent, when Miriama and one of her female cross-cousins quietly and matter-of-factly entered the camp and began taking down Miriama's tent, not more than 10 meters away from us. No greetings were exchanged, there was no display of any emotion whatsoever, and we looked straight ahead in silence. The two women left with the tent poles and mats, and Zuher's mother deftly picked up the conversation where we left off, with no mention of the women's actions. After a month and a half, the couple got back together again, and began living together in Miriama's tent, at her mother's camp.

Every now and then, a Twareg woman finds it necessary to replace one of her large tent mats or needs an additional quilt. Quilting and large weaving jobs are often handled through a women's work party (*tasarrer-it*), which is organized by the woman who needs to make the quilt or mats. Other groups within Twareg society also organize work parties. Male pastoralists sometimes have work paties to dig out wells that have caved in or to administer vaccinations to livestock. Blacksmiths (*inadan*) organize a work party (*tadgelshet*) to forge anvils or to manufacture large, complex objects such as camel saddles. In the past, women formed work parties in order to sew clothing for their husbands and children. Most Twareg men now have their robes, shirts, and pants sewn by tailors who use sewing machines. Quilting, also, is less common now, although I did record a women's work party in 1977 at Ajjab, south of In Gall that was formed to produce two quilts. Mat-making is still common; all Twareg women, including noble Ighalgawan women, made their own mats before the 1950s and 1960s when the expansion of sheep- and cattle-raising increased pastoralist cash flow and made it possible for many women to buy ready-made mats at the markets in Agadez and In Gall. The Twaregs' poverty following the last two droughts has made it necessary for many women to begin making their own mats again, and most of the women's work parties that take place are for the purpose of making mats, often on the occasion of a daughter's upcoming marriage. The majority of work parties are held during the rainy season when it is necessary to produce mats, quilts, and new clothing quickly for the wedding and festivities that occur at that time.

Sometime before the day of the work party, the organizer will have her husband purchase a sufficient quantity of fronds (*tafle*) of the duhm palm tree (*tednƐst*) for the mats, or black and white lengths of cotton fabric and thread for the quilts (usually old clothing is used for the thermal filling), plus a large quantity of tea, sugar, and tobacco to maintain the participants' energy during the work. A substantial amount of millet, butter, onions, dried tomatoes, chili pepper, and salt are set aside for the occasion in order to feed the workers. The day before the event, the organizer will call upon as many as ten or fifteen of her female relatives and friends camped nearby to form the one-day work party, which lasts from about 7:30 a.m., when the milking is done, until sundown. While a woman is away at a work party, her older children or husband will tend to her usual work at home.

On the day of the work party, the organizer may disassemble the bed in her tent in order to provide a larger work space. She sweeps out the tent and lays the palm fronds, which have been soaked in water to soften them, in neat bundles on one side of the tent. The participants arrive in pairs or small groups from the neighboring camps, bringing their mat-making knives or sewing needles with them, and arrange themselves in a tightly seated group inside and around the tent of the hostess. The organizer distributes a bundle of palm fronds to each participant, or parcels of cloth to pairs or small groups of women, and the women set to work almost immediately. Each woman contributes her talents to the communal effort. The work is often divided up by type among the women in a production line fashion. The organizer or one of her daughters busies herself with making tea for the workers throughout the day, and prepares a noontime feast for them.

With quilt making and the sewing of clothing, some women occupy themselves with cutting the pieces while others sew; some sew seams, others specialize in hems, and some sew the designs into the quilt (*tabarde*). The prepared fabric is stretched out over a low smoothed mound of clean sand, and the seamstresses take positions around it, much like American women who come together in quilting bees, each worker taking a corner or a particular area in sewing and embellishing the fabric. Twaregs prefer quilts that are black on one side and white on the other, with black stitching contrasting on the white side, and vice versa. Stitched designs generally consist in zig-zag and parallel lines made by running stitches.

In mat-making, the women begin by preparing the duhm palm fronds for weaving by cutting off the stiff base of the frond, and slicing the frond into two to five strips, each 3 to 4 millimeters wide, using a small double-edged pointed knife (*tatǝnut*), which is also used to part and coif the hair. The prepared strips are then gathered into small bunches, measured out by placing the thumbs together and joining the forefingers around the opposite side of the bundles, and tied together using a single palm frond. Each woman takes one bundle and weaves (*tezate*) one long band (*efalanfal*) about 10 cm. in width and as much as 6 to 10 metres in length, which will later be sewn (*asharad*) side by side with other bands using a large hand-crafted iron needle (*ǝnazmay*). The connected bands form a long rectangle, either for the mat that arches over the top of the tent from front to back (*esǝlamamas*), or for one of the two mats that wrap around the sides of the tent and forms the tent walls (*ǝgheli*). The bands may otherwise be connected end to end and sewn together into a spiraling oval, as with early American rugs, to form one of the large mats (*tǝsalat*) for the tent roof. Toward the end of the afternoon, when the women have finished weaving their separate bands, each woman stretches out her woven band across the ground, and the women inspect each other's work. An impromptu judge, usually an elderly woman, makes a pronouncement on the quality of their work, and announces the merits of the best worker, while the rest of the women ululate in her honor.

The work party, which would otherwise be very boring, is given an air of festivity by the availability of an abundant supply of chewing tobacco and tea, and the heavy gossip and joking behavior that ensues. Late in the morning, when the women have been enjoying each other's company for several hours and their spirits are high with tobacco and tea, they begin to discuss their prospects for getting a contribution of a sheep or goat from the men sitting around camp for their noontime feast. Twareg feasts by custom usually require the sacrifice of a goat or sheep.[2] Any men they see nearby may be hailed with loud shrills of ululation, shouted insults and demands for meat (*isan*) from the entire group of women. While the work party is going on, the men in camp generally stay away from it.

Some of the young women fashion a kind of doll, whose body consists of a wooden bed post set upright in the middle of a large flat basket (*tesseyt*) used for separating and sifting grain. The bed post is dressed in women's clothes, including a skirt (*teri*), which is laid around the pillar in the bottom of the basket, and a blouse (*aftǝk*), pulled over the base of the pillar. A necklace (*tadnit*) is attached to the neck of the pillar. A pair of large silver earrings (*tezabit*), attached at each end of a single duhm palm frond strip, is suspended from the top of the bedpost so that they dangle at the sides of it. A woman's head cloth (*adalil*) is draped on top of the post, and a face is painted on it, using the same make-up the women wear, kohl (*tazolt*). The bedpost (*tesɇtkɇlt*), thus bedecked, is now called *ewajakkan* (in some areas, *ejawakkan*). When it is finished, the odd-shaped pillar dressed in women's clothing with a dark face smeared across the front of it is other-worldly. It is grotesque and eerie.

One of the younger women, a daughter of the woman hosting the event or some other young woman, raises the female effigy above her head and, while the others ululate loudly behind her, runs with it to where the men are sitting, and shouts: "*Nɇgga-r-kawan s-ewajakkan!*" ('We're doing an *ewajakkan* on you!'), or "*ɇnta da, tamtut-nawan*" ('Here's your (pl.) wife!'), or else, "*ɇnta da, tabarart-nawan*" ('Here's your (pl.) daughter/young woman!'). Men who see the women coming with their effigy attempt to get out of their path. They respond with a whoop (*teghɇrit*) a lot like the American cowboy yell, jump to their feet laughing, and move quickly away. The effect is something like a game of "tag"; once the effigy has intruded into the men's social area, it is as if they were "tagged." The women continue to ululate and shout demands at the men, and the men by custom must respond with gifts for the work party.

The net result of this dramatic confrontation is a contribution from each of the men caught in the vicinity of the *ewajakkan*. Small contributions of tobacco, tea and sugar are allowable, but at least one man must donate a sheep or goat to the women for the feast. With great flourish the animal is dragged to the group by its horns or neck for the women's inspection, which stirs up another round of ululation. Then the animal is taken beyond the camp and one of the men sacrifices it according to Muslim tradition.

The confrontation varies somewhat from group to group. Once, a head cloth wrapped around a sandal was substituted for the bed post effigy, and merely waggled at the men from a distance. This caught their attention, but one of the men retorted, "What's that, a hyena? A *talaguna*?[3] That's no *ewajakkan!*" Kel Fadey informants say that, among Twareg who live in skin tents (*akkom*), women at a work party to make or repair a tent may simply throw bits and trimmings of the leather at the men. Men "tagged" by the leather must make a donation of money or other goods. This is the case with women in the Tchin Tabaraden area also (William Fitzgerald, personal communication). In the region west of In Gall, the young women dashed up and quickly deposited the female effigy on the ground in the midst of the men, and ran back to the work tent. On occasion, however, the men will chase after the young woman bearing the *ewajakkan*, and attempt to take the effigy away from her so that they may douse it with blood from the animal sacrificed, ruining the head cloth, jewelry, and the blouse put on it. Everyone enjoys this, and there is a good deal of laughing and merry-making.

In discussing the ritual significance of the *ewajakkan* confrontation, we might begin by asking why it is that the women take such dramatic action in order to obtain meat from the men. Since Twareg women own their own livestock, it appears incongruent that the hostess would not have one of her own animals sacrificed, since it is an event organized by her, for her benefit in terms of the work involved. Nor is it clear why the women would choose to make tent mats, considering the cost of the foods consumed and time invested, when they might be purchased for less at the market.

The monotonous and intense work of weaving mats is not one of the favorite occupations of Twareg women. Women who make their own tent mats, however, believe they can make finer and more durable ones than they can purchase at the market. Weaving is boring work, and the women enjoy helping one another through work parties because it gives them an excuse to leave their usual work and spend the entire day in one another's company socializing and exchanging stories and information. The creative activity of dressing up a bedpost and haranguing the men with it provides a memorable punctuation to the day's boring work. It is fun. It should be noted, moreover, that the women's demand for "meat" has distinctly sexual connotations in Tĕmaljĕq, as it does in many other languages. This behavior is not only fun, it is lewd.

The sexual connotations lead us to look at the relationship between men and women that is being acted out in the *ewajakkan* ritual. At the women's work party, women demand a gift from the men. But at men's work parties, women are not called upon to make a gift of a sheep or goat to the men, even though Twareg women make gifts and loans of their livestock to male relatives and neighbors at other times. This discrepancy points out the nature of the statement being made: husbands are expected to purchase household needs with cash from sales of their own herds. The women are effectively providing goods that men are supposed to provide--household equipment. The fact that women engage in a day's hard labor to produce such goods is, in this symbolic fashion, brought to bear on the men's sense of honor. The women seem to be taking the "initiative" in asserting their right to gifts for the work party from men who exhibit "restraint" in avoiding the work party and holding back their gifts--but this reversal only serves to affirm the sex role expectation of men as providers. In Western societies, "men as providers" generally connotes "women that are economically dependent." But among Twaregs, the role of men as providers coexists with women's right to and practice of economic independence. The structure of sexual hierarchy is there, but male oppressor-female submissiveness behavior is not.

To focus on the ritual itself, one might ask why the effigy is made from a bed post, instead of a tree branch like children's dolls or like scarecrows used by Twareg groups who keep gardens. The immediate answer is that the bed post has a good shape for the purpose. It has a roughly hourglass shape, like a woman. But, unlike a tree branch, it is not a found object -- it is selected from among the important things the wife owns: she has to partially dismantle the bed in order to get access to it. The bed post is chosen over other possibilities not simply because of its suggestive shape, but also because it is an important symbol of the marriage relationship, since it supports the conjugal bed, and of the sex role expectations involved in Twareg marriage.

The bed, in fact, is one of the few things that follows a woman through successive marriages. The millet mortar and other equipment and all the components of the tent wear out periodically and have to be replaced. The bed may become quite worn over the years, but it is sturdy and a woman may keep the same bed right up to her death. In drought years, women may sell their livestock or their jewelry if need be, but rarely ever sell their beds. The bed is both a treasured item and a personal, feminine emblem. Perhaps more than any other household artifact, the bed is symbolic of the female domain and women's power in Twareg society. For the purpose of the *ewajakkan* ritual, the bedpost is right, because it is shaped right and because it symbolizes Twareg women's domestic power and the feminine on the perceptual level.

At first glance, it would seem difficult to understand why Twareg men, who are normally reserved and aloof, do not become angry when regaled with such public silliness. On the contrary, the men are indulgent and amused at the women's rowdy display. The male code of honor prohibits any show of anger as a sign of weakness and laughable personal flaw (Murphy 1964b). Laughter is acceptable male behavior, an angry outburst is not. But Twaregs do not laugh when their blacksmiths (*inadan*) assault them in a ritual called *zakkatan* (Saenz 1980, 1986) that in some ways is similar to the bed post ritual. When the smiths feel they have not gotten their due remuneration for services they have performed or for goods they have crafted for the Twaregs, they blacken their faces with charcoal, tie old sandals to their heads like hyena (*eridal*) ears, don old rags, and come into the camp howling and grabbing at everyone in the camp until the Twaregs offer them gifts of food and livestock. In the case of the *zakkatan* mumming ritual, Twaregs maintain a serious demeanor because they consider the smiths to have secret malevolent powers (*attama* and *tɛzma*) and are fearful of losing their *albaraka* (Islamic concept of "grace").

The form of the *ewajakkan* ritual, and its social content, suggest that it is a type of mumming. Mumming often involves a ritual confrontation between two opposing social categories, one politically or economically dominant and the other subordinate in terms of some social status such as age or social class -- or, in the case of the bed post ritual, sex -- and the resolution of their differences through a prestation. Mumming is an expression of social conflict. The subordinate group makes use of culturally recognized symbols such as masks, costumes, effigies and so forth, in creating a liminal state in which there emerge temporary status changes in both groups. In peripheral areas of the British Isles, in certain rural areas of Europe, Africa, and the Americas, mumming is still practiced. Young people dressed in disguises and carrying effigies such as the hobby horse go through the streets knocking on doors and chanting rhymes, and are offered gifts of money or food. Halloween, of course, is the chief mumming ritual in America, and there are elements of mumming in workers' protests associated with strikes.

Just as kinship "resolves a contradiction within the natural order" (Murphy 1971:211, restating Schneider 1968:115), mumming resolves a contradiction within the social order. Rites of passage, which include such rites of intensification as mumming, resolve crises in the social field caused by changes in individual status, a point inherent in the work of Arnold van Gennep (1960[1909]) and elaborated upon by Eliot D. Chapple and Carleton S. Coon (1942). Max Gluckman (1963[1954]:110-136) describes a South-East African ritual in which sex roles are reversed and women temporarily "assert license and dominance as against their formal subordination to men." This agricultural ritual was performed in honor of Nomkubulwana, a fertility goddess.

> The most important of these rites among the Zulu required obscene behaviour by the women and girls. The girls donned men's garments, and herded and milked the cattle, which were normally taboo to them. . . At various stages of the ceremonies women and girls went naked, and sang lewd songs. Men and boys hid and might not go near. (Gluckman 1963[1954]:113)

Gluckman termed this a "ritual of rebellion" (1963[1954]:112), which he defines as "an instituted protest demanded by sacred tradition, which is seemingly against the established order, yet which aims to bless that order to achieve prosperity" (1963[1954]:114). Basic to this genre of ritual are role reversal, and lewd, aggressive behavior. In Twareg society, both the smiths' *zakkatan* performance and the women's *ewajakkan* ritual have these characteristics. Smith men act like women in wearing skirts and crying. Both smiths and women assume a dominant role in relation to men, and exhibit raucous and sexually suggestive behaviors. The ritual brings about a catharsis and, therefore, a temporary solution to the conflict.

The basic tension between male and female on the biological level, which has been described by Murphy (1977:17) as male "initiative" and female "restraint," is resolved through a whole matrix of cultural behavior -- which in turn produces further sexual contradictions and oppositions. In the case of Twaregs, male aggressiveness is mediated by a code of honor symbolized in the men's raised face veil that prescribes an attitude of negative affect (Murphy 1964a), especially toward women, while maintaining dominance in the political affairs and economic responsibility in the domestic realm. Female restraint is mediated through female domination of the domestic sphere, and insistence on female participation and influence in the public domain. The conflict occurs as a result of the culturally subordinate status of women coupled with their relatively great power and influence, and resolves itself at least temporarily through role reversal in aggressive confrontation and interplay with the men, in the form of the mumming ritual described above.

The *ewajakkan* ritual is a model of Twareg male-female relations. It is not merely a means of obtaining some meat for the feast or remuneration for household items the women have fabricated, nor is it simply a display of power by women in a society where men dominate politically -- although it does have all these aspects. The themes of social play and sexual antagonism are as much a part of the ritual as the underlying economic and political motives. The bed post ritual is a social drama in which men and women act out the contradictions between sex role norms and social actions.

FOOTNOTES

Acknowledgement: This paper was written in Agadez, Niger, during my 1984-86 dissertation research among Twareg pastoral nomads. I gratefully acknowledge the funding for this research from the Social Science Research Council, the Fulbright-Hays Dissertation Fellowship Abroad Program, and the Woodrow Wilson Women's Studies Program. I would like to thank Candelario Sáenz, Robert and Yolanda Murphy, and Elizabeth Warnock Fernea for their comments on earlier drafts. My research among Twaregs includes the summer of 1974 among Ifoghas and Ahaggar Twaregs camped near Tamanrasset, Algeria, and twenty-one months during 1976 and 1977 among Kel Fadey Twaregs in Niger. Transcription of Twareg words is in Western Aîr dialect.

[1] The (*adalil*), a long cloth folded over itself and worn on top of the head by Twareg women, must not be confused with the veils worn by many other Muslim women. Because it could be construed by some as a kind of "veil," I have used the term "head cloth" to distinguish it from a veil as commonly conceived. It is not designed to hide the face, neck, or shoulders. Twareg men's faces are customarily covered; that is, they wind their turbans (*tagélmust*) so that one winding of it (*témedért*) comes down from the crown of their head and crosses their faces, bandit-style, leaving only the eyes showing. Thus, Twareg men are "veiled," and Twareg women are not.

[2] Twaregs raise livestock primarily for milk production. The consumption of meat is usually reserved for festive occasions, when animals are sacrificed according to Muslim tradition.

[3] There are other effigies used by the Twaregs. One motif is the jackal (*eridal*), in which an individual ties sandals to the sides of his head to symbolize jackal ears. Twareg blacksmiths may use this representation to frighten their patrons into giving them gifts. Twareg mothers may combine the use of sandals as ears with a face mask made of a piece of old leather with holes for the eyes, to scare recalcitrant children. The disguise is called a *talaguna*.

18

MOULAY ABEDSALEM:
AN ETHNOGRAPHIC FICTION

Vincent Crapanzano
CUNY Graduate Center

"I will tell you everything that happened to me in France, and God will bear witness to its truth," Moulay Abedsalem said. "During the time of the Sultan Moulay Yusuf, the French were fighting a great war in their country. They needed men in Bordeaux. They stationed an Algerian in the Jma' el Fna in Marrakech. I used to go to his office every day and tell him I wanted to sign up, but when he would ask my name, I'd tell him I wasn't crazy. I'd never go to France. Then, on the day that Allah willed it, ten of us went to the Algerian's office. We had decided to sign up the night before. We didn't tell our fathers. Early that morning we went to the sanctuary of Sidi Belabes, and there, before the saint, we all vowed to carry out our decision. Then we went to the Algerian's. His name was Meshmasha. It means apricot. It was very hard for us to answer all his questions. We didn't know our house numbers. There were none in those days. We only knew the name of our streets.

"Meshmasha told us to report back at seven the next morning. We were to take the Marrakech-Casablanca road, in some Spanish mule carts. We arrived at six and found many peasants there already. There were about sixty of them. We were each given fifty francs. Then someone led us to Caid Tusi's house. He didn't live very far from the train station at Ben Griri. It took us three days. At Ben Griri they gave us tickets, and we got on the train. It was a little tiny train. It took us seven days to get to Casablanca. By foot it would have taken a halfday! At every hill the train would begin to roll backwards, and so we'd all have to get out and march up the hill next to it.

"When we got to Casablanca, an Algerian took us to the depot, where we were assigned wooden beds. They make us go into a room and take off our clothes, and a doctor examined us. They gave us a shirt, striped pants, in the French style, and a jacket. Then they took us to another room and gave us shoes that fit, socks, and a thick black shirt that we had to wear between the white shirt they had already given us and the jacket. We had to leave our old clothes behind. The quarter master give us pillows, sheets, and a mat. We waited for two weeks at the depot for other volunteers. We spent the first day and the second day and the third day learning our numbers. My number was 36,631. The Algerian put us in lines, four by four. He would call our number, and we would say, 'na ^{c}am.' He would say, 'Forget na ^{c}am and say *présent*.' Everyone laughed at our uniforms. We looked like red and white French chickens. People told us we'd never see the sun in France.

"Finally they gave us another fifty francs and packed us into a boat. We marched to it, four in a line. Beside the Algerian adjutant, there was a French lieutenant who spoke Arabic and could write our numbers and read our script. The name of the boat was 'Babour Chawiya.' It was later destroyed by the Germans. We took it to Marseille. It took four days. We all got sick, in one corner. Around Gibraltar, it was terrible. We weren't even afraid. We thought we were dead. We were not allowed on deck. We were always in the hole, just like animals, and some of us didn't even eat.

"When we got to Marseille, we left the boat in groups, four by four, and were taken to another depot. We found a lot of young men from Algeria. They were all eighteen, and so we called them the *Ouled Dix-Huit*. There were men from Senegal. And there were the *Allumettes*, 'matches,' literally Annamites from Indo-China. They were all the same color and size. They had black teeth and slanted eyes. There were also Chinese. We were called *Sidi Maruk*.

"At the depot there was an Algerian who had worked in Morocco for seven years. He sold us watches, which, he said, had already been used in Tantan, in Morocco. He told us that to make us buy them because we missed our country so much.

"We were each given a plate. We ate at tables, seven of us at each table. They gave us potatoes, cheese, sardines, and jam. The tables were long, and it was hard for the men at the ends to reach the food. With forks and knives we were always spilling our food.

"After seven days, they called a hundred Sidi Maruk, a hundred *Dix-Huit*, a hundred Senegalese, a hundred Chinese, and a hundred *Allumettes*. We marched, four by four, to the train station. The train moved so fast that the earth looked like it was rolling. We couldn't open the windows. We were given four boxes of cheese, four boxes of sardines, four boxes of potatoes, four boxes of meat, and two large loaves of bread. This was to last us for four days. It was during the World War, and there was supposed to be nothing to eat in France! We were also given four boxes of jam.

"The factory where we were going to work was very long. The Moroccans threw iron into a furnace and stoked it with coal. When the iron got very hot, we pushed a button, and a strainer separated the iron from the earth. Someone would then press another button, and a cup

290

scooped up the iron and poured it into moulds, which were moving along on belts. One of us was responsible for filling the moulds and another lifted the moulds with pincers and plunged them in water. Once the moulds were empty, they were used again. We loaded the grenades -- we were making grenades -- onto a little wagon, and they were taken to other Moroccans who filled them smooth. Then they were put on a second wagon. A bell rang, and the work of the Senegalese began. They filled the grenades with sulphur. They pressed it in with little mallets. Other Senegalese put bands of iron around them. The *Ouled Dix-Huit* made the caps, because they were educated, and they soldered them on. Then the grenades went to European women -- there were also a hundred of them -- who charged them with fuses. Now the grenades were ready. They were taken to the *Allumettes*, who were carpenters. They made boxes for them. It was the Chinese who cut the wood.

"Suddenly, one day, we were all told to pack our things. The Germans had discovered the factory! We were sent to a town near Paris where we also made grenades. There were a lot of French there, with no training, who wanted to fight the Germans. 'Waw, waw, waw' was their battle cry. There were also German prisoners who were charged with cleaning up our quarters. We weren't even allowed to give them any bread.

"It was cold there. There was snow for three months, and you could see men with frozen moustaches. We were given wooden shoes and three pairs of socks to wear at the same time. Water couldn't get into those shoes.

"Then we were sent to Bordeaux. I spent a month there and did nothing. If German planes flew over us, we had to walk in the streets to make them look crowded with civilians so that the Germans wouldn't drop any bombs. The French trembled. They were always scared.

"Buildings in Bordeaux had elevators, and we stayed in one of them -- in a long room next to the *Allumettes*. We were always distant. We always kept a pickaxe next to our pillows when we slept. If the *Allumettes* ever attacked you, they would tear off your skin with their fingernails. Their nails were very long! They would stick them in our eyes or nose. When they fought, they would take off their shirts, tie them around their waists, and go *tatata*. We used to break their hands with police clubs. There was a lot of bad feeling between us, and the police were always around. It all began in Marseille because the *Allumettes* lived near the kitchen and got their food first, and we got ours last.

"The *Allumettes* had been conscripted by force. So were the Algerians, but relations between us were good. I had some friends from Algeria, ben Ramadan and ben Abdelkader, and we swore an oath of friendship before Sidi Abdelkader Jilali. Relations with the Senegalese were also good. There were Bambara who spoke Arabic. Their cheeks were all scarred. There were also Mossi -- their name means Jewish --

and Fulani, who were descendents of the prophet and had a ring of hair.

"In Marrakech, we had signed a contract. We were to work for six months and then do a year of military service. When we had only three more months of work, they told us about the military service. We were very upset. (We were always together. We had no problem remembering our numbers because only the first of us had to remember it all. The other numbers followed.) We told our lieutenant that we didn't want to join the army. All we wanted to do was to go back to Morocco. He told us we had to join up. We would receive wages like all the other soldiers. I was the secretary of our group. I marked off the days of service we had left. Every day, my friends would ask me how much more time we had to go, and I told them. You know, in Marrakech we used to say prayers to make the Europeans sick. Well, we were the sickness. We used to get six francs an hour for overtime. We wanted to join up -- we wanted the money -- but we were afraid we would never see our families again. We received letters from them. The French brought four scribes who wrote letters for us. They always arrived, but the letters we wrote privately never arrived. They were always returned to us."

*****

I met Moulay Abedsalem for the first time in 1967 in the police station in Meknes. He had been summoned by the assistant pasha, along with the two local leaders of a mystical Islamic brotherhood, a band of exorcists really, called the Hamadsha, to answer my questions. He was quicker than the others and seemed to understand the absurdity of my position. We were in a room filled with plainclothesmen who pretended to be working while they listened in on us. Several times one or another of them burst out laughing. I had come to Meknes with a letter from the Minister of the Interior, giving me permission to work with the Hamadsha. I had been instructed to report to the governor of the province. He had introduced me to the pasha of the city, who introduced me to the assistant pasha, who invited me to dinner that night and asked me countless questions about my research, none of which I managed to answer to his satisfaction. What, in fact, was an American doing in a garrison city -- an American who claimed to be studying a dying band of exorcists whose existence most modern Moroccans preferred to deny? It was only when I happened to mention that my father was a psychiatrist that the assistant pasha relaxed. He now had something to report. A careful man, however, he arranged for my interviews at the police station. I left the station with a sunken heart. How could I ever expect any confidence from people who associated me with the police?

Moulay Abedsalem was waiting for me when I turned the corner. So, I thought, it is he who is working for the police. I decided to play along, and invited him to tea. We did not talk about what had happened in the police station. We never did. We talked about Marrakech, where Moulay Abedsalem had been born, and about the Tafilelt, the Sahara, where his grandfather had been born. And as we talked and I looked into watery brown eyes that seemed to express a kind of transcendent resignation, I decided, quite irrationally, I suppose, that he was no police spy, that he had waited for me because he knew I had learned nothing of any interest, and that he was dissatisfied with what he had told me.

*****

I could not take notes in the café where we were drinking tea. We would have been even more conspicuous than we in fact were -- a *nasrani*, a European, as the Moroccans say, a Christian, talking to an old shroud maker from Marrakech. But I remember that hour more vividly that many of the hours I spent with Moulay Abedsalem, writing down everything he said. Whenever I returned to my field notes, I am reminded of a conversation I had with him later. In my notes, Moulay Abedsalem seems like a collection of words. Whatever life these words have seems to come from the silences between them. They, the words, orient me, but they are somehow far removed from the Moulay Abedsalem I remember.

With the exception of those words given to Mohammed by Allah, Moulay Abedsalem had said, all words betray the world Allah created. I was not sure I understood. "Betray" seemed an awfully strong word -- a word of a fanatic -- and Moulay Abedsalem was no fanatic. "Distort," yes, "color," "transform," but "betray," no. I resisted.

"Then, you mean to say, each time we speak we betray God's creation?"

"Yes," Moulay Abedsalem answered stubbornly.

Had he trapped himself in his own rhetoric? I wondered.

"Ought we to be silent, always?" I asked.

"Silence too is a way of speaking."

"And so it too is a way of betrayal?"

"Yes."

"But, may I ask a question?" my friend Lhacen put in. The three of us were sipping sweetened mint tea in the courtyard of Lhacen's house. Lhacen always added a little extra sugar to the tea he served when Moulay Abedsalem was his guest. He knew how poor Moulay Abedsalem was. "Are not the words we speak the gift of Allah?"

"Yes." "And are not the gifts of Allah good?" I expected Lhacen to ask. He had, at times, the style of a Socrates. But, instead, he asked, "Then, it is Allah's gift that we betray His creation?"

"Who can know the ways of Allah?" Moulay Abedsalem answered, and he quoted from out of the litanies the Hamadsha chant, "I take refuge, O God, from created evil in Your words, perfect and divine."

"Then we have only to repeat the divine and perfect words of God?" I asked stupidly.

"That would not be enough."

"Is there then no way not to betray God's creation?"

"Through giving a sacrifice," Moulay Abedsalem answered elliptically.

"I do not understand."

"When we give a sacrifice, we create a bond with Allah and His saints. We fix a promise. But most men's promises are worth nothing."

And Moulay Abedsalem changed the subject.

After Moulay Abedsalem had left, I asked Lhacen what he thought.

"Perhaps, there is truth in what he says," Lhacen began. And then, after one of the long pauses that always preceded something delicate Lhacen had to say, he added, "But, perhaps, he was referring to the notes you take."

"But, what am I to do? He never objected to my taking notes." I was a little frightened. Moulay Abedsalem had helped me a lot in my Moroccan research. I liked him immensely.

"Oh, he is not objecting now. If he did not want you to take notes, he would have told you. Perhaps, he is orienting you." Lhacen used the same word the Hamadsha used when they talked about how to discover the particular musical phrase that pleased a demon who had taken possession of their patient. Lhacen and I had discussed the word several days earlier. He had been surprised by my surprise that the Hamadsha used such a word to describe their diagnostic procedures. I had assumed that they were as blind to the influence of their diagnoses on their patient's illness as American doctors were. There was, at any rate, irony in Lhacen's words.

*****

I had not expected such attention to language, such subtlety of argument, from a shroud maker, whose only formal education had been a few years in a Koranic school in Marrakech. He talked about a room crowded with boys of all ages and proficiency. There he had learned to decipher the letters of the alphabet, to sign his name, and to recite the first chapters of the Koran -- without any understanding. They were written in classical Arabic, which bore about as much resemblance to his Moroccan Arabic as Latin does to Spanish. His teacher was more concerned with rapping his knuckles when he mispronounced a word than with explaining the meaning of the verses he recited. Understanding could come only after years of rote learning -- more years, certainly, than his teacher had spent on them. What was important was the resonance -- the materialization through sound -- of the written word, its possession. We *nasrani* learn to read for information and in doing so we tear the meaning of the word from its written or phonic contours in ways which would seem foolish -- blasphemous perhaps -- to Moulay Abedsalem if we described our "reading" to him. For Moulay Abedsalem, the power of the word, the Koranic word at least, was precisely in the unity of sound, script, and meaning.

Moulay Abedsalem often talked about the efficacy of the word -- not, to be sure, in linguistic terms, but when he talked about magic. An old man (as far as I could determine he was in his eighties), he had spent hours listening to tales of magic and collecting apotropaic formulae and recipes for charms and amulets from the Hamadsha and adepts of other brotherhoods, from Koranic scholars, like his teacher, who supplemented the little they earned from their pupils paid them by selling magic and from oracular seers and sorcerers who saw perhaps in Moulay Abedsalem a gift for magic.

Of course I do not know whether any of the magicians really did see a gift for magic in Moulay Abedsalem. He could not make such an observation about himself. He was not given to self-reflection. We never discussed how he was viewed by anyone else -- except once, by a holy fool. I do not know whether it was I -- my questions, my presence -- who precluded self-reflection or whether it was simply a matter of character, cultural style, or sensibility. Certainly the absence of reflection flattened the stories Moulay Abedsalem told me. It gave them an autonomous, an arbitrary quality, reminiscent of fairy tales, which somehow supported the fatedness -- the writtenness, as the Moroccans say -- the inevitability of one's ordinary life and the resignation that implies.

Moulay Abedsalem himself never practiced magic, so he assured me. When he brought an amulet to Lhacen's little niece who was pale and feverish from an infection of the middle ear, it was not an amulet he himself had prepared but one he had purchased from a local scholar of some repute. "I can give advice," he told me once. "I have learned many things in my life, but I do not have *the* learning to write." By "to write," he meant to write verses from the Koran, which are placed in the phylacteries that protect Moroccans from witchcraft, the evil eye, the anger of the *jnun* -- the demons -- and from the less easily embodied bad luck that seems to them to pervade the world. He did not have the learning to write verses, again from the Koran, on bits of the blue paper in which the sugar cones Moroccans buy in the souk to sweeten their tea are wrapped. The paper is efficacious. It is left in a glass of water until all the ink -- the sacred words -- are dissolved, and then the water is drunk by the sufferer. The paper is dried and burned -- Moulay Abedsalem insisted on the importance of this -- in case there are any traces of the words left, traces a sorcerer might use for evil purposes. When Moulay Abedsalem was little, his father cured him of night terrors -- Moulay Abedsalem had seen "someone," a spirit, one of the *khabatin* who gravitate to toilets and drains -- by sponging his son's body with vinegar, reading the Koran over him, and writing some verses on a scrap of paper which he tore in half. He put one half of the paper in an amulet that his son wore for years and burned the other half, forcing Moulay Abedsalem to breathe in the words that were in the smoke.

Moulay Abedsalem did not like school and often ran away to his mother's sister's house. She would protect him from his father's wrath. "Once I had such a bad fight with my father that I knew I would never be able to look him in the eyes again. I hid in the countryside near where my father worked the land." Although Moulay Abedsalem's father was a saddlemaker, he worked in the fields around Marrakech at harvest time. "I told the farmers that my father had sent me. One of them went to my father and told him that he would not be responsible for me, if I got killed along the road. My father said he had been looking for me for four days. They arranged to bring me home. The farmer said we were taking milk and butter to the market. Had I known where we were going, I would have run away again. My mother scolded me -- she had a temper like my father's -- and she wanted to hit me just as my father and a holy man, a *sherif* -- "a descendent of the Prophet" -- walked in from the shop. My father told me that he had used up all of his money lighting candles for me at every saint's sanctuary he could think of and was about to make an *ar* -- a promise to sacrifice a ram to Moulay Brahim if I were found. He had looked for me among the beggars and the whores. Oh, how he wanted to beat me, but the *sherif* stopped him. And I never had to go back to school."

Moulay Abedsalem was so caught up in his story that he did not show any of his usual regret at not having learned the entire Koran by heart. He did have a prodigious memory, and I have pages of stories, chants, and legends that he recited to me. To know, for Moulay Abedsalem, was to know by heart. His litanies were like an encyclopedia. I asked him once if he had ever heard of a particular saint, and he answered that it was possible. I waited for him to tell me what he knew, but instead he began to recite one of the litanies he knew. He went faster and faster, like a tape recorder at fast forward. I could barely distinguish one word from another. Suddenly he stopped, back tracked, and repeated what he had just said slowly, listening, as it were, for the significance. The verses described the saint, and then Moulay Abedsalem told me what he knew about the saint. For him the sounds contained in his memory were like the written texts we read; they contain information that we can extract when we have to, but that, without the word itself, is a distortion -- a perversion -- of the meaning the word contains. Translation would clearly pervert meaning -- which I believe, is why explanations are not given to school boys. They would be translations.

There is in this unity of sound, script, and meaning -- for me at least -- an intolerable involution. In its cohesion, the word does not resonate with the world around it. It dictates a world but it does not disclose a world that exists. It shows up that world. Self-contained, it can only relate to the world through the power it is believed to have -- through rhetoric and magic. As the gap between the cohesive word and the "real world" becomes greater -- through such disruptive processes, for example, as colonization and decolonization -- rhetoric and magic become more and more extravagant, violent in their possibility. Those who adopt such an attitude to the word, implicitly to be sure, are caught between a kind of stubborn fundamentalism -- a nativism, if you will -- and an equally stubborn figurativism with revolutionary possibility.

I did not, of course, think of any of this when I was listening to Moulay Abedsalem talk. I did note a difference in his attitude toward the word which was reflected in the stories he told and in the way he constructed his relationship to me and to the other Moroccans with whom I saw him. He seemed, at times, to be more caught up in his stories than I would have been if they were my stories, and at other times less caught up in them than I would have been. Sometimes, he used words in such a figurative way that they seemed to lose all contact with reality (as I declared reality to be) but promoted a quite pleasing relationship with me. At other times he insisted on a literalness that seemed to preclude any understanding between us. Most of the time, of cause, we just talked, ignoring the shadows cast by our different attitudes to the word, to story and rhetoric, to the world they evoked. We assumed the transparency of language, the possibility of dialogue and the feasibility of translation.

*****

"When I was little, all the boys in Marrakech carried daggers. I had one. My father had given it to me. I polished it each morning. I showed it to my friends. I swaggered about with it. But I never had an occasion to use it." Moulay Abedsalem began one afternoon this way. He was relieved. He had remembered a story he knew would charm me. I had been asking about what he had done once he had left school, and he seemed particularly uninterested in my questions. I was, in fact, never able to learn how he became a shroud maker. He must have apprenticed with someone, but with whom, and for how long, I never found out. Sometimes he implied that his father and grandfather had been shroud makers and sometimes he insisted that they had always been saddle makers. It is unlikely that they carried on in both professions. Moulay Abedsalem liked mystery. He always made himself, in his youth, a bit of an adventurer.

"One day a man led a burro carrying some filth past our house. Some of the filth fell to the groud. I asked the man what he thought he was doing. 'Why don't you pick it up?' I shouted. He cursed me and continued on his way. I waited for him to get past our house, and then I pulled out my dagger and stabbed him in the back."

I looked at Moulay Abedsalem in amazement. He showed no particular concern for what he had done, no shame, no moral culpability. He was telling a story, exactly what kind of a story I do not know, but it was not confessional and he made use of none of the rhetorical figures -- sin, guilt, depression, expiation -- that I associate with confession.

"The dagger went in so deep that I had trouble pulling it out. Finally I managed to and ran into the house. The man had collapsed. My mother called the *moqaddem* -- district leader -- and the *moqaddem* called an ambulance. Then he wrote down what had happened.

"At the time there lived in Marrakech a certain Moulay Hasan. He was very rich. People used to say that the sky belongs to Allah and the earth to Moulay Hasan. He used to free people who were imprisoned. He would see them as they were being marched off to jail and ask them what they had done and for how long they were sentenced. Then, he would buy them liberty. Whenever the pasha heard that Moulay Hasan was interested in a prisoner he would release him."

"Why did Moulay Hasan want to free the prisoners?" I asked.

"That was his way," Moulay Abedsalem said. He was anxious to get on with his story. "He was a just man, and he knew how little justice there is in the world.

"My father was Moulay Hasan's friend. He had been a guard in the palace, and Moulay Hasan was a chamberlain. It was there that they had met. My father went directly to Moulay Hasan when he learned what I had done. Moulay Hasan told him to bring me to his house. My father disguised me as a woman, and I accompanied my mother. My father walked ahead of us. 'What have you done?' Moulay Hasan asked me. I told him everything just as it occurred and then I added that the man had thrown a rock at me. Moulay Hasan asked where the rock had hit me. I pointed to my back."

Moulay Abedsalem pointed to the exact spot on his back where earlier he said he had stabbed the man.

"Moulay Hasan examined me carefully. He could find no mark on my back. He called in a servant and ordered him to fetch the wounded man's wife and children. When they arrived, he gave them new clothes. He told the woman to visit a certain man who would give her five dirhams a day -- that was a lot of money in those days -- and he ordered the hospital to give the man a good room and to do everything possible for him. He promised to pay for everything. In twenty days the man was completely cured. Moulay Hasan gave him new clothes, a *jallaba*, pants, slippers, everything. He also gave him one of his shops.

"He sent for me -- I had been hiding at a neighbor's -- and he had me stretched out by four huge men so that he could beat me. I felt like a sacrifice. My mother did not want me beaten. Moulay Hasan had told her to hide in another room and to come out and throw herself on me when she thought I had had enough. (I did not know about this.) When I was all stretched out, Moulay Hasan came up to me, carrying a whip, threatening me. 'You think you are the strongest man in the world,' he said. I did not answer. 'The next time you want to stab a man, take two daggers, one in each hand like this.' He showed me how, menacingly. Then he gave me such a slash with the whip that my hair stood on end. My mother jumped out of her hiding place and threw herself on me. 'Do not beat him,' she cried. 'Beat me instead.' Moulay Hasan stopped. 'I swear by Allah that if you ever stab another man, I'll kill you,' he said. Then he turned to my mother in a fury and asked her how she had managed to get into his house. 'Had I known you were there, I would never have beaten your son -- in your eyes,' he apologized. He had just wanted to scare me, he explained. He ordered me to leave. I kissed his hand, and he gave me five dirhams. 'Go to the steam baths,' he said, 'and wash away your tears.' As I was leaving, he added, 'if you ever stab a man again, I shall hang you by your feet, cut off the lower part of your body, make brochettes with it, and feed them to you.' After that I quieted down. Whenever I passed the injured man's shop, I gave him whatever money I had. Now when someone insults me, I only thank him. I did not want to be made into brochettes."

Moulay Abedsalem laughed. I did not. I was used to his convoluted stories, but I wondered whether he understood Moulay Hasan's perversity. I felt it strongly -- the show of strength, the threatened punishment, the beating, the humiliation of Moulay Abedsalem's mother, the tawdry theatricality of the whole affair. But I imagined that for Moulay Abedsalem it was simply power or his fantasy of power.

"If a lion approaches and hears you cry," Moulay Abedsalem concluded, "he will leave and never come back. If a jackal hears you cry, he will move away and approach again later. I had had the knife for two months and thought of nothing else. It was *shitan* who made me do it. I was the eldest son."

Moulay Abedsalem must have added the conclusion for my benefit. My questions, and my reactions, must have always seemed strange to him. He was, I must assume, never sure that I had understood him. The jackal is a lowly creature, he explained. The lion is a noble one. *Shitan* is the devil, I knew, and many Moroccans hold him or his off-spring, the *shi-tani*, responsible for their misdemeanors. An eldest son has at once to be man and to submit to his father like a child. He has to bear the jealousy of his younger brothers. I know Moroccan men of thirty or forty who would put out a cigarette when their father entered the room.

Moulay Abedsalem often talked about his father's temper. He explained that anger, rage really, mounts from a vein in the small of the back which contracts when people are irritated or humiliated. This is why their eyes turn red, this is why they see red, this is why they feel their head swell. They cannot control themselves. They are not responsible for what they do. "You have seen enraged women in Sidi Baba," Moulay Abedsalem said, referring to one of the shanty towns on the outskirts of Meknes. He knew I spent a lot of time in Sidi Baba and had often seen women fall into tantrums there. They were almost daily occurrences. "Those women will scream at a neighbor for hours because she didn't keep her children from fighting with their children. They can't stop until they have had enough -- until their blood cools down."

"Are they possessed?" I asked.

"Sometimes. But possession is different. When you are possessed, it is the one inside you who causes the rage, who makes the head swell and the blood mount. But for these women it is the way their children were treated that makes the vein contract. When I ran away, it was *that* that made my father's head swell."

"But such anger is dangerous," Lhacen, who was with us that day said.

"Why?" I asked.

"When you are enraged, the invisible ones attack." Moulay Abedsalem said. "You don't know what you're doing then and so you risk offending them. They are easily offended."

*****

Moulay Abedsalem traveled a great deal as a young man. His travels were, I suppose, a way to escape from his father's control and from the growing jealousy of his two younger brothers. They were step-brothers, and their mother was always advancing their claims at Moulay Abedsalem's expense. He talked about them so rarely that it was only after I had known him for quite some time that I realized he had actually had a stepmother and stepbrothers. He did not mention them at all when I asked for his genealogy. Lhacen, who had also had a jealous stepmother, was interested in their intrigues. He was convinced that Moulay Abedsalem left home because he was afraid his stepmother would poison him. Tales of poisoning are frequent, but Moulay Abedsalem never mentioned the possibility of poisoning to me.

Morocco was turbulent when Moulay Abedsalem was growing up. The Spanish in the North and the French in the South had taken the country under their "protection." There were opportunities for work all over the country. They were disruptive of family and tradition, and Moulay Abedsalem tried to take advantage of them all. He worked in Casablanca -- without much success -- as a saddlemaker, in Tetouan as a waiter, in the Rif and in the High Atlas mountains selling food to soldiers, and in France. He often conflated events in his life, and, like other Moroccans of his generation, he was never particularly concerned about chronology. He seemed less interested in continuous biography than in the rhetorical force of the singular event. He did not link events together in his stories in some progressively determining fashion, creating, as we do in our biographical narratives, an always somewhat vulnerable sense of personal consistency. Rather he used them to define a particular context, to determine a relationship, or comment on a matter of concern he shared with those with whom he was talking. As such his stories about himself were a bit like a parable; they ceased, at any rate, to be mere personal reminiscences. With them he created a tactful distance and preserved a sense of dignity that is so frequently lost in our more confessional modes of talk.

"There was a *sherif* named Moulay Khalifa in Tetouan. He had a big restaurant where all the Spanish soldiers used to go. He got very sick; his back was covered with boils. He asked me to look after his restaurant. I had worked for him before and had come back to Tetouan when Abd el-Krim was fighting the Spanish. Abd el-Krim was in the area at the time. He used to disguise himself to spy on the Spanish. He covered his scalp with a sheep's stomach. It looked as though he had ringworm. He also wore a ragged cloak. The Spanish were fighting in the mountains, and I followed them, cooking for them. Moulay Khalifa had arranged this; he liked the way I had managed his restaurant. I had five mules and a team of five men who would bring up the food from Tetouan. At first I had not wanted to follow the soldiers. I was afraid of getting killed. I told Moulay Khalifa, but he assured me that I would be in no danger because I would be well behind the front lines."

Still, the war had its effect on Moulay Abedsalem. He said he was enraged in Tetouan. He had seen so many people killed in the mountains. Many of them had been his customers in the restaurant or had bought food from him in the field.

"The war was terrible. Everytime I fell asleep, I dreamed about it -- about the people I had known who were now dead. I couldn't stand it. I talked to a *sherif* from Marrakech who was living there. He took me to the sanctuary of Sid l-Mendri who can free you of bad dreams. I spent three nights there, and sacrificed a black he-goat. On the first night I dreamed of the war. On the second night and the third I did not dream of the war at all. I slept soundly for the first time in weeks. Before leaving the sanctuary, I threw some salt on the saint's tomb. I was better, but I never went back to the war. I grew less angry."

Moulay Abedsalem explained that what one dreams is what the soul, the *ruh*, has witnessed. Dream distortions result from *c aqel's*, from mind's, inability to translate accurately what the soul has experienced. Moulay Abedsalem added that insofar as mind has to make use of words to convey dreams, it is the words that distort them.

"So when you dreamed of the war in the Rif, your soul was there?"

"Yes. That is why dreams can tell us what will happen."

"But sometimes you dream of the past," I said. "Didn't you dream of soldiers you knew who had already died?"

"Many times. Sometimes you dream of past events. You can dream of what is happening elsewhere and what will happen.

"Dreams have power. They are like gifts. You give blessing or harm to the first person you tell a dream to. You should always tell a bad dream to a rock before you tell it to some one. If you dream of a saint and he commands you to do something, you must do it. Otherwise you will suffer great harm."

And Moulay Abedsalem began a tale of great importance to him. It reminded me of one of the myths that are supposed to tell us why the world is the way it is. Although at times his recitation had the mechanical cadence of the *déjà racconté*, of words that an actor has spoken once too often, or a neuropath had used so many times to explain himself that they no longer resonate with his desired self-image, Moulay Abedsalem seemed to have more invested in his story -- psychologically, as we but not he would say -- than he had in any of the other stories he told me. He told it, however, with dignity, and even distance.

Moulay Abedsalem had come to Meknes as a shroud maker, pall bearer, and body washer during a terrible epidemic, perhaps the influenza epidemic of 1918. All the body washers of Meknes had died. The dead were accumulating. Their stench was everywhere. The pasha of Meknes wrote to the pasha of Marrakech praising his body washers, and asking him to send just three to bury the dead so that their disease would spread no further. Once they had taught their skills to apprentices, they could return home. They would be given a place to live, food, and a handsome salary during their stay.

The pasha of Marrakech ordered the leader -- the *amin* -- of the body-washers' guild to send three of his guild members to Meknes. The *amin* called all the bodywashers together and asked for volunteers. There were none. "We all had families," Moulay Abedsalem said. "We were very busy. People were dying in Marrakech as well as in Meknes. And Meknes was far away. The air was supposed to be good there, but we didn't know anyone." The *amin* had the bodywashers draw straws, and Moulay Abedsalem was one of the unfortunate three who was forced to go to Meknes. He had just been married for the third time -- his father had arranged it -- and his wife was pregnant. "We were sent to Meknes by train. The pasha of Meknes paid for our tickets! He greeted us when we arrived. He told us the bodywashers of Marrakech were famous all over the world."

The three bodywashers went to work and soon all the dead were buried and the apprentices trained. Two of them returned to Marrakech, but Moulay Abedsalem remained. He had been given a nice house and a shop and was well paid. His wife had come from Marrakech and though she missed her mother, she was happy in Meknes. "Life was freer," Moulay Abedsalem said. He went to Hamadsha meetings. The brethern welcomed him. They were interested in their confreres in Marrakech.

Months went by. Each day Moulay Abedsalem promised to leave on the next and on the next the next. His wife returned to Marrakech to give birth to a son. Moulay Abedsalem brought her back when Sidi Driss was three months old. He could not bring himself to return to Marrakech, but he knew he had to, eventually. The pressures of an aging father, a scheming stepmother and two jealous stepbrothers, left him no choice. He went to the bus terminal and bought two tickets for Marrakech.

"I told my wife that I wanted to leave. She packed everything. Then we went to sleep and had the same dream. It was very hot. I dreamed that I had come to the courtyard in front of the sanctuary of the Perfect Sheikh" -- Sidi Mohammed ben Isa, Meknes' most important saint. "Then the walls were even higher than they are today. There I found a well-swept place. It was well-washed. There was a pole in the center. 'This place is clean. There is a pole. If the people dance (the sacred trance-dance of the disciples of ben Isa), I'll stay here and watch,' I said to myself. 'perhaps someone will bring a horse and attach it to the pole. He may have cleaned the place for it. If someone brings a horse, then I'll leave.' I sat down and suddenly I saw someone come out of the window next to the door of the sancturary. The man was tall. He was dressed in white; he had a hammer in his hand. He came up to the pole and looked at me. 'Are you not ashamed? You do not want to stay.' He hammered the pole until it was all the way down into the earth. When the pole was in, he said, 'You can stay or leave.' The man disappeared. My wife dreamed she had seen a woman, an Isawiyya (a follower of the Perfect Sheikh) dancing. The woman said to her, 'Welcome and rest assured you will not leave.' In the morning my wife waited for me to leave, but I couldn't even get up until after the sun had risen. The bus had already gone. Then I told my wife to unpack."

The man in white was the Perfect Sheikh, Moulay Abedsalem said. Many people have seen him come out of that window. He had hammered the pole so that Moulay Abedsalem would not be able to leave. If he and his wife left Meknes after their dreams, they would have incurred the saint's anger. "Perhaps the bus would have had an accident or a car would have hit me. God shows us things that are true in our dreams." Once his relatives knew of the dream, they could not expect him to return to Marrakech. "Even now, when I go to Marrakech and stay for two months," Moulay Abedsalem said, "I get nervous and want to come back to Meknes."

It is always presumptuous to describe another's faith. It may be impossible to describe one's own, for descriptions of faith can become assertions *about* faith that mask its shifting, often contradictory *Alltäglichkeit*, its everydayness. Moulay Abedsalem did not talk about his faith nor did he talk about the faith of others. He certainly told me many things he believed in and discussed the beliefs of others. He never asked me what I believed. He respected the seriousness with which I listened to his words, and I respected the seriousness with which he answered my questions. I was his student. I felt comfortable in that role.

I was also, I suppose, a sort of son for him. He had two sons, Sidi Driss and Sidi Mohammed, and they were not much interested in him. They were both civil servants, stationed in remote areas of the Anti-Atlas mountains, waiting to be called to one of the plains' cities. Moulay Abedsalem rarely talked about them, and when he did, I thought I heard a disappointment in his words. His sons were the new -- the modern -- Moroccans who had abandoned (less successfully, perhaps than they realized) the world as Moulay Abedsalem knew it. Colonialism had declared their father's culture inferior -- at best of anthropological interest -- but had denied them any real access to the culture that was "superior," and now they were caught in that post-colonial dilemma of condemning the imperialist culture and at the same time emulating it. They were petty bureaucrats with a French veneer. Gogol would have enjoyed describing them. They played at a culture they did not really understand with a confidence they did not have either. The style they assumed fit them poorly. In Moulay Abedsalem's eyes they were spiritually hollow, and, thinking back on them now, I see them as ready victims of some fundamentalism or another. They manipulated what little power they had by being arbitrary with that power (I have often thought that the ultimate gauge of power in Morocco is arbitrariness). To preserve their illusions of power, modernity, and superiority they took advantage of and often harmed people who had neither the where-with-all nor the capacity for those illusions. Sidi Mohammed, Moulay Abedsalem implied on more that one occasion, was corrupt.

Moulay Abedsalem was attached to the Perfect Sheikh -- it was the Sheikh who had bound him to Meknes -- but he was a follower of Sidi Ali and Sidi Ahmed, the two saints who had founded the Hamadsha brotherhood in the early Eighteenth century. Moulay Abedsalem seemed spiritually closer to them and, quoting one of the litanies dedicated to them, he called them his pillar. Several times a year he visited their sanctuaries on the Jebel Zerhoun, the sacred mountain northwest of Meknes, and he always accompanied the tens of thousands of pilgrims who made their way there each year to venerate the saints in collective ardor -- in a frenzied enthusiasm bordering on violence. Moulay Abedsalem himself referred to the annual pilgrimage, the *musem*, as it is popularly called, by another word that suggested plenitude. "Once, I was in Marrakech at the time of the pilgrimage," he told me. "I had decided not to go, but the saints called. I could not help myself. I was drawn to them. I took a bus and arrived there on the second day of the pilgrimage. When I saw the sanctuaries, gleaming white in the distance, my heart was lightened."

Moulay Abedsalem's father had taken him as a boy to a Hamadsha meeting house in Marrakech, and there he became an adept; he was made to bow over a little iron halberd with which some of the adepts slashed their heads when they fell into trance, and to kiss the earth before a fig tree sacred to the brotherhood's saints. Although he himself never fell into deep, frenetic trances, he did experience a lightness of heart, a falling out of time and space, a gentle ecstasy, a warmth the spread through his body, -- a promise, he sometimes called it -- whenever he chanted the litanies, the *hizb* and the *dhikr*, of his brotherhood. "Allah, our Lord, our Master, fill us with Your generosity. O Generous One. O Sublime One. When the promise comes, when rising from my feet, it reaches my chest, when it settles there in my chest, then am I freed of all anguish ..." "There are times when I am one with the words of the *dhikr*", he said, "at one with the words of Allah."

There were times, too, when Moulay Abedsalem was one with the words, the song, the melody, of a demoness, a *jininiyya* called Aisha Qandisha, and thus with Aisha Qandisha herself. Moulay Abedsalem had a special relationship with Aisha Qandisha. He would talk about her obliquely, never mentioning her name, in a hushed, awed voice that, were it not for a certain detectable terror, would have been melodramatic. He kept a shrine for her behind his house. It consisted of a pile of stones, a pocket mirror, a jar in which he put flowers, and a little bowl in which he burned the black incense that particularly pleased her. He would see Aisha Qandisha there, and he always marvelled at the apparition. He never described Aisha to me, but other Moroccans did, and Moulay Abedsalem agreed with their description. She could appear as beauty or she could appear as a hag with medusa curls, pendulous breasts, and long, clawing fingernails. Whatever form, she had a cloven foot which she always hid under flowing robes. She was jealous, quick-tempered, ready to seduce, eager to enslave. She was likely to render anyone who insulted her impotent or sterile or to take possession of him. Some of the Hamadsha said that when they danced their exorcism, it was Aisha Qandisha who made them slash their heads until blood flowed. She had never taken possession of Moulay Abedsalem, and he did not have to appease her by falling into trance when he heard her special song -- any demon worthy a name is said to have a favorite song -- or by wearing the bright red and black that were her special colors. Moulay Abedsalem did see her at exorcisms when, hours after the dancing and trancing had begun, the lights suddenly went out and the dancers sang to her at a fevered, anticipatory pitch until she "showed" herself in what seemed to me a kind of collective hallucination. "Welcome, O Daughter of the river. Allah! Allah! Lady Aisha! She has come! *She* has come! She has come! Lady Aisha!"

If it did not sound melodramatic, I would say that in that hushed, awed voice with which Moulay Abedsalem spoke about Aisha Qandisha, in the terror I detected, there was a primal, a chthonian eroticism. For Moulay Abedsalem, at least as he described Aisha Qandisha to me (and I do not think he made any special effort to transforms her for my sake), Aisha represented the terrifying allure, the enchantment, of the never-to-be trusted woman. This was the Moroccan male's insistent sterotype of women. And it was Moulay Abedsalem's no less than anybody else's. He was an old man when I knew him -- involved and suspicious as old men tend to be. Talking about women, he talked mechanically, in generalities, and often with disdain. Women had irrisistible power over men. They were never satisfied. They were faithless. Their word meant nothing.

Occasionally Moulay Abedsalem would mention the woman who lived in his house. He was not married to her and he never said he lived *with* her. He expressed no affection for her, no real interest in her. She was just there. She carried water to his house. She cooked for him. She washed his clothes. I saw her once or twice from a distance. She was very old and very poor -- the kind of woman Moroccan call an ^{c}*aguza*, a witch, an old hag. I think it was out of charity, and not convenience, that Moulay Abedsalem had given her a room. She had sold tiny quantities of rotting vegetables in a market where the poorest people in Meknes bought their food. She disappeared one day, and Moulay Abedsalem never explained why. She may have died.

Moulay Abedsalem had married three times. He never said much about his last two wives. They were both cousins, and his father had arranged his marriage to them. He did talk about his first wife, Tuda, and when he talked, he expressed some of the excitement that Moroccan men usually express when they talk about their adventures with prostitutes. He had married Tuda of his own choice when he was very young and selling food in the High Atlas to the *goumi* -- those Moroccan soldiers who were helping the French pacify the mountain Berbers. His parents did not approve of the marriage. They had wanted him to marry a cousin, the one he eventually did marry, and not an Ait Atta woman, a woman of one of the fiercest Berber tribes, a woman whose face was covered with strange tattoos, a woman who had never worn the veil. Ait Atta women were known for their savage sexuality, their infidelity, and their warrior wrath. Above all, Moulay Abedsalem's parents disapproved because their son had chosen without asking their permission. He was wayward.

"The *goumi* had to buy food from traveling vendors like me. The French gave them the money for it. I used to leave some of my supplies with a man, an Ait Atta, when I went up into the mountains. He never touched anything I left with him. He had a daughter, and after a while, I asked him for her. He agreed, and I took her to Marrakech -- to learn to cook, to learn the ways of the city. Whenever I returned to the mountains from Marrakech, I'd bring her mother a present. She always wanted to know how my mother was treating her daughter."

"And how did your mother treat her?" I asked.

"She was waiting to see a grandson," Moulay Abedsalem answered. In other words, his mother had not treated Tuda well.

"Finally, after many months, when I had stopped selling food to the *goumi*, my father invited her family to Marrakech. We had a big wedding, Marrakech style. It lasted seven days. We were married for three years, and then she died in childbirth along with our daughter. Something went wrong with her womb."

Moulay Abedsalem's voice cracked. He was silent for a few minutes.

"My father arranged for me to marry again -- a cousin. He knew I had experienced marriage and would chase after women if I weren't married again soon. The woman couldn't have children. We went to a lot of saint's sanctuaries, to Moulay Brahim, to Sidi Rahal, to Moulay Idriss. We went to the magicians. And she went to an ^{c}aguza who could cure barren women. We invited the Hamadsha, and we even went to Sidi Ali and the grotto there."

Moulay Abedsalem was referring to a grotto under an enormous fig tree on the Jebel Zerhoun, near the Hamadsha sanctuaries, where Aisha Qandisha is said to live. His wife promised to sacrifice a goat to the demoness if she had a baby. It was Moulay Abedsalem's first trip to the sanctuaries, and he and his wife spent several days there.

"Nothing helped. So I divorced her. Then my father arranged for me to marry another cousin -- two months later. She was the mother of my sons, and when she died I lived alone."

Moulay Abedsalem's voice was cold. Perhaps he had had too much contact with death. It was many years since he had worked as a pall bearer or a body washer. He now devoted himself entirely to making shrouds. His eyesight was poor, and he had to depend on the two little apprentices who threaded his needles and did most of the sewing. They lived in the back of his shop and worked for ten hours a day for some stale bread and a cup of vegetable soup. Moulay Abedsalem taught them how to make shrouds, how to count the right number of stitches, how to wash the bodies of the dead, how to straighten limbs twisted in *rigor mortis*, how to say the correct prayers and express the appropriate grief. He told them about the afterlife: how the souls of the dead remain in a beehive-like structure until the day of judgment, how the two angels who accompany a human being throughout his life report on the good and the bad deeds of their companion, how the dead must cross over the fires of hell on a bridge "finer than a hair and sharper that a razor" to have those deeds weighted, one against the other, and how the dead whose good deeds outweigh their bad deeds are escorted by the sensuous houris to one of the seven levels of Paradise appropriate to their virtue and status. (When Moulay Abedsalem told me about the afterlife, he forgot to mention what happens to women.) And he explained to his apprentices the physiology of death. Death starts in the big toe and mounts slowly, ever so slowly, like ants crawling, up the legs to the navel and once beyond the navel -- the dying can still talk but cannot hear -- to the lungs when the death rattle begins. Passing through the throat, the soul leaves the body by the mouth. It is then that a few drops of water should be squeezed from a damp cloth into the mouth of the dying; for death has pulled a heavy, sharp-edged chain up the throat of those who have eaten such forbidden food as pork and scraped it raw. One never knows, Moulay Abedsalem always said, who has eaten such food.

*****

In all ethnographic encounters there is a moment of exhaustion. Words lose their resonance -- their ability to sustain what in reality was always an artificial bond. The anthropologist and the people with whom he has been working are saddened both by the certainty of having heard it all and by the certainty that something critical has been omitted. Such moments are dangerous because they can lead to a break, but they are also full of possibility -- they can herald a new, more intimate rapport, a friendship.

On one of our first meeetings Moulay Abedsalem told me that he had been to France. I had trouble imagining him there, but I did not ask him about his trip. He had been talking about a holy fool, a *mejdub*, who had sat in front of the mosque in Marrakech where Moulay Abedsalem's father prayed on Fridays. One Friday, when Moulay Abedsalem was small, the fool had grabbed him by the head and pressed his temples hard and cried out: "How much is going to happen to this head! How much is going to happen to this head! In the end, everything will be well." It was then that Moulay Abedsalem mentioned his trip to France. "It is true. Much has happened to me. I have been to France." But he went on to tell me about holy fools. He did not mention his trip again until we reached the moment of exhaustion when it seems there is nothing else to say. "I will tell you everything that happened to me in France, and God will bear witness to its truth. . ." Moulay Abedsalem began solemnly. He had never spoken like that before. His words were stilted, and though he seemed to take a certain delight in his story, he was at the same time horribly removed from it.

"Once the ten of us from Marrakech drank a lot and went to a river at the bottom of a ravine. There was a European who was walking with his wife. The ten of us looked at him and told him to run or we'd have his life. Then all ten of us took the woman, once each. She had perfume on. At first she moved, but then she just trembled. '*Marie, Marie*,' her husband cried. '*Nom de dieu, viens ici.*'

I had never heard Moulay Abedsalem speak French before. His voice was absolutely flat.

'*Il n'y a rien a faire. Sauve-toi,*' she screamed back. We had numbers on our jackets, and the European saw them. The next day he complained to the captain. The captain liked us. He could never leave the base on Sundays, and so we always brought him something from town. We were eating lunch, the captain's adjutant called out our numbers. Food stuck in our throats. The adjutant wore a red sash that we had given him along with his belt. He was French and he also liked us. He took us to the captain's office and asked the captain to excuse us. He said we were only following the custom of our country. We did not understand what the captain said. We asked the adjutant what he'd said. 'It's nothing,' the adjutant said. 'The captain told the European that we were Moroccans and had come as volunteers to help France in the war and that there was nothing to be done about it.' If we had been conscripted, they could have punished us. 'They came here freely,' he told the European, 'They work for us and have a right to our women.'

"There was also a brothel in every town. The one in Bordeaux had four floors. You'd go into a large room with chairs. A woman would press a button, and girls would come in. If you liked one of them, you went with her. If you didn't like them, the woman would press another button. There were French girls, Spanish girls, and Algerian girls. I preferred the Algerian ones because they spoke Arabic. If the girl was pretty, you paid more than if she was ugly. You always had to pay first. Service always comes after money. If the girls were good, you gave them a little extra, which they hid in their stockings."

Moulay Abedsalem listed prices the girls cost. He did not like European women; he did not like their style of making love. "They would sit on your lap and suck saliva from your mouth."

Moulay Abedsalem stopped talking. I couldn't think of anything to say. He poured more tea and went on with his story.

"We never had to join the army. When our six months were over, we were sent back to Marrakech. Our boat was attacked near Gibraltar. A lookout with binoculars caught sight of a German plane. The captain made the boat go so fast that you could see the ocean escaping behind you. Both motors were hit, first one and then the other. The boat began to sink. Fortunately, a Spanish boat came up, and we were loaded on board. We moved at unbelievable speed. They gave us jackets made of cork. None of us lost any of our clothing or any money.

"The Spanish police had helmets which they wore backwards when they were on duty. We spent three days near Gibraltar. You could see Tangier. We ate nothing but sardines -- they weren't even cooked -- and jam. There was also a light bread but it made me sick. We wanted to go to town to buy our own food but the Spanish wouldn't let us. Not even a mosquito could get by them. They were afraid we'd run away.

"Finally a boat came to get us. When we got to Casablanca, we were each given a few thousand francs. The French did this to attract more volunteers. There were over four hundred of them from my quarter of Marrakech alone. When I got to Marrakech, I knocked at our door. My step-mother asked who it was. I told her. She told my sister not to open the door. She would do it herself. She hugged me. She held my hands all the way to the center of the house. I tried to give money to my father. He told me to keep it. I would need it because I had no work in Marrakech. Everyone thought I was a rich man from Bordeaux and had a lot of money to spend. 'Thank God you are home and alive,' my father said. 'If you had been killed there, you would have been buried with Europeans.' I understood his words. 'I thought of you,' I said to him, 'but it interested me there a lot.'"

*****

I did not see Moulay Abedsalem again for almost two weeks. His story had exhausted me. I could not get rid of it. I could hear the emasculating panic, the terror in Marie's husband's words, "*Marie, Marie, nom de dieu, viens ici*," -- all the panic, all the terror that was missing in Moulay Abedsalem's uncomprehending repetition. He had never spoken French to me before. He never did again. Was his French frozen in these seven words? And there was Marie's cry, "*Il n´y a rien a faire. Sauve-toi*," and Moulay Abedsalem's laughter.

When I did see Moulay Abedsalem again, there was a lot of excitement in Menes. The king's son was about to be circumcised in the great sanctuary of Moulay Idriss on the Jebel Zerhoun, and I had promised to take Moulay Abedsalem to the celebration. The road was lined with armed soldiers. They saluted me, a *nasrani*, as I drove by them. I must, after all, have been important. Moulay Abedsalem said little. When I asked him if he thought the king's son was really going to be circumcised in the shrine, he shrugged, indifferent. I had heard that the king's son had already been circumcised in a hospital in Rabat, that the king was only pretending to have him circumcised in the sanctuary to keep his reputation with the people. As we approached the turn-off to the Hamadsha shrines, Moulay Abedsalem asked if we could visit them first. I agreed. He went directly to Aisha Qandisha's grotto, and there he sat for almost an hour, opposite the fig tree -- lost either in himself or in the demoness's charm. I didn't know. Finally, he got up and pulled a bit of cloth from his purse -- it was cloth from a shroud, perhaps -- and tied it to one of the gnarled roots of the tree. The cloth was an *ar* -- that I knew. It was a vow to sacrifice something to the demoness if she would grant whatever it was that Moulay Abedsalem was seeking.

We drove on to Moulay Idriss by the back road and were able to get closer to the village than if we had come by the main road. The crowds were tremendous. So was the noise they made. We could not get near the sanctuary -- it was too well guarded -- and we could see nothing. We heard that the king had sacrificed a giant black bull. Moulay Abedsalem was soon tired. We walked back to the car. We were surrounded by parked cars, hobbled donkeys, and street vendors -- of candles, *kebab*, and candies -- who had set up shop wherever they could find the space. We couldn't leave. We sat in the shade, and I asked Moulay Abedsalem about the meaning of circumcision. He said it was a sign of a father's promise to raise his son as a good Muslim. It was like *ar*, he added, but when I asked what was being sought, he hesitated for a long time before answering. I expected him to say God's blessing or a place in heaven. He said, instead, "to be able to keep the word of God in place." I wondered what he had sought from Aisha Qandisha.

Before we left Moulay Idriss, a government official, a minister perhaps, certainly a man of importance (his chauffeur had called some soldiers and he waited for them to clear the road), greeted Moulay Abedsalem and kissed his hand. Moulay Abedsalem blessed the man with cool dignity, but I saw the excitement in his face. He was pleased, I am sure, that I had seen him greeted by such an eminent *personage*.

*****

I met with Moulay Abedsalem many more times before I left Meknes. He recited litanies which I recorded, and he helped me with the technical lexicon of the Sufi brotherhoods, but he never again talked about his life. Nor did I ask him to. He blessed me the day I left, and when I said I hoped to see him again soon, he answered, conventionally, "God willing," but I saw in his eyes the knowledge that we would never meet again.

Several years later I returned to Meknes and went at once to find Moulay Abedsalem. His shop was deserted, as I must have known it would be, and so was the hovel he lived in behind the city dump. I shouted for him, and finally a prostitute emerged from a nearby shack and asked me (a bit salaciously) what I wanted. I told her I wanted Moulay Abedsalem. At first she did not know whom I was talking about, and then, when she did, she said "Ah, you mean the old sorcerer who used to live here. He died a long time ago." I thanked her, numb, and as I turned to go I noticed a little pile of rocks behind Moulay Abedsalem's house. There were a few dried flowers in a broken jar.

REFERENCES CITED

Abadan-Unat, Nermin
    1981 "Social Change and Turkish Women." In, Nermin Abadan-Unat,
        ed., *Women in Turkish Society*. Leiden: E.J. Brill.

Abbeville, C.
    1945 *História da missão dos Padres Capuchinos na Ilha do Maranhão*.
        São Paulo: Livraria Martins.

Acuña, C.
    1859 "A new discovery of the great river of the Amazons." In
        Expeditions into the Valley of the Amazons. Trans. by C.
        Markham. London: Hakluyt Society.

Ahmed, Leila
    1984 "Mysticism, Female Autonomy and Feminism in Islam."
        Presented at the Middle East Studies Association Meetings. San
        Francisco.
    1985 "The Next Arab Decade: Alternative Futures. Arab Women in
        1995." Presented at the Middle East Studies Association Meet-
        ings. New Orleans.

Al-Alusi, Manal
    1980 Speech Delivered at the Ninth Conference of the General
        Federation of Iraqi Women. Baghdad.

Al-Hassan, Ihsan
    1980 *The Effects of Industrialization on the Social Status of Iraqi
        Women*. Baghdad: General Federation of Iraqi Women.

Al-Hibri, Azzizah.
    1982a *Women and Islam*. New York: Pergamon Press.
    1982b "A Study of Islamic Herstory: Or How Did We Ever Get Into
        This Mess." In, Azzizah Al-Hibri, ed., *Women and Islam*.
        New York: Pergamon Press.

Al-Sayyid-Marsot, Afaf.
    1979 *Society and the Sexes in Medieval Islam*. Malibu, CA: Undena
        Publications.

Allen, L.A.
1975 *Time Before Morning: Art and Myth of the Australian Aborigines*. New York: Thomas Y. Crowell Co.

Allen, M.R.
1967 *Male Cults and Secret Initiations in Melanesia*. Melbourne: Melbourne Univ. Press.

Almeida, C.M.
1874 *Memórias para a história do extincto Estado do Maranhão*. Vol. 2. Rio de Janeiro.

Alwaya, Semhai
1977 "Formulas and Themes in Contemporary Bedouin Oral Poetry," *Journal of Arabic Literature*, viii. 48-76.

Antoun, Richard T.
1968 "On the Modesty of Women in Arab Muslim Villages: A Study in the Accomodation of Traditions," *American Anthropologist*, 70, no. 4, 671-97.

APE (Arquivo Público do Estado -- São Luís, Maranhão)
1834 Magistrados, vol. 2, doc. no. 91.
1839 Magistrados, vol. 14, doc. no. 114.
1840 Magistrados, vol. 14, doc. no. 145.
1854 Magistrados, vol. 114, doc. no. 53.
1874 Chefe de Polícia, vol. 24, p. 374.
1880 Magistrados, vol. 49, p. 241.
1885 Diversas Províncias, pp. 105-106.

Ardener, E.
1972 "Belief and the problem of women." In *The Interpretation of Ritual*, edited by J.S. La Fontaine. Tavistock.

Arhem, Kaj
1981 *Makuna Social Organization*. Uppsala, Sweden.

Arnaud, E.
1981/82 O direito indígena e a ocupacão territorial: o caso dos índios Tembé do Alto Guamá (Pará). *Revista do Museu Paulista*, n.s., vol. 28:221-233.

Arnaud, E. and E. Galvão
1969 Notícia sobre os índios Anambé (Rio Caiari, Pará). *Boletim do Museu Paraense Emílio Goeldi, Antropologia*, no. 42. Belém.

Arvelo-Jimenez, Nelly
1971 "Political Relations in a Tribal Society: A Study of the Ye'cuana Indians of Venezuela." *Cornell University Latin American Studies Program Dissertation Series 31.*

Aspelin, Paul
1979 "Food Distribution and Social Bonding among the Mamaindê of Mato Grosso, Brazil." *Journal of Anthropological Research* 35: 309-327.

Attir, Mustafa O.
1985 "Ideology, Value Changes, and Women's Social Position in Libyan Society." In *Women and the Family in the Middle East: New Voices of Change.* Austin: University of Texas Press.

Auerbach, Judy, et al
1985 "On Gilligan's *In A Different Voice,"* *Feminist Studies* 11 (1): 149-161.

Ayres, Barbara
1974 "Bride Theft and Raiding for Wives in Cross-Cultural Perspective." *Anthropological Quarterly* 47: 238-252.

Azevedo, J.L.
1930 *Os Jesuitas no Grã-Pará.* Coimbra.

Baena, A.L.M.
1969 *Compêndio das eras da Província do Pará.* Belém: Universidade Federal do Pará.

Bailey, Clinton
1972 "The Narrative Context of the Bedouin Qasidah-Poem" *Journal of the Folklore Research Center,* iii, 67-105. Jerusalem.

Baksh, Michael
1984 Cultural Ecology and Change of the Machiguenga Indians of the Peruvian Amazon. Ph.D. Dissertation. Los Angeles: University of California.

Balandier, George
1965 "The Colonial Situation." In, Pierre L. Van den Berghe (ed.), *Africa: Social Problems of Change and Conflict.* San Francisco: Chandler.

314

Balée, William
  1984a The persistence of Ka´apor culture. Ph.D. dissertation, Colum-
         bia University, New York.
  1984b "The Ecology of Ancient Tupi Warfare." In *Warfare, Culture,
         and Environment.* R.B. Ferguson, ed., pp. 241-265. Orlando:
         Academic Press. Pp. 241-265.
  1985   "Ka´apor ritual hunting." *Human Ecology* 13(4):485-510.

Bamberger, Joan
  1974   "The Myth of Matriarchy: Why Men Rule in Primitive Society."
         In *Women, Culture, and Society.* M. Zimbalist Rosaldo and L.
         Lamphere, eds., pp. 263-280. Stanford: Stanford University
         Press.
  1979   "Exit and Voice in Central Brazil: The Politics of Flight in
         Kayapó Society." In *Dialectical Societies: The Gê and Bororo
         of Central Brazil.* D. Maybury-Lewis, ed., pp. 130-146. Cam-
         bridge: Harvard University Press.

BAP (Biblioteca do Arquivo Público - Belém, Pará)
  1825   Códice 429, doc. no. 1.

Barker, James
  1959   "Las Incursiones entre los Guaika." *Boletin Indigenista Venezo-
         lano* 7: 151-167.

Barnouw, Victor
  1977   *Wisconsin Chippewa Myths and Tales.* Madison: University of
         Wisconsin Press.

Basso, Ellen
  1973   *The Kalapalo Indians of Central Brazil.* New York: Holt,
         Rinehart and Winston.

Batatu, Hannah
  1979   "Class Analysis and Iraqi Society." *Arab Studies Quarterly.*
         1(3):229-44.
  1981   "Iraq's Underground Shi'i Movement: Characteristics, Causes and
         Prospects." *The Middle East Journal.* 35(4):578-694.

Bauer, Janet
  1983   "Poor Women and Social Consciousness in Revolutionary Iran."
         In, Guity Nashat, ed., *Women and Revolution in Iran.* Boulder:
         Westview Press.

Beckerman, Stephen
  1980 "Fishing and Hunting by the Bari of Colombia." In *Working Papers on South American Indians*, vol. 2. R. Hames, ed., pp. 67-111. Bennington: Bennington College.
  1983 "Carpe Diem: An Optimal Foraging Approach to Bari Fishing and Hunting." In *Adaptive Responses of Native Amazonians*. R. Hames and W. Vickers, eds., pp. 269-299. New York: Academic Press.

Bennett Ross, Jane
  1977 "An Assessment of the Nutritional and Health Status of an Aguaruna Jívaro Community, Amazonas, Peru." *Ecology of Food and Nutrition* 6: 69-81.
  1980 "Ecology and the Problem of Tribe: A Critique of the Hobbesian Model of Preindustrial Warfare." In *Beyond the Myths of Culture: Essays in Cultural Materialism*. E. Ross, ed., pp. 33-60. New York: Academic Press.
  1984 "Effects of Contact on Revenge Hostilities among the Achuara Jívaro." In *Warfare, Culture, and Environment*. R.B. Ferguson, ed., pp. 83-109. Orlando: Academic Press.
  1986 Revenge Feuding among the Achuara Jívaro of the Northwest Peruvian Amazon. Doctoral Dissertation, Department of Anthropology, Columbia University. Elois and E. Markell Markell.

Berger, Iris
  1976 "Rebels or Status Seekers?" In *Women in Africa*, Nancy J. Hafkin and Edna G. Bay, eds., Stanford Stanford University Press, Stanford, p. 172.

Berndt, R.M.
  1962 *Excess and Restraint*. Chicago: Univ. of Chicago Press.

Bernstein, Basil
  1961 "Aspects of Language and Learning in the Genesis of the Social Process," *Journal of Child Psychology and Psychiatry* 1: 313-324.
  1970 "Social Class, Language, and Socialization." In *Language and Social Context*, edited by Pier Paolo Giglioli. Penguin.

Bernus, Edmond
  1981 *Touaregs Nigeriens: Unite Culturelle et Diversite Regionale d'un Peuple Pasteur*. Memoires ORSTOM n. 94. Paris: Editions de l'Office de la Recherche Scientifique et Technique Outre-Mer.

Berredo, B.P.
1849 *Annaes históricos do Estado do Maranhão.* 2nd ed. São Luis:
Typographia Maranhense.

Betendorf, J.F.
1909 *Chrónica da missão dos Padres da Companhia de Jesus no
Estado do Maranhão.* In *Revista do Instituto Histórico e
Geográphico.* Tomo 72, ser. 1, vol. 119. Rio de Janeiro.

Bettleheim, B.
1962 *Symbolic Wounds: Puberty Rites and the Envious Male* New
York: Collier Books.

Biocca, Ettore
1971 *Yanoama: The Narrative of a White Girl Kidnapped by Amazonian Indians.* New York: E.P. Dutton.

Boddy, Janice
1982 "Womb as oasis: the symbolic context of Pharaonic circumcision
in rural Northern Sudan," *American Ethnology,* 9: 682-698.

Bonaparte, Marie
1953 *Female Sexuality,.* New York: International Universities Press.

Borker, Ruth
n.d. "Domestic/Public: Concepts and Confusions," paper presented at
the Annual Meetings of the American Anthropological Association, Washington, D.C., 1985.

Briggs, Lloyd Cabot
1958 *The Living Races of the Sahara Desert.* Peabody Museum. Vol.
XXVII, 2. Cambridge: Harvard University Press.

Broughton, John
1983 "Women's Rationality and Men's Virtues: A Critique of Gender
Dualism in Gilligan's Theory of Moral Development," *Social
Research* 50 (3): 597-642.

Broverman, Inge et al.
1970 "Sex-Role Stereotypes and Clinical Judgments of Mental Health,"
Journal of Consulting and Clinical Psychology 34.

Brown, Judith
1970 "A Note on the Division of Labor by Sex." *American Anthropologist* 72:1073-1078.

Brown, P.
1964 "Enemies and Affines." *Ethnology* 3:335-336.

Bryk, Felix
1934 *Circumcision in Man and Women: Its History, Psychology and Ethnology*, D. Berger, trans. New York: American Ethnological Press.

Burton, Richard F.
1885 *The Book of the Thousand Nights and a Night*, Benares, Kama-shastra Society 5: n. 4.

Calame-Griaule, Genevieve
1965 *Ethnologie et langage*, Paris: Gallimard.

Carneiro, Robert
1970 "A Theory of the Origin of the State." *Science* 169:733-738.
1983 "The Cultivation of Manioc among the Kuikuru of the Upper Xingú." In *Adaptive Responses of Native Amazonians*. R. Hames and W. Vickers, eds., pp. 65-111. New York: Academic Press.

Chagnon, Napoleon
1967 "Yanomamo Social Organization and Warfare." In *War: The Anthropology of Armed Conflict and Aggression*. M. Fried, M. Harris, and R. Murphy, eds., pp. 109-159. Garden City, NY: Natural History Press.
1972 "Tribal Social Organization and Genetic Microdifferentiation." In *The Structure of Human Populations*. G.A. Harrison and A.J. Boyce, eds., pp. 252-282. Oxford: Clarendon Press.
1973 "The Culture-Ecology of Shifting (Pioneering) Cultivation among the Yanomamo Indians." In *Peoples and Cultures of Native South America*. D. Gross, ed., pp. 126-142. Garden City, NY: Natural History Press.
1974 *Studying the Yanomamo*. New York: Holt, Rinehart and Winston.
1975 "Genealogy, Solidarity, and Relatedness: Limits to Local Group Size and Patterns of Fissioning in an Expanding Population." *Yearbook of Physical Anthropology* 19: 95-110.
1977 *Yanomamo: The Fierce People*, Second edition. New York: Holt, Rinehart and Winston.
1979 "Is Reproductive Success Equal in Egalitarian Societies?" In *Evolutionary Biology and Human Social Behavior*. N. Chagnon and W. Irons, eds., pp. 374-401. North Scituate, Mass.: Duxbury Press.
1980 "Highland New Guinea Models in the South American Lowlands." In *Working Papers on South American Indians*, vol. 2.

R. Hames, ed., pp. 111-130. Bennington: Bennington College.

1981 "Terminological Kinship, Genealogical Relatedness and Village Fissioning among the Yanomamo Indians." In *Natural Selection and Social Behavior: Recent Research and New Theory.* R. Alexander and D. Tinkle, eds., pp. 490-508. New York: Chiron Press.

1983 *Yanomamo: The Fierce People*, Third edition. New York: Holt, Rinehart and Winston.

Chapple, Eliot D. and Carleton S. Coon
1942 *Principles of Anthropology.* New York: Henry Holt & Co.

Charrad, Mounira
1984 "The Politics of Family Law: The Tunisian Example." Presented at the Middle East Studies Association Meetings. San Francisco.

Chernela, Janet
1983 Hierarchy and Economy of the Uanano (Kotiria) Speaking Peoples of the Middle Uaupes Basin, Columbia University Dissertation, University Microfilms International.

1984a "Why One Culture Stays Put: a Case of Resistance to Change in Authority and Economic Structure in an Indigenous Community in the Northwest Amazon." In *The Frontier After a Decade of Colonisation: Change in Amazonia, V. II*, edited by John Hemming, Manchester University Press.

1984b "Sexual Ideologies in Lowland South America," *Working Papers on South American Indians*, Bennington College, Number 5.

1985 "The Sibling Relationship among the Uanano of the Northwest Amazon: the case of Nicho," *Working Papers on South American Indians*, Benningon College, Number 7.

1986 "Righting History in the Northwest Amazon." In *Rethinking Myth and History*, ed. Jonathon Hill, University of Illinois Press. Forthcoming.

Chodorow, Nancy
1974 "Family Structure and Feminine Personality." In *Woman, Culture, and Society*, edited by Michelle Rosaldo and Louise Lamphere. Stanford University Press.

1978 *The Reproduction of Mothering.* University of California Press.

Clastres, Pierre
1972 "The Guayaki." In *Hunters and Gatherers Today: A Socioeconomic Study of Eleven Such Cultures in the Twentieth Century.* M.G. Bicchieri, ed., pp. 138-174. New York: Holt, Rinehart and Winston.

Clough, Paul and Gavin Williams
n.d. Marketing with and without Marketing Boards. Oxford University mimeo.

Collier, Jane, and Sylvia Yanagisako (eds.)
1987 *Gender and Kinship.* Stanford University Press.

Comrie, Bernard
1976 *Aspect: An Introduction to the Study of Verbal Aspects and Related Problems.* Cambridge: Cambridge University Press.

Crocker, Christopher
1969a Review of "Yanomamo: The Fierce People." *American Anthropologist* 71: 741-743.
1969b "Men's House Associates among the Eastern Bororo." *Southwestern Journal of Anthropology* 25: 236-260.

Cruz, E.
1973 *História do Pará.* Vol. 1. Belém: Governo do Estado do Pará.

d'Azevedo, W.L.
1973 "Mask Makers and Myth in Western Liberia." In *Primitive Art and Society,* edited by A. Fordge. Oxford: Oxford Univ. Press, pp. 126-150.

Daly, Mary
1978 *Gyn/Ecology: The Metaethics of Radical Feminism,* Boston: Beacon Press.

DeBoer, W.
1981 "Buffer Zones in the Cultural Ecology of Aboriginal Amazonia: An Ethnohistorical Approach." *American Antiquity* 46(2):364-377.

Diário do Maranhão
1897 Extraccão de borracha. 23 de Septembro. São Luís.

Dillon, Richard
1980 "Violent Conflict in Metá Society." *American Ethnologist* 7: 658-673.

Divale, William
1975 "An Explanation for Matrilocal Residence." In *Being Female: Reproduction, Power, and Change.* D. Raphael, ed., pp. 99-108. The Hague: Mouton.

Divale, William, and M. Harris
1976 "Population, Warfare, and the Male Supremacist Complex." *American Anthropologist* 78: 521-538.

Divale, William, F. Chameris and D. Gangloff
1976 "War, Peace, and Marital Residence in Pre-Industrial Societies." *Journal of Conflict Resolution* 20: 55-62.

Dodt, G.
1939 *Descripcão dos Rios Paranaíba e Gurupy.* In *Colecão Brasiliana*, vol. 138. São Paulo: Cia. Editora Nacional.

Dole, Gertrude
1973 "Shamanism and Political Control among the Kuikuru." In *Peoples and Cultures of Native South America.* D. Gross, ed., pp. 294-307. Garden City, NY: Natural History Press.
1983-84 "Some Aspects of Structure in Kuikuru Society." *Anthropologica* 59-62: 309-329.

Domingues, V.
1953 *O Turiaçu.* São Luís.

Doughty, C.M.
1926 *Travels in Arabia Deserta*, New York: Boni & Liveright

Douglas, M.
1975 *Purity and Danger.* London: Routledge and Kegan Paul.

Dufour, Darna
1983 "Nutrition in the Northwest Amazon: Household Dietary Intake and Time-Energy Expenditure." In *Adaptive Responses of Native Amazonians.* R. Hames and W. Vickers, eds., pp. 329-355. New York: Academic Press.

Dundes, Alan
1976 "To Love My Father All: A Psychoanalytic Study of the Folktale Source of King Lear." *Southern Folklore Quarterly* 40:353-366.

Durkheim, Emile
1965 *The Elementary Forms of the Religious Life.* New York: The Free Press.

Dworkin, Andrea
1976 *Our Blood*. New York: Harper and Row.

Echols, Alice
1983 "Cultural Feminism: Feminist Capitalism and the Anti-Pornography Movement," *Social Text* 7: 34-53. Spring/summer. (Revised version, "The New Feminism of Yin and Yang," in *Powers of Desire: The Politics of Sexuality*, edited by Ann Snitow, Sharon Thompson, and Christine Stansell. Monthly Review Press. 1983.)

El Saadawi, Nawal
1980 *The Hidden Face of Eve*. London: Zed Press.
1982 "Women and Islam." In, Azzizah Al-Hibri, ed., *Women and Islam*. New York: Pergamon Press.

Ember, Carol
1974 "An Evaluation of Alternative Theories of Matrilocal versus Patrilocal Residence." *Behavior Science Research* 9: 135-149.

Ember, Carol, M. Ember and B. Pasternak
1974 "On the Development of Unilineal Descent." *Journal of Anthropological Research* 30: 69-94.

Ember, Melvin, and C. Ember
1971 "The Conditions Favoring Matrilocal versus Patrilocal Residence." *American Anthropologist* 73: 571-594.

Engels, Frederick
1884/1972 *The Origin of the Family, Private Property and the State*. 2nd ed., Leacock, Eleanor B. ed. Int'l Pubs Co.

Esposito, John L.
1982 *Women in Muslim Family Law*. Syracuse: Syracuse University Press.

Estado do Pará.
1920 *Os Índios Urubus em Bragança*. 22 de outubro. Belém.

Etienne, Mona and Eleanor Leacock (eds.)
1980 *Women and Colonization: Anthropological Perspectives*. Praeger Publications.

Evans-Pritchard, E.E.
1940   *The Nuer.* New York: Oxford University Press.

Farah, Madelain
1984   *Marriage and Sexuality in Islam.* A Translation of al-Ghazzali's Book on the Etiquette of Marriage from the Ihya. Salt Lake City: University of Utah Press.

Ferdows, Adele K. & Amir H. Ferdows
1983   "Women in Shi'i Fiqh: Images through the Hadith." In, Guity Nashat, ed., *Women and Revolution in Iran.* Boulder, CO: Westview Press.

Ferguson, R. Brian
1983   "Warfare and Redistributive Exchange on the Northwest Coast." In *The Development of Political Organization in Native North America: 1979 Proceedings of the American Ethnological Society.* E. Tooker, ed., pp. 133-147. Washington: American Ethnological Society.
1984a "Introduction: Studying War." In *Warfare, Culture, and Environment.* R.B. Ferguson, ed., pp. 1-81. Orlando: Academic Press.
1984b "A Reexamination of the Causes of Northwest Coast Warfare." In *Warfare, Culture, and Environment.* R.B. Ferguson, ed., pp. 267-328. Orlando: Academic Press.
1986   "Explaining War." Paper presented at the conference on the anthropology of war, sponsored by the Harry Frank Guggenheim Foundation, at the School of American Research, Santa Fe, New Mexico, March 24-28, 1986.

Fernandes, F.
1975   *A investigacão etnológica no Brasil e outros ensaios.* Petrópolis, Rio de Janeiro: Vozes.

Flowers, Nancy
1983   "Seasonal Factors in Subsistence, Nutrition, and Child Growth in a Central Brazilian Indian Community." In *Adaptive Responses of Native Amazonians.* R. Hames and W. Vickers, eds., pp. 357-390. New York: Academic Press.

Flowers, Nancy, D. Gross, M. Ritter and D. Werner
1982   "Variation in Swidden Practices in Four Central Brazilian Societies." *Human Ecology* 10: 203-217.

Folha do Norte
1920 *Osselvícolas do Gurupy.* 26 de janeiro. Belém.

Friedl, Ernestine
1975 *Women and Men: An Anthropologist's View.* New York: Holt, Rinehart and Winston.

Frikel, Protásio
1985 "Notes on the Present Situation of the Xikrín Indians of the Rio Caeteté." In *Native Americans: Ethnology of the Least Known Continent.* P. Lyon, ed., pp. 358-369. Prospect Heights, Ill.: Waveland Press.

Fróes Abreu, S.
1931 *Na terra das palmeiras.* Rio de Janeiro: Oficina Industrial Gráphica.

Fromm, Erich
1948 "The Oedipus Complex and the Oedipus Myth." In, Ruth N. Anshen, ed. *The Family: Its Function and Destiny.* New York: Harper & Brothers.

Fry, Peter
1982 *Para ingles ver: identidade e political na cultural brasileria.* Rio de Janeiro: Zahar Editores.

Gallop, Jane
1982 *The Daughter's Seduction, Feminism and Psychoanalysis.* Cornell University Press.

Gebhart-Sayer, Angelika
1984 *The Cosmos Encoiled: Indian Art of the Peruvian Amazon.* New York: Center for Inter-American Relations.
1985a "Some Reasons Why the Shipibo-Conibo (Eastern Peru) Retain their Art." Paper presented at the 45th International Congress of Americanists, Bogota, 1985.
1985b "The Geometric Designs of the Shipibo-Conibo in Ritual Context." *Journal of Latin American Lore* 11:2 (1985), 143-175.

General Federation of Iraqi Women
1980a *A Practical Translation to the Objectives of the Revolution in Work and Creativity.* Beirut: Dar Al Afaq al Jadidah, Dar-Lubnan.
1980b Summary. The Report of the Illiteracy Eradication Secretariat.

Gilligan, Carol
1982 *In A Different Voice*. Harvard University Press.

Glasse, R.
1968 *Huli of Papua*. Paris: Mouton.

Glaze, A.J.
1981 *Art and Death in A Senufo Village*. Bloomington: Indiana Univ. Press.

Glazier, Stephen G.
1983 *Marchin' the Pilgrims Home; Leadership and Decision-Making in an Afro-Caribbean Faith*. Westport, Conn.: Greenwood Press.

Gluckman, Max
1963[1954] "Rituals of Rebellion in South-East Africa." In *Order and Rebellion in Tribal Africa*. M. Gluckman, ed., pp. 110-136. London: Cohen & West.

Godelier, M.
1976 "Le Problem des Formes et des Fondaments de la Domination Masculine: Les Baruya." *Les Cahiers du Centre d'Etudes et de Researches Marxist*. 128:1-42.
1977 *Perspectives in Marxist Anthropology*. Cambridge Studies in Social Anthropology 18. Cambridge Univ. Press.
1982 *La Production de Grands Hommes, Pouvoir et Domination Masculine chez Les Baruya de Nouvelle-Guinea*. Paris: Fagard.

Goldman, Irving
1963 *The Cubeo: Indians of the Northwest Amazon*. Urbana: University of Illinois Press.

Gomes, M.
1977 The ethnic survival of the Tenetehara Indians of Brazil. Ph. D. dissertation, University of Florida. Gainesville.
1980 "Relatório sobre o contato e a necessidade de transferência de 27 Índios Guajá do Igarapé Timbira . . ." unpublished ms., on file at FUNAI. São Luis.

Goody, Jack
1983 *The Development of Family and Marriage in Europe*. Cambridge: Cambridge University Press.

Gotlieb, Yosef
1981 "Sectarianisms and the Iraqi State." In, Michael Curtis, ed., *Religion and Politics in the Middle East.* Boulder: Westview Press.

Gran, Peter
1979 *Islamic Roots of Capitalism. Egypt 1760-1840.* Austin: University of Texas Press.

Gray, L.
1924 "Circumcision, Introductory Note." In, J. Hastings, (ed) *Encyclopedia of Religion and Ethics*, New York: Scribner, 659-70.

Gregor, Thomas
1977 *Mehinaku: The Drama of Daily Life in a Brazilian Indian Village.* Chicago: University of Chicago Press.
1985 *Anxious Pleasures: The Sexual Lives of an Amazonian People.* Chicago: University of Chicago Press.

Gregory, James
1984 "The Myth of the Male Ethnographer and the Woman's World," *American Anthropologist* 86(2): 316-327.

Grenand, P.
1982 *Ainsi parlaient nos ancêtres.* Travaux et documents de L'ORSTOM, no. 148. Paris: ORSTOM.

Griaule, Marcel
1965 *Conversations with Ogotemmeli.* Oxford, Clarendon Press.

Griaule, Marcel and Germaine Dieterlen
1965 *Le Renard Pale.* Paris: Institute d'Ethnologie.

Gross, Daniel
1979 "A New Approach to Central Brazilian Social Organization." In *Brazil: Anthropological Perspectives, Essays in Honor of Charles Wagley.* M. Margolis and W. Carter, eds., pp. 321-342. New York: Columbia University Press.
1982 "The Indians and the Brazilian frontier." *Journal of International Affairs* 36(1):1-14.

Guimarães, J.
1887 "Relatório da commissão de reconhecimento do R. Parauá e suas margens." In, Relatório do Presidente da Província do Maranhão (Anexo), *Jose Bento de Araújo*, pp. 62-67. São Luís.

Haddad, Yvonne
1985 "Islam, Women and Revolution in Twentieth-Century Arab
Thought." In, Yvonne Yazbek Haddad and Ellison Banks
Findly, eds., *Women, Religion and Social Change*. Albany:
State University of New York Press.

Hage, P.
1981 "On Male Initiation and Dual Organization in New Guinea."
Man (N.S.) 16:268-275.

Halila, Souad
1984 "From Koranic Law to Civil Law: Emancipation of Tunisian
Women Since 1956." *Feminist Issues* 4(2):23-44.

Hames, Raymond
1983 "A Settlement Pattern of a Yanomamo Population Bloc: A
Behavioral Ecological Interpretation." In *Adaptive Responses of
Native Amazonians*. R. Hames and W. Vickers, eds., pp. 393-
427. New York: Academic Press.

Hamilton, James
1856 *Wanderings in North Africa*, London: John Murray, 1856.

Harding, Sandra
1986a "The Instability of the Analytic Categories of Feminist Theory,"
Signs 11 (4): 645-664.
1986b *The Science Question in Feminism*. Cornell University Press.

Harding, Sandra, and Merrill B. Hintikka (eds.)
1983 *Discovering Reality*. Reidel.

Harner, Michael
1973 *The Jívaro: People of the Sacred Waterfalls*. Garden City, NY:
Anchor Books.

Harris, Marvin
1974 *Cows, Pigs, Wars, and Witches*. New York: Random House.
1977 *Cannibals and Kings*. New York: Random House.
1979a "The Yanomamo and the Causes of War in Band and Village
Societies." In *Brazil: Anthropological Perspectives, Essays in
Honor of Charles Wagley*. M. Margolis and W. Carter, eds., pp.
121-132. New York: Columbia University Press.
1979b *Cultural Materialism: The Struggle for a Science of Culture*.
New York: Random House.
1984 "A Cultural Materialist Theory of Band and Village Warfare: The
Yanomamo Test." In *Warfare, Culture, and Environment*. R.B.
Ferguson, ed., pp. 111-140. Orlando: Academic Press.

Hartsock, Nancy
1983   "The Feminist Standpoint: Developing the Ground for a Specifically Feminist Historical Materialism." In *Discovering Reality*, edited by Sandra Harding and Merrill Hintikka. Reidel.

Hatem, Mervat
1985 "Egyptian Middle Class Women and Views of the Sexual Division of Labor in the Nationalist Personalized Patriarchal System." Presented at the Middle East Studies Association Meetings. New Orleans.
forthcoming "The Enduring Alliance of Nationalism and Patriarchy in Muslim Personal Status Laws: The Case of Modern Egypt." *Feminist Issues*.

Hawkes, Kristen
1981   "A Third Explanation for Female Infanticide." *Human Ecology* 9: 79-96.

Hegland, Mary E.
1983 "Aliabad Women: Revolution as Religious Activity." In, Guity Nashat, ed., *Women and Revolution in Iran*. Boulder: Westview Press.
1986 "The Political Roles of Aliabad Women in Community Politics and in the Iranian Revolution." MERIP Reports.

Hemming, J.
1978   *Red gold*. Cambridge, MA: Harvard Univ. Press.

Henry, Jules
1964   *Jungle People: A Kaingáng Tribe of the Highlands of Brazil*. New York: Vintage.

Herdt, G.H.
1981   *Guardians of the Flutes* (vol 1). New York: Macmillan.

Hill, Jonathan, and E. Moran
1983   "Adaptive Strategies of Wakuénai Peoples to the Oligotrophic Rain Forest of the Rio Negro Basin." In *Adaptive Responses of Native Amazonians*. R. Hames and W. Vickers eds., pp. 113-135. New York: Academic Press.

Hill, Kim and K. Hawkes
1983   "Neotropical Hunting among the Aché of Eastern Paraguay." In *Adaptive Responses of Native Amazonians*. R. Hames and W. Vickers, eds., pp. 139-188. New York: Academic Press.

Hill, Kim, H. Kaplan, K. Hawkes, and A.M. Hurtado
1985 "Men's Time Allocation to Subsistence Work among the Aché of Eastern Paraguay." *Human Ecology* 13: 29-47.

Hill, Kim, K. Hawkes, A.M. Hurtado, and H. Kaplan
1984 "Seasonal Variance in the Diet of Aché Hunter-Gatherers in Eastern Paraguay." *Human Ecology* 12: 101-135.

Hill, Polly
1972 *Rural Hausa.* Cambridge: Cambridge University Press.
1977 *Population, Prosperity and Poverty.* Cambridge: Cambridge University Press.

Hobsbawn, E.J.
1964 "Custom, Wages and Work-load." In *Labouring Men.* New York: Basic Books, pp. 344-70.

Hobsbawn, E.J. and G. Rude
1975 *Captain Swing.* New York: Norton.

Holmberg, Allan
1969 *Nomads of the Long Bow: The Siriono of Eastern Bolivia.* Garden City, NY: Natural History Press.

Horton, Donald
1963 "The Mundurucu." In *Handbook of South American Indians*, vol. 3. J. Steward, ed., pp. 271-282. Smithsonian Institute, Bureau of American Ethnology, #143.

Horton, Robin
1969 "Types of Spirit Possession in Kalabari Region." In, John Beattie, and J. Middleton, eds., *Spirit Mediumship and Society*, London.

Hosken, Fran P.
1976 "Genital Mutilation of Women in Africa." *Munger Africana Library Notes*, #36, October, p. 6.

Hugh-Jones, C.
1978 "Food for Thought -- Patterns of Production and Consumption in Pirá-Piraná Society." In *Sex and Age as Principles of Social Differentiation.* J.S. LaFontaine, ed., pp. 41-66. New York: Academic Press.

Huizinga, Johan
1955 *Homo Ludens: A study of the Play Elements in Culture*. Boston: The Beacon Press.

Hurly, J.
1928 *Nos sertões do Gurupy*. Belém.
1932a *O Rio Gurupy*. Belém.
1932b *Chorographia do Pará e Maranhão*. Belém.

Hurtado, A.M., K. Hawkes, K. Hill and H. Kaplan
1985 "Female Subsistence Strategies among Aché Hunter-Gatherers of Eastern Paraguay." *Human Ecology* 13: 1-28.

Hussein, Aziza
1985 "Recent Amendments to Egypt's Personal Status Laws." In, Elizabeth Fernea, ed., *Women and the Family in the Middle East*. New Voices of Change. Austin: University of Texas Press.

Huxley, F.
1957 *Affable savages*. NY: Viking Press.

Iraq, Ministry of Planning
1965 General Population Census. Baghdad.
1977 Annual Abstract of Statistics. Baghdad.
1978 Annual Abstract of Statistics. Baghdad.

Ismael, Jacqueline
1980 "Social Policy and Social Change: The Case of Iraq." *Arab Studies Quarterly*. 2(3):235-248.

Ismael, T. Y.
1976 *The Arab Left*. Syracuse: Syracuse University Press.

Jackson, Jean
1974 "Language Identity of the Colombia Vaupes Indians." In, R. Bauman and J. Sherzer, eds., *Explorations in the Ethnography of Speaking*. Cambridge Univ. Press.
1975 "Recent Ethnography of Indigenous Northern Lowland South America." *Annual Review of Anthropology* 4: 307-340.
1983 *The Fish People: Linguistic Exogamy and Tukanoan Identity in Northwest Amazonia*. New York: Cambridge University Press.

Johnson, Allen
1975 "Time Allocation in a Machiguenga Community." *Ethnology* 14: 301-310.
1983 "Machiguenga Gardens." In *Adaptive Responses of Native Amazonians.* R. Hames and W. Vickers, eds., pp. 29-63. New York: Academic Press.

Johnson, Allen and Michael Baksh
1987 "Ecological and Structural Influences on the Proportions of Wild Foods in the Diets of Two Machiguenga Communities." In, Marvin Harris and Eric Ross, eds., *Food and Evolution: Toward a Theory of Human Food Habits.* Philadelphia: Temple University Press.

Johnson, Allen and Timothy K. Earle
1986 *The Evolution of Human Societies: From Foraging Group to Agrarian State.* Stanford: Stanford University Press.

Johnson, Orna R.
1978 Interpersonal Relations and Domestic Organization Among the Machiguenga Indians of the Peruvian Amazon. Ph.D. Dissertation. New York: Columbia University.
1980 "The Social Context of Intimacy and Avoidance: A Videotape Study of Machiguenga Meals." *Ethnology* 19:353-366.

Johnson, Orna, and A. Johnson
1975 "Male/Female Relations and the Organization of Work in a Machiguenga Community." *American Anthropologist* 2: 634-648.

Joseph, Suad
1978 "Muslim-Christian Conflict in Lebanon: A Perspective on the Evolution of Sectarianism." In, Suad Joseph and Barbara L.K. Pillsbury, eds., *Muslim-Christian Conflicts: Economic, Political and Social Origins.* Boulder, CO: Westview Press.
1982 "The Mobilization of Iraqi Women into the Wage Labor Force." *Studies in Third World Societies.* 16:69-90.
1983 "Working Class Women's Networks in a Sectarian State: A Political Paradox." *American Ethnologist.* 10:1:1-22.
1984 "The Literature on Women, Family and the State." Berkshire Women's History Conference. Smith College.
1985a "Family Structure and the State: The Lebanese and Iraqi Cases." Middle East Studies Association Meetings. New Orleans.
1985b "Family and State: European and Middle Eastern Models." Duke University Symposium on Family, Class and Production. Durham.
1986a "Women and Political Movements in the Middle East: Agendas

for Research." MERIP Reports.

1986b "Ruling Elites and the Young: A Comparison of Iraq and Lebanon." In, Larry Michalak, ed., *Tools for Development, Tools for Domination: Social Legislation in the Contemporary Middle East*. Berkeley: Institute of International Studies. University of California.

Kandiyoti, Deniz
1984 "From Empire to Nation State: Transformations of the Women Question in Turkey." Presented at the University of California, Berkeley. Forum on Current Research on Middle Eastern Women.

Kang, Gay Elizabeth
1979 "Exogamy and Peace Relations of Social Units: A Cross-Cultural Test." *Ethnology* 18: 85-99.

Kaplan, Hillard, and K. Hill
1985 "Food Sharing among Aché Foragers: Tests of Explanatory Hypotheses." *Current Anthropology* 26: 223-246.

Kaplan, Joanna
1972 "Cognation, Endogamy, and Teknonymy: The Piaroa Example." *Southwestern Journal of Anthropology* 28: 282-297.
1973 "Endogamy and the Marriage Alliance: A Note on the Continuity in Kindred-Based Groups." *Man* 8: 555-570.
1975 *The Piaroa: A People of the Orinoco Basin*. Oxford: Clarendon Press.

Keenan, Jeremy
1977 *The Tuareg: People of Ahaggar*. New York: St. Martin's Press.

Keesing, Roger
1985 "Kwai Women Speak: The Micropolitics of Autobiography in a Solomon Island Society." *American Anthropologist*, Vol. 87, Number 1.

Kensinger, Kenneth
1975 "Studying the Cashinahua." In, Kensinger et al., *The Cashinahua of Eastern Peru*. Providence: The Haffenreffer Museum of Anthropology, Brown University.
1984 "Marriage Practices in Lowland South America" (editor). *Illinois Studies in Anthropology* no. 14. Urbana: University of Illinois Press.

Kenyatta, Jomo
1962 *Facing Mount Kenya*, New York, Vintage Books.

Khomeini, Ayatollah
1982 "The Question of Women (A Selection of Interviews and Speeches." In, Azar Tabari and Nahid Yeganeh, eds., *In the Shadow of Islam*. London: Zed Press.

Kiemen, M.
1954 *The Indian policy of Portugal in the Amazon region, 1614-1693*. Washington, D.C.: Catholic Univ. of America Press.

King, William J. Harding
1903 *A Search for the Masked Tawareks*. London: Smith, Elder & Co.

Kohut, Heinz
1984 *How Does Analysis Cure?* Chicago: University of Chicago Press.

Kracke, Waud
1976 "Uxorilocality in Patriliny: Kagwahiv Filial Separation." *Ethos* 4: 297-310.
1978 *Force and Persuasion: Leadership in an Amazonian Society*. Chicago: University of Chicago Press.

Kuhn, Annette and Ann Marie Wolpe
1978 *Feminism and Materialism: Women and Modes of Production*. London: Methuen.

Labov, William
1969 "The Logic of Nonstandard English," *Georgetown Monographs on Language and Linguistics*, 22: 1-31.

Lamphere, Louise
1974 Strategies, Cooperation and Conflict Among Women in Domestic Groups. In, Michelle Rosaldo and Louise Lamphere, eds., *Women, Culture and Society*. Stanford: Stanford University Press.

Langness, L.L.
"Sexual Antagonism in the New Guinea Highlands: A Bena Bena Example." *Oceania*, 37:161-77.

LaPoint, Jean
1970   Residence Patterns and Wayana Social Organization. Doctoral
       Dissertation, Department of Anthropology, Columbia Univer-
       sity.

Lasch, Christopher
1979   *The Culture of Narcissism.* W.W. Norton & Co.

Lathrap, D.
1970   *The Upper Amazon.* New York: Praeger.

Lave, Jean
1971   "Some Suggestions for the Interpretation of Residence, Descent
       and Exogamy among the Easter Timbira." Verhandlungen des
       XXXVIII Internationalen Amerikanistenkongresses, Band III:
       pp. 341-345.

Lazreg, Marnia
1985   "You Don't Have to Work, Sisters!   This is Socialism." Presented
       at the Middle East Studies Association Meetings. New Orleans.

Leach, E.
1954   *Political Systems of Highland Burma.* A study of Kachin Social
       Structure. London: The London School of Economics and Polit-
       ical Sciences/ Bell and Son.

Leacock, Eleanor B.
1972   Introduction. In *The Origin of the Family, Private Property and
       the State*, by Frederick Engels, pp. 7-67. New York; Interna-
       tional Publishers.

Leacock, Seth and Ruth Leacock
1972   *Spirits of the Deep: A study of an Afro-Brazilian Cult.* Garden
       City, N.Y.: Doubleday Natural History Press.

Lebanon, Ministry of Planning
1969, 1973   Recueil de statistique libanaises: Annee 1969; Annee 1973.
       Beirut.

Lee, Richard.
1984.   *The Dobe !Kung.* New York: Holt, Rinehart, Winston.

Leeds, Anthony
1961   "Yaruro Incipient Tropical Forest Horticulture." In *The Evolu-
       tion of Horticultural Systems in Native South America: Causes
       and Consequences.* J. Wilbert, ed., pp. 13-46.   Caracas:
       Sociedad de Ciencias Naturales la Salle.

Lennihan, Louise
1983 *Origins and Development of Agricultural Wage Labor in Northern Nigeria*, 1886-1980. Ph.D. dissertation, Department of Anthropology, Columbia University.
1987 "Agricultural Wage Labor in Northern Nigeria." In, M. Watts ed., *State Oil and Agriculture in Nigeria*. Berkeley: Institute of International Studies, University of California Press.
forthcoming "The Wages of Change: The Unseen Transition in Northern Nigeria." *Human Organization*.

Levinson, David
1985 "On Wife-beating and Intervention." *Current Anthropology* Vol. 26, No. 5, pp. 665-666.

Levi-Strauss, C.
1962 *Totemism*. Beacon Press. (*Le totémisme aujourd'hui*. Presses Universitaires de France, 1962.)
1963 "The Structural Study of Myth." *Structural Anthropology* 1. New York: Basic Books.
1964 Mythologiques I : Le cru et le cuit. Paris: Librairie Plon.
1966 Mythologiques II : Du miel aux cendres. Paris: Librairie Plon.
1967 "Social Structures of Central and Eastern Brazil." In *Structural Anthropology*. C. Levi-Strauss, ed., pp. 116-127.
1968 Mythologiques III: L'origine des maniéres de table. Paris: Librairie Plon.
1971 Mythologiques IV : L'homme nu. Paris: Librairies Plon.

Lewis, I.M..
1971 *Ecstatic Religion: An Anthropological Study of Spirit Possession and Shamanism*. Harmondsworth, England: Penguin Books.

Lhote, Henri
1955 *Les Touaregs du Hoggar*. Paris: Payot.

Lisboa, M.A.
1935 "A bacia do Gurupy e suas minas de ouro". In *Departamento Nacional da Producão Mineral*, Boletim no. 7. Rio de Janeiro.

Lizot, Jacques
1977 "Population, Resources and Warfare among the Yanomami." *Man* 12: 496-517.

Llewellyn-Davies, Melissa
1978 "Women, Warriors and Patriarchs," in Kuhn and Wolpe: *Feminism and Materialism* 330-358.

Lloyd, Genevieve
1983 "Reason, Gender and Morality in the History of Philosophy,"
Social Research 50 (3): 490-513.
1984 *The Man of Reason: "Male" and "Female" in Western Philosophy.*
University of Minnesota Press.

Lopes, R.
1916 *O torrão maranhense.* Rio de Janeiro: Typographia do Jornal do
Commercio.

Lyons, Harriet
1981 "Anthropologists, moralities, and relativities: the problem of genital mutilations." *Canadian Review of Sociology and Anthropology,* 18: 499-518.

MacCormack, Carol, and Marilyn Strathern (eds.)
1980 *Nature, Culture, and Gender.* Cambridge University Press.

Maltz, Daniel
n.d. "Analytical Concepts and Their Semantic Ambiguity: Public and
Domestic with Some Insights from Scotland." Paper presented
at the Annual Meetings of the American Anthropological Association, Washington, D.C., 1985.

Marchant, A.
1942 "From barter to slavery". In *Johns Hopkins University Studies in
Historical and Political Science,* ser. LX(1):1-160. Baltimore:
Johns Hopkins Press.

Marks, Elaine, and Isabelle de Courtivron (eds.)
1981 *New French Feminisms.* New York: Schocken.

Márques, C.
1870 *Diccionário histórico-geográphico da Província do Maranhão.* Rio
de Janeiro.

Martin, M. Kay
1969 "South American Foragers: A Case Study in Cultural Devolution." *American Anthropologist* 71: 243-260.

Marx, Karl
1967 *Capital.* Vol. 1. New York: International Publishers.

Marx, K. and F. Engels.
1974 *The German Ideology*. New York: International Publishers.

Maybury-Lewis, David
1971 "Some Principles of Social Organization among the Central Gê."
Verhandlungen des XXXVIII Internationalen Amerikanistenkongresses, Band III: 381-386.
1974 *Akwê-Shavante Society*. New York: Oxford University Press.
1979a "Conclusion: Kinship, Ideology, and Culture." In *Dialectical
Societies: The Gê and Bororo of Central Brazil*. D. Maybury-
Lewis, ed., pp. 301-312. Cambridge: Harvard University Press.
1979b *Dialectical Societies: The Gê and Bororo of Central Brazil* (editor). Cambridge: Harvard University Press.

Mbiti, John S.
1970 *African Religions and Philosophies*, New York: Anchor Books,
Doubleday, 158.

Mead, Margaret.
1935. *Sex and Temperament*. New York: William Morrow and Co.

Meeker, Michael
1979 *Literature and Violence in North Arabia*. Cambridge University
press, Cambridge.

Meggers, B.
1971 *Amazonia: Man and Culture in a Counterfeit Paradise*. Arlington
Heights, ILL: AHM Publishing Corp.

Meggitt, M.J.
1964 "Male-Female Relationships in the Highlands of Australian New
Guinea." *American Anthropologist* 66: #4 Part 2: 204-224.

Meillassoux, Calude
1983 *Maidens, Meal and Money : Capitalism and the Domestic Community* (Femmes, Greniers et Capitaux, 1975). Cambridge
University Press.

Messing, Simon D.
1980 "The Problem of 'Operations Based on Custom' in Applied
Anthropology: The Challenge of the Hosken Report on Genital
and Sexual Mutilations of Females." *Human Organizations*, Vol.
39, No. 3, p. 296

Metraux, Alfred
1948 "The Guarani." In *Handbook of South American Indians*, vol. 3.
      Ed. by J.H. Steward. Washington, D.C.: Smithsonian Institution.
      pp. 69-94.
1963a "The Tupinamba." In *Handbook of South American Indians*, vol.
      3. J. Steward, ed., p. 95-133. Smithsonian Institute, Bureau of
      American Ethnology, #143.
1963b "Warfare, Cannibalism, and Human Trophies." In *Handbook of
      South American Indians*, vol. 5. J. Steward, ed., pp. 383-409.
      Smithsonian Institute, Bureau of American Ethnology.

Milton, Katharine
1984 "Protein and Carbohydrate Resources of the Maku Indians of
      Northwestern Amazonia." *American Anthropologist* 86: 7-27.

Minces, Juliette
1978 "Women in Algeria." In, Lois Beck and Nikki Keddie, eds.,
      Women in the Muslim World. Cambridge: Harvard University
      Press.

Ministério de Agricultura
1915 Relatório do Ministério de Agricultura. Rio de Janeiro.
1917 Relatório do Ministério de Agricultura. Rio de Janeiro.

Mirani, S. Kaveh
1983 "Social and Economic Change in the Role of Women, 1956-1978."
      In, Guity Nashat, ed., *Women and Revolution in Iran*. Boulder,
      CO: Westview Press.

Mitchell, Juliet, and Jacqueline Rose (eds.)
1983 *Feminine Sexuality, Jacques Lacan and the école freudienne.*
      New York: W.W. Norton.

Moren, Emilio
1983 "Mobility as a Negative Factor in Human Adaptability: The Case
      of South American Tropical Forest Populations." In, *Rethinking
      Human Adaptation: Biological and Cultural Models*. R.
      Dyson-Hudson and M. Little, eds., pp. 117-135. Boulder:
      Westview Press.

Morey, R. and J. Marwitt
1975 "Ecology, economy, and warfare in lowland South America." In
      War, its Causes and Correlates. Ed. by M.A. Nettleship, R.D.
      Givens, and A. Nettleship. The Hague: Mouton. pp. 439-450.

338

Morey, Robert, and D. Metzger
1974 "The Guahibo: People of the Savanna." *Acta Etnologica et Linguistica* #31.

Morgan, Robin
1978 *Going Too Far*. New York: Random House.

Mortimore, M.J. and J. Wilson
1965 *Land and People in the Kano Close-settled Zone*. Zaria, Nigeria: Department of Geography, Ahmadu Bello University.

Moura, P.
1936 O Rio Gurupy. In, Servico Geológico e Mineralógico, Boletim no. 78. Rio de Janeiro.

Mueller, Eric
1985 "Revitalizing Old Ideas: Developments in Middle Eastern Family Law." In, Elizabeth Fernea, ed., *Women and the Family in the Middle East*. Austin: University of Texas Press.

Muniz, P.
1925 *Municipio de Ourém*. Belém.

Murphy, Robert F.
1956 "Matrilocality and Patrilineality in Mundurucu Society." *American Anthropologist* 58: 414-434.
1957 "Intergroup Hostility and Social Cohesion." *American Anthropologist* 59: 1018-1035.
1958 "Reply to Wilson." *American Anthropologist* 60: 1196-1199.
1958 *Mundurucu Religion*. Berkeley and Los Angeles: University of California Press.
1959 "Social Structure and Sex Antagonism." *Southwestern Journal of Anthropology* 15: 89-98.
1960 *Headhunter's Heritage: Social and Economic Change among the Mundurucu Indians*. Berkeley: University of California Press.
1964a "Social Structure of the Southeastern Twareg." Paper presented at Wenner-Gren Symposium No. 24 on Pastoral Nomadism, July 15-16, 1964.
1964b "Social Distance and the Veil." *American Anthropologist* 66: 1257-1274.
1967 "Tuareg Kinship." *American Anthropologist* 69:163-170.
1970 Basin Ethnography and Ecological Theory. In Earl H. Swanson, Jr. ed., *Languages and Cultures of Western North America*. Pocatello: Idaho State University Press, pp. 152-71.
1971 *The Dialectics of Social Life: Alarms and Excursions in Anthropological Theory*. New York: Basic Books, Inc. Publishers
1974a "Deviance and Social Control, II: Borai." In *Native South*

Americans, ed. Patricia J. Lyon, 202-8. Boston: Little Brown.

1974b "Deviance and Social Control I: What Makes Warú Run?" In *Native South Americans*, edited by Patricia J. Lyon, pp. 195-202. Boston: Little, Brown and Company.

1977 "Man's Culture and Woman's Nature," *Annals of the New York Academy of Sciences*. Vol. 293, 15-24.

1978 "Man's Culture, Woman's Nature." *New York Review of Sciences*.

1979 "Lineage and Lineality in Lowland South America." In *Brazil: Anthropological Perspectives, Essays in Honor of Charles Wagley*. M. Margolis and W. Vickers, eds., pp. 217-224. New York: Columbia University Press.

1979 *An Overture to Social Anthropology*. Englewood Cliffs, NJ.: Prentice-Hall, Inc.

Murphy, Robert F. and Yolanda Murphy
1980 "Women, Work, and Property in a South American Tribe." In, Stanley Diamond ed., *Theory and Practice: Essays Presented to Gene Weltfish*. New York: Mouton, pp. 179-94.

Murphy, Robert, and B. Quain
1955 "The Trumai Indians of Central Brazil." Monographs of the American Ethnological Society 24.

Murphy, Robert F. and Julian H. Steward
1956 "Tappers and Trappers: Parallel Processes of Acculturation." *Economic Development and Cultural Change* 4: 335-55. Weltfish. S. Diamond, ed., pp. 179-194. Mouton: New York.

Murphy, Yolanda, and Robert F. Murphy
1974 *Women of the Forest*. New York: Columbia University Press.
1985 *Women of the Forest*, Second Edition. New York: Columbia University Press.

Murray-Brown, Jeremy
1980 *Kenyatta*. London, George Allen & Unwin Ltd.

Musil, Alois
1928 *The Manners and Customs of the Rwala Bedouin*. American Geographical Society, New York.

Nashat, Guity
1983 "Women in Pre-Revolutionary Iran: A Historical Overview." In, Guity Nashat, ed., *Women and Revolution in Iran*. Boulder, CO: Westvaiew Press.

Needham, Rodney
1964   "Descent, Category, and Alliance in Siriono Society."
        Southwestern Journal of Anthropology 20: 229-240.

Nelson, Cynthia
1973   "Women and Power in Nomadic Societies in the Middle East".
        In *The Desert and the Sown: Nomads in the Wider Society*, ed.
        by C. Nelson, pp. 43-59. Berkeley: Institute of International
        Studies, University of California.

New York
1980   *New York Times* July 18, B4.

Nicolaisen, Johannes
1963   *Ecology and Culture of the Pastoral Tuareg.* Copenhagen:
        National Museum.

Nicolas, Francis
1946   *Tamesna: Les Ioullemmeden de l'Est. ou Tuareg "Kel Dinnik,"*
        Cercle de T'awa--Colonie du Niger. Paris: Imprimerie
        Nationale.

Nimuendaju, C.
1946   *The Eastern Timbira.* University of California Publications in
        American Archaeology and Ethnology, vol. 41. Berkeley.
1948   "The Turiwara and Aruã." In *Handbook of South American Indi-*
        ans, vol. 3. Ed. by J.H. Steward. Washington, D.C.: Smithsonian
        Institution. pp. 193-198.
1963   "Tribes of the Lower and Middle Xingú River." In *Handbook of*
        South American Indians, vol. 3. J. Steward, ed., pp. 213-243.
        Smithsonian Institute, Bureau of American Ethnology, #143.
1967   *The Apinayé.* Anthropological Publications: Oosterhout N.B.,
        The Netherlands.
1983   *Os Apinayé.* Belém: Conselho Nacional de Desenvolvimento
        Científico e Tecnológico; Museu Paraens Emílio Goeldi.

Norman, David
1972   "An Economic Survey of Three Villages in Zaria Province". 3
        vols. *Samaru Miscellaneous Papers* 37, 38, 39. Samaru: Insti-
        tute of Agricultural Research.

Noronha, J.M.
1856   "Roteiro da viagem da cidade do Pará até as últimas colonias dos
        domínios portuguezes em os Rios Amazonas e Negro." In
        Notícias para a História e Geographia das Nacoẽs Ultramarinas,
        vol. 6. Lisbon.

Norris, H .T.
1975 *The Tuaregs: Their Islamic Legacy and its Diffusion in the Sahel.* Warminster, England: Aris and Phillips.

Nurbakhah, Javad
1983 *Sufi Women.* Khaniqahi-Nimatullahi Publications.

O Correio da Manhã
1928 Os índios Urubus: O terror das regiões maranhenses do alto Gurupy. 13 de janeiro. Rio de Janeiro.

O Correio da Tarde
1912 Os índios do Gurupy. 12 de janeiro. Rio de Janeiro.

O Globo
1929 Nos sertões do extremo Norte. 14 de janeiro. Rio de Janeiro.

O Paiz
1929 A pacificacão dos índios Urubus. 17 de dezembro. Rio de Janeiro.

Oberg, Kalervo
1973 "Types of Social Structure among the Lowland Tribes of South and Central America." In *Peoples and Cultures of Native South America.* D. Gross, ed., pp. 189-212. Garden City, NY: Natural History Press.

Ortner, Sherry
1974 "Is Female to Male as Nature is to Culture?" In *Woman, Culture, and Society,* edited by Michelle Rosaldo and Louise Lamphere. Stanford University Press.

Otterbein, Keith
1968 "Internal War: A Cross-Cultural Study." *American Anthropologist* 70: 277-289.
1973 "The Anthropology of War." In *Handbook of Social and Cultural Anthropology.* J. Honigmann, ed., pp. 923-958. Chicago: Rand McNally.
1977 "Warfare: A Hitherto Unrecognized Critical Variable." *American Behavioral Scientist* 20: 693-710.
1985 *The Evolution of War: A Cross-Cultural Study,* second edition. New Haven: HRAF Press.

Otterbein, Keith, and C. Otterbein
1965 "An Eye for an Eye, a Tooth for a Tooth: A Cross-Cultural Study of Feuding." *American Anthropologist* 67: 1470-1482.

Pacere, T.F.
1979 *Ainsi on a assassine tous les Mosse*, Sherbrooke, Quebec, Canada: Editions Naaman, C.P. 697; 105-109.

Paige, Karen
1985 "Gender, Family Systems and the State: The Case of Egypt." Presented at the Middle East Studies Association Meetings. New Orleans.

Pakizegi, Behnaz
1978 "Legal and Social Positions of Iranian Women." In, Lois Beck and Nikki Keddie, eds., *Women in the Muslim World*. Cambridge: Harvard University Press.

Peteet, Julie
1986 "Gender and Politics: The Palestinian National Movement." MERIP Reports.

Piaget, Jean
1971 *The Construction of Reality in the Child*. New York: Random House, Inc.
1974 *The Origins of the Intelligence in Children*. New York: International Universities Press.

Price, Barbara
1982 "Cultural Materialism: A Theoretical Review." *American Antiquity* 47: 709-741.

Price, David
1981 "Nambiquara Leadership." *American Ethnologist* 8: 686-708.

Rahman, Fazlur
1980 "A Survey of Modernization of Muslim Family Law." *International Journal of Middle East Studies*. 11:4: 451-65.
1983 "Status of Women in the Qur'an." In, Guity Nashat, ed., *Women and Revolution in Iran*. Boulder, CO: Westview Press.

Ramos, A.
1972 The social system of the Sanumá of northern Brazil. Ph.D. dissertation, Univ. of Wisconsin, Madison.
1978 "Mundurucu: Social Change or False Problem?" *American Ethnologist* 5: 675-689.

Reddy, William M.
1984 *The Rise of Market Culture. The Textile Trade and French Society*, 1750-1900. New York: Cambridge Univer. Press.

Reichel-Dolmatoff, G.
1971 *Amazon Cosmos: The Sexual and Religious Symbolism of the Turkano Indians*. Chicago: Univ. of Chicago Press.

Ribeiro, D.
1956 "Convìvio e contaminacão: efeitos dissoaciativos da depopulacão provocada por epidemias em grupos indìgenas." *Sociologia* 18 (1): 3-50.
1970 *Os ìndios e a civilizacão*. Rio de Janeiro: Civilizacão Brasileira.

Ribeiro, J.P.
1913 "Exposicão nacional da borracha de 1913: Maranhão." In, Ministério de Agricultura, Indústria e Commercio, monographia no. 4. Rio de Janeiro.

Rich, Adrienne
1976 *Of Woman Born*. New York: W.W. Norton.

Riesman, David
[1950] 1961 *The Lonely Crowd*. Yale University Press. (Abridged edition with new forward, 1961.)

Rivet, P.
1924 "Les Indiens Canoeiros." *Journal de la Société des Americanistes de Paris*, n.s., 16:169-181.

Riviere, Peter
1969 *Marriage among the Trio*. Oxford: Clarendon Press
1970 "Factions and Exclusions in Two South American Village Systems." In *Witchcraft Confessions and Accusations*. M. Douglas, ed., pp. 245-255. New York: Tavistock.

Rivlin, B. and J.S. Szyliowicz
1965 *The Contemporary Middle East: Tradition and Innovation*, Random House, New York.

Rodd, Francis Rennell
1926 *People of the Veil*. London: Macmillan and Co.

Rodinson, Maxime
1973 *Islam and Capitalism.* Austin: University of Texas Press

Rodrigues, A.D.
1984/85 "Relacões internas na família linguística Tupi-Guarani." *Revista de Antropologia,* vols. 27/28:33-53.

Rodrigues, J.B.
1875 *O Rio Capim.* Rio de Janeiro: Typographia Nacional.

Roe, Perter G.
1982 *The Cosmic Zygote.* New Brunswick, N.J.: Rutgers University Press.

Rogers, Susan
1978 "Women's Place: A Critical Review of Anthropological Theory." *Comparative Studies in Society and History 20*: 123-162.

Roosevelt, Anna
1980 *Parmana: Prehistoric Maize and Manioc Subsistence along the Amazon and Orinoco.* New York: Academic Press.

Ruddick, Sara
1980 "Maternal Thinking." *Feminist Studies* 6 (2).
1986 "Remarks on the Sexual Politics of Reason," to appear in *Women and Moral Theory*, edited by Eva Kittay and Diana Meyers. Rowman and Allenheld.

Sabbah, Fatna A.
1984 *Woman in the Muslim Unconscious.* New York: Pergamon Press.

Sacks, Karen
1974 "Engels Revisisted: Women, the Organization of Production, and Private Property." In, Michelle Rosaldo and Louise Lamphere eds., *Women, Culture and Society.*

Saenz, Candelario
1980 "Kinship and Social Organization of the *Inadan.*" Paper presented at Table Ronde de la Parente Touareque, CNRS, Gif/Yvette, Paris, 23-26 September 1980.
1986 They Have Eaten Our Grandfather! The Special Status of Twareg Smiths. Ph.D. Thesis, Columbia University, New York City.

Saffirio, Giovanni, and R. Scaglion
1982 "Hunting Efficiency in Acculturated and Unacculturated Yanomamo Villages." *Journal of Anthropological Research* 38: 315-327.

Sahlins, Marshall
1961 "The Segmentary Lineage: An Organization of Predatory Expansion." *American Anthropologist* 63: 332-345.

Sanasarian, Eliz
1982 *The Women's Rights Movement in Iran: Mutiny, Appeasement, and Repression from 1900 to Khomeini.* New York: Praeger.

Sanday, Peggy
1973 "Toward a Theory of the Status of Women." *American Anthropologist* 75: 1682-1700.
1981. *Female Power and Male Dominance.* Cambridge: Cambridge University Press.

Schimmel, Annemarie
1982 "Women in Mystical Islam." In, Azzizah Al-Hibri, ed., *Women and Islam.* New York: Pergamon.

Schlegel, Alice
1975 Three Styles of Domestic Authority: A Cross-Cultural Study. In *Being Female: Reproduction, Power, and Change*, Dana Raphael, ed., pp. 165-176. The Hague, Paris: Mouton Publishers.

Schneider, David M.
1968 *American Kinship: A Cultural Account.* Englewood Cliffs, N.J.: Prentice-Hall.

Scott, James C.
1972 "The Erosion of Patron-Client Bonds and Social Change in Rural Southeast Asia." *Journal of Asian Studies* XXXII, 1 (November): 5-37.

Shapiro, Judith
1972 Sex Roles and Social Structure among the Yanomamo Indians of Northern Brazil. Doctoral Dissertation, Department of Anthropology, Columbia University.
1974 "Alliance or Descent: Some Amazonian Contrasts." *Man* 9: 305-306.
1975 "Alliance or Descent: Some Amazonian Contrasts (Rejoinder)." *Man* 10: 624-625.

Sharara, Yolla
  1978 "Women and Politics in Lebanon." *Khamsin. Journal of Revolutionary Socialists of the Middle East* 6:6-15.

Sharqi, Amal
  1982 "The Progress of Women in Iraq." In, Tim Niblock, ed., *Iraq: The Contemporary State.* London: Croom Helm and Exeter: Center for Arab Gulf Studies.

Shenton, R.W.
  1985 *The Development of Capitalism in Northern Nigeria.* London: James Currey.

Shenton, R.W. and L. Lennihan
  1981 "Capital and Class: Peasant Differentiation in Northern Nigeria." *Journal of Peasant Studies* 9, 1 (October).

Siskind, Janet
  1973a *To Hunt in the Morning.* New York: Oxford University Press.
  1973b "Tropical Forest Hunters and the Economy of Sex." In *Peoples and Cultures of Native South America.* D. Gross, ed., pp. 226-240. Garden City, NY: Natural History Press.
  1978 "Kinship and Mode of Production." *American Anthropologist* 80: 860-872.

Smith, Jane, ed.
  1980 *Women in Contemporary Muslim Societies.* London: Associated University Presses.
  1985 "Women, Religion and Social Change in Early Islam." In, Yvonne Yazbeck Haddad and Ellison Banks Findly, eds., *Women, Religion and Social Change.* Albany: State University of New York Press.

Smith, M.G.
  1955 *The Economy of Hausa Communities of Zaria.* London: HMSO.

Smith, Mary
  1954 *Baba of Karo.* London: Faber.

Smole, William
  1976 *The Yanomama Indians: A Cultural Geography.* Austin: University of Texas Press.

Soffan, Linda
1980 *The Women of the United Arab Emirates*. London: Croom Helm.

Sorensen, Arther P.
1967 "Multilingualism in the Northwest Amazon," *American Anthropologist*, Vol. 69, pp. 670-684.

Spencer, R.
1959. *The North Alaskan Eskimo*. Washington, D.C.: Smithsonian Institution.

Sponsel, Leslie
1983 "Yanomama Warfare, Protein Capture, and Cultural Ecology: A Critical Analysis of the Arguments of the Opponents." *Interciencia* 8: 204-210.

Steward, Julian
1938 *Basin Plateau Aboriginal Sociopolitical Groups*. Washington, D.C.: Smithsonian Bureau of American Ethnology. Bulletin 120.
1955. "The Great Basin Shoshonean Indians: An Example of a Family Level of Sociocultural Integration." *Theory of Culture Change*. Urbana: University of Illinois Press. pp. 101-121.

Steward, Julian, R.A. Manners, E.R. Wolf, E. Padilla, S.W. Mintz, and R.L. Scheele
1956 *The People of Puerto Rico*. Urbana: University of Illinois Press.

Stoler, Ann L.
1980 "Social History and Social Control: A Feminist Perspective on 'Facts' and Fiction." *Research Seminar on Women's Struggles and Research*. Institute of Social Studies, The Hague.

Stork, Joe
1982 "State Power and Economic Structure: Class Determination and State Formation in Contemporary Iraq." In, Tim Niblock, ed., *Iraq: The Contemporary State*. London: Croom Helm and Exeter: Center for Arab Gulf Studies.

Strathern, Marilyn
1972 *Women in Between*. New York: Seminar Press.
1976 "An Anthropological Perspective," in *Exploring Sex Differences*, edited by B. Lloyd and J. Archer. Academic Press.
1980 "No nature, no culture: the Hagen case." In *Nature, Culture, and Gender*, edited by Carol MacCormack and Marilyn Strathern. Cambridge University Press.
1987 "An Awkward Relationship: The Case of Feminism and

Anthropology." *Signs* 12 (2).

Sweet, D.G.
1975 *A rich realm of nature destroyed: the middle Amazon valley, 1640-1750.* Ph.D. dissertation, University of Wisconsin, Madison.

Tabari, Azar and Nahid Yeganeh, eds.
1982 *In the Shadow of Islam. The Women's Movement in Iran.* London: Zed Press.

Tabatabai, Shahin Etezadi
1982 "Understanding Islam as the Only Way to Understand Women's Role." In, Azar Tabari and Nahid Yeganeh, eds., *In the Shadow of Islam. The Women's Movement in Iran.* London: Zed Press.

Taylor, Kenneth, and A. Ramos
1975 "Alliance or Descent: Some Amazonian Contrasts (Reply)." *Man* 10:128-130.

Tekeli, Serin
1981 "Women in Turkish Politics." In, Nermin Abadan-Unat, ed., *Women in Turkish Society.* Leiden: E.J. Brill.

Teleghani, Ayatollah
1982 "On Hejab." In, Azar Tabari and Nahid Yeganeh, eds., *In the Shadow of Islam. The Women's Movement in Iran.* London: Zed Press.

Tessler, Mark with Janet Rogers and Daniel Schneider
1978 "Women's Emancipation in Tunisia." In, Lois Beck and Nikki Keddie, eds., *Women in the Muslim World.* Cambridge: Harvard University Press.

Thoden Van Velzen, H.U.E., and W. Van Wetering
1960 *Residence, Power Groups and Intra-Societal Aggression: An Enquiry into the Conditions Leading to Peacefulness within Non-Stratified Societies.* International Archives of Ethnography 59: 169-200.

Thompson, E.P.
1974 "Patrician Society, Plebian Culture." *Journal of Social History* (Summer).
1976 "The Grid of Inheritance." In, J. Goody, J. Thirsk, and E.P. Thompson eds., *Family and Inheritance -- Rural Society in Western Europe.* Cambridge: Cambridge University Press, pp.

328-360.
1978 "Eighteenth-Century English Society: Class Struggle without Class?" *Social History* 3, 2 (May).

Toral, A.
1985 "Avá-Caneiro: Os índios na clandestinidade." In CEDI, Aconteceu, Especial 15. São Paulo: Sagarana Editora Ltda. pp. 274-275.

Turnbull, C.
1961 *The Forest People*. New York: Simon and Schuster.

Turner, Terence
1971 "Northern Kayapó Social Structure." Verhandlungen des XXXVIII Internationalen Amerikanistenkongresses, Band III: 365-371.
1979 "The Gê and Bororo Societies as Dialectical Systems: A General Model." In *Dialectical Societies: The Gê and Bororo of Central Brazil*. D. Maybury-Lewis, ed., pp. 147-178. Cambridge: Harvard University Press.

United Kingdom
1926 *Colonial Record Office*, Kew Gardens. C0536. 147/14386. Uganda: Memorandum on the Beating of Women.

United Nations, Department of International Economic and Social Affairs (UNIESA).
1982 Demographic Indicators of Countries: Estimates and Projects as Assessed in 1980. New York.

van Gennep, Arnold
1960[1909] *The Rites of Passage*, transl. by Monika B. Vizedom and Gabrielle L. Caffee. Chicago: University of Chicago Press.

Viana, A.
1975 *As epidemias do Pará*. Belém: Universidade Federal do Pará.

Vieira, A.
1925 *Cartas do Padre Antônio Vieira*. Ed. by J.L. Azevedo. vol. 1. Coimbra.

Villas Boas, Orlando, and C. Villas Boas
1973 *Xingú: The Indians, Their Myths*. New York: Farrar, Straus, and Giroux.

Vincent, Joan
1971   *African Elite: The Big Men of a Small Town.* Columbia University Press. Viveiros de Castro, E.
1986   *Arawete: Os deuses canibais.* Rio de Janeiro: Jorge Zahar, Ed.

Wada, Shohei
1984   "Female Initiation Rites of the Iraqw and the Gorowa." *Senri Ethnological Studies* 15, Africa 3, National Museum of Ethnology, Tokyo.

Wagley, C. and E. Galvão
1949   *The Tenetehara Indians of Brazil.* NY: Columbia University Press.

Wagley, Charles
1983   *Welcome of Tears: The Tapirape Indians of Central Brazil.* Prospect Heights, Ill.: Waveland Press.

Warren, Kay, and Susan Bourque
1985   "Gender, Power, and Communication: Women's Responses to Political Muting in the Andes," in *Women Living Change*, edited by Susan Bourque and Donna Robinson Divine. Temple University Press.

Watson, J.
1952   Cayuá culture change. In *Memoirs of the American Anthropological Association* 73 (54), no. 2, part 2.

Watts, Michael
1983   *Silent Violence: Food, Famine and Peasantry in Northern Nigeria.* Berkeley: University of California Press.

Wehr, Hans
1961   *A Dictionary of Modern Written Arabic*, Cornell University Press, Ithaca, N.Y.

Werner, Dennis, N. Flowers, M. Lattman Ritter, and D. Gross
1979   "Subsistence Productivity and Hunting Effort in Native South America." *Human Ecology* 7: 303-315.

White, Elizabeth
1978   "Legal Reform as an Indicator of Women's Status in the Muslim Nations." In, Lois Beck and Nikki Keddie, eds., *Women in the Muslim World*. Cambridge: Harvard University Press.

Whiting, John W. M. and Beatrice B. Whiting.
    1975. "Aloofness and Intimacy of Husbands and Wives: A Cross-Cultural Study." *Ethos* 3:183-207.

Whorf, Benjamin Lee
    1941 "The Relationship of Habitual Thought and Behavior to Language," in *Language, Culture, and Personality, Essays in Memory of Edward Sapir*, edited by Leslie Spier. Menasha, Wisconsin: Sapir Memorial Publication Fund. (Reprinted in *Language, Thought, and Reality, Selected Writings of Benjamin Lee Whorf*, edited by John B. Carroll.)

Williams, Gavin
    1983 *Why There is No Agrarian Capitalism in Nigeria*. St. Peter's College, Oxford. Mimeo.

Wilson, H. Clyde
    1958 "Regarding the Causes of Mundurucu Warfare." *American Anthropologist* 60: 1193-1196

Yost, James, and P. Kelley
    1983 "Shotguns, Blowguns, and Spears: The Analysis of Technological Efficiency." In *Adaptive Responses of Native Amazonians*. R. Hames and W. Vickers, eds., pp. 189-224. New York: Academic Press.